PRIMARY
COMPUTING & DIGITAL
TECHNOLOGIES

SAGE was founded in 1965 by Sara Miller McCune to support the dissemination of usable knowledge by publishing innovative and high-quality research and teaching content. Today, we publish over 900 journals, including those of more than 400 learned societies, more than 800 new books per year, and a growing range of library products including archives, data, case studies, reports, and video. SAGE remains majority-owned by our founder, and after Sara's lifetime will become owned by a charitable trust that secures our continued independence.

Los Angeles | London | New Delhi | Singapore | Washington DC | Melbourne

7TH EDITION

PRIMARY COMPUTING & DIGITAL TECHNOLOGIES

KNOWLEDGE, UNDERSTANDING & PRACTICE

KEITH TURVEY
JOHN POTTER
JEREMY BURTON
WITH JONATHAN ALLEN
& JANE SHARP

SAGE | LearningMatters

Learning Matters
An imprint of SAGE Publications Ltd
1 Oliver's Yard
55 City Road
London EC1Y 1SP

SAGE Publications Inc.
2455 Teller Road
Thousand Oaks, California 91320

SAGE Publications India Pvt Ltd
B 1/I 1 Mohan Cooperative Industrial Area
Mathura Road
New Delhi 110 044

SAGE Publications Asia-Pacific Pte Ltd
3 Church Street
#10–04 Samsung Hub
Singapore 049483

Editor: Amy Thornton
Production controller: Chris Marke
Project management: Deer Park Productions,
Tavistock, Devon
Marketing manager: Lorna Patkai
Cover design: Wendy Scott
Typeset by: C&M Digitals (P) Ltd, Chennai, India
Printed and bound by CPI Group (UK) Ltd, Croydon,
CR0 4YY

Library of Congress Control Number: 2016944009

British Library Cataloguing in Publication Data

A catalogue record for this book is available from the
British Library.

ISBN 978-1-4739-6156-2
ISBN 978-1-4739-6687-1 (hbk)

At SAGE we take sustainability seriously. Most of our products are printed in the UK using FSC papers and boards.
When we print overseas we ensure sustainable papers are used as measured by the PREPS grading system.
We undertake an annual audit to monitor our sustainability.

Contents

Acknowledgements

We would like to thank Amy Thornton who has provided invaluable editorial support and assistance in the ongoing updating of this book. Similarly a number of colleagues in Initial Teacher Education have also supported this publication contributing their insights through various vignettes of classroom practice and projects. These include Lis Bundock and Pippa Totraku. Finally, we owe our gratitude to all of the children, teachers and schools referred to throughout this book, without whose partnerships the ongoing development of professional practice in primary computing and ICT would not be possible.

About the authors

Keith Turvey is Principal Lecturer in Education at the Education Research Centre in the School of Education, University of Brighton. He teaches on a range of undergraduate and postgraduate courses, and plays a leading role in the MA Education course. As a primary school teacher of 15 years he led successfully a range of subjects, including music, ICT and mathematics, and took on a number of senior management roles both in the UK and abroad. Since joining the University of Brighton in 2003, he has researched and published widely in the fields of digital technologies, pedagogy and teacher education. He completed a PhD in 2011 focusing on teachers' professional learning and digital technologies. Keith has provided research, CPD and consultancy on digital technologies in education, and on primary computing for a number of national and international agencies including local authorities, schools, the European Commission and UNESCO.

John Potter is Reader in Media in Education at University College London Institute of Education (UCL IOE). He works in the UCL Knowledge Lab and was a founder member of the Digital Arts Research in Education collaborative (DARE). His research and publications are in the fields of: media education, new literacies, creative activity and learner agency; digital video production by young learners; the use of social software and online networks for publication and learning; and the changing nature of teaching and learning in response to the pervasive use in the wider culture of media technologies in formal and informal settings. Before becoming an education researcher and academic John worked as a primary school teacher in East London and, later, a local authority advisory teacher for ICT. He currently teaches on the MA in Digital Media Culture and Education and supervises doctoral students in the fields of learning, media and technology at the UCL IOE.

Jeremy Burton is Senior Lecturer in Computing Education in the School of Education, University of Brighton. He leads the computing subject group and teaches on both undergraduate and postgraduate courses. While working as a primary school teacher and ICT co-ordinator, Jeremy developed a passion for digital media education. A self-taught web designer and developer, he coded his school's first website in 1998 and has since worked freelance for private clients. His experience in this area, and in digital media production more broadly, has informed his teaching of ICT/computing to student teachers. Jeremy is a co-founder of NumeracyReady (a web-based tuition package that prepares candidates for the Numeracy Skills Test) and Staffrm (an online professional network for teachers).

Jonathan Allen is Strategic Lead for Teacher Education at the UCL Institute of Education. He was previously Director for Initial Teacher Education, involved across Primary, Secondary and Post-compulsory programmes, as well as in e-learning projects. Before joining the IOE Jonathan held posts responsible for Primary ICT in teacher education at University of Reading and Oxford Brookes University.

Jane Sharp is a Learning Development Tutor at Bishop Grosseteste University, working with students at all levels to develop the academic practices, skills and attributes needed for effective study at university. Her current research centres on the academic writing experiences of students studying education at university. Jane was formerly Senior Lecturer in Primary Education and ICT at the University of Winchester and a researcher at the University of Exeter involved in innovative and largescale computing projects in schools.

Introduction

About this book

This book has been written to support primary teacher trainees and newly qualified teachers in developing their knowledge and understanding of both computing and the broader pedagogical issues concerning the ways in which Information and Communications Technology (ICT) can support children to develop confidence, capability and competence as lifelong learners in the information society. The requirements of teachers in England are clearly identified in the National Curriculum and the Teachers' Standards. This book identifies clear links with these requirements, but also addresses the wider context in which ICT has an impact on learning and teaching. For this reason, we use both ICT and computing as terms throughout this book. That is by ICT we mean the broader context of technology-enhanced learning as children learn to use digital technologies effectively and critically across many domains of learning and curricula. Indeed, the terms ICT and digital technologies are used interchangeably throughout the book. By the term computing we mean the more tightly focused core knowledge and understanding identified in the National Curriculum programme of study (DfE, 2013). As we will explore later, these two are intricately linked, but focusing only on the subject of computing as now defined in the new National Curriculum (DfE, 2013) does not adequately address the need for 'high-quality training and support that prepares trainees with the skills they need to use a range of approaches to teaching and learning, including information and communication technology (ICT) and educational technology where relevant' beyond the remit of the computing National Curriculum (Ofsted, 2012, p.33).

With these issues in mind we have structured this book into three clear sections: A, B and C. We have found over the years that the first concern of many trainees is often how to make effective use of the digital technologies they may have access to in their school placements. Thus Section A of this book focuses primarily on what trainees need to know in order to begin to utilise digital technologies effectively in their wider pedagogical practice. Section B concentrates on the National Curriculum for computing and should provide trainees with the knowledge and understanding to plan activities that engage children with computing in ways that fuel their understanding of the subject and develop their capability to apply this knowledge critically and creatively. Section C introduces trainees to some of the wider issues regarding the professional use of digital technologies and ongoing professional development.

At the time of writing this edition, as at various other times in education, significant policy changes continue to be implemented that remove the statutory status of the National Curriculum for some schools such as academies and free schools. The government that took office in May 2010 introduced many reforms to education during their tenure including reform of Early Years policy that will affect the Early Years Foundation Stage (EYFS) and a review of the primary National Curriculum (DfE, 2013). These significant changes to the National Curriculum and EYFS Framework have continued to impact on the assessment of children's attainment in the Early Years and at Key Stages 1 and 2. Many of the legislative changes in education through this period have been intensified since the 2015 general election. Despite the introduction of the revised National Curriculum (DfE, 2013) adjustments continue to be made to the curriculum and assessment which have ongoing implications for teaching and learning. This is particularly heightened with regards to ICT and computing as new digital technologies and practices are also continually evolving.

This book includes references to the statutory programmes of study for computing in the National Curriculum, which should be regarded as a minimum entitlement for children, to the areas of learning in the Early Years Foundation Stage and to the systems of assessment that relate to these. In any period, you will need to understand what curriculum and assessment requirements were in place before the new arrangements, and teachers you work with may retain in their practice elements of the earlier ways of working. You will certainly hear colleagues discussing the differences between curriculum initiatives and referring to former frameworks, for example the Primary National Strategy for Teaching Literacy and Mathematics, and also perhaps to the earlier QCA Scheme of Work for ICT, discussed later in this introduction in the section on curriculum context.

We have focused in this book on giving you insights into the development of the theory behind the core areas of computing that you will need to inform your practice as you plan to promote the capability of the children you work with. This is essential to ensure that they develop effective skills of using and applying digital technologies as they build on their knowledge and understanding of computing and its broader significance in a digital age.

Features of the main chapters of this book include:

- clear links with the Teachers' Standards in the introduction to each section of the book;
- references to required knowledge and understanding, both of computing as a subject and of the broader use of digital technologies to support teaching and learning in other subjects;
- research summaries that give insights into how the theory has developed, including studies on how children's computing capability develops and on the development of the use of different applications and technologies;
- examples of practice in the classroom to illustrate important points;
- suggestions for developing the use of digital technologies in your own practice;
- reminders of how planning for teaching computing and the broader use of digital technologies fits in with the bigger picture, across the curriculum and with other aspects of school life;
- reflective tasks and practical activities for you to undertake;
- a summary of key learning points;
- references to key texts and suggestions for further reading.

For those undertaking credits for a Master's degree, we have included suggestions for further work and extended study at the end of each chapter in a section called 'M-Level Extension'.

This introduction will briefly discuss some of the significant national policies and initiatives regarding the changes from ICT to computing in schools in order to set the background. The concept of ICT capability as defined in the 1999 National Curriculum (DfEE, 1999) will be explored as will the recent shift in emphasis towards computer science in the most recent iteration of the National Curriculum for computing (DfE, 2013). There will then be a broader discussion of the features of digital technologies, which make a distinctive contribution to learning and teaching. Consideration will be given to the Professional Standards for QTS, which form part of an ongoing continuum of professional development for pre-service and in-service teachers. The Standards require all teachers in all subjects and phases to use digital technologies appropriately and effectively in their work. This is a much broader brief than the focus on computing expressed in the National Curriculum. Despite the rebalancing of the programme of study for computing it remains important to consider the wider application of digital technologies in some detail in order to develop an understanding of the conceptual framework which needs to underpin a teacher's professional capability with digital technologies.

Teachers' Standards

This book has been written with the Teachers' Standards firmly at its core. The *Teachers' Standards in England* (DfE, 2011c) came into force from 1 September 2012, replacing the standards for Qualified Teacher Status (QTS), the Core Professional Standards and the General Teaching Council for England's *Code of Conduct and Practice for Registered Teachers.* These standards define the minimum level of practice expected of all teachers from the point of being awarded QTS. At the beginning of each section of this book we offer a synopsis of how the content of the section relates to and addresses the Teachers' Standards.

It is well established that digital technologies have the potential to empower children with a wide range of learning needs through their interactivity and adaptability. Indeed, it could be argued that digital technologies have made most impact in education in the area of special educational needs where software, hardware and peripherals can be designed to bypass a number of physical and cognitive learning difficulties. Thus technology has a significant role to play with regard to inclusion and facilitating accessibility in education. Consequently, it is the responsibility of thinking teachers to use their professional skills, knowledge, understanding and judgement as to how digital technologies may or may not be appropriate within these contexts.

Auditing

Your tutor will be able to outline how the audit is carried out in your particular institution. If you feel, in discussion with your mentor, professional tutor or other colleagues, that you have covered aspects of the audit of your development according to the Teachers' Standards, then make a note of it, copy the plan, attach any relevant photographs or printouts as further evidence and cross-reference it with your audit in your portfolio of evidence. Remember that a good plan, a good lesson activity and detailed evaluation may provide evidence that you are operating at a good level within one or more Standard.

Curriculum context

There has been significant government expenditure on ICT infrastructure, which is indicative of the important role many believe technology can play in education. Now no longer in existence, the National Grid for Learning (NGfL), established in 1998, was managed and funded through the then government's agency for ICT, the British Educational Communications and Technology Agency (Becta). This was essentially an online portal to web-based resources for teachers and children. Similarly, other linked services emerged, such as the Virtual Teacher's Centre (VTC), also no longer in existence. The main thrust of government policy at this time was to connect every primary school to the internet and ensure that all teachers had a basic level of ICT competencies. In-service training was offered to schools by a variety of providers funded through the National Lottery's New Opportunities Fund (NOF). However, the potential of these initiatives was limited by the lack of access to broadband connectivity in schools. This prompted a second wave of national investment that was directed again mainly at infrastructure and hardware, with broadband connectivity and interactive whiteboards introduced into many schools. In the later years of the 1997–2010 Labour government two reviews of the primary curriculum were also undertaken. The Rose Review (Rose, 2009) was commissioned by the 1997–2010 Labour government and suggested, among other things, that the status of ICT should be raised to that of core subject in the National Curriculum. The Cambridge Primary Review (Alexander, 2010), an independent review led by the University of Cambridge and funded by the Esmée Fairbairn Foundation, also envisaged an important role for ICT as a tool across eight distinctive domains of learning as well as being located as a subject within the specific domain of 'Language, oracy and literacy'. What these preceding curriculum reviews and national initiatives indicate is the ongoing problematic role of both computing as a subject and ICT more broadly in education.

The contested role of ICT and computing continued to characterise the most recent curriculum developments and debate under the 2010 coalition government. A report by the expert panel for the National Curriculum Review (DfE, 2011a) recommended that the structure of the Key Stages changed to Key Stage 1 for 5–7 year olds (Years 1 and 2), Lower Key Stage 2 for 7–9 year olds (Years 3 and 4) and Upper Key Stage 2 for 9–11 year olds (Years 5 and 6). The report reaffirmed that the National Curriculum is a minimum entitlement for children and that schools have the flexibility and freedom to design a wider school curriculum to meet the needs of their pupils and decide how to teach it most effectively. In the Framework for the National Curriculum (DfE, 2011a) the Expert Panel for the National Curriculum Review recommended that ICT be reclassified from a core subject to part of the Basic Curriculum and that requirements should be established so that ICT permeates all National Curriculum subjects. As a component of the Basic Curriculum, ICT would remain compulsory, but schools themselves would be able to determine the specific nature of the provision.

The establishment of ICT as a component of the Basic Curriculum, underpinning the core and foundation subjects, was challenged by two further reports: one by the Royal Society and the Royal Academy of Engineering (2012), and another funded by Nesta (Livingstone and Hope, 2011). These two reports have possibly had the most significant impact on the status and conception of ICT in the most recent iteration of the National Curriculum (DfE, 2013), including its renaming as a subject from 'ICT' to 'computing'. Livingstone and Hope (2011), who approached their review from the perspective of the video games industry, made several recommendations regarding ICT in schools, including calls to 'bring computer science into the National Curriculum as an essential discipline' (p.7). This report also recognised the cross-disciplinary and applied nature of ICT and computing recommending that schools 'encourage art-tech crossover and work-based learning through school clubs' (ibid.). The report from the Royal Society and the Royal Academy of Engineering also suggested a need for greater emphasis on computer science in any new programme of study for ICT. This report also recommended that ICT as a subject in schools be renamed computing to align it more closely with computer science, 'a rigorous academic discipline on an equal footing with other disciplines such as mathematics, physics, chemistry, geography or history' (p.10). Indeed, the Royal Society and the Royal Academy of Engineering led a group of representatives from organisations such as Naace (ICT Subject Association), ITTE (Association of Information Technology in Teacher Education), BCS (Chartered Institute for IT) and Computing at Schools (CAS) to produce the initial draft of the new programme of study, which was accepted with some modifications.

The recommendation that ICT as a subject should be renamed computing was accepted by the coalition government and as we will see next in a closer analysis of the new programme of study for computing much greater emphasis is placed on computer science at both Key Stages 1 and 2. However, in other ways it can be argued that the focused and specific construction of the new programme of study for computing as a subject (DfE, 2013) now leaves more room for innovation in ICT, which, as mentioned earlier, we define throughout this book as the broader application of digital technologies to enhance learning throughout and beyond the curriculum. That is, in freeing the broader application of digital technologies from specific curricular restraint there can be more scope for the exploration of the ways in which technologies have the potential to enhance learning (Twining, 2013).

From ICT to computing

As suggested earlier in this introduction, the question over whether the subject is best represented by calling it ICT or computing is redundant. In the most recent changes to the National Curriculum (DfE, 2013), ICT as a subject has been renamed computing and, as we will see it has also been given a tighter focus on a core of knowledge and understanding with greater emphasis on aspects of computer science. However, ICT as the broad application of digital technology remains an important concept used widely in the worlds of commerce, business, science, media and the arts, not to mention the many applications within people's leisure and social lives; there are many areas of people's work and leisure that require effective and critical engagement with digital technologies. There is also a clear indication from the DfE (2013) and Ofsted (2011) that, although not detailed in the National Curriculum, teachers are expected to use digital technologies broadly to enhance their teaching and children's learning where appropriate. So how has the National Curriculum for computing changed other than being renamed?

Table 0.1 sets out the previous programme of study and the new programme of study alongside each other for comparison. Immediately evident in comparing and contrasting the left- and right-hand columns of Table 0.1 is the tighter focus in the scope of knowledge, understanding and skills that is specified. But again it should be emphasised that this is a minimum requirement. Take some time to study Table 0.1.

It is worth considering in more depth how the old and new programmes of study are both similar and different. Both programmes of study avoid a purely skills-based computing curriculum. Such a notion is flawed because the work and leisure spaces that today's children will inhabit throughout their lives will be technologically very different from the present and subject to change – consider how networks have transformed many people's work and leisure practices in the last two decades, and more recently how

Table 0.1 Comparison of programmes of study for Key Stages 1 and 2 in 1999 and 2014

Programme of Study (ICT) 1999 Key Stage 1 *Pupils should be taught:*	Programme of Study (Computing) 2014 Key Stage 1 *Pupils should be taught to:*
Finding things out ➤ How to gather information from a variety of sources ➤ How to enter and store information in a variety of forms ➤ How to retrieve information that has been stored **Developing ideas and making things happen** ➤ To use text, tables, images and sound to develop their ideas ➤ How to select from and add to information they have retrieved for particular purposes ➤ To try things out and explore what happens in real and imaginary situations **Exchanging and sharing information** ➤ How to share their ideas by presenting information in a variety of forms ➤ To present their completed work effectively **Reviewing, modifying and evaluating work as it progresses** ➤ To review what they have done to help them develop their ideas ➤ To describe the effects of their actions ➤ To talk about what they might change in future work **Breadth of study** ➤ Working with a range of information to investigate the different ways it can be presented ➤ Exploring a variety of ICT tools ➤ Talking about the uses of ICT inside and outside school	➤ understand what algorithms are; how they are implemented as programs on digital devices; and that programs execute by following precise and unambiguous instructions ➤ create and debug simple programs ➤ use logical reasoning to predict the behaviour of simple programs ➤ use technology purposefully to create, organise, store, manipulate and retrieve digital content ➤ use technology safely and respectfully, keeping personal information private; know where to go for help and support when they have concerns about material on the internet ➤ recognise common uses of information technology beyond school
Key Stage 2 **Finding things out** ➤ To talk about what information they need and how they can find and use it ➤ How to prepare information for development using ICT, including selecting suitable sources, finding information, classifying it and checking it for accuracy **Developing ideas and making things happen** ➤ How to develop and refine ideas by bringing together, organising and reorganising text, tables, images and sound as appropriate	**Key Stage 2** ➤ design, write and debug programs that accomplish specific goals, including controlling or simulating physical systems; solve problems by decomposing them into smaller parts ➤ use sequence, selection and repetition in programs; work with variables and various forms of input and output ➤ use logical reasoning to explain how some simple algorithms work and to detect and correct errors in algorithms and programs

> How to create, test, improve and refine sequences of instructions to make things happen and to monitor events and respond to them

> To use simulations and explore models in order to answer 'What would happen if …?' questions, to investigate and evaluate the effect of changing values and to identify patterns and relationships

Exchanging and sharing information

> How to share and exchange information in a variety of forms, including e-mail

> To be sensitive to the needs of the audience and think carefully about the content and quality when communicating information

Reviewing, modifying and evaluating work as it progresses

> To review what they and others have done to help them develop their ideas

> To describe and talk about the effectiveness of their work with ICT, comparing it with other methods and considering the effect it has on others

> To talk about how they could improve further work

Breadth of study

> Working with a range of information to consider its characteristics and purposes

> Working with others to explore a variety of information sources and ICT tools

> Investigating and comparing the uses of ICT inside and outside school

> understand computer networks including the internet; how they can provide multiple services, such as the world-wide web; and the opportunities they offer for communication and collaboration

> use search technologies effectively, appreciate how results are selected and ranked, and be discerning in evaluating digital content

> use technology safely, respectfully and responsibly; know a range of ways to report concerns and inappropriate behaviour

> select, use and combine a variety of software (including internet services) on a range of digital devices to accomplish given goals, including collecting, analysing, evaluating and presenting data and information

mobile technologies such as smartphones and tablets are facilitating new ways of interacting both professionally and socially. Consequently both programmes of study avoid specific reference to particular hardware, software or skills. This is not to say that teachers do not need to teach or model specific skills to children when operating specific software and applications, but it does indicate that in itself merely teaching a set of skills is not enough to enable children to develop autonomy in their learning with and about digital technologies and computing. Children need a much deeper knowledge and understanding of the role that technologies might play in their own and others' lives as well as an understanding of how they are designed and created.

This is perhaps where the new and old programmes of study begin to differ in emphasis. The previous programme of study for ICT emphasised the digital literacy elements of ICT. The key strands – finding things out, developing ideas and making things happen, exchanging and sharing information, reviewing, modifying and evaluating work as it progresses (Table 0.1) – place emphasis on the fundamental processes underlying why and how we use technology critically and effectively – that is digital literacy. These four strands within the old programmes of study for ICT encompass a range of skills and higher-order knowledge and understanding. For example, on one level, in order to use ICT to 'find things out' using the internet, children need to know how to use the tools on a navigation bar – whether it be Internet Explorer, Safari, Firefox, Google Chrome and so on. However, they also need to be able to identify what information they need, search effectively and efficiently for it and interpret that information accurately, taking into account the validity and reliability of the source. This level of higher-order thinking is dependent on a deep understanding of the ways in which information is managed, structured and published online in comparison with other sources of information. Similarly, if children are going to be able to use technology throughout their lives to 'share and exchange information', they will need to develop a deep understanding of the ways in which information can be created and manipulated to communicate effectively with different audiences. In these ways the old programme of study defined ICT capability broadly in terms of developing children's critical understanding of how they use and apply a range of technologies, placing emphasis on the development of children's digital and media literacy as well as their skills. As Loveless (2003) notes, such a broad ICT capability requires children to develop a deeper understanding of where, when and why to use digital technologies as well as how.

The new programme of study for computing, in contrast, emphasises some of the fundamental processes of computer science such as programming and using logical reasoning as illustrated in the first three statements in the new programme of study at both Key Stages 1 and 2 (Table 0.1). There is also a deliberate use of terminology such as 'algorithms' and 'decomposition' in the new programme of study, which are common terms within the specific discipline of computer science and which we explore in more depth in Chapters 8 and 9. However, it should be stressed that the new programme of study for computing also recognises the importance of digital literacy which is encapsulated by the aspects of the new programme of study which refer to children being able to use technologies 'purposefully', 'safely', 'effectively', 'discerningly' across a range of digital devices (Table 0.1). Indeed online safety, which is dealt with in detail in Chapter 17, is explicitly mentioned in the new programme of study (DfE, 2013) as this is an extremely important area that schools and teachers need to address with children. Essentially the new programme of study for computing delineates the computer science and digital literacy elements of computing more precisely than the previous programme of study, as will become more apparent as you read Section B of this book. As well as developing their knowledge and understanding of digital and media literacy by using technologies effectively and safely with purpose, children are expected to develop a much deeper understanding of how the applications they are using actually work. We often take for granted the technological tools we use in our every-day lives, but the burgeoning array of digital technologies and applications has prompted those designing the new curriculum to question the extent to which we are preparing children to become creators as well as users of new digital technologies. For example, it is argued that learning about computer science has the potential to help children and young people to become the future 'technology designers and creators rather than merely technology users – a philosophy of creativity and expression rather than mere productivity' (Royal Society and Royal Academy of Engineering, 2012, p.290).

As suggested before in this introduction, this reframing of ICT as computing and the tighter focus on a body of core knowledge surrounding how digital technologies and applications are created as well as their effective use brings a new opportunity to enrich the teaching of computing as a subject in schools, while also perhaps creating the space for teachers and children to experiment more with new technologies throughout learning and teaching. However, there is also a risk that the good work that many schools have already developed in relation to computing as a subject and ICT more broadly throughout their practice is abandoned rather than built upon. Trainees will become aware in schools that there has been much debate around the role and status of ICT/computing in schools and this will no doubt continue to a certain extent as policies continue to develop and change. But it is important also to point out that in relation to the teaching of ICT throughout primary schools in the previous National Curriculum (DfEE, 1999) Ofsted reported that in two-thirds of primary schools inspected from 2008 to 2011 the practice of ICT was 'good' or 'outstanding' (Ofsted, 2011). As with any new policy development in education, it is important to recognise and build on the most successful aspects of what has already been achieved.

From this perspective you may find that some schools and individual teachers you work with are still using whole units, adapted units or elements of schemes of work in their medium- and long-term planning for computing and ICT. Furthermore, some of these schemes of work may have been adapted from the QCA scheme of work (QCA, 1998, revised 2002, 2003), which was developed to support the 1999 National Curriculum (DfEE, 1999).

The QCA scheme of work for Key Stages 1 and 2

In order to facilitate the implementation of the previous National Curriculum for ICT (DfEE, 1999) and develop children's ICT capability through challenging and relevant experiences, an ICT Scheme of Work was published by the Department for Education and Skills (DfES) and the Qualifications and Curriculum Authority (QCA). However, this was not statutory and many schools developed their own schemes of work as teaching for creativity and creative teaching with ICT requires teachers to think imaginatively about where purposeful links might be made between ICT and other curriculum areas. The QCA scheme of work provided a sequence of units and is still available via the National Archive (online – see references). While there may be some useful ideas here for trainees to adapt which could provide opportunities for addressing some elements of the new programme of study, it should be stressed that the QCA scheme of work no longer fulfils the requirements of the new programmes of study for computing (DfE, 2013).

Early Years Foundation Stage

The *Statutory Framework for the Early Years Foundation Stage* (DfE, 2014a) identifies features of good practice for the education and care of young children and sets out the early learning goals that most children should achieve by the end of their Reception year in the context of six areas of learning. From September 2008, children in the EYFS have been assessed against a comprehensive Early Years Foundation Stage Profile, the main purpose of which is to provide Year 1 teachers with reliable and accurate information about each child's level of development as they enter Key Stage 1. A number of reforms to the EYFS have been implemented in response to the Tickell Review, *The Early Years: Foundations for Life, Health and Learning* (Tickell, 2011). For example, it recommended that the EYFS reform changes the six areas of learning in development into three prime areas and four specific areas in which the prime areas are applied:

Prime areas:

- personal, social and emotional development
- communication and language
- physical development.

Specific areas:

- literacy
- mathematics
- expressive arts and design
- understanding the world.

As this edition was written, the government announced some more of the details regarding its reform of Primary Assessment and Accountability Measures (DfE, 2014b) which have significant implications for the Early Years and Foundation Stage. From September 2016, the government intend the Early Years Foundation Stage Profile to become non-statutory and be replaced by a Reception Baseline Assessment. There is much debate and some significant apprehension among teachers regarding the implications of this move, based on concerns that the proposed approach is more akin to testing than assessment.

Digital technologies: tools for learning

In the Classroom

In the corner of a classroom, Albert (a Second World War veteran) is searching the Commonwealth War Graves Commission database (**www.cwgc.org**/) with a group of Year 6 children. They are searching for information about local people from the village who lost their lives in the Second World War, people Albert grew up with and went to school with. The children are fascinated by the information Albert shares with them about these people who until now were merely names engraved on the War Memorial in the centre of the village. However, Albert is equally fascinated as the children demonstrate how they can access information about how, when and where these people fell and where their graves are. Albert wants to know more and so do the children. These children go on to create a multimedia presentation with images, text and audio from interviews with Albert about the plight of local people during the Second World War.

Encapsulated within this brief extract is the power of technology to act as a catalyst for rich educational experiences for all generations. This snapshot offers a glimpse of the important role technology has to play in lifelong learning – both the children and the 85-year-old were united in their quest for information. Digital technology can have relevance for all, in different contexts and in whatever phase of life they may be. This raises important and challenging issues for people undertaking primary teacher training and embarking on their careers as newly qualified teachers.

How can digital technologies enhance teaching and learning?

Such a question prompts us to examine our values and beliefs about the purposes of education, the contexts in which people learn and the roles that teachers might play in facilitating such rich educational opportunities described in this classroom example. Digital literacy will no doubt be a vital factor in enabling both teachers and children to exploit the creative potential of new technologies throughout their learning lives, and this is complicated by the fact that technologies are in a constant state of change and pervade all areas of our lives from work to leisure. Teachers' appropriation of technological tools into their professional practice is a complex process affected by a range of factors (Fisher, Higgins and Loveless, 2006; Somekh, 2007; Turvey, 2013). As Loveless and Williamson state (2013, p.158), 'being *ready, willing and able* to teach, calls for a reading of the world in which content, context and tools can be orchestrated with skill and purpose'. Teachers themselves are linchpins in the turning of technological tools into effective pedagogical tools that support learning.

Despite there remaining a significant digital divide between those with access to technology in the home and those without, many children in our society enjoy rich digital lives outside of school, downloading and sharing music, interacting in online multi-user games environments, and engaging in various forms of communication through a range of digital devices. So, what can we as teachers learn from these informal uses of technology outside of school and what effect might the constantly changing technological landscape have on our own uses of technology within school? Teachers need an understanding of the ways in which they can use information and communications technology (ICT) to support and enhance their teaching across the curriculum and in a range of contexts. They also need an understanding of how children develop an ICT capability which enables them to deal with information critically in a rapidly changing world. These are pedagogical issues and indeed the development of new technologies often necessitates a shift in pedagogical approach in order to exploit fully the educational potential of the technology. To support your professional judgement about how digital technologies can be integrated into your teaching and children's learning it is useful to consider the characteristics that any new technology or application bring that can be exploited for pedagogical gain, as we examine now.

Key characteristics of digital technologies as learning tools

Many teachers, teacher-educators and policy-makers have grappled with the question of what contribution new technologies bring to learning and teaching. The plethora of technological tools now available, from web-based tools (blogs, social networking, content management) to mobile devices such as tablets, smartphones, electronic voting systems and digital video cameras has led many to look for new ways of describing and classifying the role of digital technologies in learning and teaching. The term 'e-learning' is often used in education and encompasses learning and teaching strategies which draw on a range of digital and networked technologies. As teachers you need to exercise critical judgement, confidence and expertise in applying e-learning strategies throughout your work to improve the quality and standard of children's education. Teachers need to have knowledge, skills and understanding of the ways in which digital technologies can support their professional practice. That is, teachers should be able to make informed decisions about when, when not and how to use digital technologies effectively in their teaching and children's learning. Indeed, Turvey and Pachler (2016) call for an approach that treats the introduction of digital technologies in formal education as creating 'problem spaces' that offer both opportunities and tensions in practice. In order to unpick this issue, it is useful to begin to consider the features of ICT, which can make a distinctive contribution to practice or a specific subject. That is the characteristics that can be exploited in order to make a contribution as a resource, as a tool and as a catalyst for new ways of working in the curriculum. These characteristics can be broadly categorised as *interactivity*, *provisionality*, *multimodality*, *automaticity* and *mobility*.

Interactivity can engage users at a number of levels, from the playing of a computer game to investigating the geographical features of the Himalayas via Google Earth. Both of these activities have in common the ways in which digital technologies can give immediate and dynamic feedback to decisions and actions made by the user. Whether undertaking a search of the internet, investigating a graph of the changes detected by a temperature sensor over a period of time or editing a multimedia presentation, these activities enable children to make decisions, see the consequences and act on feedback accordingly. However, the degree to which children engage and interact will very much depend on the way in which the teacher has framed these activities. Furthermore, the role of the teacher in encouraging the children to explore, to learn from dead ends and frustrations and to develop perseverance in trying out ideas and learning from feedback is vital in maximising the educational value of the experience for the children. Interactivity is more than passive engagement with digital technologies.

The *provisionality* of ICT enables users to make changes, try out alternatives and keep a track of their developmental ideas. The advantages of this can be recognised immediately in the writing of text for a report or a blog. Word processing in these ways can facilitate continual editing and development of ideas. Advances in the speed and storage capacity of computers have extended this feature to the digital manipulation of still images, moving images and sound or the designing and programming of computer games. Such advances put within children's and teachers' grasp a range of new modes of expression and enable them to become creators of rich multimedia. However, as with interactivity, teachers have a vital role to play in promoting positive attitudes to working with and exploiting the provisionality of digital technologies. They can model, discuss and make explicit the processes of evaluation, changing ideas and reviewing work, whether this is with text, still images, moving images, sound or adapting and debugging an algorithm that is not providing the expected outcome in a game they have created.

Multimodality is another key characteristic of digital technologies. The capacity and range it offers for multimodal ways of representation enables children and teachers to access vast amounts of digital information in the form of text, visual images and sound. As file capacity and processor speed increase across the range of technologies from mobile phones to desktop computers, increasingly multimodality becomes the norm. However, with this increasing multimodality comes the need for children to be able to make sense of this information and critically evaluate its authority and authenticity. While teachers continue to play a vital role in enabling children to make sense of text from an early age, reading images (still, moving and animated) and considering the impact of sound in a multimodal text will also be key to children's capacity to make sense of an increasingly rich multimodal world. It is also important for teachers to consider if there are circumstances in which such multimodality can distract from or confuse the conceptual knowledge being taught.

Automaticity or the speed and automatic function of ICT allow tasks of storing, changing and displaying information to be carried out by technology, enabling users to read, observe, interrogate, interpret, analyse and synthesise information at higher levels. Many routine activities such as capturing and organising data, monitoring change, carrying out calculations, drawing graphs and presenting findings can be done using digital technologies, leaving the children time to ask questions and think about the meaning of the information with which they are presented.

The characteristic *mobility* of many digital technologies perhaps most clearly illustrates the tensions and opportunities (Turvey and Pachler, 2016) they bring in terms of teaching and learning. The ubiquitous nature of the internet combined with the portability of small yet powerful digital devices such as tablets and smartphones in theory offers a seamless connection between sites of both formal and informal learning (schools, homes, museums, educational trips, connections to the wider world). But mobility also brings tensions as children's and teachers' personal/social networks converge with their professional or formal learning networks. Teachers need to think carefully about how they can safely exploit the mobility of digital technologies to enhance the quality of teaching and learning.

These distinctive characteristics of digital technologies offer a useful framework for teachers in thinking about the broader contribution of digital technologies to learning and teaching throughout the curriculum as well as in their wider professional role. However, it is important to understand that these features do not lie solely within the technology. It takes a thinking and skilful teacher to realise and exploit the full potential offered by these key features of digital technologies.

Outcomes

As you read this book it will become clear that it is grounded in a view of computing and digital technologies as both a subject and a powerful teaching and learning tool throughout the school curriculum and beyond into many areas of children's learning lives. The emphasis is placed on children becoming discerning and creative users of technology as opposed to passive consumers. In order for children to develop such critical, confident and expansive dispositions towards technology they need opportunities to develop their capabilities over time, through using and applying their skills, knowledge and understanding across a range of purposeful and meaningful contexts. The new National Curriculum for computing (DfE, 2013) has introduced the need for children to develop a knowledge and understanding of how technology works through aspects of computer science as well as how it is used effectively and critically (digital literacy). However, it is also clear that there is an expectation that schools will continue to create opportunities for children to develop a broad ICT capability through the integration of a range of digital technologies into their learning, which reflect the 'increasingly digital and connected world' in which they live (DfE, 2013, n.p.). The challenge for teachers is to develop children's knowledge and understanding through planning and providing meaningful opportunities for sustained engagement with technology, opportunities in which children themselves are required to explore, create, reflect, review, ask questions and share ideas openly. Trainees and new teachers also need to take responsibility for the development of their own capability, through personal study, working with others, planning classroom experiences and developing networks of professional support, providing strong role models for the children as they themselves become confident, informed and critical users of digital technology.

By using this book to support your own subject knowledge development, you will be able to learn the knowledge and develop the understanding that you require to teach primary computing, develop your professional use of ICT and consider the appropriate elements of the EYFS areas of learning.

So that you can check on how well you have assimilated the subject knowledge and test your understanding, you may wish to try the self-assessment questions related to the different aspects of computing and ICT application that we address. You will find these in a section at the end of the book. The answers follow.

For those undertaking credits for a Master's degree, we have included suggestions for further work and extended study at the end of each chapter in a section called 'M-Level Extension'.

To support you in understanding the curriculum context, you may find it helpful to refer further to some of the documentation that we have mentioned in this introduction (see References).

REFERENCES REFERENCES **REFERENCES** REFERENCES **REFERENCES** REFERENCES

Alexander, R. (2010) *Cambridge Primary Review Final Report: Children, Their World, Their Education*. Available online at **www.primaryreview.org.uk/**.

DfE (2011a) *The Framework for the National Curriculum. A Report by the Expert Panel for the National Curriculum Review*. London: DfE.

DfE (2011c) *Teachers' Standards.* Available at **www.education.gov.uk/publications**.

DfE (2013) *Digital Technology in Schools*. Available at **www.education.gov.uk/a00201823/digital-technology-in-schools**.

DfE (2014a) *Statutory Framework for the Early Years Foundation Stage.* London: DfE. Available at **www.education.gov.uk/publications**.

DfE (2014b) *Reforming Assessment and Accountability for Primary Schools*. Available at **www.gov.uk/government/consultations/new-national-curriculum-primary-assessment-and-accountability**.

DfEE (1999) *National Curriculum Handbook for Key Stages 1 and 2*. London: HMSO.

Fisher, T., Higgins, C. and Loveless, A. (2006) *Teachers Learning with Digital Technologies: A Review of Research and Projects*. Bristol: Futurelab.

Livingstone, I. and Hope, A. (2011) *Next Gen. Transforming the UK into the World's Leading Talent Hub for the Video Games and Visual Effects Industries*. London: NESTA. Available online at **www.nesta.org.uk/publications/next-gen**.

Loveless, A. (2003) *The Role of ICT*. London and New York: Continuum.

Loveless, A. and Williamson, B. (2013) *Learning Identities in a Digital Age: Rethinking Creativity, Education and Technology*. London and New York: Routledge.

Ofsted (2011) *ICT in Schools 2008–11*. Available at **www.ofsted.gov.uk/resources/ict-schools-2008-11**.

Ofsted (2012) *Initial Teacher Education Inspection Handbook*. London: Ofsted.

QCA (1998, revised 2002, 2003) *Scheme of Work for ICT*. London: QCA. Available online at **http://webarchive.nationalarchives.gov.uk/20090608182316/http://standards.dfes.gov.uk/schemes2/it/?view=get**.

Rose, J. (2009) *Independent Review of the Primary Curriculum Final Report*. Available online at **www.educationengland.org.uk/documents/pdfs/2009-IRPC-final-report.pdf**.

Royal Society and Royal Academy of Engineering (2012) *Computing in Schools: Shut Down or Restart? The Way Forward for Computing in UK Schools*. Available online at **http://royalsociety.org/education/policy/computing-in-schools/report/**.

Somekh, B. (2007) *Pedagogy and Learning with ICT: Researching the Art of Innovation*. London: Routledge.

Tickell, C. (2011) *The Early Years: Foundations for Life, Health and Learning. An Independent Report on the Early Years Foundation Stage to Her Majesty's Government*. London: DfE.

Turvey, K. (2013) *Narrative Ecologies: Teachers as Pedagogical Toolmakers*. London and New York: Routledge.

Turvey, K. and Pachler, N. (2016) '"Problem spaces": a framework and questions for critical engagement with learning technologies in formal educational contexts', in N. Rushby and D. Surry (eds), *The Wiley Handbook of Learning Technology*. Hoboken, NJ: John Wiley & Sons.

Twining, P. (2013) *ICT Is Dead – Long Live ICT*. Available online at **http://edfutures.net/ICT_is_dead_-_long_live_ICT**.

FURTHER READING   FURTHER READING   FURTHER READING   FURTHER READING

Duffty, J. (2006) *Primary ICT: Extending Knowledge in Practice*. Exeter: Learning Matters.

Selwyn, N. (2011) *Schools and Schooling in the Digital Age: A Critical Analysis*. London and New York: Routledge.

Section A
Digital Technologies in Teaching and Learning

Trainees' first concerns when they begin teaching are often how to make effective use of the digital technologies they very quickly find themselves needing to use. Although digital technologies are often described as tools, this description can conceal or downplay the knowledge and skills that teachers require to make effective use of digital technologies to promote children's learning. Thus Section A is concerned with issues related to planning, organising and teaching for effective learning with digital technologies. The curriculum for the Early Years will also be addressed in a separate chapter on digital technologies in the Early Years Foundation Stage. As good planning depends on a thorough analysis of the situation before you even start working, Chapters 1–3 provide a consideration of the background knowledge you need to acquire in order to deliver appropriate learning opportunities for the children you teach. In Chapters 4 and 5 we then consider some of the more specific technologies such as Interactive Whiteboards and tablet devices that trainees may need to integrate into their professional practice and children's learning.

In 'Organising digital technologies in your classroom' we will consider the physical management of a range of technologies in learning areas. The different levels of resourcing will be characterised so that you can begin to assess the situation in your placement school more quickly. We will consider what the various strategies are for dealing with high-, medium- and low-resource situations. For example, we will consider the very different management strategies to be employed when working with children in a primary school with a network room full of computers or when working with one stand-alone machine in the classroom.

In the chapter 'Planning for digital technologies across the curriculum', we will consider the potential to integrate digital technologies in all subjects of the National Curriculum, so this section will also look at how to plan within the core curriculum (English, maths and science) and within the foundation subjects in order to maximise the potential for all learners.

'Planning to use digital technologies in the Early Years Foundation Stage' will look specifically at ICT in the context of the *Statutory Framework for the Early Years Foundation Stage* (DfE, 2014).

The final two chapters in Section A (Chapters 4 and 5) focus specifically on 'Interactive display technologies' and 'Mobile technologies' respectively. These are two vital areas that trainees need to reflect on critically if they are to appropriate the various tools effectively into their practice. It is essential that trainees understand the various features of digital technologies such as Interactive Whiteboards (IWBs), visualisers and tablets in order to make sound judgements about what they may or may not lend to the teaching and learning context.

Chapter Objectives are highlighted at the start of each chapter. You can find the relevant references in *Teachers' Standards* (DfE, 2011) applying to all of the chapters in this section.

However, Chapter 1 focuses mainly on Teachers' Standards 1, 5 and 7, whereas Chapters 2, 3, 4 and 5 concentrate on Teachers' Standards 1, 2, 3 and 4 as set out below.

TEACHERS' STANDARDS

A teacher must:

1. **Set high expectations which inspire, motivate and challenge pupils**

- establish a safe and stimulating environment for pupils, rooted in mutual respect
- set goals that stretch and challenge pupils of all backgrounds, abilities and dispositions
- demonstrate consistently the positive attitudes, values and behaviour which are expected of pupils.

2. **Promote good progress and outcomes by pupils**

- be accountable for pupils' attainment, progress and outcomes
- demonstrate knowledge and understanding of how pupils learn and how this impacts on teaching
- encourage pupils to take a responsible and conscientious attitude to their own work and study.

3. **Demonstrate good subject and curriculum knowledge**

- have a secure knowledge of the relevant subject(s) and curriculum areas, foster and maintain pupils' interest in the subject, and address misunderstandings
- demonstrate a critical understanding of developments in the subject and curriculum areas, and promote the value of scholarship

4. **Plan and teach well structured lessons**

- impart knowledge and develop understanding through effective use of lesson time
- promote a love of learning and children's intellectual curiosity
- contribute to the design and provision of an engaging curriculum within the relevant subject area(s).

5. **Adapt teaching to respond to the strengths and needs of all pupils**

- have a secure understanding of how a range of factors can inhibit pupils' ability to learn, and how best to overcome these
- demonstrate an awareness of the physical, social and intellectual development of children, and know how to adapt teaching to support pupils' education at different stages of development
- have a clear understanding of the needs of all pupils, including those with special educational needs; those of high ability; those with English as an additional language; those with disabilities; and be able to use and evaluate distinctive teaching approaches to engage and support them.

7. **Manage behaviour effectively to ensure a good and safe learning environment**

- manage classes effectively, using approaches which are appropriate to pupils' needs in order to involve and motivate them

As far as possible throughout the parts of chapters which are concerned with resources, we have attempted to be completely generic. That is to say we have not specified a particular platform (Microsoft, Apple, etc.). Some example titles of software, apps or other specific resources may be given, but only where absolutely necessary to explain a concept further. There is so much software available for schools at all levels for all of the computer platforms that it would be impossible to create a list that would be applicable or viable in all settings. Also, a great deal of software these days is web-based and does not require installation on individual computers.

REFERENCES REFERENCES **REFERENCES** REFERENCES REFERENCES REFERENCES

DfE (2011) *Teachers' Standards.* Available at **www.education.gov.uk/publications**.

DfE (2014) *Statutory Framework for the Early Years Foundation Stage.* London: DfE. Available at **www.education.gov.uk/publications**.

1
Organising digital technologies in your classroom

Chapter objectives

When you have completed work on this chapter, you will have:

- thought about the organisational issues around teaching with digital technologies in your primary classroom;
- considered the practical aspects of locating equipment and how this impacts on planning;
- looked at organising the different levels of resources present in schools/settings;
- examined how best to meet children's needs and to enable them to benefit from and enjoy using digital technologies in their learning.

Introduction

First, to look back at the recent past, new entrants to the teaching profession are fortunate to be joining it at a time following continuing, well-funded change in ICT in schools. Since the late 1990s in England, there has been significant spending on ICT infrastructure, hardware and software in schools. However, change on such a large scale is not without its logistical difficulties and much still depends on how the additional spending on ICT in schools has been managed at school level, local authority (LA) level and in the case of academies, the priorities of the academy trusts to which they belong.

The national background

The evidence, from inspections by Ofsted and others, has suggested year on year that the use of computers and other digital technologies in schools, such as interactive whiteboards, is, in some cases, becoming more prevalent and better integrated into subject teaching. However, there is concern at the widening gap between schools that are at the cutting edge and using digital technologies widely and pervasively and those that have not yet fully integrated them into their teaching and learning. Even in areas where there is rich provision of resources, it is possible to find evidence that ICT is not always fully or usefully integrated into the broader curriculum.

Part of the issue lies with the variation in the quality of the development plans at local and at school level as well as with the wide variation in support to schools. In turn, some of the variation can be put down to the 'bid culture' in which the innovation has taken place. In some initiatives, LAs made bids for funding to central government on the basis of a costed development plan. Schools sometimes had to bid to LAs for a share, and so on. No two neighbouring LAs managed this in exactly the same way, so you will notice variations when you move between your placement schools. The recent move to free schools and academies has only added to this complexity and variation.

Allied to the expansion in hardware provision was the connection of every school to the internet and to subsequent opportunities for collaboration and communication, as well as home–school links. This used to be referred to as connecting schools to the National Grid for Learning (NGFL) and you may still see references to this now-defunct initiative in school documentation. To this end, LAs in many parts of the country aligned themselves with the emergent 'Regional Broadband Consortia' (RBCs) which were public-private partnerships providing fast, relatively low-tariff internet access for schools and, in many cases, a virtual learning environment (VLE) of one kind or another through which the learning community interacts. Most also assisted schools in protecting children from unsuitable content through the deployment of firewalls and servers which screen sites and searches.

A further major element of spending early on was an acknowledgement of the need to train teachers in schools. The New Opportunities Fund (NOF) was set up with Heritage (Lottery) money. Again, although NOF funding and training have now ceased, you may well encounter references to it in staffroom documentation or in conversation.

A further intention of government policy under the New Labour Government from 1997 to 2010 was to provide subsidised laptops for teachers. Significant pilot projects, such as the Becta multimedia Portables for Teachers pilots, had found that giving teachers laptops greatly increased their use of digital technologies in the curriculum for teaching and administration. In order to benefit from the scheme teachers had to be part of a school which was registered with the above-mentioned NOF training scheme. Some of the teachers with whom you will be working may well have benefited from this scheme.

Other major initiatives have had differing levels of emphasis in different local authorities. In some LAs, personal ownership of computers was pursued in the form of projects which focus on the use of hand-held equipment such as PDAs (personal digital assistants). In other LAs, the use of laptops was seen as something to be encouraged through bulk purchase schemes alongside trolleys for the storage and charging of the equipment. The aim here was to diversify ICT provision away from the static fixed computer lab and put the technology in the hands of the learners. More recently some schools have moved towards exploring the use of tablet devices such as iPads and other such devices, in order to exploit the mobility and flexibility offered by such devices. Similarly trainees might come across schools which operate what is called a 'bring your own device' strategy (BYOD) in which children may be encouraged to bring their own devices to school (e.g. smartphone, iPod touch) which can be linked to the school network and used for researching on the internet and to support learning. This is more common in secondary schools and does of course bring with it issues of equal opportunity for learners.

You may well also encounter local projects and initiatives based in the realm of digital media, recording and presenting video and audio resources, digital movie-making, podcasting and so on. There is a fuller discussion of this in future sections.

The local background

There has been a perceived lack of confidence with the integration of ICT on the part of some teachers. Occasionally, this is characterised as 'reluctance'. It is certainly true that some teachers find it enormously threatening to be delivering a subject or using technological tools which employ skills which they do not feel that they themselves have but which the children may possess.

There may also be no support structure for teachers in their school situation. At school level, there may be no ICT or computing co-ordinator. Good ICT and computing subject leaders who attend training and pass it on to colleagues and who give generously of their time and knowledge are not always readily available. At LA level, it may be that there is no active advisory team encouraging good practice and recommending hardware and software. In both these cases there has been a failure of management to see the necessity of putting money into human resources. Too much time and money can sometimes be spent on hardware and software and not enough on the human resources needed to develop and promote excellence in ICT and computing in the classroom. You may well see evidence of this in your placement school. The recent emphasis on computer science and programming in the National Curriculum has also exacerbated this issue.

One other issue to note is the perceived 'skills gap' between teachers and children at home. Year on year, home ownership of computers and digital devices is increasing. It would be wrong to assume that it was all going into the study bedrooms of middle-class students. It is possible to find levels of computer ownership in deprived areas of Inner London, for example, where six-year-old children are experienced users of the latest software. As alluded to above, it would be wrong for teachers to allow the feeling to grow that children know more than they do. What children do not know, and the reason why they need the teacher to be using digital technologies with them, is how to apply it critically in their developing subject knowledge. Marc Prensky (2001) popularised the term 'digital natives' to refer to the apparent ease with which children and young people who have grown up in technology-rich contexts relate to digital technologies and appropriate them. However, this term is often used far too loosely and naively in relation to children and young people's use of digital technologies and their safe, critical and effective use of digital technologies cannot be assumed. Bennett et al. (2008) offer a more critical view on the debate about so-called 'digital natives' and the implications for education.

Resource levels in schools: a rough guide

This section attempts to categorise schools according to the resource settings at different levels. Three types of resource setting are described on a continuum from high resource to medium resource to low resource (see Table 1.1). It is useful to characterise resource settings in this way because you will be able to make a judgement about particular organisational strategies if you can learn to observe and sum up the situation in a placement school quickly.

Table 1.1 Resource-level definitions

High-resource setting

Portable computers such as laptops or tablets and handheld devices are used around the school and throughout the curriculum. There is a network room used by groups and the wider community (sometimes) as a hub for ICT development activities.

Printing – in colour when necessary – is available at every station.

There is a fast broadband connection and wireless connectivity throughout the school.

There is a technician who regularly attends to maintain equipment in good working order. Digital cameras and digital video cameras are available for use by teachers and children. There are interactive whiteboards or visualisers in most teaching spaces and their use is informed by good pedagogical decisions, not always teacher-led; children often have control of the resource.

A range of appropriate software is available for every age phase.

There are also stations connected to the network available in the classroom to carry on with work begun in the network room or computer suite. These may be in the form of rechargeable laptops or tablet devices such as iPads.

Programmable toys and other robotics or electronics equipment are available for exploring programming and aspects of computer science.

The school is implementing a cohesive strategy for the use of ICT and the teaching of computing, including an ongoing development plan.

There is a policy for acceptable internet use and comprehensive safeguarding procedures.

There is a fully implemented scheme of work that is regularly reviewed and updated.

Teachers, children and the wider community make use of the VLE where the school has a vibrant and well-used web presence.

Suitability for placement as a trainee:

This is an excellent setting for learning how to integrate digital technologies fully into the curriculum and develop your ICT capability at the same time.

Medium-resource setting

There is a working computer and printer in every classroom.

There is a network room with computers connected to the Internet that is partially timetabled for each year group.

Some programmable toys are available.

A digital camera is available to borrow and some short video clips are sometimes used.

Repairs to equipment are dealt with fairly promptly.

Interactive whiteboards (IWBs) are present in some classrooms and are sometimes used by children.

A scheme of work for computing is being implemented.

The school has a development plan in operation and is considering how to integrate digital technologies more fully through the use of flexible and mobile technologies such as laptop trolleys or class sets of tablet devices.

ICT and computing are valued and within the next two or three years the school will move forward and become a high resource setting.

A policy on safe and acceptable internet use is being developed and there are plans to upgrade the school website soon.

Suitability for placement as a trainee:

Although not at the very cutting edge, this is a good situation in which to develop skills of organising for the use of digital technologies and a trainee may still learn and even contribute something to the placement school.

Low-resource setting:

There is an older, frequently broken computer in the classroom or one between two. There are a few interactive whiteboards that are used infrequently or ineffectively.

Overhead projectors are used on the whiteboard surface.

There may be low staff morale, low spending on digital technologies, no ICT co-ordinator, no technician.

There is no scheme of work in place for computing.

Printers are shared and are not always properly serviced.

Poor software results in children from Year 1 to Year 6 doing the same thing on the computer (copy typing, doodling in a Paint package, playing a number or spelling game, possibly the same one each time).

The school website is rarely updated.

In Ofsted terms, the school is not providing the full entitlement to computing and ICT for its children and staff are not receiving their entitlement to professional development.

Suitability for placement as a trainee:

Hopefully, there are very few settings like this left as this is a very difficult placement in which to gain the required standard in computing or the effective use of digital technologies in teaching and learning. You would be heavily dependent on your institution for support.

The school in which you are placed will be somewhere along the line of development and will not necessarily have all elements of the different resource settings represented. Furthermore, schools develop and change year on year.

A further issue – which is partly included below – is the human resource levels in the school. A school with very low levels of ICT equipment may still be doing well in ICT and computing due to excellence in the organisation and involvement of all staff. Similarly a school which looks good with a network room full of computers and trolleys of iPads may in fact be keeping the door locked and doing nothing with them. The situation is complex.

PRACTICAL TASK PRACTICAL TASK PRACTICAL TASK PRACTICAL TASK

Observing the ICT setting 1: The computers and other hardware

Schools have a degree of choice over how they organise their resources for computing and ICT and this early observation task is designed to raise awareness about the organisation and use of digital technologies in teaching and learning. The sections which follow will take up issues around school organisation and discuss how they may have come to certain pedagogical decisions.

Although in itself computing is a foundation subject, ICT or digital technologies can be integrated into every subject area across the curriculum and you will see it being used in a range of settings, including in areas of learning in the Early Years Foundation Stage. Make notes on what is being used and on where it is being used. Use these questions as prompts for your note-taking. Have a look at all of the places in the school where digital technologies may be in operation.

- What do you see?
- Is there a computer in the classroom?
- Or are all the computers grouped in an ICT/computer suite?
- Is there a mixed provision of some in the classroom and some in an ICT suite?
- Are there any portable computers available, either laptops or tablets?
- Is there an interactive whiteboard in the classroom or the EYFS setting?
- How is it being used?

- Who is using it?

- Are there scanners or digital cameras or digital video cameras?

- Can children and teachers access the internet easily?

- Is the internet available in the classroom or ICT suite or both?

- Does this appear to be a quick connection?

- Is there wireless connectivity throughout the school?

- Is the internet filtered in any way to protect the children?

- Does it go straight onto the internet or special local authority network?

- Does the school use a virtual learning environment (VLE)?

- Does there appear to be interesting primary school software around in the school?

- How does it appear to be organised?

- Has the school subscribed to appropriate web-based software for learning? Find out what is available and, if you can, list six to eight titles with their subject area and age range.

The notes which you make should be brief and comprise up to two sides of A4. They should be written with enough detail to give you a snapshot of digital technologies in use across the curriculum in your school. Read them again in the context of the opening sections of this chapter. What do your observations and reflections tell you about the kind of ICT setting in which you will be operating?

Observing the ICT setting 2: Human resources for ICT

Observe how the class teachers organise the digital technologies for their children.

Observe the children themselves as they work with digital technologies in the school. They are the best source of information about what is going on with ICT in the classroom. They know about the equipment. If it is old, they know which keys stick. They tend to know how to get round the deficiencies of the equipment, such as the printer which jams regularly. The games-playing children, those who have computer game consoles at home of one kind or another, often have a robust attitude towards computers of all sorts. They are aware of 'cheating' to get to different levels. Sometimes they will indulge in various key presses which may cause havoc with onscreen displays; sometimes they may discover for the class, newer, more efficient ways of doing things. Whatever the situation, it is always worth listening to what children say about computers and considering and valuing their contributions to the whole class body of knowledge about computing and ICT.

Observe the classroom and learning support assistants wherever possible. Where available, they are a valuable source of knowledge and support about digital technologies in the classroom. Listen to what they say and involve them in your planning. Mutual respect and good communication are the keys to working well with teaching assistants in all areas of the curriculum.

How do the children and adults use the interactive whiteboard? Is the teacher always in control? Which curriculum areas predominate? Do they use the software that comes with the board or do they sometimes show web pages, images and DVDs through the projector?

Find out about the parents and governors and ICT. Parents, like children, have a wide range of ability and experience and an even wider range of concerns with computing and ICT. Some parental concerns will be around the use of the internet in your school, how it is organised and so on. They may ask whether or not the school has an acceptable use policy and adequate protection for their children from unsuitable material. Governors may raise many of the same issues with you as the school will be held responsible for the materials which the children may, in all innocence, be accessing if the school is not providing access through an education provider or through a filter which it is maintaining itself.

Make notes about your findings, including who the computing and ICT subject leader is, how to report faults/maintenance issues, for example to a technician or via the school office, and who you can talk to if you have queries on policies that relate to digital technologies.

RESEARCH SUMMARY RESEARCH SUMMARY **RESEARCH SUMMARY** RESEARCH SUMMARY

Bridget Somekh (Somekh and Davis, 2007) characterises three ways in which teachers approach the use of ICT. In the first two of these, teachers use ICT either as a tutorial tool, delivering content to pupils, or as a tool for carrying out tasks in 'content-free' software that does not necessarily depend on fully exploiting the features of ICT (she calls the computer a neutral tool in this mode). Finally, the third way of using the computer is as a cognitive tool to support active learning on the part of the children concerned (see Somekh and Davis, 2007). These provide a useful framework for examining practice, either your own or observed in school.

Organisational strategies for different resource settings

Computing as a subject and the appropriate use of digital technologies in teaching and learning is an entitlement no matter which situation you are working in. In all settings there are organisational issues which need to be addressed. This section looks at organising digital technologies in low-resource and high-resource settings. As mentioned in the Introduction we use the terms ICT and digital technologies interchangeably throughout this book except when referring to the previous National Curriculum.

Organising digital technologies in high-resource settings

In a high-resource setting, it is quite likely that you will be able to share the experience of the lesson with the children by means of a large display. This will be in the form of a large monitor, projector and screen or an interactive whiteboard (IWB). There could be software installed on the system that enables the teacher to take control of the screens at the individual stations, temporarily replacing them with the teacher's or another child's screen, in order to model something to the rest of the class. In any school where there is no such display facility, you will have to gather the children together in a space in front of one of the monitors. Teaching in network rooms without a large display is very difficult and you will need to learn strategies for overcoming this from observing the other teachers and/or teaching assistants.

Remind the children that they do not have to sit at the same machine each week and about the importance of their password. Here are some different models of practice.

- Whole-class logon with the same username and password into a general area on the network for that class.
- Children with a unique username and password.
- Children with group logon names and passwords.

Before teaching the children on a network, make sure that you understand the process of logging on yourself. Ask the computing and ICT subject leader or technician before starting. Remember to ask for your own username and password as a guest on placement at the school. Children are often given their own area on the network in which to save their work. It is important that you follow the same protocols that they are used to. Every school network is slightly differently organised and you will need to take time to learn this for yourself so as not to make potentially serious mistakes such as losing work. Also, when working as a whole class in a computer suite children should be encouraged to develop independent problem-solving skills. Strategies such as 'ask three and then me' are useful in managing the learning environment so that the teacher is not seen as the only source for support and learning. For example, a child who is stuck with a task or technical issue considers first if they can solve the problem themselves, secondly if another child can help them and thirdly perhaps another child or teaching assistant can help, before asking the teacher.

As a rule, unless the children are very young, they should be taught how to log on and log off by themselves. This is part of learning about network literacy. One strategy is to have all the passwords and usernames on index cards, used at the beginning of the session and collected at the end.

Whole-class demonstrations can, and should, still take place, but they need to be a sensible length, enabling the children to make the best use of the time available.

In a school where there is access to distributed technology, such as laptops or tablet devices, many of these issues do not arise at all. In their place, other factors need to be taken into account, such as battery life, ownership, sharing, storing and so on. At any rate, it is important that you follow the protocols of the school in this area as in others. Many teachers remark on how much simpler it is to integrate the use of technology when mass access to portable or hand-held computers is available, rather than having to take everyone down to a computer suite. It becomes as much a part of the provision as the use of traditional items in the classroom.

Later chapters will look in detail at how to manage ICT resources to approach knowledge and skills across the curriculum as well as when teaching computing as a subject. It is important to remember that children can contribute to the whole-class understanding and skills development with digital technologies and that there should be an opportunity for them to do so at times during, or at the close of, the session. The plenary, for example, can really come alive in a networked environment if the children are encouraged to use software for the presentation of their projects for all to see. Schools in high-resource settings which are capable of publishing on the internet or their own intranet will be able to further enrich the motivational opportunities for children writing or creating multimedia work for a wider audience.

Organising digital technologies in low-resource settings

Low-resource settings are far less common. However, they still exist and can also pertain in a school when a network room or set of laptops is out of use or block-booked by another teacher. In a setting in which a single computer is shared by a class of 30 children, first bring the computer to the carpet area where it can be seen by everybody. There may, of course, be physical reasons why you cannot do this. If there are, do what you can to overcome them or borrow areas big enough to do it somewhere else in the school. Just getting started with a piece of software should involve the whole class. When beginning with software that children have not encountered before and the screens look very unfamiliar to the class, it would be worth spending time on them.

The aim is still to allow the computer to be more fully a part of the general resource provision of the classroom. A question-and-answer style lends itself to this situation. Allow the children to contribute, even to provide tips for other users. Discuss with them the difficulties that they have overcome in familiarising themselves with the onscreen layout of the particular piece of software. Whole-class sessions can be enhanced by the following examples and principles.

- Ask the children to discover during the session, and then report back on, different ways of doing the same thing. In a writing program for example, how can they make text appear in a different font size or colour?
- Stress regular, practical instructions. One such regularly repeated instruction should be 'Save before you print' in order to avoid the inevitable heartache which arises when a document gets lost.
- As is the case with all good primary practice, question children who don't always jump up and down with the answer (don't favour the loud over the quiet). Your school may even operate a no hands up policy where children are chosen randomly to respond to questions (e.g. named lolly sticks).
- Do not allow one gender or group of children to dominate.
- Stress the team-building aspects of sharing strategies so that they/we can all use the computer efficiently and safely.
- Involve children in a discussion about safety – monitor position, length of time, seating and so on. If they are using the internet for research, monitor their search strategies and approaches.
- Value what children contribute even when it is patently wrong. Help them to discover a better way constructively (e.g. 'That's a good suggestion but …').
- Draw on children's experience of digital technologies at home or in other community settings.

The suggestions in the list above are part of good practice for any teaching situation. There is no reason why the use of technology should result in adopting different values around communication and sharing. Technology sometimes challenges assumptions that we have of teaching and learning. Indeed it often stimulates debate about the first principles of education, but it should never be an end in itself. There has to be a sound pedagogical reason for using ICT in a given situation.

Regular whole-class input increases the shared level of knowledge in the classroom about the use of digital technologies and will reduce the number of times that you have to say the same thing over and over again to groups of two to three children.

Becoming independent and increasingly competent in basic ICT skills will engender in the children a sense of responsibility for their work. It may be something that many of the children know from home but there will be others for whom you are providing the only access to newer technology. From an early age, as children progress through the school, they are expected to take on more responsibility for knowing where their equipment is, where their possessions are, where they're going next and so on. It should be the same for ICT. Children can be shown the importance of looking after digital forms of their work, just as they learn the importance of looking after their books. They will often need to be shown how to save and retrieve their work and the importance of backing up work.

An alternative model of instruction, a version of the cascade model or peer teaching, whereby one or two children learn it and teach others, can allow the more negative messages about digital technologies to be disseminated and should be used cautiously. Among these more negative messages are:

1. There are ICT experts who know everything and must always be consulted before you do anything.
2. ICT is something that happens in a corner of the room away from the mainstream and is never discussed and nothing to do with the rest of the school day.

Show children that you are also a learner. Using digital technologies in your own practice will be less threatening to you as a teacher if you enter into the situation as a learner alongside them. It is wrong to give children the impression that you or anyone else knows all they need to know about computers. Frustrating as it may be, the truth of the matter is that we are all always learning about digital technologies. Once one thing is learned you can be sure another parameter will enter the equation. It is OK to make mistakes. If the basic care of the equipment is known and respected, there is not much harm that can be done by trying different solutions to problems.

At the same time it is important in the low-resource setting to establish and maintain a rota. Rotas ensure that there is equality of access and of opportunity in the classroom. However, they should not be set in stone. The acquisition of ICT skills is a dynamic process, always changing. After whole-class input when beginning to work with a new piece of software or hardware, children need time to practise. Longer rota periods can be gradually shortened as children gain more skills and independence.

Organising digital technologies for children with special educational needs

Children who have special educational needs have the right of access to the whole curriculum including computing and the use of digital technologies. Often, the use of ICT as a tool has been identified as being of particular benefit to a given learner in a given situation. Sometimes, if the child is on the SEN register, they will have ICT hardware and software use identified as part of their Individual Education Plan (IEP) and you will need to incorporate this in your planning and organisation. Some examples might include:

- software which addresses the needs of a dyslexic child;
- hardware which allows access to the computer for a child with motor impairment;
- browser windows which open up in larger fonts for visually impaired children;
- portables or laptops with specialist software loaded for very particular needs (this might include one specialist device or laptop assigned to one child in particular);
- specialist hardware for those who are wheelchair users, e.g. specialist keyboard mounts or switching devices.

THE BIGGER PICTURE THE BIGGER PICTURE THE BIGGER PICTURE THE BIGGER PICTURE

Some companies are dedicated to finding solutions for access for children with SEN and they will welcome enquiries about their software and suggestions for future development. They are usually smaller companies who depend on a close relationship with the schools and children with whom they work. The annual British Educational Technology and Training exhibition (known as the BETT show and held in January in London each year) includes a Special Needs Village for you to examine at first hand such solutions.

For children with SEN in your class, it is important to discover if they require any additional access to the computer in the form of hardware that makes it easier to point and click at menu items or enter text. Some examples include:

- *A concept keyboard* – a device which allows touch-sensitive areas to be created on a flat A4 or A3 board which can be set up to input particular items of text or commands. Teachers can tailor the concept keyboard to the particular needs of an individual child using authoring software provided. The software also includes printing facilities.
- *A touch window* – a device which attaches to the front of a monitor allowing the user to touch areas of the screen as a replacement mouse click to gain access to the menus in given software.
- *Big keys* – a larger-format keyboard for children with fine motor control difficulties.
- *Switches* – on/off rack-mounted switches for wheelchair users and others which equate to left and right mouse clicks.
- *Trackballs* – large inverted mouse systems where the user is able to move a larger ball over a bigger area to point and click.
- *Small mice* – smaller point-and-click devices for those children with motor control difficulties, for example children with muscular dystrophy.
- *Dictation/speech-to-text software* – the accuracy of such software has increased significantly over recent years.

In terms of software for special educational needs, there is a very wide range available. There is also a case for appropriate tutorial software for some children with dyslexia or language delay because it will address very specifically the multi-sensory approach needed to allow such children to acquire strategies to catch up with language development.

REFLECTIVE TASK

When organising ICT for children who have special educational needs

- **Find out about children in your class with SEN.**
- **Does their IEP require that they use particular digital technologies?**
- **Is there dedicated equipment for use by one child?**
- **Would this be hardware, software or both?**
- **Does the child have a special needs assistant who will work with them on their skills in using the digital technologies?**
- **How does their need for specialist ICT input impact on your organisation of the class?**

- Is there a programme of review for determining success levels of the digital technologies with their special educational need?

- Is there someone you can discuss the situation with, for example the ICT/Computing subject leader or the special needs co-ordinator (SENCO)?

- What are the feelings of the parent on the use of digital technologies by their child during the week? Do they have materials or equipment at home which they are using to support their child? Does it complement what you are doing or do you need to make adjustments?

RESEARCH SUMMARY RESEARCH SUMMARY **RESEARCH SUMMARY** RESEARCH SUMMARY

Research by Lie et al. (2000) in Scottish schools showed that, although word processing is believed to have a positive effect on the compositional process for children with specific writing difficulties, there are further significant background factors around motivation, cognition, medical factors and the whole learning environment.

The argument throughout this book and this chapter in particular is about seeing the possibilities for ICT use within the context of the whole class, or, in this case, the individual learner with special educational needs. ICT is a tool for the enhancement of the learner's education within the context of the whole child and not simply an intrinsically 'good thing'.

Organising digital technologies for children with English as an additional language

Digital technologies offer many benefits to young learners in the primary classroom who are learning and using English as an additional language (EAL). The internet brings many audio and video resources across the curriculum within reach. Children who are learning English at the earliest stages can access parts of the curriculum by means of such media.

As a child begins to acquire more English, the computer, if properly managed, allows them to experiment with forms of written and spoken English in an unthreatening and motivating environment. Some additional tutorial software may be appropriate but talking word processors can be just as effective, with immediate feedback provided on composition. The biggest benefit is in areas where the child can experiment with open-ended software alongside peers.

Community languages with their own alphabets and letter systems are available through font add-ons in Office software. Among other uses, these can be employed to produce signs and instructions in the appropriate language. In turn, this goes some way to demonstrating that the language of that child is valued in the context of the school.

For younger children in this context, sensitive adult intervention and peer support are crucial. There should be plenty of opportunity to try to move conceptual development along by talk in the home language alongside support for learning English.

The choice of software or web-based resource should include elements which allow for the child to choose menu items by pointing and clicking, to have sections of text spoken, and to allow access to pictures, music and video. Multimedia authoring packages, including some digital video activities, can be useful in this context. There is enormous potential for producing home-grown resources in dual language format. This would be an exciting project for a Year 6 class undertaking a unit on multimedia authoring. Resources could be created for any age in the school by the older children asking parents, siblings and other adults to help to record in the home language.

Organising digital technologies for children with English as an additional language carries the same responsibilities and requirements as for organising any area of the curriculum for them, namely:

- Never assume the level of language-learning – find out.
- Differentiate for levels of English appropriately – do not assume that all EAL learners are the same.
- Make sure that children with EAL understand all of the processes involved in switching on and off, logging on and off and saving work.
- Check and recheck understanding with sensitive questioning.

THE BIGGER PICTURE   THE BIGGER PICTURE   **THE BIGGER PICTURE**   THE BIGGER PICTURE

Lani Florian writes: 'It has been suggested that technology is a great equalizer, that for many people with disabilities technology can serve as a kind cognitive prosthesis to overcome or compensate for differences among learners' (Florian and Hegarty, 2004, p.10). While she advises caution over fixed and finite approaches to SEN and ICT she also identifies several useful ways in which digital technologies may be exploited for meeting the different needs of children with SEN. She describes these as:

- **Used to tutor**
- **Used to explore**
- **Applied as tools**
- **Used to communicate**
- **Used for assessment**
- **Used as a management tool**

While these should not be seen as mutually exclusive or exhaustive, think about the ways in which ICT can be used to support children with a range of SEN and explore this within your school-based context.

A SUMMARY OF **KEY POINTS**

➢ **There has been significant investment in digital technologies nationally.**

➢ **Progress in this varies from local authority to local authority and school to school.**

➢ **Teachers differ in their levels of capability and their confidence in using digital technologies to support children's learning and their own teaching.**

➢ **Schools vary in their levels of resourcing, both in terms of equipment and human resources, and this will impact on your planning.**

> ➤ When organising digital technologies for children with SEN, there are ranges of hardware, software and peripherals available to support their access to the curriculum and to enhance their learning.

> ➤ When organising digital technologies for children with EAL, there are many resources available that will support their language development and allow them to participate in lessons alongside their peers.

M-LEVEL EXTENSION > > M-LEVEL EXTENSION > > M-LEVEL EXTENSION

Research further the range of ways in which digital technologies can be used to support various Special Educational Needs. Read the introductory chapter of *ICT and Special Educational Needs* by Lani Florian and John Hegarty (2004) or the article 'Special educational needs and technology' by Christina Kuegel (2015).

REFERENCES REFERENCES **REFERENCES** REFERENCES **REFERENCES** REFERENCES

Bennett, S., Maton, K. and Kervin, L. (2008) 'The "digital natives" debate: a critical review of the evidence', *British Journal of Educational Technology*, 39(5), pp.775–86.

DfE (2011) *Teachers' Standards.* Available at **www.education.gov.uk/publications**.

Florian, L. and Hegarty, J. (2004) *ICT and Special Educational Needs: A Tool for Inclusion*. Buckingham: Open University Press.

Kuegel, C. (2015) 'Special education needs and technology', in S. Younie, M. Leask and K. Burden (eds), *Teaching and Learning with ICT in the Primary School*, 2nd edn. Abingdon: Routledge.

Lie, K., O'Hare, A. and Denwood, S. (2000) 'Multidisciplinary support and the management of children with specific writing difficulties', *British Journal of Special Education*, 27 (2), June.

Prensky, M. (2001) 'Digital natives, digital immigrants', *On the Horizon, 9(5), pp.1–6.*

Somekh, B. and Davis, N. (eds) (2007) *Using IT Effectively in Teaching and Learning: Studies in Pre-service and In-service Teacher Education.* London: Routledge.

FURTHER READING FURTHER READING **FURTHER READING** FURTHER READING

Ager, R. (2003) *ICT in Primary Schools*. London: Routledge.

Duffty, J. (2006) *Primary ICT: Extending Knowledge in Practice*. Exeter: Learning Matters.

Florian, L. and Hegarty, J. (2004) *ICT and Special Educational Needs: A Tool for Inclusion*. Buckingham: Open University Press.

Freedman, T. (1999) *Managing* ICT. London: Hodder & Stoughton.

Lie, K., O'Hare, A. and Denwood, S. (2000) 'Multidisciplinary support and the management of children with specific writing difficulties', *British Journal of Special Education*, 27 (2), June.

Younie, S., Leask, M. and Burden, K. (eds) (2015) *Teaching and Learning with ICT in the Primary School*, 2nd edn. Abingdon: Routledge.

2
Planning for digital technologies across the curriculum

Chapter objectives

When you have completed work on this chapter, you will have:

- considered planning for the use of digital technologies in subject teaching, focusing on enhancing the subjects;
- looked at opportunities for the use of digital technologies in the core subjects;
- examined opportunities for cross-curricular use of digital technologies to support the foundation subjects;
- considered how using digital technologies across the curriculum can contribute to the development of children's digital literacy;
- noted the differences in school settings with different levels of resourcing.

Introduction

While learning how to integrate digital technologies in subject teaching, you will be cognisant of the need to know about the children's digital literacy in order to pursue opportunities to exploit and extend it. It will be part of a set of factors that make up good lesson planning, in the same way that planning a useful mathematics lesson in shape and space, for example, takes into account the children's wider experiences, mathematical capabilities and opportunities to enhance and develop them. They do not exist in a separate world: they are inextricably linked. You must look at the features of the digital technologies which make them an appropriate learning tool – one among many – and decide on whether it is appropriate to the learning outcome for which you are currently planning. At the same time, unless other factors are taken into account (and, as previously stated this means, as a minimum, knowing about the extent of children's existing digital literacy and the resources available in the school), planning will be, at best, ineffective and, at worst, potentially counterproductive. The primary curriculum offers a rich context in which to develop children's digital literacy, but what is digital literacy?

Hague and Payton (2010, p.2) define digital literacy broadly, stating that:

> To be digitally literate is to have access to a broad range of practices and cultural resources that you are able to apply to digital tools. It is the ability to make and share meaning in different modes and formats, to create, collaborate and communicate effectively and to understand how and when digital technologies can best be used to support these processes.

Many characterise digital literacy in terms of the capacity to actively create digital artifacts and participate in a society in which digital technologies make the means of production increasingly accessible to all (Facer, 2011; Hague and Payton, 2010; Belshaw, 2012; Savage and Barnett, 2015). Potter (2012) highlights the pressure and tensions that new digital media practices exert on traditional framings of what it means to be literate in a digital age. You will become aware of these tensions as you read this chapter and also as you begin to explore the use of digital technologies in your own practice to support children's learning throughout the curriculum. As you will see, the ways in which we appropriate digital technologies into our pedagogical practice require us to consider the extent and range of our own, as well as the children's, digital literacy. The theme of digital literacy is addressed more fully throughout Section B of this book as it represents a significant element of the computing curriculum. However, it cannot be ignored as we prepare to think critically about how we use digital technologies to support children's learning throughout the primary curriculum.

This chapter addresses the issues of integrating digital technologies in subject teaching, beginning with the core curriculum and moving through to the foundation subjects. Throughout, while the emphasis is on how the digital technologies support the learning in each of these subjects, there is clearly a parallel development going on of your own digital literacy as teachers.

Digital technologies in English and literacy

In support of the requirements for National Curriculum English, lessons in literacy were introduced as part of the National Literacy Strategy, and continued under the primary national strategies (DfES/QCA, 2006). Although the requirement to have regard for the primary national strategies has been discontinued and a new national curriculum has placed a greater emphasis on systematic synthetic phonics in decoding language, you may find that schools and individual teachers you work with are still using elements of the national strategies. For example, it is likely that the three-part literacy lesson will still be used to some extent, which included a whole-class starter session on text-level, sentence-level or word-level work, main follow-up activities often with group or individual work, and a plenary review. The national curriculum for English (DfE, 2013) breaks the subject into:

Spoken Language

Reading

1. *word (decoding)*
2. *comprehension (reading for meaning)*

Writing

1. *transcription (spelling, handwriting)*
2. *composition*
3. *vocabulary, grammar and punctuation*

The main differences between the recent national curriculum for English and the Primary National Strategy (2006) is a greater emphasis on systematic synthetic phonics but many of the previous requirements can still be traced if you compare the new structure with the previous requirements. For example:

Speaking and listening for a wide range of purposes in different contexts

- *Speaking*
- *Listening and responding*
- *Group discussion and interaction*
- *Drama*

Reading and writing for a range of purposes on paper and on screen

- *Word recognition: decoding (reading) and encoding (spelling)*
- *Word structure and spelling*
- *Understanding and interpreting texts*
- *Engaging and responding to texts*
- *Creating and shaping texts*
- *Text structure and organisation*
- *Sentence structure and punctuation*
- *Presentation*

(DfES, QCA, 2006)

The issue for those planning to work with digital technologies in literacy sessions is how to integrate it effectively. The solution to this issue will, as usual, be different in almost every setting and contingent on the resources available in all the categories: human resources, hardware resources and software resources.

Here, we look at how you might approach the use of digital technologies in support of literacy sessions in low- and high-resource settings.

Group activities – low-resource setting

To take an aspect of a literacy session – the group activity – we can see that this lends itself to the use of the computer. In a low-resource setting, with one computer in the corner of the classroom, there will need to be some creativity with the planning. Depending on the nature of the task and of the software being used, it could be possible to split a group of six into two lots of three with ten minutes each. This group would then become part of the working week in the normal way and the whole class rotated through in a week.

In some ways, this is an example of the atomised curriculum at its worst, with children not being able to develop any real digital literacy skills in such short bursts. It also has high planning 'overheads' because of the need to plan something for the children to do while they are waiting for their turn. On the other hand, there are activities which lend themselves to shorter amounts of time at the computer. With tutorial software there might be short activities and investigations around a particular learning objective, such as learning the sounds of English. The most recent debates in teaching literacy in primary schools has brought to prominence the teaching of synthetic phonics in a systematic way. Software publishers have not been slow to exploit this and a whole range of titles and online areas is emerging which aim to provide multimedia reinforcement for learning sounds. An onscreen exercise, for example, to identify parts of words and break them down into constituent sounds would be one. Clearly, pointing and clicking on items in a menu or a game in such software is not doing a great deal to advance the knowledge and understanding of digital technologies. However, literacy provision itself might be enhanced by the regular presence of reinforcement of learning objectives which rely on heard sounds and take children away from photocopied worksheets.

Another idea is to use open-ended software in this situation to create your own short activities. For example, using a word processor, a document template could be created which allowed children to search and replace nouns with pronouns, or the thesaurus facility might be used to develop a wider vocabulary. Another could allow children to highlight all the verbs in sentence-level work and change the font in some way. At this level of resourcing, activities are going to be low-level with some element of repetition and reinforcement. However, in the example with open-ended software, the technology is being used to provide stimulus and variety and one more planning option for the hard-pressed class teacher. It can also legitimately be said to be providing variety for the children and giving them different ways to access the curriculum.

THE BIGGER PICTURE   THE BIGGER PICTURE   THE BIGGER PICTURE   THE BIGGER PICTURE

When you are planning to use digital technologies to support cross-curricular literacy work, consider how writing frames developed for literacy sessions could help to support less able or less confident writers in your class, including those children with additional and special educational needs. For example, a frame to structure and record research could be useful when undertaking a project on healthy lifestyles that includes work in science (healthy eating – food as fuel), personal, social and health education (good mental health, the dangers of alcohol, drug and substance abuse) and PE (the benefits of health-related exercise).

If considering such a project, you may find it helpful to visit the MEND programme website (see **www. mendprogramme.org**). MEND (Mind, Exercise, Nutrition ... Do it!) is a joint initiative between local authorities, NHS primary care trusts and other partners to work together to combat the causes of child obesity and successful elements include the healthy schools programme, extended schools activities and school sport partnerships.

The plenary in a low-resource setting

If you have access to presentation software and the computer is accessible to the carpet area, then in a given week children could be preparing small presentations on the learning objective for the plenary each day. This is potentially the highest-order development of digital literacy skills, and perhaps also of the literacy focus. As the class teacher familiar with the children concerned, you would be in a position to determine which of the children would benefit from this. It need not always be the most able. In this situation, having an adult helper who is also familiar with the software would allow the children who are struggling with a given concept to reinforce their learning by having to construct a presentation for others.

The situation in this resource setting could be as described in Table 2.1.

Table 2.1

Activity	Software	Literacy/ICT potential
Ten-minute onscreen reinforcement of learning objective	Tutorial program, focused aims, revision in a game-style environment	High literacy Low-level digital literacy skills
Ten-minute onscreen search and replace, reinforcement of learning objective	Word processing	High literacy Higher-level digital literacy skills
Collaborative work on presentation for the plenary about a particular learning objective	Presentation Word processing	High literacy High-level digital literacy skills

A literacy lesson in a high-resource setting

Looking at the other extreme, where a school is a high-resource setting, there is inevitably more scope for using digital technologies in a literacy lesson.

In the simplest example, if there are more computers in the classroom (perhaps three) then a group can work in pairs for the whole independent activity, undertaking any of the examples illustrated above at a higher level due to the extended time available.

If the high-resource setting manifests itself in the form of a collection of hand-held devices, laptops or tablets (Apple or Android), there is very great potential. If working with tablet devices, children might work with mind-mapping tools to plan a piece of writing. There are various apps to support literacy work including tools for storyboarding. Apps such as Puppet Pals HD allow the children to create and record an animated puppet show, creating their own characters and backgrounds and recording their own narrative. Such tools can be extremely motivating for children. A collection of wirelessly connected laptops or tablet devices allows much more flexibility for integrating digital technologies in English or literacy.

In a computer suite, it could be possible to run an entire literacy lesson there at regular intervals. Each child would have access to the computers, and plenaries could be held using the large monitors, interactive whiteboards, visualisers or screen control software. The opening sections of the literacy lesson could be presented to the children using hypermedia resources, perhaps containing scanned parts of books. These activities have a high overhead in terms of staff training and confidence. In a high-resource setting which fully integrates digital technologies into the good practice of the school and where the children are using the network room confidently, ICT has much to offer literacy, specifically:

- it provides a different resource base for the literacy session, a break from the classroom;
- it allows children to develop digital literacy skills alongside literacy skills (except in the case of tutorial software);
- it reinforces the message that digital technologies offer a medium in which to carry out work of different kinds;
- it provides the opportunity for children to combine text, graphics, sound and video in different software packages.

Table 2.2

Activity	Software and hardware	Literacy v. Digital literacy potential
Group/independent activity reinforcing learning objective for 20 minutes	Three computers, tutorial program or word processing	High literacy Low-level digital literacy skills (tutorial) Higher-level digital literacy skills (word processing)
Group activities on search and replace, guided writing, storyboarding/mind mapping	Tablet devices (Android/IOSApple) or laptops available for groups	High literacy Higher-level digital literacy skills
Collaborative work throughout literacy session on learning objective, used on the interactive whiteboard and perhaps published online on the school website	Computer suite Presentation software, html editors, etc. Word processing software Online blog	High literacy High-level digital literacy skills

Table 2.2 summarises literacy teaching in the high-resource setting.

The internet and literacy – publication and exhibition issues

In a reliable high-resource setting, the internet is an area of significant potential. Very large numbers of teachers and children are already sharing ideas online. Many of these are downloadable without charge and provide a basis for planning, though some require subscription. Other sites provide onscreen activities with immediate feedback. School web pages, class blogs or local authority intranets can provide rich sources of material and opportunities for publication, including many examples of good practice in literacy teaching and learning. In many schools, teachers are using blogging tools such as WordPress, Edublogs and Tumblr to create school or class blogs. These can offer incentives and an authentic context for writing, especially if used in collaboration with a partner school in another location or country. Similarly, there are new opportunities for collaborative writing through facilities such as Googledocs or Wikis which allow multiple users to edit the same document at the same time, or various wikis which also allow multiple editors albeit at different times. Such tools can be particularly useful for collaborative homework tasks allowing small groups of children to share and work on a document beyond the normal school times and at a distance. Of course, as with any online tools, these need to be monitored carefully by teachers and an appropriate code of conduct set up with the children.

Finally, as noted above, the idea that children can now publish their own work within secure online environments means that the distance between objective, idea and final publication is shortened. There is a real meaning in which this publication and the commentaries provided on it allow for a sense of audience and purpose to be built up, which motivates and increases children's concept of personal authorship (see Chapters 12 and 13 for more on this).

Planning to use digital technologies to support literacy teaching

PRACTICAL TASK PRACTICAL TASK PRACTICAL TASK PRACTICAL TASK

Look at your school's scheme of work for literacy or English and choose a particular year group. Consider the learning objectives in relation to the children you are working with.

- **Decide on what level of activity you could aim at, according to whether you are in a high-resource setting or a low-resource setting.**
- **Design an activity for five or six children for the 20 minutes of group/independent activity.**
- **Remember to discuss the current capabilities of the group with the class teacher and target the actual content appropriately.**

Here is an example of a Year 3 activity for sentence-level work on verbs, which is planned to support the following learning objective:

Children should learn to use verb tenses with increasing accuracy in speaking and writing, e.g. catch/caught, see/saw, go/went, etc., using past tense consistently for narration ...

In a low-resource setting, where there is one computer to the 30 children in the class, consider getting the children to work on a pre-prepared Word template file which contains, say, ten sentences with verbs in the present tense. Have a series of regular and irregular examples differentiated for different groups through the week. Ask the children to identify the verbs in the text and change them into the past tense using the features of the word processor.

In a high resource setting, in a network room, prepare templates for the whole class and ask them to search and replace. Alternatively, ask children to investigate the patterns in pre-prepared onscreen texts and prepare a presentation about it.

Some questions to ask yourself after the activity, some of which follow the usual pattern for the use of digital technologies while some have been adapted for the purpose of this activity, could be as follows.

- **How was the activity integrated into the normal running of the classroom?**
- **What skills did I need in order for the activity to succeed?**
- **What skills did the children need?**
- **How did I ensure that all children had access to the activity?**
- **What were the learning outcomes for the children in literacy and did the use of digital technologies facilitate or even hinder this in any way?**
- **What digital literacy skills were the children able to practise or develop?**
- **What assessment opportunities were there?**
- **How does this experience add to my understanding of using digital technologies in subject teaching?**
- **What will I do next time?**

Digital technologies in English and literacy across the curriculum

It is worth spending some time considering briefly how to use digital technologies in the teaching of English in a wider sense. Beyond the structure of their literacy lessons, children are using English in a cross-curricular way, for example:

- publishing a science report;
- creating a local area guide book in geography;
- writing school web pages;
- writing a class blog;
- generating a historical account;
- writing about their beliefs in RE;
- creating rules for classroom and playground behaviour in PSHE;
- generating captions to explain findings in maths data handling;
- reading for information in any of the foundation subjects, science and maths.

The issue for planning to use digital technologies to support these wider uses of English is, as usual, how to operate in the differing resource settings. Higher-resource settings are going to allow for much greater exploration of the provisional nature of information, simply because faster, more distributed internet access through a school means that greater numbers of teachers and children can become involved. In lower-resource settings, where one computer is shared between the class, there are still opportunities for engagement with the wider English curriculum; for example, in speaking and listening (encouraging children to defend choices made in simulations and adventure games), reading (whole-class reading sessions from the screen) and writing (using the word processor as an aid to drafting materials and understanding the writing process better).

The cross-curricular opportunities for developing English teaching which uses digital technologies are many and varied and the limit to what is feasible will be determined largely by the access to the software, hardware and the internet which the children have, as well as your professional decisions about the extent to which the use of the technology supports their learning in English.

REFLECTIVE TASK

Consider a curriculum area in which you are expecting the children to write at the computer (fixed PC, laptop or tablet device). It could be taken from the list already suggested:

- **publishing a science report;**
- **creating a local area guide book in geography;**
- **writing school web pages;**
- **generating a historical account;**
- **writing about their beliefs in RE;**
- **creating rules for classroom and playground behaviour in PSHE;**
- **generating captions to explain findings in maths data handling;**
- **reading for information in any of the foundation subjects, science and maths.**

Create a lesson plan which focuses on the specific areas of development of the writing itself which you are developing using the digital technologies. The following pro forma of a lesson plan is offered as a prompt based on an example for a Year 4 geography lesson.

LESSON OVERVIEW

Include here the English element, the element from the other subject and the digital technologies to be used. For example, a lesson overview for 'Creating a local area guide book in geography' for Year 4 might describe the ICT element as using desktop publishing software and digital images. The geographical element could be from the work on localities described in the National Curriculum (see below). The English element is the developing sense of audience and of how to present information in a clear and accessible manner as well as assessing and evaluating their writing.

SCHOOL/CLASS CONTEXT

What size is the school? Is it inner-city, urban, rural? How many children are there in the class? What are the characteristics of the class (SEND, EAL etc.)?

LEARNING NEEDS OF THE CHILDREN

Note these in the cross-curricular contexts.

GROUPING/TIMING

Think about different groupings from literacy lessons if your class employs ability groups. Children should experience a range of working partnerships and not always be grouped with the same children. We know from our understanding of the ways in which children learn that they need to interact with one another and learn in the context of talk with a whole range of peers of different abilities.

RESOURCES

Make the most of information collected on local area trips, in particular digital images, video clips and sound recordings, which could be incorporated into the work on the computer. Consider working with a multimedia-authoring package to produce a multimedia version of the guidebook if you are fortunate enough to be in a highly resourced setting.

THEORETICAL CONTEXT

What is the justification for using digital technologies in this subject context? What will it add to their understanding of the subject? Henry (2015) argues that such activities enable children to become creators of content. Likewise, various research and theory highlights the importance of embedding the use of digital technologies in meaningful and purposeful activities (Morris et al., 2015).

NC/EYFS CONTEXT

For Geography: from the programmes of Study for Key Stage 2, in their study of localities and themes, pupils should: 'understand geographical similarities and differences ...' For English: from the programmes of study for Key Stage 2, children should 'assess the effectiveness of their own and others' writing, suggesting improvements ...'

Although computing is not the key focus here it is relevant to refer to the computing programme of study Key Stage 2, for example: 'select, use and combine a variety of software (including internet services) on a range of digital devices to accomplish given goals, including collecting, analysing, evaluating and presenting data and information.'

SCHEME OF WORK CONTEXT

Make reference here to the school's schemes of work for English and geography.

Make notes under the following headings to help you plan the lesson:

- **Your own learning needs**
- **Organisational memory joggers**
- **Other adults**
- **Learning objectives/intentions**
- **Differentiation**
- **Learning needs – SEN**
- **Learning needs – EAL**
- **Assessment opportunities**
- **Key questions**
- **Lesson format**
- **Evaluating the lesson (1) – operational issues**
- **Evaluating the lesson (2) – learning outcomes**
- **Evaluating the lesson (3) – next time**

Digital technologies in mathematics

In support of the requirements for National Curriculum mathematics, lessons in numeracy were introduced as part of the National Numeracy Strategy, and continued under the primary national strategies (DfES/QCA, 2006). Although the requirement to have regard for the primary national strategies has been discontinued, you may find that schools and individual teachers you work with are still using elements of them, including the three-part mathematics lesson, which included a whole-class starter session on mental mathematics, main follow-up activities often with group or individual work, and a plenary review. The new programme of study for mathematics (DfE, 2013) differs mainly in the way it breaks down the various thematic topics and nomenclature, and sets out the programme of study on a year-by-year basis. For example, at Key Stage 1, the topic of number is broken down into place value, addition and subtraction, multiplication and division, and fractions. Also, there is a renewed emphasis on children developing fluency in mental arithmetic. The new National Curriculum for mathematics also advises against using calculators until the end of Key Stage 2 where they are recommended for developing 'pupils' conceptual understanding and exploration of more complex number problems, if written and mental arithmetic are secure' (DfE, 2013, n.p.). Consequently it is anticipated that many teachers will continue to draw on previous materials using whole or adapted units in their planning for:

- *Using and applying mathematics*
- *Counting and understanding number*
- *Knowing and using number facts*
- *Calculating*
- *Understanding shape*
- *Measuring*
- *Handling data*

(Primary National Strategy, 2006)

Technology can be incorporated into most parts of the mathematics lesson. An opening section on mental maths can be varied in its use of resources by the inclusion of an interactive whiteboard (see also Chapter 4 on using the IWB). The same applies to the plenary, where the strands of the lesson can be drawn together by the use of electronic media, either by the teacher or by groups of children presenting their work to the rest of the class. Tablet devices with screen capture apps such as Explain Everything (see **www.explaineverything.com**/) could be utilised by children or the teacher to reinforce and model understanding of mathematical processes.

However, it is the central part of the lesson which lends itself most readily to the integration of digital technologies, including all of the available audio-visual aids and, of course, calculators should the teacher judge that such devices can add to or develop children's understanding. For the computer, several different types of program are suitable for this section of the lesson, including:

- software to explore number patterns, including the use of spreadsheets;
- tutorial software for practising a particular skill, with rapid assessment;
- data-handling software;
- software for giving instructions of movement and turn in order to develop subject knowledge in, for example, measurement of distance and angle;
- software for transforming shapes;
- software for branching and sorting in order to develop logical thinking and problem-solving;
- screen capture software to model processes.

Some of these possible uses have the potential to develop high-order digital literacy skills. However, it is worth remembering that the focus of the lesson has to be mathematics specifically and the lesson succeeds or fails partly by the way in which the teacher can draw the class together in a plenary at the end of the session. If the activity has moved out of the realm of the initial focus and is meeting some other planning requirement, the quality of the mathematical experience may decline.

The potential for digital literacy skills development and maths together is summarised in Table 2.3, where, as for literacy, it is possible to see little in the way of such skill development in the use of tutorial software.

Table 2.3

Software type in mathematics	Digital literacy skills, knowledge and understanding
Software to explore number patterns (tutorial)	Low-level digital literacy skills
Tutorial software for practising a particular skill, with rapid assessment	Very low-level digital literacy skills
Software for transforming shapes	Middle-range digital literacy skills (depending on the package being used – some are much more complex than others)
Data-handling software	High-level digital literacy skills
Using spreadsheets to explore number patterns	High-level digital literacy skills
Software for giving instructions of movement and turn in order to develop subject knowledge in, for example, measurement of distance and angle	High-level digital literacy skills (link with programming)
Software for branching and sorting in order to develop logical thinking and problem-solving	High-level digital literacy skills

THE BIGGER PICTURE   THE BIGGER PICTURE   THE BIGGER PICTURE   THE BIGGER PICTURE

When you are planning for mathematics, you need to plan suitable activities that will include all children and ensure that every child makes progress. You are likely to have children in your class or group who have additional and special educational needs. You may also have in the same group or class children who are mathematically able, gifted and talented. Talk to class teacher colleagues, take advice from the inclusion leader or teacher responsible for children with special needs and discuss the children with any teaching or learning support assistants who know them well to see what they suggest will help. See also *Teaching Primary Special Educational Needs* (Glazzard et al., 2010). When you have identified links from your mathematics topics to other areas of the curriculum, don't forget to look out for opportunities to develop mathematical learning when planning other subjects. It is important to include mathematics in other subjects to improve all children's transference skills and allow them to rehearse, reinforce, consolidate and extend what they have learned in mathematics lessons. Seeing the uses and applications of mathematics in other areas of the curriculum makes it more 'real' and often more enjoyable, and demonstrates the need for functional numeracy. Examples could include opportunities to apply number work and calculation in science, using concepts of shape, space and measures in design technology, identifying patterns and sequences in music and art, and handling data in geography and history.

In a low-resource setting it is possible to become dependent on poorer-quality tutorial software of a very basic drill-and-practice type. Where this is focused (on reinforcing a topic which is under development) and targeted (at children who need it), such software can be useful. As we have seen in earlier chapters, where this software is used to keep certain children busy or as a reward or sanction, there is little justification for using it in pursuit of real learning objectives.

In a high-resource setting, in a network room or similar, all children could experience some mathematics lessons with access to the relevant software and hardware. The whole lesson could be run in the computer suite from time to time (timetabling allowing).

REFLECTIVE TASK

In a low-resource setting, or one where the children's experience of using digital technologies is limited, collect simple data about the packed lunches brought to school across a given week. Ask children to enter the information and display it in data-handling software. This could be done using a simple graphing tool or using a more complex data-handling package.

For a medium-resource setting, where there is regular access to the computer and the children have already gained experiences of simple graphing, extend their knowledge by building a more complicated database based on the different methods which children use to come to school each day.

In either case, in your planning, develop questions which exploit the learning opportunities offered by the digital technologies alongside the mathematical learning opportunities. Table 2.4 characterises some of these sorts of questions.

Table 2.4

Example digital literacy knowledge questioning	Example mathematics knowledge questioning
Which graph shows the information best?	Do most children walk to school? How do we know?
What did we have to do after entering each piece of information?	How many more children walk to school than come by car?
How did we add to the file the next day?	What would happen if it were a wet day?

In this way, digital technologies support the subject and the subject supports very important conceptual developments in digital literacy.

Questions worth asking as a result of the activity include the following.

- How was the activity integrated into the normal running of the classroom?
- What skills did I need in order for the activity to succeed?
- What skills did the children need?
- How did I ensure that all children had access to the activity?
- What were the learning outcomes for the children in mathematics?
- What were the learning outcomes for the children's digital literacy?
- What assessment opportunities were there?
- How does this experience add to my understanding of digital technologies in subject teaching?
- Did the ends justify the means in terms of time costs?
- What will I do next time?

Digital technologies in science

There is the opportunity to make good use of the very wide potential of digital technologies to support the teaching of science. There is ample opportunity for both subjects to support each other. Planning for science with ICT means identifying the sorts of activities where digital technologies can support and enhance the learning of science. As with the rest of the core subject provision discussed above, some activities develop the scientific knowledge, skills and understanding of children but do not necessarily generate further digital literacy development. There are other activities which develop much higher-level digital literacy skills alongside scientific skills of enquiry and hypothesis. To take a simple example, programs which are tutorial in nature and which describe and then question the user about certain concepts do not necessarily advance the digital literacy skills of the user who is, as in all tutorial software, rehearsing skills of navigation over and over again. On the other hand, an activity which requires that the user set up and maintain a monitoring situation with data-logging equipment and software is clearly requiring a higher level of skills in both subjects.

Whether low-level digital literacy skills or much higher-level skills are being employed, the decision to make in terms of lesson planning is to focus on the appropriate activities in the whole scheme of work for the children. Is it the case that you need a context for developing their awareness of databases? Have they browsed websites at length? Do you now need, in terms of the science, to deepen their awareness of subject knowledge in classification by asking them to work with the data they are collecting? Scientific enquiry and the application and development of digital literacy skills and understanding can usefully go hand in hand within many particular science units of work, as can be seen in Table 2.5, which breaks down some of the various units of work for science in the new National Curriculum (DfE, 2013) and highlights some indicative activities for integrating digital technologies.

Table 2.5

Key Stage	Science unit of work	Indicative links and activities integrating digital technologies
1	Plants	Use digital microscopes to look closely at the different parts of plants found in their locality.
		Use digital cameras to take photographs and compare different plants.
		Label pictures using publishing software.
		Explore examples of time-lapse photography illustrating how things grow, e.g. seed germination.
	Animals, including humans	Use various 3D apps on a tablet device to explore and compare the different parts of the body of various animals.
		Use storyboarding software on a desktop computer or a tablet to represent various life cycles. Create a poster with a graphics package to illustrate life cycles.
	Everyday materials	Use a branching database to classify different materials and their properties.
	Seasonal changes	Use a simple database to keep a record of the weather throughout the year.
	Living things and their habitat	Use the internet and video to explore local and non-local habitats to identify how living things are adapted to their environments.

2	Plants	Use a digital microscope to observe the different parts of flowering plants.
	Animals, including humans	Capture or use existing digital film footage of animals on the move, e.g. film some of the pupils running and use editing software to slow the footage down to compare and analyse movement in different animals.
	Rocks	Examine different rocks and soils under a digital microscope. Use publishing software to label and explain the physical properties of different rocks and soils.
	Light	Test the reflective properties of different materials by setting up a fair test and using a data-logger to measure and record light levels. Use graphing software to analyse and interpret the results.
	Forces and magnets	Capture the effects of different forces, including magnetism on different objects, using video camera. Playback and analyse the results.
	Living things and their habitat	Use a database and digital camera to capture and classify a wide selection of living things and their habitats. Keep a diary to monitor changes to the environment over time.
	States of matter	Use a temperature probe and data-logger to record, capture and observe the melting of ice in a cool environment (e.g. outdoors). Repeat the experiment but in a warmer environment (e.g. indoors). Compare and analyse the results.
	Sound	Use a digital audio recorder that captures sound waves and represents them graphically. Analyse and compare the relationship between the graphical representation and the features of the sounds created, e.g. volume, pitch.
	Electricity	Use a simulation package to explore and construct different types of circuits. Record these circuits using conventional symbols for components. This should not replace the actual constructing of physical circuits using batteries, bulbs, wires and switches. Use a micro controller device (e.g. Crumble, Makey Makey) to explore electrical inputs and outputs such as light emitting diodes and motors (see Chapter 9 – *Physical Computing*).
	Earth and space	A simulation package or app could be used to explore and model phenomena such as night and day, changes of seasons, phases of the Moon.
	Evolution and inheritance	Children could use the internet and other sources to research evolution and the work of key scientists such as Mary Anning, Charles Darwin and Alfred Wallace.

There are many ways in which digital technologies can support science more generally: for example, with the use of templates and scaffolding as a form of writing so as to further structure scientific thought and develop skills of planning and enquiry.

Above all, the use of digital technologies in science should be seen as something in which the scientific learning is the focus; it should be a key to opening up the world of scientific development and not an end in itself. There are benefits for both subjects in close integration.

PRACTICAL TASK PRACTICAL TASK **PRACTICAL TASK** PRACTICAL TASK

Choose a unit of work from your school's science scheme of work for which you have access to the appropriate software and hardware. Plan for one session within the unit to have a major input involving digital technologies. Use the links suggested in this section to help you. When you evaluate the session, consider the following aspects.

- Make a judgement, in conversation with your mentor and/or tutor, about the contribution of the digital technologies to the subject knowledge in the sessions.
- Did the ends justify the means?
- Would you use digital technologies to work with this particular concept or unit again?
- If yes, would you do anything differently?
- If no, why would you prefer not to use digital technologies in this way again?

Digital technologies in the foundation subjects

Planning for the use of digital technologies in the foundation subjects, as for the core curriculum, means identifying those activities where digital technologies provide an essential part of the learning experience. In other words, it means identifying the lessons in the foundation subjects where the learning opportunities are enhanced in depth, range and quality. The following examples given under the relevant subject headings are by no means an exhaustive list. They are intended to be starting points for planning for the use of digital technologies in the foundation subjects.

Art and design

Some of the foundation subjects depend on a sophisticated understanding of how the ICT works and of how it uniquely contributes to the learning in that subject area. One example would be art, where the understanding of what is happening in a graphics package is crucial to understanding the contribution which it makes to the subject.

Image-editing packages, in spite of their onscreen appearance with virtual canvases, virtual paint pots and virtual pencils, represent a different medium for artists. They may look as though they are replacing the physical world of brushstrokes and charcoal marks. The fact is that they are not. The way that they work is by arranging digital information on screen.

RESEARCH SUMMARY RESEARCH SUMMARY **RESEARCH SUMMARY** RESEARCH SUMMARY

Avril Loveless in 'Working with images, developing ideas' (2007) builds an argument about helping children and teachers to understand that they are interacting with a new medium, rich with different possibilities. She writes that 'IT has the potential to be a catalyst in the development of new ways of expressing a visual language' and goes on to define the central role that the teacher has in the process:

> *It is the interaction of the facilities of IT, the children's ability to explore and extend their visual ideas and the teacher's pedagogy that can improve the quality of teaching and learning.*
>
> (Loveless, 2007)

The use of digital still and video cameras to record observations and keep a diary of the creative process and ideas can go hand-in-hand with more traditional forms of working such as developing a sketchbook for experimenting with different media and processes. Similarly, the internet can be used as a medium for children to explore the work and styles of many different genres across the world. With bandwidth and distribution of the internet around schools improving all the time, virtual art galleries represent a significant contribution to the art and design curriculum. The faster transfer of much bigger files is of particular benefit in this area because the files are so much larger than with other uses of ICT, for example word processing.

In terms of planning appropriately, the usual judgements apply about how the subject is enhanced and which digital literacy skills are being utilised and developed. Purposeful exploration of painting packages, image-recording devices and websites which bring art into the classroom in ways which were not possible before are all unique to ICT and can enrich children's learning in art and design. The important thing to remember for your planning is the word 'purposeful' and all that implies. Of particular importance is the notion that the digital technologies are adding to the potential achievement and learning by the children in the given subject.

Geography

History and geography are two subjects in which digital technologies can make a contribution to the enhancement of the learning process. We have seen, in the section on English and literacy across the curriculum earlier in this chapter, an example of a connection between a geographical activity and a unit of work integrating digital technologies.

The internet brings much potential to the teaching of geography. The subject itself offers a context for developing skills of searching, e-mailing and publishing. Similarly, early understanding of mapping and routes can be enhanced by the use of a programmable toy. The National Curriculum for geography (DfE, 2013) organises the curriculum into the specific areas of:

Locational knowledge

Place knowledge

Human and physical geography

Geographical skills and fieldwork

Clearly, as tools, digital technologies have much to contribute to the enrichment of these areas. From the local to the global, digital cameras could be used to record events outside the classroom, while the internet could be used to obtain comparative weather information from around the world.

THE BIGGER PICTURE THE BIGGER PICTURE **THE BIGGER PICTURE** THE BIGGER PICTURE

When you are planning to use digital technologies in support of geography, the internet has a wide range of sources that you will find useful. Try some of the following:

- Blogs on geography: http://primarygeogblog.blogspot.com
- Google Earth: www.google.com/earth/index.html
- Google Street View: http://maps.google.co.uk/
- Worldmapper: www.worldmapper.org/index.html

Beyond comparative weather data comes the whole series of possibilities raised by e-mail or video conference contact with children and teachers in other localities. E-mailed questions about what you can see from your window on a given day generate vast amounts of interesting information between children of the same age, across the world, very quickly. Similarly a class blog could be used to facilitate links with other schools and children from other locations and countries.

Geographical resources which were not available before – detailed maps and aerial photographs of most of the world – are now accessible online and offline. The skill in terms of the teaching will be to integrate these resources usefully into planning. You will need to identify opportunities for learning which are uniquely offered by the technology. As in all areas, if you are in a high-resource setting with large numbers of computers and good internet access your problems are significantly reduced. In some cases the availability of tablet or hand-held devices with mapping software connected to a global positioning system (GPS) can also enhance the experience of geography.

History

History can be brought to life by the carefully planned use of digital technologies. The internet brings not only art galleries into the school, but also museums and archival resources of all kinds, many of which are free to use in educational settings. Incorporating ICT into history lessons, as with all subject areas, becomes an issue depending on the resource setting in which trainees, teachers and children are working.

Some of the links between history and ICT are simply related to the resource capabilities of ICT, as for example in finding out about significant people in the past. Another example of quite low-level digital literacy use would be in using digitised maps in a local enquiry.

Higher-level digital literacy skills are demanded by the sophisticated use of databases which could be exploited at Key Stage 2 to study patterns of change over time. History provides us with an example of the need to be very clear about the order of skills in both the curriculum subject and digital literacy which are to be developed in a given lesson. This area was explored previously in the section on planning for mathematics, where we saw a trade-off between higher-level digital literacy skills and content browsing.

Design and technology

ICT and specifically computing offers much to teachers of design and technology in the primary school. The area of most potential is probably that of computing and control technology, where children learn that they can control devices and models which will respond to external instruction and inputs (see Chapter 9 on physical computing). Children already know that such devices exist. A quick concept map at the start of work on this subject will bring to mind TV remote controls, washing machine programmes, central heating timers, games consoles and controllers, burglar alarms and a whole host of other devices.

Additionally, when creating or developing ideas for themselves, children could be encouraged to make use of digital technologies in the design process as well as think about how they can incorporate computing into their creations. The programmes of study for Key Stage 2 (DfE, 2013) make explicit reference to this idea, pointing out the link back to ICT and computing in the following statements:

Pupils should be taught to:

generate, develop, model and communicate their ideas through discussion, annotated sketches, cross-sectional and exploded diagrams, prototypes, pattern pieces and computer-aided design

apply their understanding of computing to program, monitor and control their products

It is difficult to imagine being able to meet the needs of young learners in design and technology and their curriculum entitlements without significant levels of ICT use. It is important to find out what is available to resource control technology in your placement school.

A further issue is the availability of support in terms of expertise. Although relatively simple-to-use software is involved, many teachers are deterred from including this area in their planning. Most teachers who do take it on find that the equipment and software working together are highly motivating for children and stimulate a great deal of interest and creative learning potential. Further support for this area can be found in Chapter 9 on physical computing.

Music

Digital technologies have for a long time enjoyed a close relationship with music in primary schools. Tape recorders and CD players have been used in schools for many years to:

- bring children into contact with music from different times and different cultures;
- record children's own compositions;
- provide resources for learning songs;
- provide a resource for budding instrumentalists to record and assess their work;
- provide accompaniment to dance (link to PE);
- provide a source of music for assemblies and performances.

Additionally, schools with electronic keyboards have been able to extend the performance aspects of music. Keyboards with sound modules in which real instrument voices have been stored allow children to explore the different timbres and possibilities of different instruments.

In terms of computer use, there are software packages available which allow children to explore composing. The feedback which they gain from such software is immediate and the performing and appraising aspects of the curriculum are therefore made similarly immediate. As was the case for art and design, there is no suggestion of the computer-based musical tools replacing hands-on experience with the whole range of instruments found in primary schools. Instead, the suggestion is that digital technologies can be used to enhance the learning process.

Children learn that computers are capable of storing more than just text and images and that they can be used to record and manipulate sound. They learn that sound can be represented and stored digitally, in which form it can be transformed in many different ways.

Computers are now the medium of choice in professional and home recording studios for composing and arranging music. Children will be aware of the possibilities of mixing and remixing songs as they hear different versions of their favourite songs produced. Some children may have access to simple tools on mobile phones or tablet devices for music editing, or at least know of them. The learning curve for non-specialist teachers who are seeking to use music composition software and keyboards at this higher level is sometimes perceived to be quite steep and requiring specialist training. However, once the basic concepts are mastered, such devices open up a whole range of possibilities for young composers in both key stages but particularly upper Key Stage 2, and there are increasingly simplified yet powerful tools to use for this (see Chapter 11 for more on this).

The opportunities to use digital technologies to support the programmes of study for music are numerous. For example, at Key Stage 1 (DfE, 2013) children should be taught to:

> *listen with concentration and understanding to a range of high-quality live and recorded music*
>
> *experiment with, create, select and combine sounds using the interrelated dimensions of music*

ICT can enrich both of these areas of activity and understanding. Similarly at Key Stage 2 children should be taught to develop their level of performance as expressed in the statement that they should be taught to:

> *play and perform in solo and ensemble contexts, using their voices and playing musical instruments with increasing accuracy, fluency, control and expression*

The link here is the use of recording equipment for analysing and reviewing work so that they can further develop their level of performance.

The resource setting is one potential obstacle to fully exploiting these links between music and digital technologies. Another is teacher confidence and appropriate training, as well as access to hardware and software. However, at even the most basic level of using recording equipment, ICT enhances subject teaching in music in powerful ways.

RE, PSHE and Citizenship

In terms of its access to resources on the internet, ICT is a major contributing factor to growing subject knowledge and understanding in the interlinked areas of RE, personal, social and health education (PSHE) and citizenship. The diversity of world religions can be explored and children can have a context for their writing which extends their sphere of personal expression into that of personal belief.

The potential of the internet to link to other cultures and belief systems can engender respect. Digital technologies bring these worlds within reach in a unique way.

For the non-statutory areas of PSHE and citizenship, ICT remains an important tool. One example is that of developing relationships through work and play, for example communicating with children in other countries by through video calls, online discussion or e-mails.

Children are aware that the school holds information about them from the earliest years. They can be explicitly made aware of the uses of digital technologies in gathering and processing this information. Later, they could discuss the ethical and confidentiality issues raised by large databases being held by companies and government agencies full of personal information.

PE

There is a place on the PE curriculum for the use of digital technologies, certainly in terms of devices which can help to record movement for children to analyse later. For example, in dance and gymnastics children could use videos of movements and actions to develop their ideas and improve their performance.

Further cross-curricular opportunities exist in the analysis of the effects of exercise which can be carried out using sensors. The potential link to science has already been outlined above. The potential to link with maths in the exploration of data in spreadsheets is also clearly there.

Clearly, it would be unwise to make strong claims for all-day, everyday pervasive links in planning between ICT and PE. However, there will be times, particularly when tackling the issue of assessment in PE, when digital technologies can make a vital contribution. The contribution of digital video in particular is noted in Chapter 11.

Languages and digital technologies

ICT has great potential to support the teaching of languages in primary schools. The National Curriculum (DfE, 2013) introduces the teaching of a foreign language at Key Stage 2. It should be noted that some schools introduce a foreign language in Key Stage 1. The teaching of European and other languages can be supported and enhanced by the use of high-quality CD- and DVD-based resources, which, alongside websites, can be incorporated into lessons.

Some learners will benefit from simpler drill-and-practice vocabulary reinforcement and extension. For others, the opportunity to explore scenarios and solve problems in other languages online and in collaboration with other learners will be highly significant and a genuinely useful context for technology such as video-conferencing.

Increasingly, the sophisticated operating systems of both Windows and Mac computers have simplified the use of a variety of language fonts both European and worldwide, making multilingual publishing in the classroom a real possibility. Similarly, tools such as

Google Translate have emerged but these should be used with caution due to issues of accuracy. Such tools may have their place from time to time but should not replace the practice of learning to speak and listen to a foreign language. Where ICT has the most potential is perhaps in putting children in direct contact with native foreign language speakers through, for example, a school-to-school video conference link.

REFLECTIVE TASK

If you are on a course which requires you to develop a specialism, use your specialist subject as the basis for the following activity. Use the school scheme of work for the subject to complete it.

Identify a unit of work. Consider the opportunities for using digital technologies to support children's learning in this unit of work. Think about the balance between the level of digital literacy and the subject knowledge being developed. Plan a series of four to six lessons or activities which develop the subject knowledge of the children alongside their digital literacy skills.

At the end of the sequence, address the following issues as an overview of all the sessions:

- **Were the learning objectives achieved? How?**
- **Which aspects of digital literacy did the children develop rather than just reinforce?**
- **What operational difficulties were encountered (if any) during the activity?**
- **Make a judgement, in conversation with your mentor and/or tutor, about the contribution of the digital technologies to the subject knowledge in the sessions.**
- **Was this an effective use of time?**
- **Would you use ICT to work with this particular concept or unit again?**
- **If yes, would you do anything differently?**
- **If no, why would you prefer not to use ICT in this way again?**

A SUMMARY OF **KEY POINTS**

- ➢ **The use of digital technologies can promote knowledge, skills and understanding in both core and foundation subjects.**
- ➢ **The levels of resourcing available in the school setting can affect how ICT can be used within other subjects and this must be taken into account in your planning.**
- ➢ **Planning should ensure that children's digital literacy is enhanced as well as learning in the other subjects, even where there is only the potential for lower levels of ICT skills.**

M-LEVEL EXTENSION > > M-LEVEL EXTENSION > > M-LEVEL EXTENSION

Look back over the sections on the use of ICT to support the core subjects. Is it possible to devise schemes of work that develop higher-order skills in both the subject and ICT? Would this be viable for all groups of children? Would there be any drawbacks in such schemes of work?

REFERENCES REFERENCES **REFERENCES** REFERENCES **REFERENCES** REFERENCES

Belshaw, D. (2012) *What Is 'Digital Literacy'? A Pragmatic investigation.* Doctoral thesis, Durham University. Available at **http://etheses.dur.ac.uk/3446/**.

DfE (2011) *Teachers' Standards.* Available at **www.education.gov.uk/publications**.

DfE (2013) *National Curriculum in England: Primary Curriculum.* London: DfES. Available at **www. gov.uk/government/collections/national-curriculum#programmes-of-study-by-subject**.

DfES/QCA (2006) *Primary Framework for Literacy and Mathematics*. London: DfES.

Facer, K. (2011) *Learning Futures: Educational, Social and Technological Futures*. London and New York: Routledge.

Glazzard, J. et al. (2010) *Teaching Primary Special Educational Needs*. Exeter: Learning Matters.

Hague, C. and Payton, S. (2010) *Digital Literacy Across the Curriculum*. Bristol: Futurelab. Available at **www.futurelab.org**.

Henry, M. (2015) 'Learning in the digital age', in S. Younie, M. Leask and K. Burden (eds), *Teaching and Learning with ICT in the Primary School*, 2nd edn. Abingdon: Routledge.

Loveless, A. (2007) 'Working with images, developing ideas', in A. McFarlane (ed.), *Information Technology and Authentic Learning: Realising the Potential of Computers in the Classroom*. London: Taylor & Francis.

Morris, D., Uppal, G. and Ayres, D. (2015) 'Being creative with technology', in S. Younie, M. Leask and K. Burden (eds), *Teaching and Learning with ICT in the Primary School*, 2nd edn. Abingdon: Routledge.

Potter, J. (2012) *Digital Media and Learner Identity: The New Curatorship*. Basingstoke: Palgrave Macmillan.

Savage, M. and Barnett, A. (2015) *Digital Literacy for Primary Teachers*. Norwich: Critical Publishing.

FURTHER READING FURTHER READING **FURTHER READING** FURTHER READING

Savage, M. and Barnett, A. (2015) *Digital Literacy for Primary Teachers*. Norwich: Critical Publishing.

3
Planning to use digital technologies in the Early Years Foundation Stage

Chapter objectives

When you have completed work on this chapter, you will have:

- considered the differences between the Early Years Foundation Stage and the National Curriculum;
- thought about the theories of child development that underpin the organisation of the Early Years environment;
- noted the importance of talk in relation to the use of digital technologies in the Early Years Foundation Stage;
- examined the opportunities for using digital technologies to support young children's learning in the Prime and Specific areas of learning set out in the EYFS curriculum.

(DfE, 2014)

Introduction

Under the Labour government (1997–2010) the *Statutory Framework for the Early Years Foundation Stage* (DCSF, 2008) identified features of good practice for the education and care of young children and set out the early learning goals that most children should achieve by the end of their Reception year in the context of six areas of learning. From September 2008, children in the EYFS were assessed against a comprehensive Early Years Foundation Stage Profile, the main purpose of which was to provide Year 1 teachers with reliable and accurate information about each child's level of development as they enter Key Stage 1. The current government have brought in some changes to the EYFS curriculum (DfE, 2014) but, in terms of the EYFS curriculum the reforms do not mark a significant change of direction as we will see.

The Early Years Foundation Stage (EYFS) continues to be based on an entirely different structure from the National Curriculum. If you are not an Early Years specialist but you find yourself in a placement in an Early Years setting, you need to familiarise yourself with the guidance provided. In particular, you need to become attuned to a setting which looks at key early learning goals for young children rather than at explicit programmes of study and schemes of work.

The definition of the early learning goals is informed by Early Years specialists' understanding of the ways in which young children think and learn. They are also intended as laying the foundation for the child's future engagement with the curriculum in the mainstream primary setting. Table 2.1 shows the early learning goals as they were mapped out for the EYFS in six developmental areas in 2008 and as they are now defined (DfE, 2014).

Table 3.1

EYFS (DCSF, 2008)	EYFS (DfE, 2014)
• personal, social and emotional development; • communication, language and literacy; • problem-solving, reasoning and numeracy (PSRN); • knowledge and understanding of the world; • physical development; • creative development.	Prime areas: • communication and language; • physical development; and • personal, social and emotional development. Specific areas: • literacy; • mathematics; • understanding the world; and • expressive arts and design.

The changes highlighted above were triggered by the Tickell Review, *The Early Years: Foundations for Life, Health and Learning* (Tickell, 2011), which recommended a number of changes for EYFS reforms. The Tickell Review prompted the change of the six areas of learning in development into three prime areas and four specific areas in which the prime areas are applied (DfE, 2014).

Key issues

The key issue for practitioners who are seeking to use digital technologies to support young children's development in these areas of learning is how to merge its use with the philosophy and methodology of planning for young learners.

Adults who work in EYFS settings, planning for and interacting with young children, set out their environment to maximise the opportunities for learning to take place. This is not a simple template for daily use of a space with young learners; it is an environment underpinned by knowledge of how children develop skills, explore and grow in under-standing of key concepts. Learning happens both in the opportunity for play and in the interaction between people – all people – in learning spaces.

RESEARCH SUMMARY RESEARCH SUMMARY **RESEARCH SUMMARY** RESEARCH SUMMARY

The theories of Vygotsky are important here as a major component of the theory underpinning the mapping out of Early Years settings. He believed that children are continually refining their growing understanding through a sort of innate, inner speech or dialogue. Learning potential is enhanced in settings where children verbalise their inner speech and test and retest it in their interaction with others. This happens in what Vygotsky characterised as the 'zone of proximal development'. Many texts are available which explore these concepts in some depth. One example would be the book by David Wood (1997) *How Children Think and Learn.* Early Years specialists will also be familiar with the work of Sandra Smidt in *A Guide to Early Years Practice* (Smidt, 2007), which looks at the theories of how very young children learn.

Vygotsky's theories underpin the Early Years setting. As a result, such environments are rich in opportunities for play (the context for the inner speech of children) and in opportunities for interaction (in the zone of proximal development).

Where – and indeed should – digital technologies fit into this environment? Plowman et al. (2010) found significant ambivalence among parents regarding the introduction of digital technologies to very young children. Furthermore for the children themselves, playing with digital technologies was often not their preferred choice or a high priority. With its associated certainties and appearance of rigidity and non-fluid thinking, the computer appears to contradict widely held views of the way in which young children learn in the zone of proximal development. Some writers (Crook, 1996; Mercer and Fisher, 1997) have, however, attempted to analyse the working of the computer and digital technologies in the zone of proximal development and to look at the key features of talk around children working with computers. Their work suggests that computers and digital technologies are particularly rich in their possibilities for collaborative learning in the zone of proximal development.

The above research suggests that the best organisational strategies for the Early Years are the same, in many respects, as for the classroom. At the most basic level, this means making the computer more a part of the general experience of play and dialogue alongside the writing area, the modelling, the books and the play equipment. It means making the computer accessible for use in a range of contexts, both collaboratively and singly, with an adult and without an adult, in the same way as any Early Years activity might be designed to maximise learning opportunities.

THE BIGGER PICTURE THE BIGGER PICTURE THE BIGGER PICTURE THE BIGGER PICTURE

When teaching children in the Early Years Foundation Stage, remember to build on their high levels of engagement by giving them opportunities to interact with a wide range of media and technologies. When you are developing a dramatic play area, remember to make this as realistic and up to date as possible by including a range of information and communication technologies. In the hairdressing salon or boarding kennel, include a laptop so that the children can take bookings and make appointments. In a coffee shop or restaurant, include an electronic till, a basic calculator to add up the bills and an up-to-date looking telephone or mobile. In a hotel reception area, include a computer so that the children can print customers' accounts. Photocopy or scan and print the children's work to include in a class book or to be sent home to share with parents.

Clearly, giving children and the adults around the computer the space to talk and play is crucial. Placing the computer or digital technologies in, for example, a role-play situation, building a small office play environment around it and running open-ended software on it could be a starting point for stimulating much of the inner dialogue and talk in the zone of proximal development.

From the planning point of view, it is important to be clear about how each of the defined areas of learning can be enriched and enhanced. It means thinking about digital technologies throughout the areas of learning and development (DfE, 2014). With regard to the prime areas of learning and development the following activities are indicative of the kinds of experiences that practitioners could facilitate.

Encouraging children's development of 'Communication and language' in the Early Years means planning opportunities for children to participate in the following activities.

- Write messages, label pictures with their name and otherwise engage with the communicative aspects of ICT. They do not have to get it right in the same way as a writing area doesn't exclude children who can't yet form letters. The uncritical nature of the digital technologies can prove extremely motivating (particularly when the computer is in a role-play area and the child is experiencing an impetus to try from the imaginative play).
- Experience the notion that computers (including any device, e.g. IWB, smartphone, tablet) can communicate words and pictures from books. If an adult helper, parent or older child is present, much useful talk and discussion about books and print, words and sounds, computers and communication can occur.
- Communicate with friends, relatives and peers in other settings nearby and very far away if possible. Children know that the computer is one among many tools for communication over distance and time. If the computer cannot deliver the necessary experiences then other ICT equipment such as a digital camera, video camera or tape recorder may be able to.

For children's 'physical development' it can be useful to consider some of the following.

- Encourage children to monitor and regulate the amount of time they might spend using and exploring digital technologies;
- Use technologies such as digital cameras to capture and celebrate the physical outdoor activities the children engage with.
- Digital cameras could also be used to capture and celebrate the healthy choices children make in relation to food.
- The use of ICT equipment can promote and develop fine motor skills for all children, in particular the use of the mouse.
- For children who are experiencing difficulties in fine motor skills across the whole range of severity, access devices such as brightly coloured, larger keyboards, touch windows and trackballs can all be used. Concept Keyboards which contain teacher-defined touch areas, touch screens and big switches which can be wheelchair-mounted and others all allow for inclusion and development within the Early Years setting.

For 'Personal, social and emotional development' this could mean planning opportunities for any of the following to occur.

- learning how to share the ICT equipment and take turns to allow children to establish constructive relationships with each other and with other adults;
- using the computer or digital technologies to encourage collaboration between children and between adults and children in problem-solving (even at the basic level of switching on, selecting an item from a menu, clicking on a name);
- using ICT to explore worlds beyond the Early Years;
- using the computer as a tool to encourage collaboration between children who are experiencing difficulties and others in the Early Years setting (using alternative access devices alongside mice and keyboards).

In terms of the specific areas of learning and development there may well be cross-over with the activities and ideas suggested above. For example, in terms of 'literacy', the strategies discussed above for 'communication and language' may be relevant.

For children's 'mathematics', the following strategies might be useful.

- **Plan to use software which allows children to experience situations of counting and sharing and identifying numbers, e.g. in counting items for a picnic.**
- **Use software which relates a counting song or nursery rhyme known to the children to reinforce early counting concepts and which allows the children to have some free play. If children are working with parent helpers or other adults and making conscious what they understand, much constructive dialogue can take place, which takes the child forward.**

Digital technologies can develop children's 'understanding of the world' including their skills of enquiry in many ways. Some of the following might be used to plan to address this key learning area.

- **As mentioned above, include digital technologies within a role-play area. Consider settings with which the children are familiar such as libraries, doctors' surgeries and any kind of office. This creates a powerful context for imaginative play because the computer reinforces the 'reality' of the situation for the child. It is a powerful stimulus for the inner speech and the outer dialogue in the zone of proximal development.**
- **The computer provides everyone in the Early Years Setting with a means of recording in writing, orally and visually (still and full motion), the children's experiences as learners. Digital cameras are highly significant tools in this context, with their capacity for immediate feedback.**
- **The capacity for ICT to provide access to activities for many children with special educational needs (including sensory impairment, physical and behavioural problems) allows for activities which promote knowledge and understanding of the world to be planned for all.**
- **There is plenty of scope for the internet to bring experiences of other cultures and other worlds into the Early Years setting.**

For children's 'expressive arts and design', ICT brings into the world of the Early Years setting experiences with new media which can be used alongside the range of traditional, hands-on experiences. For example:

- **The use of graphics software is an area of great potential in the Early Years setting. The medium in which the learner operates is infinitely editable and scalable. Colours in areas of the onscreen canvas can be varied at the click of a mouse. Shapes can be created with and without filled areas. With support from an adult or working with a friend, the child can be encouraged to verbalise their thoughts on the image they are making. Digital cameras allow images of the child themselves and other people and objects from the environment to become part of the onscreen canvas.**
- **Digital technologies also offer the Early Years setting the potential to be creative with sound and video. Simple musical composition software allows young learners to see that you can do more than just paint and write at a computer. A recording studio is another imaginary scenario in which to explore and develop.**

REFLECTIVE TASK

Choose one of the EYFS areas of learning and development. Identify, with the help of the Early Years team at the school, an appropriate piece of software with which the children are already familiar.

Set up the computer within some kind of role-play context if possible (if space allows and if it fits with the current planning in the setting). Observe the children working with the software over a period of a few days for a few minutes each day. Ask for one or other of the co-workers in the setting to do the same. Collate your observations.

How has the presence of the computer assisted in generating talk around the area of learning? Have you been able to observe any interactions in which peer learning was evident? Did the children work in the ways in which you expected? Were there any surprising outcomes?

Were there any overlapping areas of development from the other areas of learning and development?

THE BIGGER PICTURE THE BIGGER PICTURE THE BIGGER PICTURE THE BIGGER PICTURE

When you are planning in the Early Years, think about planning across all of the areas of learning rather than just one. For example, when planning for mathematics, think about how mathematical concepts might fit into a wider topic or unit of work. Comparing eye and hair colour and measuring heights and using a basic graphing program (see Chapter 14) to display results might fit in with the theme of 'Ourselves' that also includes creative development work on drawing self and others and communication, language and literacy work on children's families. Investigating patterns and tessellations might form part of a half-term's focus on 'Buildings' that includes finding out about homes in different parts of the world or at different times in history. Collecting data on favourite foods or numbers of different types of animal might both be included in a cross-area plan based on 'Food and farming' that includes research on farming in different parts of the world.

RESEARCH SUMMARY RESEARCH SUMMARY RESEARCH SUMMARY RESEARCH SUMMARY

Research has been carried out on the importance of talk around the computer which is of particular interest to Early Years practitioners as they plan for contexts in which young learners express their 'inner speech' (Smidt, 2007). In Wegerif and Scrimshaw's *Computers and Talk in the Primary Classroom* (1997) a number of projects are outlined which analyse talk in and around computers according to a variety of frameworks. In one example Eunice Fisher reports on the influence of software type on the kinds of talk generated (Mercer and Fisher, 1997). A pattern of talk emerges in the use of less open-ended software which is quite different from the wide-ranging exploratory talk in evidence when open-ended software is being used by children. Wegerif responds in the chapter which follows, making a case for exploratory talk which is generated around closed software and which actually extends children and 'leads to the educationally valuable combination of directive teaching software with children's active peer learning' (Wegerif, 1997, p.99).

A SUMMARY OF **KEY POINTS**

> ➤ **Planning for ICT should be based on an understanding of the ways in which young children think and learn.**

> ➤ **The talk and play around digital technologies is an important element in the planned outcomes.**

> ➤ **Each of the areas of learning and development can be supported with planned use of digital technologies.**

M-LEVEL EXTENSION > > M-LEVEL EXTENSION > > M-LEVEL EXTENSION

In the light of this chapter it should be clear that there can be an important role for digital technologies in the Early Years Foundation Stage. However, this is a contested area with many justifiably raising concerns about the developmental appropriateness of the use of digital technologies with very young children. Read this informative policy document from the National Association for the Education of Young Children (2012) in the USA, at the following link **www.naeyc.org/files/naeyc/file/positions/PS_technology_WEB2.pdf**. What issues does it identify?

Compare the position taken with a similar policy statement from UNESCO (Kalaš, 2012) about the exposure of very young children to digital technologies at this link: **http://iite.unesco.org/pics/publications/en/files/3214720.pdf**.

REFERENCES REFERENCES **REFERENCES** REFERENCES **REFERENCES** REFERENCES

Crook, C. (1996) *Computers and the Collaborative Experience of Learning.* London: Routledge.

DCSF (2008) *Statutory Framework for the Early Years Foundation Stage.* London: DCSF.

DfE (2011) *Teachers' Standards.* Available at **www.education.gov.uk/publications**.

DfE (2014) *Statutory Framework for the Early Years Foundation Stage.* London: DfE. Available at **www.education.gov.uk/publications**.

Kalaš, I. (2012) *Policy Brief: ICTs in Early Childhood Care and Education.* Moscow: UNESCO Institute for Information Technologies in Education. Available at **www.iite.unesco.org/pics/publications/en/files/3214720.pdf**.

Mercer, N. and Fisher, E. (1997) 'The importance of talk', in R. Wegerif and P. Scrimshaw (eds), *Computers and Talk in the Primary Classroom.* London: Multilingual Matters.

NAEYC (2012) *Technology and Interactive Media as Tools in Early Childhood Programs Serving Children from Birth through Age 8.* Washington, DC: NAEYC. Available at **www.naeyc.org/files/naeyc/file/positions/PS_technology_WEB2.pdf** (accessed 18 March 2015).

Plowman, L., Stephen, C. and McPake, J. (2010) *Growing Up with Technology: Young Children Learning in a Digital World.* London: Routledge.

Smidt, S. (2007) *A Guide to Early Years Practice.* London: Routledge.

Tickell, C. (2011) *The Early Years: Foundations for Life, Health and Learning. An Independent Report on the Early Years Foundation Stage to Her Majesty's Government.* London: DfE.

Wegerif, R. (1997) 'Children's talk and computer software: a response to Fisher', in R. Wegerif and P. Scrimshaw (eds), *Computers and Talk in the Primary Classroom.* London: Multilingual Matters.

Wegerif, R. and Scrimshaw, P. (eds) (1997) *Computers and Talk in the Primary Classroom.* London: Multilingual Matters.

Wood, D. (1997) *How Children Think and Learn.* London: Wiley Blackwell.

FURTHER READING FURTHER READING **FURTHER READING** FURTHER READING

Basford, J. and Hodson, E. (2008) *Teaching Early Years Foundation Stage.* Exeter: Learning Matters.

Plowman, L. (2016) 'Learning technology at home and pre-school', in N. Rushby and D. Surry (eds), *Wiley Handbook of Learning Technology.* Hoboken, NJ: John Wiley & Sons.

4
Digital display technologies

Chapter objectives

When you have completed work on this chapter, you will have:

- considered the different types of digital display technologies such as interactive whiteboards and visualisers often available in schools;
- thought critically about the opportunities digital display technologies offer to support teaching and learning across the curriculum;
- noted the practicalities of using digital display technologies in the primary classroom;
- examined critically the idea of interactivity often associated with digital display technologies and considered the different ways of appropriating IWBs and visualisers into your pedagogical practice;
- reflected critically on some of the claims made about the potential of digital display technologies to impact on learning and begun to consider the nature of this impact.

Introduction

Large-format display technologies – interactive or otherwise – have been a long-standing feature of classrooms for many years. From the chalkboard to the dry-wipe whiteboard, the floor-standing flipchart to the overhead projector (OHP) and the more recent interactive whiteboards (IWBs) to visualisers, display technologies offer opportunities to model concepts and processes as well as the chance for children to interact with and share these processes and concepts themselves. It may seem strange from an Anglo-centric perspective, where the vast majority of schools have digital display technologies like IWBs and visualisers, to reflect on chalkboards. However, chalkboards are still in use in many countries including many economically developed countries such as Japan, where they remain the display technology of choice in many schools (Emerling, 2015). We mention this because it is worth thinking for a moment about how the effective use of any display technology in the classroom is in essence contingent upon the teacher's and to some extent the children's technical and pedagogical mastery of the technology to explain, illustrate or model conceptual knowledge and processes appropriately, regardless of whether the technology is analogue or digital. In some respects, a traditional chalkboard, it could be argued, can be more interactive than a digital interactive display used only to present slides, because the user is required to create their own content (diagrams, timelines, text and so on). Furthermore, Emerling (2015, n.p.) writes: 'Japanese educators possess a unique technical vocabulary for describing chalkboard teaching practices, called *bansho* (board-writing) and *bansho-keikaku* (board-writing planning).' These practices have emerged from the great care that is taken in planning and analysing how the chalkboard can be used to support teaching and learning in Japan. It is worth reading Emerling's (2015) article in full (see: **https://larrycuban.wordpress.com/2015/04/26/lessons-learned-from-a-chalkboard-slow-and-steady-technology-integration-bradley-emerling/**)

**Figure 4.1 New and old technology in a Japanese classroom.
Image courtesy of Professor Yoichi Nonaka.**

as he suggests this is a model that could be adapted to the use of digital technologies in the classroom. Where digital display technologies are integrated into Japanese schools they are often integrated in ways that enable synergy between the old and new technologies as can be seen from the photograph in Figure 4.1. Professor Yoichi Nonaka, from Yokohama National University in Japan, explains that 'in this social studies lesson, the scenario is projected onto the green chalkboard and children's names on white card are attached to the board against the ideas and opinions they have expressed.'

We argue throughout this chapter for careful and critical analysis of how you and your children might engage with interactive display technologies for learning. In the context of schools in the UK, it is most appropriate to focus on interactive whiteboards (IWBs) as this is perhaps the dominant technology that student teachers will encounter. However, at points throughout the chapter we also discuss visualisers, as schools are increasingly seeing the educational potential of these. Despite the focus of this chapter on digital display technologies we would also encourage student teachers to learn from the case of Japanese schools and not neglect the old analogue display technologies such as A1 flip-charts or dry-wipe whiteboards. There can be good pedagogical reasons for choosing to use these over digital technologies in some contexts or to think about how you use them in conjunction with the digital display technologies you may have access to. We will also examine some of the claims made about IWBs in the light of recent evidence and developments in order to help student teachers develop a more critical and reflective approach to the appropriation of the IWB or any digital display technology in their practice.

Digital display technologies and the National Curriculum

Digital display technologies such as the interactive whiteboard are akin to the traditional chalkboard or whiteboard in that they are genuinely a cross-curricular tool. It is not useful to think of their implementation as grounded in the computing subject content. Both the IWB and visualiser have application across the curriculum although they differ considerably.

The positioning of the teacher when operating an IWB is more akin to the traditional chalk-board whereas operating the visualiser is more akin to using an OHP in that there is more opportunity for the teacher to face and address the class. Both of these technologies might be used to model processes. For example, a teacher might demonstrate the dissection and labelling of the parts of a real flower under the visualiser or a graphic representation of the parts of a flower on an IWB (Science). Or in mathematics, a child might demonstrate to the class how to measure an angle using a real protractor, pencil and paper under a visualiser. Using an IWB they could demonstrate this process using the IWB's inbuilt interactive mathematics program, manipulating a virtual protractor to model the process to the rest of the class. There are myriad opportunities to integrate these technologies into the curriculum.

It is also arguable that good classroom use of any digital display technology can contribute to any aspect of the computing programme of study. For example, it could be used to facilitate whole-class or small group analysis of the programming within a particular Scratch project that a child has created. Equally another student might use the IWB to explain and model how they have used a variable in their Scratch game to keep the player's score. Similarly, a teacher might want to use a visualiser to illustrate and discuss the circuitry and components within a small digital device like the BBC micro:bit or the inside of a broken mobile phone. These examples could address the computer science aspects of the programme of study that we discuss in Section B of this book. An interactive whiteboard or a visualiser could be employed to facilitate most aspects of the computing programme of study, again depending on the teacher's pedagogical design of the activity.

What are interactive whiteboards and visualisers?

Interactive whiteboards (IWBs) are touch-sensitive boards which allow teachers and children to engage directly with digital content projected on a screen from a computer via a data projector. They have their conceptual origins in commercial contexts where they were introduced to enliven presentations and dialogue in the boardroom and elsewhere. In large part due to the 1997–2010 Labour government policy, they have now been widely adopted in schools in the UK. The most common types of IWB found in UK schools are those developed by Smart Technologies referred to as a SmartBoard (see **http://smart tech.com/gb**) and another type developed by Promethean referred to as an ActivBoard (**www.prometheanworld.com/gb/english/education/home/**). An exploration of these two companies' websites will also reveal that development in touch sensitive (haptic) technologies for education is a fast-moving field, one of the latest developments being what are referred to as multi-touch tables which allow learners to interact synchronously around a horizontal surface. Such technologies are expensive at the moment, and there is not a great deal of research about their educational value. However, it is reasonable to assume that like IWBs and other educational technologies, once the 'wow' factor has waned it is the pedagogy that is vital if the technology is to be effective.

Visualisers (also referred to as document cameras) contrast significantly to IWBs in that they tend to be used to capture and manipulate real artifacts. They consist of a powerful digital camera mounted above a lit workspace or display space. Most visualisers offer the facility to zoom in close on the workspace area. The higher the quality of the optical zoom of the visualiser's camera, the higher the quality of the images. Higher-quality visualisers can act like a microscope, giving very high-quality and detailed close-up images of objects, which can be displayed to the whole class. Still images and video can be captured of the activity being demonstrated in the workspace. Of course it is important to note that many schools and teachers may already have digital technologies such as older digital video cameras, tablet devices or mobile phones that can be repurposed or set up to act as a visualiser, as you will see from the following task.

PRACTICAL TASK PRACTICAL TASK PRACTICAL TASK PRACTICAL TASK

Firstly, watch the demonstration of some of the different ways in which you can use a visualiser in the classroom, at the following link or search online for video of teachers demonstrating how they use visualisers in their classrooms:

www.youtube.com/watch?v=gFxkguEskYU. Secondly, watch the following video by teacher José Picardo (2014) on 'Using your iPad as a visualiser' (at **https://vimeo.com/97250314**).

Some practicalities about using interactive whiteboards in the classroom

Technically, interactive whiteboards work by enabling the teacher and children to control the computer by touching the board, either with a special pen or with their finger. The touch is understood by the computer in the same way as it recognises mouse movement and clicks.

There are two main technologies that have been implemented in the design of IWBs used in the classroom, which can broadly be characterised as 'hard' or 'soft' boards. Hard boards have a grid of copper wire behind the solid surface. These boards need special pens which are tracked by the grid using electromagnetism. Soft boards use 'resistive' technology. The board has a polyester surface membrane which is flexible, though strong, and separated from a rigid second layer by a small air gap. As the finger or pen is used to depress the surface, the contact is registered by the board and transmitted to the computer.

The 'feel' of the two different boards is quite distinctive, and teachers usually decide that they have a preference for one type of board rather than the other. Sometimes this partiality may simply be the result of familiarity. It can also be influenced by the software that is provided with the board. The software is not interchangeable, although there has been considerable convergence in functionality as the different manufacturers have recognised the utility of particular tools. Teachers need to consider that, if they build up a bank of resources for one type of board, it will not easily be converted to the other.

Another vital area to consider is the physical set up of the IWB. While you will not have much if any control over this as a student teacher it is worth considering the set up of the IWB you inherit so that you are aware of the issues that can arise and affect your lesson, as we will explore next.

The components of an IWB set-up

In order to use an interactive whiteboard three items of equipment are necessary: the whiteboard itself, a computer and a data projector. The computer is connected to both the projector and to the interactive whiteboard. The physical organisation of this equipment is important. When IWBs were first introduced decisions had to be taken as to whether the equipment should be fixed or mobile, with the IWB held on a trolley and the data projector and computer moved around with it. Schools now tend to arrange for their IWBs to be permanently installed on a wall, as mobile systems proved to be cumbersome and time consuming. If at all possible, ceiling mounting the data projector is preferable, too, although more recently all-in-one systems have become available in which the projector is mounted on an arm that reaches out from the whiteboard with a short-throw projector mounted at the end of the arm. The advantage of this is that it is easier to interact with the board, without blocking the projected image. Health and safety concerns would support this option too as there is less risk of the user looking directly into the projector. Trailing leads should always be avoided in the classroom and trunking used for cables where at all possible. An additional benefit to a fixed installation is that encasing the projector in a ceiling-mounted unit provides security for what is otherwise an attractive, portable target for thieves.

The computer used to control the IWB can be a standard desktop computer. Its positioning will to a certain extent depend on the geography of the classroom; there is no need for it to be close to the whiteboard. Many schools use laptops for this purpose, which have the benefit of enabling teachers to prepare resources away from the classroom. Similarly it is increasingly becoming possible to link up tablet devices to projection facilities.

The positioning of the board in the classroom needs careful consideration. There must be sufficient space on either side of the board for the teacher or children to stand and avoid being in the path of the projector. The projected light will be affected by other light sources such as windows and overhead lights. Blinds or curtains may be necessary. The height of the board is also a factor. At the very least the teacher must be able to reach the top of the board, both to calibrate it and to access menu items in program windows, and as far as is practical the children should be able to use as much of the board as possible. However, the board also needs to be visible to the class. In many classrooms benches or small platforms have been set up so that shorter users can write on the whole board. There is an obvious safety consideration here; balancing on a stool is not an acceptable alternative.

The size of the board is important. Generally speaking, the larger the board, the easier it will be for the class to use. Detail will be difficult to make out on a small board from the back of the room. While this may not be problematical when using resources designed specifically with the whiteboard in mind, the size of text will be a concern when, for example, demonstrating menu items in a program window. Needless to say there is a cost implication involved in opting for a larger board.

Increasingly, schools are recognising that the full potential of an interactive whiteboard is realised only if good-quality audio equipment has been integrated. Many programs and web pages that might be used on the interactive whiteboard depend to a greater or lesser extent on audio facilities, sometimes to give feedback on choices that the user has made. It is important that the sound can be heard by the whole class, and ideally the source should be close to the board itself, rather than the computer, so that there is close identification of sound and projected image.

The IWB should not be used with conventional whiteboard pens. Although the IWB can be wiped, marks will inevitably be left and will be picked out by the light from the projector.

Wherever space has allowed, teachers have tended to retain their old whiteboard, or use a whiteboard (or paper flipchart) mounted on an easel, in addition to the IWB.

RESEARCH SUMMARY RESEARCH SUMMARY **RESEARCH SUMMARY** RESEARCH SUMMARY

In the early research into the use of interactive whiteboards, among the general benefits that were concluded were motivation, which was widely reported (e.g. Levy, 2002), the efficiency with which teachers were able to present web-based and other resources (Walker, 2003) and the opportunities for interaction and discussion in the classroom. Factors that support effective use include, significantly, the importance of teachers becoming familiar with the technology (Levy, 2002; Glover and Miller, 2001) and also practical considerations such as the position of the boards to avoid sunlight and any obstructions (Smith, 2001). More recently research has highlighted the importance of distinguishing between levels and types of interactivity, suggesting that interactivity for its own sake may not necessarily lead to increased cognitive engagement with the learning process (Kennewell et al., 2007; Beauchamp, 2011). Indeed, this is one area where visualisers may be seen to have an advantage over IWBs. Mavers (2009) carried out research into the use of visualisers and found that the display of the the teacher's fine motor skills together with the representation of the actual through the visualiser aided students in making meaning and understanding the processes and conceptual knowledge being modelled.

What are the key ways of using an interactive whiteboard?

There are two main ways in which a teacher may use an interactive whiteboard. It can be used very effectively with the pen or finger simply replacing the mouse. For example, a PowerPoint presentation can be managed at the board, clicking for each new slide, rather than the teacher needing to go to the computer in order to move on. This becomes particularly useful for the children if the presentation has been designed to include choices activated by hyperlinks, so that the children are able to decide or at least to see what option has been taken. Similarly, for the teacher to work at the board to show the children how to use software has more impact, and can help to maintain the momentum of a lesson, compared with the teacher demonstrating remotely, hoping that the children can follow the pointer.

Alternatively, the teacher can use the native software of the whiteboard. At its most straightforward, the software provides a selection of tools that enable annotation and other manipulation such as gradually revealing parts of the desktop. These tools can be used in 'real time', and combined with the strong visual impact of what is on screen, perhaps from a web page, can make for lively lessons that engage the children well. However, the software can also be used to prepare resources in advance of the lesson to create files that will be used interactively with the children. In SMART, these files are known as notebooks, while in Promethean they are flipcharts. RM offer an alternative software called Easiteach. Creating notebooks, flipcharts or Easiteach files with interactive features is not difficult, but time spent becoming familiar and adept with the software will be repaid.

PRACTICAL TASK   PRACTICAL TASK   **PRACTICAL TASK**   PRACTICAL TASK

Spend some time exploring the IWB resources at the following websites and consider how you could use them or adapt them for use in your own teaching.

ActivBoard Promethean: **www.prometheanplanet.com/en-gb/**

SmartBoard: **http://exchange.smarttech.com/#tab=0**

Depending on the digital display technology you have access to, download any teacher support software you can access. On placement set aside some time to practise using the IWB in your classroom. Familiarise yourself with the features such as any built in software. Try using the onboard screen capture facility to record a process you will need to model to the class in mathematics.

What do interactive whiteboards contribute to teaching and learning?

It is worth briefly considering the claims noted by the National Whiteboard Network (2006, p.193) in relation to the potential of interactive whiteboards. These opportunities were summarised by the National Whiteboard Network, the arm of the Primary National Strategy charged with supporting the introduction of IWBs into schools, as the potential to:

- *Improve the quality of interactions*
- *Improve teacher assessment through the promotion of effective questioning*
- *Enhance modelling*
- *Redress the balance of making resources and planning for teaching*
- *Increase the pace of learning*

(National Whiteboard Network, 2006)

Four of the five refer to gains that may be made over 'traditional' teaching approaches. The judgement that a particular technology offers an improvement over teaching by alternative means is always a good litmus test: if ICT does not bring an enhancement, then why bother with it?

Perhaps the most important of the five gains is the **increased pace of lessons** that IWBs allow, although it should also be remembered that increased pace may not always be desirable or indeed synonymous with increased learning. Sometimes teachers slow the pace of a lesson to try to address misconceptions or deepen the children's understanding of a concept. Nevertheless, the potential for increased pace has been widely reported by teachers. If the lesson is well prepared, the teacher will be able to use resources quickly and smoothly to move from one point to another. File organisation on the computer is important for quick access, and it will usually be helpful to organise desktop shortcuts in advance of the lesson. The teacher also needs to know how to use the resource itself. This is not as straightforward as it may seem. Some resources may have been created with a lot of thought but are not necessarily intuitive to use. Planning, and specifically consultation of the supporting guides, will help to ensure that the lesson itself maintains good pace where desirable.

If the teacher has sufficient digital resources to hand and knows how they intend to use them, then the pace of the lesson that follows can be varied accordingly to make space for two other of the benefits identified by the National Whiteboard Network, namely *improving the quality of interactions* and *improving teacher assessment through the promotion of effective questioning*. Indeed, the importance of the quality of pedagogical interactions when using the interactive whiteboard and maintaining a focus on learning goals are important factors as confirmed by Kennewell et al.'s findings (2007) and also Beauchamp's research (2011).

The final claim of the National Whiteboard Network, that IWBs have the potential to *redress the balance of making resources and planning for teaching*, is perhaps more contentious. Resources are increasingly available for downloading from the internet, and many of these are of high quality or can be adapted easily. There are also some proprietary software titles, designed with IWB use particularly in mind, which may be purchased. However, searching for the right resource takes time and in some circumstances it may be quicker, and provide a tailor-made outcome, to create the resource from scratch. Once the teacher has a file for use on the interactive whiteboard, though, it is recyclable, and the initial effort made to secure exactly the right material will be repaid in subsequent years. Within a school, teachers may also share resources and develop online libraries, using filing systems provided by the IWB software.

Modelling is well suited to work on the interactive whiteboard. For young children, to see and manipulate representational images and icons has a strong impact and will often make the teaching point much more clearly than verbal or textual explanations. The technology self-evidently lends itself to whole-class teaching more than to group work. Even if a teacher decided to work with one group at the IWB while the rest of the class was occupied in other activities, there would be the likelihood of children being distracted, especially if sound and video were involved. As with any whole-class work, the teacher needs to ensure that all of the children are engaged. Planned and targeted questioning will be a key technique to this end. Ironically, the children's physical interactivity with the board may not be as fundamental. In the early days of the introduction of IWBs it was reckoned that giving the children direct access to the board would be central to the success of the technology. However, it became apparent that bringing young children, especially, frequently to the front of the class incurred a time overhead and distracted from the learning objectives of the lesson – the very benefit that the IWB is supposed to bring. Obviously there is a balance to be struck.

Another surprising consideration is whether the interactive whiteboard is genuinely being used interactively (Kennewell et al., 2007; Beauchamp, 2011). If the data projector is essentially only beaming what is on the computer desktop, or if the interactivity is low level, such as moving on slides sequentially in a PowerPoint presentation, then it is questionable whether the IWB is necessary. At a more sophisticated level, some schools are exploring the potential of wireless devices such as remote tablet devices or slates, that can be passed around the room but enable the children to interact with the interactive whiteboard. The intention here is for the input equipment to be passed around the class, without the children coming to the board. This provides an interesting alternative approach, but in the primary classroom, at least, there will be a concomitant loss of physical connection directly between the teacher or children and the board which might represent a pedagogical disadvantage. As we can see, the effective integration of a technology such as the interactive whiteboard is pedagogically complex and requires a critical approach to one's practice.

Break down the elements of a lesson you have observed (or given) in which extensive use was made of the interactive whiteboard. Identify which parts of the lesson were necessarily interactive and which were more a matter of projecting images or text or making use passively of other multimedia resources.

Interactive whiteboards and the core subjects

On the face of it, interactive whiteboards are cross-curricular and it is possible to conceive of resources being prepared for any subject. However, it is noticeable that many of the available resources focus on the core subjects.

THE BIGGER PICTURE   THE BIGGER PICTURE   THE BIGGER PICTURE   THE BIGGER PICTURE

When planning and drafting shared writing and going on to develop it further through revising and editing it, the IWB can be integral in engaging and motivating children. It can be used to record their contributions, give vocabulary choices, draft sentences and cut and paste them to re-sequence the piece, until everyone is happy with the result. The children can then move to working further on the same text or developing one of their own in groups on the classroom computer or in your school's ICT suite.

THE BIGGER PICTURE   THE BIGGER PICTURE   THE BIGGER PICTURE   THE BIGGER PICTURE

There are many programs available as secondary sources to illustrate phenomena that are not possible to recreate in the classroom, both for use with the whole class on the IWB and for children to use in groups on the class computer. These can make mathematics and science fun while providing useful models and simulations. Make sure that you know what is available in school and also consider the internet. When you plan to use secondary sources, remember that there are colleagues in school who can advise you on what is available, and check the school's long/medium-term planning in case it identifies available resources before deciding whether you will need to source any additional materials yourself. Always pre-view video clips and TV programmes, simulations and models and use programs hands-on to ensure that they are appropriate for your requirements and suitable for the children's needs.

Provision of free resources for science is not as well developed. Partly this may be for reasons of cost. Interesting and accurate representations of scientific phenomena and experiments take time to produce. Again, it may be more appropriate to use a visualiser with the children to record and produce your own representations of scientific phenomena and experiments. However, there is good proprietary software available from companies such as Sherston, 2Simple, CATS, 4Learning, Kar2ouche, ClicSoft, Boardworks, The Big Bus and Inclusive Technology. Also when using secondary sources on an IWB it is worth remembering that they are a representation of a real-world artifact or process. So, for example, if you plan to use a science electricity simulation, think about what is lost in comparison to using actual batteries, bulbs and wires. A visualiser or an iPad connected to the display can be used to illustrate electrical circuits to the whole class, using the actual components rather than virtual components. The advantage of this is that actual components such as batteries and bulbs behave as they do in the real world, whereas virtual batteries never run down and virtual bulbs never blow. These real-world characteristics provide opportunities for learning. Similarly, a simulated protractor on an IWB is not the actual tool, so think about how modelling the use of a protractor by using a simulated protractor on the IWB might actually confuse some children further rather than help them.

A SUMMARY OF **KEY POINTS**

➢ **Digital display technologies can be useful tools to support teaching and learning across the curriculum, if teachers reflect critically on how to appropriate them into their practice.**

➢ **IWBs and visualisers are the most common digital display technologies found in schools but this area is under constant development.**

➢ **The positioning of the digital display technology, the computer and the data projector requires careful thought to ensure that this is optimal in supporting teaching and learning.**

➢ **There are five main benefits of using IWBs identified by research projects, including the pace of learning, the enhancement of modelling, improving the quality of interactions, assessment through effective questioning, and redressing the balance between making resources and planning.**

➢ **Teachers need to think critically about the concept of interaction through digital display technology. Physical interaction with an IWB is not necessarily synonymous with increased learning.**

➢ **Digital display technologies should not replace analogue display technologies but be used in careful connection with them.**

M-LEVEL EXTENSION > > M-LEVEL EXTENSION > > M-LEVEL EXTENSION

Teachers often liken their 'performance' in the classroom to a stage role in which the success of a lesson is in part gauged by how well they have engaged their audience of children. If teachers include an interactive whiteboard as one of their props, then it is important that it is used effectively and efficiently. This does not mean that the whole lesson is scripted. Indeed, one of the exciting aspects about the use of an interactive whiteboard is that the opportunity is there to respond quickly and easily to the questions or suggestions of the audience, following hyperlinks and creating searches. Make a point of observing a range of colleagues teaching with the IWB in as many subjects as you can make arrangements to see. Read as widely as possible about the IWB as a tool to improve the quality of teaching and learning (see Moss et al., 2007; Somekh et al., 2007).

REFERENCES REFERENCES **REFERENCES** REFERENCES **REFERENCES** REFERENCES

Beauchamp, G. (2011) 'Interactivity and ICT in the primary school: categories of learner interactions with and without ICT', *Technology, Pedagogy and Education*, 20(2), pp.175–90.

DfE (2011) *Teachers' Standards*. Available at: **www.education.gov.uk/publications**.

Emerling, B. (2015) 'Lessons learned from a chalkboard: slow and steady technology integration'. Available at: **https://larrycuban.wordpress.com/2015/04/26/lessons-learned-from-a-chalkboard-slow-and-steady-technology-integration-bradley-emerling/**.

Glover, D. and Miller, D. (2001) 'Running with technology: the pedagogic impact of the large-scale introduction of interactive whiteboards in one secondary school', *Journal of Information Technology for Teacher Education*, 10(3), pp.257–76.

Kennewell, S., Tanner, H., Jones, S. and Beauchamp, G. (2007) 'Analysing the use of interactive technology to implement interactive teaching', *Journal of Computer Assisted Learning*, 24(1), pp.61–73.

Levy, P. (2002) *Interactive Whiteboards in Learning and Teaching in Two Sheffield Schools: A Developmental Study*. Sheffield: Department of Information Studies, University of Sheffield.

Mavers, D. (2009) 'Teaching and learning with a visualiser in the primary classroom: modelling graph making', *Learning Media and Technology*, 34(1), pp.11–26.

Moss, G. et al. (2007) *The Interactive Whiteboards, Pedagogy and Pupil Performance Evaluation: London Challenge*. London: School of Educational Foundations and Policy Studies, IOE. Available at **http://webarchive.nationalarchives.gov.uk/20130401151715/https://www.education.gov.uk/publications/eOrderingDownload/RR816%20Report.pdf**.

National Whiteboard Network (2006) *An Interactive Whiteboard; What Is It?* Available at **http://web.archive.org/web/20051222045729/http://www.nwnet.org.uk/**.

Picardo, J. (2014) 'Using your iPad as a visualizer'. Available at **https://vimeo.com/97250314**.

Smith, A. (2001) *Interactive Whiteboard Evaluation*. Available at **www.mirandanet.ac.uk/publications/smartboard.htm**.

Smith, H. (2001) *SmartBoard Evaluation: Final Report*. Kent NGfL. Available at **http://www.kentict.org.uk/kentict/kentict_iwb_smart_final**.

Somekh, B. et al. (2007) *Evaluation of the Primary Schools Whiteboard Expansion Project (SWEEP)*. Manchester: Metropolitan University/SWEEP/DfES. Available at **http://webarchive.national archives.gov.uk/20130401151715/https://www.education.gov.uk/publications/eOrderingDownload/SWEEP-Report.pdf**.

Walker, D. (2003) 'Quality at the dockside', *TES Online*, 3 January, pp.66–7.

FURTHER READING FURTHER READING **FURTHER READING** FURTHER READING

Barber, D., Cooper, L. and Meeson, G. (2007) *Learning and Teaching with Interactive Whiteboards*. Exeter: Learning Matters.

5
Mobile technologies

Chapter objectives

When you have completed work on this chapter, you will have:

- familiarised yourself with a range of mobile technologies used in education;
- considered the potential that mobile technologies offer for teaching and learning both in the classroom and beyond;
- thought about some of the issues involved with incorporating mobile technologies into classroom practice;
- considered how mobile technologies could support your own professional development.

Introduction

One of the exciting aspects of computing is that the technology itself is evolving quickly and providing opportunities for innovation and experiment. In this chapter we will summarise the different kinds of mobile technology that are currently available, conscious that the picture is constantly changing. We will go on to review some of the ways in which mobile devices might be utilised in primary schools. What we will encounter is considerable variety in the contexts in which mobile technology can be applied, which leads to consideration of the implications for primary teachers and subject leaders in taking strategic decisions about the equipment that is important and relevant for them.

What are mobile technologies?

In the last few years there has been significant development in the range and diversity of ICT equipment that is small enough to be carried around conveniently, and it is to these recent innovations that the term 'mobile technologies' is usually applied. Early developments saw the emergence of what were called personal digital assistants (PDAs) which incorporated various facilities such as calendars, satellite navigation and internet connectivity. However, many of these applications have now converged into one device, with the development of smartphones, MP3 players such as Apple's iPod and Apple/Android/Windows tablets (e.g. iPad, Galaxy, Surface). We will also refer to laptops, or 'notebook' computers, and tablet PCs, although strictly these are 'portable' rather than 'mobile', due in part to their physical size (Anderson and Blackwood, 2004).

Mobile technologies and the National Curriculum

Neither the programmes of study for computing nor any other area of the National Curriculum make any direct reference to mobile technologies. However, mobile technology has become commonplace in our lives and you may find yourself in a school that actively incorporates the use of mobile technologies into teaching and learning. Accordingly, including the use of mobile technologies in curriculum activities is only a reflection of what is happening in the world beyond the school gates. How mobile technologies are used to address aspects of the curriculum including computing will depend on how they are integrated into teaching and learning. For example, if a tablet device such as an iPad is used in a history lesson to research the life of a Victorian child, using the internet and a note taking app, then there will be an opportunity to develop children's digital literacy skills alongside their historical skills as they are taught to:

- use search technologies effectively, appreciate how results are selected and ranked, and be discerning in evaluating digital content.

However, equally children might be engaged in programming an on-screen Bee-Bot to navigate a virtual maze on a tablet device and would therefore be focusing on how to:

- create and debug simple programs;
- use logical reasoning to predict the behaviour of simple programs.

Essentially, mobile devices can be used to support any aspect of the curriculum, depending on the teacher's pedagogical design of the activities.

Some practicalities about using mobile technologies in the classroom

In considering the use of mobile technologies inside – and outside – the classroom, teachers will need to establish what is practical in terms of funding. This is likely to be a team decision involving all staff. Some schools have made the choice to buy a class set of laptops or even iPads. Some schools have equipped children with iPads but at present they are a minority, especially in the UK. For an example, see José Picardo's blog at the following link in which he describes his own school's experience of a 1 to 1 tablet project: **www.josepicardo.com/2016/03/tablets-in-schools-case-study-in-success**/. Other schools have explored schemes – Bring Your Own Device (BYOD) – which actively encourage the children to bring their own mobile devices into schools in order to teach them how to use them appropriately and critically to support their learning. Of course any scheme needs to be carefully considered by the whole school in terms of issues of equal access and safety. It is unlikely that mobile devices will completely replace the school's need for desktop or laptop computers, so if a set of iPads is bought, will staff in the school as a whole have the time and commitment to explore how to appropriate them into their pedagogical practice? If not, then it is questionable whether the devices will be more than an expensive novelty. Apart from cost considerations, the increasing diversity of affordable digital technologies suggests that teachers in future will need to choose what is most appropriate for their classroom.

The range of mobile technology available is substantial and it may be useful to summarise the features of the main types of mobile equipment that are currently marketed.

A *laptop computer* in principle has all the functionality of a desktop computer but with the additional benefit of being powered by a rechargeable battery and so is transportable. With mobility in mind, the size and weight of laptops are minimised and so they usually have a smaller screen and keyboard. The reduction in size of the components makes laptops more expensive than a desktop computer of comparable specification. Laptops can also be more difficult to use. The keyboard is not raked, which makes typing physically harder, and some users have difficulty using the touch pad to control the pointer. These concerns can be overcome by attaching a standard keyboard and mouse, or by using a docking station and mouse. Laptops have the advantage of being easy to transfer from one location to another. In a school, this potentially enables more effective use of a valuable resource as the laptop is moved from one classroom to another according to need. Some schools have bought class sets of laptops which are stored on a specially designed trolley with recharging facilities, so constituting a portable computer suite. Manufacturers have recently tended to refer to laptops as 'notebooks'.

Tablets are now characterised by having a touch-sensitive (haptic) screen that also responds to various gestures, e.g. swiping. These have developed as a variation from what were often referred to as tablet PCs which often had a pen-shaped stylus as an input device. Tablets such as the iPad can be operated using a stylus and some users find the stylus easier to use than touch and hand gestures. Tablets also incorporate a range of applications (apps) to support many different activities, image capture and manipulation, sound recording and editing and note-taking to name but a few. Another advantage of a tablet device is that it can be passed around a classroom and, using a data projector and wireless connection, children can take their turns to make a contribution which will be shared instantly by the whole class. For more information about the use of tablets in education see Burden et al.'s *iPad Scotland Evaluation* (2012).

Smartphones have developed through the convergence of PDAs and mobile phones. PDAs were initially conceived as personal organisers, but their functionality was quickly extended so that they were typically supplied with simple versions of office software, internet connectivity and sound recording facilities. Mobile phone ('smartphone') capability, including photography was then incorporated into PDAs, leading to what are generally termed smartphones. Smartphones have a pop-up virtual keyboard for input via a touch screen. However, small physical keyboards can also be connected via Bluetooth to both tablets and smartphones which can be a much easier way of entering text.

The use of *mobile phones* has been considered in relation to teaching and learning. Many schools ban children from bringing their phones into the classrooms, concerned about the possible distraction and also the risk of theft. However, there is an argument that children's enthusiasm for these devices can be harnessed to support the development of their literacy and oracy skills (Attewell, 2005) and, more generally, to support teaching and learning throughout the curriculum (Burden and Maher, 2015)

MP3 players store and play audio files, usually music. MP3 is a reference to the file format which at one time was dominant for music, but the devices are perhaps better referred to as digital audio players (DAPs), as other formats such as Windows Media Audio (WMA) and Advanced Audio Coding (AAC), used on Apple's iPod, are now also popular. The hardware itself falls into three main categories. Portable CD players originally could play only purchased (or copied) CDs, but can now usually manage downloaded MP3s or other formats burned onto a CD-R. Some products are now effectively personal media players, capable of capture and playback of video and still images as well as audio files.

What are the key features of mobile technologies?

While the transportability of mobile devices is their obvious shared feature, it is also worth considering how they will be integrated with other equipment. It would probably be a mistake to think of a tablet device such as an iPad as a replacement for a fully functioning desktop (or laptop) computer. Rather, its portability can be exploited, but through synchronisation with the full-size computer; data collected 'on the move' can be processed further in the classroom. For example, if a Calendar entry – a time and date for an appointment – is made on a smartphone during a staff meeting it can later be synchronised with Calendar on the teacher's home computer (it was this kind of facility, rather than any educational application, that originally drove forward the development of PDAs and smartphones). This procedure effectively backs up the information and also makes it accessible on a large screen.

Data transfer between devices may be set up via cables but increasingly wireless connectivity can be established. There is increasing interoperability between devices with many devices offering automatic synchronising via web-based storage and services. These are often referred to as cloud-based services, the principle being that the user's data follows the user rather than being fixed by the location of a particular device. Services such as Dropbox (see **www.dropbox.com**/), Google Drive and SkyDrive are useful in this respect because they enable you to store and save all documents to one location which is always accessible from any device providing an Internet connection is available. This saves working with duplicate files and avoids losing track of the latest version of a document or file. However, it should also be noted that such facilities for cloud-based storage and synchronisation work best when there is personal ownership of the mobile device.

What do mobile technologies contribute to teaching and learning?

Investigations into the opportunities for mobile technologies to support teaching and learning have been ongoing for some time now (see Passey, 1999, for an early influential report). It is arguable, though, that evidence to support the benefits of mobile technologies for teaching and learning remains inconclusive (see Naismith et al., 2004, for an objective overview) and may have depended on resources and time that, though possible in an experimental situation, would not be scaleable. While some educationalists see potential for the use of smartphones for school use, this possibility has not been widely adopted. Technical, financial and practical constraints can all be readily identified. Ironically, it may also be that children and young people see the smartphone and technologies associated with it as representative of their independence from adults. In this case, they may be reluctant to see their phones 'hijacked' for the school's purposes. Crook (2012) identified significant tensions associated with the use of such technologies in schools and Traxler (2010, p.5) argues that the integration of mobile technologies into education offers opportunities for innovation and inclusion but also warns that it is necessary to resolve several tensions as mobile technologies are 'woven into all the times and places of students' lives.'

Nevertheless, if all these reservations can gradually be overcome, it would seem that mobile technologies offer exciting prospects by extending the classroom both spatially, or geographically, and temporally, so that learning does not have to take place within any fixed parameters of location or time. This shift to what has been dubbed 'anytime, anywhere' learning is consistent with other social trends such as '24/7' availability of services and flexible working patterns for adults.

Podcasts, which might be either sound or video files that are transferred automatically onto mobile devices (or other computers), could be exploited profitably by education. Files are offered through a feed by the information provider (which would be the school or individual teacher) to a 'subscriber' (the learner) (the idea of a subscription in this instance does not necessarily imply that a payment is made). On the internet, feed readers or 'aggregators', most popularly in RSS (Really Simple Syndication) format, are used to keep subscribers in touch with any changes made to pages. This is particularly helpful for fast-changing news websites. However, the principle could also be applied to release lessons in the form of talks or demonstrations to children which they would download and play back at a time to suit themselves. *Screencasts* use screen-capture apps now available for tablet devices, which can be used for modelling and direct instruction of specific processes, for example in mathematics. Similarly, Wishart has highlighted how the facility to capture and edit moving images and create animation through mobile devices lends itself to the educational representation of scientific concepts and process (Wishart, 2016).

PRACTICAL TASK   PRACTICAL TASK   PRACTICAL TASK   PRACTICAL TASK

Watch the video *Modelling Multiplication* (Turvey, 2013) at the following link: **http://vimeo.com/64421196**. This short video was recorded on an iPad using the app, *Explain Everything* (**www.explaineverything. com/**) and then edited using video editing software. It demonstrates how short lessons can be put together to reinforce children's learning of a particular process while also illustrating the process to parents or guardians so they can support the children's learning. Think about other ways you could use a screen-capture app like Explain Everything to model other processes.

THE BIGGER PICTURE   THE BIGGER PICTURE   THE BIGGER PICTURE   THE BIGGER PICTURE

The use of mobile technologies in and beyond the primary classroom has many exciting possibilities. The peer- and self-assessment in PE using digital video clips can be extended by utilising iPods or tablet devices to include the use of videos of good practice in a range of sports and there are apps available, many of which are free to download, that enable children to analyse performance. Relevant material can be projected onto a larger screen, such as the IWB, for wider group or whole-class discussion. The versatility of mobile devices also means they could easily be incorporated into field trips or trips to museums. Of course, a balance needs to be struck between the use of any such devices and ensuring the children make the most of the experience beyond the classroom. For example, on a trip to a science or history museum, just as giving children a worksheet to complete can detract from them fully appreciating the experience so they can also become more fixated on the technology they are using. It is possible to counter this by agreeing a clear code of conduct for how any mobile technologies are to be used on field trips.

Teacher use of mobile technologies

The value of a mobile device for a teacher's professional use should not be underestimated. Apart from providing a portable electronic diary, devices offer a range of possibilities for maintaining records or creating media-rich digital content. For example, a spreadsheet can be set up so that children's achievement during a lesson can be recorded as it happens rather than retrospectively. A discreet entry into a mobile device, taken as the lesson progresses, is much less obtrusive than making a note in a desktop or laptop computer, and can be made as the teacher moves around the class. The compactness and easy transport of mobile devices may also allow notes to be carried around during a lesson, either of the plan itself or relating to individual children. However, just as mobile technologies tend to pervade all aspects of children and young people's lives, the same can be said for teachers' own use of mobile technologies. Thus careful consideration needs to be given to how the different aspects of teachers' professional and personal lives converge through the use of mobile technologies (Turvey, 2012). Many teachers use their mobile devices to connect to personal and professional networks in order to share resources and keep up to date, for example by following other teachers through Twitter or following their blogs. We discuss this further in Chapter 16 on the professional use of ICT.

PRACTICAL TASK PRACTICAL TASK PRACTICAL TASK PRACTICAL TASK

The only practical approach to starting to think about the ways in which mobile technologies might be applied in teaching and learning is to explore them thoroughly so that you become familiar with their characteristics and limitations. Once you have done this at a personal level you will be better placed to determine a role for mobile technologies in the classroom, and to persuade others (including those in the school who manage budgets) that what you are proposing is worthwhile. Accordingly, choose one of the mobile technologies that appeals to you and which, somehow, you can finance and use it regularly over several weeks to discover its capabilities. For example, if you own a smartphone or an iPad, think about how you currently use this device. If your use is mainly personal, search for some free apps that you could use to support your professional role.

THE BIGGER PICTURE THE BIGGER PICTURE THE BIGGER PICTURE THE BIGGER PICTURE

Many schools are already using mobile technologies to keep in touch with parents, such as when they need to let families know of school closure due to bad weather, reporting the safe arrival of a school trip or text messaging when a child is absent from school. There are also services that can text or e-mail school correspondence and newsletters direct to parents. These are further developed by the use of apps. For example, ParentMail's +Pay service (see **www.parentmail.co.uk**) is a mobile phone app that sends parents information about school visits and other events and allows them to send authorisation and pay for the trip electronically, with the school being able to track payments into a central account covering extra-curricular clubs and sports teams' arrangements as well.

REFLECTIVE TASK

Talk with children about mobile technologies. With which technologies are they familiar through personal use? Do you foresee any difficulties in teaching children the technical aspects of mobile technology use? What might be some of the data protection issues with mobile technologies? Also think about online safety and the various associated risks that mobile technologies might pose. For example, is there a need for guidelines on the use of mobile devices for taking photographs in school? How and where will the photographs be stored? See Chapter 16 for more guidance on issues relating to online safety.

A SUMMARY OF **KEY POINTS**

➢ **There are many mobile technologies that could be used in primary schools, but not all educationalists are convinced of their value and purchasing class sets has obvious financial implications as does equipping children with devices.**

➢ **Some schools have invested in class sets of laptops or notebooks and use them as a mobile computer suite.**

➢ **Tablet devices can use simple versions of office software and provide internet connectivity and rich-media capability. They have touch screens and virtual QWERTY keyboard input but physical peripherals can be added via Bluetooth.**

➢ **Mobile phones and smartphones may have uses in the classroom, though some children may prefer to use these independently and their inclusion in schools can be controversial.**

➢ **Podcasts/screencasts of sound or video files could be provided by schools for use out of school hours.**

➢ **Research and studies show that the use of mobile technologies has the potential to extend learning beyond the physical boundaries of school.**

M-LEVEL EXTENSION > > M-LEVEL EXTENSION > > M-LEVEL EXTENSION

Male and Burden (2014, p.423) claim that the implications of mobile technologies for education are 'enormous and the anticipated change probably ranks alongside the introduction of the printing press in terms of historical importance'. Consider this claim and find out more about the controversy around the use of mobile technologies in the primary classroom. Use the research summaries and studies described in this chapter, together with your own further reading, to examine the debate. What are the advantages and disadvantages of utilising mobile technologies to support children's learning? What are the pros and cons of using them to support your own teaching strategies, including for assessment, recording and reporting to parents? What ethical or safeguarding concerns are raised by their use? Overall, what are your conclusions about this issue?

REFERENCES REFERENCES **REFERENCES** REFERENCES **REFERENCES** REFERENCES

Anderson, P. and Blackwood, A. (2004) *Mobile and PDA Technologies and Their Future Use in Education.* JISC Technology and Standards Watch: **www.jisc.ac.uk/**.

Attewell, J. (2005) *Mobile Technologies and Learning*. London: Learning and Skills Development Agency. Available at **http://www.m-learning.org/docs/The%20m-learning%20project%20%20 technology%20update%20and%20project%20summary.pdf**.

Burden, K. and Maher, D. (2015) 'Mobile technologies and authentic learning in the primary classroom', in S. Younie, M. Leask and K. Burden (eds), *Teaching and Learning with ICT in the Primary School*, 2nd edn. Abingdon: Routledge.

Burden, K., Hopkins, P., Male, T., Martin, S. and Trala, C. (2012) *iPad Scotland Evaluation*. University of Hull. Available at **http://www.janhylen.se/wp-content/uploads/2013/01/Skottland.pdf**.

Crook, C. (2012) 'The "digital native" in context: tensions associated with importing Web 2.0 practices into the school setting', *Oxford Review of Education*, 38(1), pp.63–80.

DfE (2011) *Teachers' Standards*. Available at **www.education.gov.uk/publications**.

Male, T. and Burden, K. (2014) 'Access denied? Twenty-first-century technology in schools', *Technology, Pedagogy and Education*, 23(4), pp.423–37.

Naismith, L., Lonsdale, P., Vavoula, G. and Sharples, M. (2004) *Literature Review in Mobile Technologies and Learning*, Futurelab Series Report 11. Available at **http://www.nfer.ac.uk/publications/FUTL15/FUTL15_home.cfm**.

Passey, D. (1999) *Anytime, Anywhere Learning Pilot Programme: Project Report*. Reading: Microsoft UK/Lancaster University.

Picardo, J. (2016) *Tablets in Schools: Case Study in Success*. Available at **www.josepicardo.com/2016/03/tablets-in-schools-case-study-in-success/**.

Traxler, J. (2010) 'Will student devices deliver innovation, inclusion, and transformation?', *Journal of the Research Center for Educational Technology*, 6(1), pp.3–15.

Turvey, K. (2012) 'Questioning the character and significance of convergence between social network and professional practices in teacher education', *British Journal of Educational Technology*, 43(1), pp.739–53.

Turvey, K. (2013) *Modelling Multiplication*. Available at **http://vimeo.com/64421196**.

Wishart, J. (2016) 'Using the cameras on mobile phones ipads and digital cameras to create animations in science teaching and learning', in H. Crompton and J. Traxler (eds), *Mobile Learning and Stem: Case Studies in Practice*. London and New York: Routledge.

FURTHER READING FURTHER READING **FURTHER READING** FURTHER READING

Heppell, S. et al. (2004) *Building Learning Futures … A Research Project at Ultralab within the CABE/RIBA 'Building Futures' programme*, p.9. Available at **http://rubble.heppell.net/places/media/final_report.pdf**.

London Mobile Learning. Available at **www.londonmobilelearning.net/#about_lmlg.php**.

Naismith, L., Lonsdale, P., Vavoula, G. and Sharples, M. (2004) *Literature Review in Mobile Technologies and Learning*, Futurelab Series Report 11. Available at **www.nfer.ac.uk/publications/FUTL15/FUTL15_home.cfm**.

Pachler, N., Cook, J. and Traxler, J. (2016) *Key Issues in Mobile Learning: Research and Practice*. London: Bloomsbury Continuum.

Section B
Primary Computing and the National Curriculum

The chapters in this section of the book will inform your development towards meeting aspects of the professional standards relating both directly and indirectly to computing-specific subject knowledge and pedagogy. Although, because of the great diversity available, subject-related educational software and hardware cannot be treated comprehensively here. Chapters 6 and 7 introduce and focus on the basics of planning and assessing primary computing.

The remaining chapters (Chapters 8 to 15) build on this foundation to equip you with both the knowledge and understanding of the key concepts in the computing curriculum as well as how this can be developed in the children you teach. To support you in the development of your knowledge and understanding of computing and how to develop this in your pupils, chapters in this section include:

- chapter objectives;
- a brief introduction and definitions;
- reference to relevant sections of the National Curriculum for computing;
- background information as appropriate;
- examples of the ways in which teachers may address the computing curriculum with specific pedagogical approaches and software/hardware;
- details of the specific functions of the software or hardware with which teachers should be familiar;
- exploration of the potential and limitations of the software/hardware used to teach computing;
- references and further reading.

It is envisaged that you will dip into the various chapters in this section based upon your own needs and also the requirements of your course. Topics covered in Section B are:

- Planning for primary computing as a subject
- Assessment in primary computing
- Computational thinking and programming
- Physical computing
- Web literacy (including coding for the web)
- Digital media/digital literacies
- Writing with digital technologies
- Social media – tools for communicating, collaborating and publishing
- Graphing programs
- Databases and spreadsheets.

After Chapter 6 and Chapter 7, there is no implied hierarchy in the order with which the various topics are introduced throughout this section. As discussed in the introduction to this book and highlighted by others (Twining, 2012; Berry, 2013), it is possible to discern three broad yet overlapping aspects to the National Curriculum for computing. There is some debate over the definition of these aspects but we draw on Twining's (2013) definitions here:

- Computer science (CS) – e.g. programming, computational thinking, algorithms, designing and problem-solving
- Information technology (IT) – e.g. understanding the assembly, deployment and configuration of digital systems to meet user needs for particular purposes
- Digital literacy (DL) – e.g. the critical, creative and safe engagement with digital technologies.

As mentioned, while it is possible to discern distinct processes and concepts associated with these different aspects, the effective teaching of computing as well as its successful application often draws on concepts and processes from across at least two or three of the aspects of CS, IT and DL. While we may as teachers focus on developing children's understanding and writing of algorithms (CS) this should have some purpose that it can be turned or applied to such as being used to design and program a computer game which will also require aspects of IT and DL at some point in the process. Throughout the chapters in Section B it is useful to keep these three strands in mind as they can help to focus both our planning and assessment of computing as we discuss in Chapters 6 and 7.

Much of the software and hardware we have chosen to cover in Chapters 8–15 of Section B has been selected for its specific character in lending itself to various uses. Its freedom from a particular context or narrow conception means that the child may well start working with a clean slate on which they must fashion a finished product. The blank page of a blog post or the sketches of a story board for an animation or computer game epitomise this situation. The child may then go through a creative journey which culminates in an outcome that represents the harnessing of the software's capability to the child's purpose. However, just as with a blank paper page, the child needs support from the teacher. This is necessary not just to set the objective and guide the process, but perhaps also to provide the scaffolding that enables the child to start in the first place.

The hardware that features in this section is similarly broad in its scope and gives rise to all sorts of creative opportunities, some of which are described in the chapters, some of which you will think of yourself.

You can find the relevant references in *Teachers' Standards* (DfE, 2011) applying to all of the chapters in this section. However, Chapters 6 and 7 focus primarily on TS 1, 2, 4, 5 and 6, whereas Chapters 8–15 focus primarily on TS 1, 3 and 8 as follows.

TEACHERS' STANDARDS

A teacher must:

1. **Set high expectations which inspire, motivate and challenge pupils**

- **establish a safe and stimulating environment for pupils, rooted in mutual respect**
- **set goals that stretch and challenge pupils of all backgrounds, abilities and dispositions**
- **demonstrate consistently the positive attitudes, values and behaviour which are expected of pupils**

2. **Promote good progress and outcomes by pupils**

- plan teaching to build on pupils' capabilities and prior knowledge
- be accountable for pupils' attainment, progress and outcomes
- demonstrate knowledge and understanding of how pupils learn and how this impacts on teaching

3. **Demonstrate good subject and curriculum knowledge**

- have a secure knowledge of the relevant subject(s) and curriculum areas, foster and maintain pupils' interest in the subject and address misunderstandings
- demonstrate a critical understanding of developments in the subject and curriculum areas, and promote the value of scholarship

4. **Plan and teach well structured lessons**

- impart knowledge and develop understanding through effective use of lesson time
- contribute to the design and provision of an engaging curriculum within the relevant subject area(s)

5. **Adapt teaching to respond to the strengths and needs of all pupils**

- know when and how to differentiate appropriately, using approaches which enable pupils to be taught effectively
- have a secure understanding of how a range of factors can inhibit pupils' ability to learn and how best to overcome these
- demonstrate an awareness of the physical, social and intellectual development of children, and know how to adapt teaching to support pupils' education at different stages of development
- have a clear understanding of the needs of all pupils, including those with special educational needs; those of high ability; those with English as an additional language; those with disabilities; and be able to use and evaluate distinctive teaching approaches to engage and support them

6. **Make accurate and productive use of assessment**

- know and understand how to assess the relevant subject and curriculum areas, including statutory assessment requirements
- make use of formative and summative assessment to secure pupils' progress
- use relevant data to monitor progress, set targets and plan subsequent lessons

8. **Fulfil wider professional responsibilities**

- take responsibility for improving teaching through appropriate professional development

REFERENCES REFERENCES **REFERENCES** REFERENCES **REFERENCES** REFERENCES

Berry, M. (2013) *Computing in the National Curriculum: A Guide for Primary Teachers*. Bedford: Computing at School. Available at **www.computingatschool.org.uk/**.

DfE (2011) *Teachers' Standards*. Available at **https://www.gov.uk/government/publications/ teachers-standards**.

DfE (2013) *National Curriculum in England: Computing Programmes of Study*. Available at **https:// www.gov.uk/government/publications/national-curriculum-in-england-computing-programmes- of-study/national-curriculum-in-england-computing-programmes-of-study**.

Twining, P. (2013) *Three Strands in Computing National Curriculum*. Available at **http://edfutures. net/Three_strands_in_computing_national_curriculum**.

6
Planning for primary computing as a subject

Chapter objectives

When you have completed work on this chapter, you will have:

- examined some of the key principles to focus on when planning for computing;
- considered the elements of effective planning;
- looked at a possible lesson-planning pro forma;
- thought about how to plan for computing as a National Curriculum subject.

Introduction

There are some key principles on which to focus when thinking about planning for computing.

High expectations must extend to the use of technology in schools in an era of continual change and adaptation and in which young learners may have access to all sorts of digital technologies at home and elsewhere away from the classroom. Having high expectations means knowing where the children are up to in the first place. It presupposes that some kind of conversation has taken place which locates the children's knowledge and experience of computing. In this way, computing is no different from any other area of learning. It needs to be mapped accurately by reference to the learners and what they bring to the setting. It will not do, for example, to teach how to underline fonts to someone who is designing and creating their own web space at home. There will have to be a different set of expectations for these learners.

You need to have a *secure knowledge and understanding of your subject* and related pedagogy. This means being aware of where to go for support in knowledge and understanding and not simply in the way of finding appropriate 'content' for subject teaching, by when and how to use that content, and with what sort of pedagogy in mind. There are very many resources produced by LAs, software publishers and the government (as well as informally through the networks which teachers establish for themselves) which lend themselves to particular visions of pedagogy.

You need to design *opportunities for learners to develop their computing skills*. This means being able to see opportunities in whatever sessions you are designing for the convergence of skills and purposeful learning with the technology in a given subject. As a concrete example, publishing small books in the classroom will give a sense of writing for a purpose, for a target audience and perhaps focusing on particular aspects of literacy teaching. At the same time, the mix of text and graphics and the negotiation with scanners, printers, cameras and other peripherals helps to develop children's computing capabilities within a real context.

You need to *use a range of teaching strategies and resources*, including e-learning. E-learning is defined here in its broadest sense for the use of both online and offline resources and as both a resource and a subset of skills in its own right. It means seeing opportunities for using web-based learning platforms, online software and resources in the classroom (including IWBs).

You need to plan for *a purposeful and safe working environment*. The word 'safe' means being physically well organised in the space, whether you are in a network room or bringing a portable resource to the classroom. It is about being aware of everything that can contribute to a safe working environment around technology. A fuller discussion appears in Chapter 17 but, at this juncture, it's worth demarcating the range of thinking in health and safety as starting from who plugs and unplugs the equipment to dealing with trailing cables, to safe, possibly height-adjustable seating, and monitoring levels of screen-time.

The word 'purposeful' relates to having some clear idea of what is happening and where it is taking the learners in terms of their knowledge and experience. More than that, as in other subjects, it means being able to communicate this. In planning terms, this means being very clear about the learning objectives and how they are related to and delineated from the National Curriculum programme of study for computing.

You need to ensure that *other adults in the classroom are fully briefed* as to your planning and their role within it. There are many occasions in classrooms where you will be responsible for the work of other adults in the setting. With computing, this means being sensitive to the needs of those teachers and helpers and being fully apprised of the situation regarding skill levels and expectations of everyone in the setting.

Effective planning – analysing the situation

Effective teaching depends heavily on effective planning. Computing is no exception to this rule. In turn, effective planning depends on a thorough analysis of the situation at the outset. Many writers have identified this link and some have produced books for teachers in training which summarise and synthesise the best of the available research.

RESEARCH SUMMARY   RESEARCH SUMMARY   **RESEARCH SUMMARY**   RESEARCH SUMMARY

Chris Kyriacou (2009) provides an overview of studies which have looked at lesson effectiveness. One of the studies reported, that of Cooper and McIntyre (1996), looked at the teaching and learning in a series of lessons in terms of what both the teachers and the pupils felt. Analysis produced the following list of key items which contributed to lesson effectiveness:

- **clear learning goals for pupil learning;**
- **helping pupils to contextualise the content in terms of their own experience and knowledge;**
- **providing a supportive social context for learning;**
- **enabling pupils to engage in the learning process in a number of different ways;**
- **willingness of the teacher to modify learning tasks in the light of pupil circumstances.**

All of these factors are of immediate direct relevance to teachers' planning for any subject in the curriculum. When it comes to computing, there is an added layer of complexity because of the impact of the resource setting of the school (see Chapter 1). Some questions need to be raised to take account of this and added to the generic areas above. At the outset, as a minimum, trainees preparing to teach computing need to be asking these questions:

- What do we know about the children's existing knowledge, skills and understanding in the subject?
- What has been their previous experience of digital technologies and computing?
- What does the computing curriculum set out for the children in this year group?
- What does the school's scheme of work require?
- What am I therefore expecting the children to achieve?
- How will I differentiate the activity to reflect the different needs and abilities in the class?
- What relevant pieces of theoretical writing and/or case studies are there to support my planning?
- What will be the demands on me in terms of my own knowledge, skills and understanding of computing?
- What is the resource setting for the school and how does this impact on what I can plan for the class?
- What are the additional time costs and constraints on me when planning to teach computing?
- What kind of grouping or organisation am I planning to use?
- How do I go about the physical management of the activity?
- Are there any further cross-curricular links I need to consider?
- How will I go about including the whole class in the activity?
- What are the assessment and record-keeping opportunities in the activity?

Planning is, of course, cyclical in nature. No sooner have you reached the last question than you realise it must be used to answer the first question in the next batch of planning. Good planning should create assessment opportunities because good assessment informs good planning.

THE BIGGER PICTURE   THE BIGGER PICTURE   THE BIGGER PICTURE   THE BIGGER PICTURE

When you are planning differentiation as part of your duty to ensure the inclusion of all children, remember that there are sources of advice within your school (class teachers and teaching or learning support assistants who work with the children, and the inclusion leader or special educational needs co-ordinator) and from local authority services (such as those for children with additional and special educational needs, for those with English as an additional language and for traveller and minority ethnic children, and a 'virtual headteacher' with responsibility for looked-after children).

It makes sense to try to collect these questions into headings which you can use to ensure that you cover all of the necessary elements each time you plan. As part of your training year, you will develop, or be given assistance in developing, lesson-planning pro formas of various kinds. Some will provide very detailed outlines of what is going on in a session, whereas others will be shorter. As you gain experience through the year, what seems like a very detailed and time-consuming activity initially will become part of your professional life and second nature to you as a practising and reflective teacher.

Without attempting to prescribe a model which works in all settings, on all courses and in all classrooms, we set out later in this chapter an example plan for a computing lesson in Key Stage 1. Most of the headings are in common use for curriculum planning in all subjects and are relatively easily adapted to computing. However, before examining more closely what a computing lesson in Key Stage 1 might look like in practice, we want to take a more detailed look at computing as expressed in the National Curriculum programme of study.

Computing as a National Curriculum subject

This chapter is concerned principally with the computing curriculum as it is outlined for children entering Year 1 of primary school up to Year 6. The curriculum for the Early Years Foundation Stage was covered in Chapter 5. We give an overview here of the computing programme of study, but more detailed information on specific activities can be found throughout the chapters in Section B of the book.

The most recent version of the National Curriculum for schools in England was published in 2013 for implementation from September 2014. As discussed in the Introduction to this book, compared to the previous Programme of Study, the latest iteration of the computing National Curriculum places more emphasis on children learning to program computers and developing computational thinking. The revised National Curriculum (DfE, 2013) sets out the purpose for computing as a subject stating that:

> *A high-quality computing education equips pupils to use computational thinking and creativity to understand and change the world. Computing has deep links with mathematics, science, and design and technology, and provides insights into both natural and artificial systems. The core of computing is computer science, in which pupils are taught the principles of information and computation, how digital systems work, and how to put this knowledge to use through programming. Building on this knowledge and understanding, pupils are equipped to use information technology to create programs, systems and a range of content. Computing also ensures that pupils become digitally literate – able to use, and express themselves and develop their ideas through, information and communication technology – at a level suitable for the future workplace and as active participants in a digital world.*

> (DfE, 2013, n.p.)

It is clear that one purpose of this programme of study is to give children a greater understanding of the ways in which computers actually work by addressing some of the fundamental concepts and processes of computer science (CS). However, there also remains a clear expectation that the curriculum will enable children to become creative and discerning users of technology, that is digitally literate (DL) users with knowledge, understanding and skills in the broad application of these across information technology (IT) systems. Figure 6.1 captures these strands and illustrates how it is useful to think of them as both distinct and overlapping. This may be a useful tool when planning as it can help you to identify whether you are addressing a particular strand of the computing curriculum or planning a more complex lesson that addresses more than one strand. For example, an online safety lesson focusing on privacy and the use of algorithms to harvest users' data for advertising purposes could well involve aspects of CS, DL and IT.

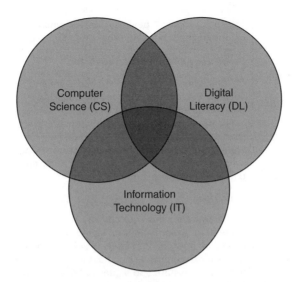

Figure 6.1 The three overlapping strands of the Primary National Curriculum for computing

Looking briefly at resource provision for planning with the National Curriculum, as a minimum, Tables 6.1 and 6.2 suggest the kind of indicative resources (hardware and software) and activities you would expect to see provided in order for children to have their entitlement to computing met. Important terms from the programme of study are also defined. Subsequent chapters in Section B of this book explore these aspects of the programme of study in more depth. As you study these tables, consider also the overlapping strands of the computing curriculum (see Figure 6.1).

Table 6.1 Key Stage 1

Area of knowledge, skills and understanding. Children should be taught to:	Resource entitlement, indicative activities and definitions	Section B – chapter cross reference
Understand what algorithms are; how they are implemented as programs on digital devices; and that programs execute by following precise and unambiguous instructions. Create and debug simple programs. Use logical reasoning to predict the behaviour of simple programs.	**Resources and indicative activities:** Children should use programmable toys such as Bee-Bots, Roamers, giving them instructions to navigate a floor map or maze. On the computer or tablet device they could use programs that allow them to give instructions to control an on-screen turtle or other controllable object. For example, apps and programs such as Hopscotch, Daisy the Dinosaur, 2Simple's 2Go or Logo could be used. Or they could create a game using software such as Kodu or Scratch. **Definitions:** *Algorithm* – a sequential set of instructions to achieve a specific goal. *Debug* – to identify and remove errors, e.g. in an algorithm.	Chapters 8, 9, 14, 15.

	Logical reasoning – being systematic when writing algorithms or debugging programs.	
Use technology purposefully to create, organise, store, manipulate and retrieve digital content.	**Resources and indicative activities:** Children should use a range of hardware and software such as word processors, desktop publishing, multimedia software, digital cameras (still and video), music/audio editing software, scanners, monitoring and data-logging equipment. For example, they might write a short report about a school trip for a class blog, or create a short film for their whole-class assembly. **Definitions:** *Digital content* – this could be any kind of digital content, for example data collected as part of a survey on how children travel to school; photographs and text for a presentation about a recent school trip to a local museum; and digital audio that the children have recorded and edited.	Chapters 10, 11, 12, 13, 14, 15.
Use technology safely and respectfully, keeping personal information private; know where to go for help and support when they have concerns about material on the internet. Recognise common uses of information technology beyond school.	**Resources and indicative activities:** Children should use the internet for finding and critically evaluating information. Opportunities can also be available for children to discuss safety issues by means of engaging in communication through a range of communication tools such as email or online forums in the relative safety of the school's virtual learning environment or blog. Teachers should discuss with the children what is meant by personal information (i.e. passwords, usernames, home town and address details) and when this should not be shared. There should be opportunities to discuss children's use of technologies beyond school. For example, safety issues surrounding the use of online games or technologies in the home such as mobile phones and tablet devices can be addressed positively through the discussion and modelling of appropriate use of such devices.	Chapters 10, 13, 17, 18.

Table 6.2 Key Stage 2

Area of knowledge, skills and understanding. Children should be taught to:	Resource entitlement, indicative activities and definitions	Section B – chapter cross reference
Design, write and debug programs that accomplish specific goals, including controlling or simulating physical systems;	**Resources and indicative activities:** Children should have the opportunity to work with a range of programming environments/languages. For example, they could work with block-based visual programming tools (e.g. Scratch, App Inventor, Kodu, Lego WeDo) to design, create and control simulations,	Chapters 8, 9, 14, 15

solve problems by decomposing them into smaller parts

Use sequence, selection, and repetition in programs; work with variables and various forms of input and output

Use logical reasoning to explain how some simple algorithms work and to detect and correct errors in algorithms and programs

apps, games and physical models or systems including robots (e.g. Dash and Dot). Similarly, they could work with flow-chart programming tools (e.g. Flowol) to control simulations such as automated lighthouses, pedestrian crossings and traffic light scenarios, which illustrate how computers can be used to automate aspects of the physical environment. Logo could also be used to create on-screen graphical objects which can be controlled and animated using a text-based programming language (e.g. MSW Logo, Testease Turtle CT). They could use a micro-controller device such as Makey Makey or the Crumble Controller to create and program inputs and outputs such as LEDs and motors.

Definitions:

Control/simulate physical systems – this refers to any simulated or physical system or model that can be linked to a computer or has a computer embedded within it e.g. traffic light system or bicycle light with different output modes.

Decomposition – the process of isolating or breaking down the various constituent parts of a computer program or problem.

Input – a signal or data entered into a computer (e.g. via the keys on a keyboard, buttons on a mouse, button on a pedestrian crossing, or a hotspot on a touchscreen device).

Output – what results when data or signals are processed and sent from a computer or program (e.g. a letter on a screen when a key on a keyboard is pressed; the wait light, amber, red and green lights on a pedestrian crossing).

Program – a collection of related algorithms/ instructions with specific outcomes.

Repetition – loops in programs are often exploited by programmers. Repeat commands can also be used to make programming more efficient.

Selection – the point within a computer program or algorithm where there is more than one possible output (e.g. conditional IF, THEN, logic).

Sequence – the order of events in a program or algorithm.

Variable – a place in a computer program where data is stored and remembered (e.g. a score in a computer game uses variables; a sold out sign in a drinks vending machine would also depend on variables that monitor how many of each drink have been sold).

Understand computer networks including the internet; how they can provide multiple services, such as the world wide web; and the opportunities

Resources and indicative activities:

Children can learn about and discuss how information is sent and received via the internet. Processes such as packet switching could be explained and explored with children through role-play activities. They should also explore the difference between the internet and the

Chapters 8, 10, 13, 17, 18

they offer for communication and collaboration

Use search technologies effectively, appreciate how results are selected and ranked, and be discerning in evaluating digital content

Use technology safely, respectfully and responsibly; know a range of ways to report concerns and inappropriate behaviour

world wide web. There are a number of online videos that explain this (e.g. **www.youtube.com/ watch?v=VXg_HGgo7Qs** and **www.youtube.com/ watch?v=C3sr7_0FyPA**). Children could be introduced to HTML code by remixing an online project using the Mozilla code editor software Thimble (e.g. **https:// thimble.mozilla.org/**).

Children should use a range of web browsers (e.g. Google Chrome, Firefox, Safari, Internet Explorer) and search engines to support their research. They could explore Boolean search strategies to narrow their searches. They could also explore how different search engines (Google, Bing, Yahoo, Ask) deliver different results and consider the reasons for this. They could also compare and check information from a range of different sources, for example books, people, information leaflets and the world wide web.

Children should have hands-on experience of strategies for keeping themselves safe online as well as opportunities to discuss issues of online safety. They could take part in an online simulation game where they have to make decisions about how to respond to a range of scenarios (e.g. from how to deal with spam email to what to do if they receive threatening or abusive text messages)

Definitions:

Boolean search strategies – these are specific strategies that enable users to perform more specific or targeted searches.

Internet – this is the infrastructure of the network, e.g. the interconnected cables, computers, servers, routers and connected networks.

Packet switching – this is the process by which data is transferred so speedily on the internet by being broken down into millions of smaller pieces of data by the sender's device and then reassembled by the receiving device. For a more detailed explanation see **www. explainthatstuff.com/internet.html**.

Search engine – a search engine is a web-based program that acts like an index in a library, returning a list of web-based documents or resources according to a keyword used to search.

Web browser – a web browser is a program that enables users to locate, access and present information on the internet.

World wide web – this is the content or the billions of digital pages on the internet.

Select, use and combine a variety of software (including internet services) Select, use and combine a variety of software (including internet services)	***Resources and indicative activities:*** Under the supervision of the teacher children could create and maintain a class blog (e.g. WordPress, Edublogs, Tumblr) to keep the wider school community (other classes, parents and family, partner school in another location or country) up to date with news of trips and what they have been learning about.	Chapters 8, 9, 10, 11, 12, 13, 14, 15

on a range of digital devices to accomplish given goals, including collecting, analysing, evaluating and presenting data and information.	This could include presenting relevant photographs provided appropriate safety procedures have been followed and permissions obtained. Children could use moving or still images combined with digital audio to create a short online safety video or presentation for other children (e.g. presentation software, video/audio editing software). Children could investigate how the school could become a more environmentally friendly community by carrying out a survey of how children travel to school. They could design a survey and make it available to the wider school community via an online form (e.g. Survey Monkey). They could evaluate and analyse the data using a database and then present their findings about the school's impact on the environment. *Definitions:* *Blog* – the word is a contraction of 'web log'. A blog is an online chronological journal/diary of individual or group reflections and observations. The most recent blog post or entry is at the top of the home page.	

From National Curriculum to lesson plan

Schools must have a scheme of work in place as a fundamental aid to planning, as a map of the learning outcomes for computing in their school and as a statement of intent and entitlement. In the past many schools used what was known as the QCA Scheme of Work for ICT (QCA, 2000), and you may find that this has been adapted to account for the changes to the National Curriculum. Other schools may have bought into a commercial scheme of work like the Switched On Computing scheme of work and resources (Berry, 2014, **www.switchedon computing.co.uk**). Try to obtain early on in your placement a copy of your school's scheme of work and use it in your planning. However please note that if it is based on the QCA model (QCA, 2000) this no longer meets key aspects of the new programme of study for computing.

Planning example for Key Stage 1

An example follows of a suggested longer-format lesson plan. It assumes a high-resource setting, a school with a networked suite of computers and multiple programmable toys/robots. The specific lesson is adapted from an idea by Kristine Kopelke (see **http://elre sources.skola.edu.mt/wp-content/uploads/2010/06/doc_669_2468_beebotguideA4v2. pdf**). The context is a unit for Year 1: Journeys – Robots Routes. This lesson could also be adapted for different contexts or smaller groups. You may also find the following video tutorial on working with programmable toys useful **http://bcove.me/oouug2wh** (Turvey, 2015). In terms of the three strands of the National Curriculum for computing (Figure 6.1) the focus of this lesson is predominantly on the computer science aspect in that the lesson is designed to develop children's understanding of algorithms, that is sequencing, logical reasoning and so on. However, through discussion with the children this lesson could be put in a broader context and used to discuss their encounters with automated machines or robots in their wider world.

LONGER LESSON PLAN FOR COMPUTING AT YEAR 1

UNIT: Journeys – Robot Routes

CROSS-CURRICULAR LINK: Mathematics

OVERVIEW: In this unit of work the children have been finding out about journeys in a range of contexts (e.g. in stories, their own lives, historical journeys). In computing they have been working with programmable toys (Bee-Bots) exploring how they can be controlled using the input keys (e.g. forward, backward, right, left). To support this work they have also been exploring non-standard units of measure in mathematics. For example, Bee-Bot moves 15cm so this unit of measure has been used to estimate the distance Bee-Bot travels. The children have also begun to explore routes on maps, using maps/plans of familiar places (e.g. plan of the school layout and simple map of the local area). In this lesson the children will design and create their own route for Bee-Bot. They will also be challenged to predict and program multi-step instructions (algorithms) for Bee-Bot to carry out as it navigates the routes they have designed. The lesson will be in two parts. In the first part, the children will work in groups to design and create a simple but multi-step route or maze for the Bee-Bot to follow. In the second half of the lesson they will devise algorithms using adapted playing cards to program the Bee-Bots to navigate the mazes/routes they have created.

SCHOOL/CLASS CONTEXT

The school is a large, inner-city primary school with a wide range of attainment. Some 20 different languages are spoken, of which the majority speak Sylheti-Bengali. There are 29 children in the class, an average size for the school. The children are all in Year 1.

LEARNING NEEDS OF THE CHILDREN

FOR COMPUTING: Most children are confident at logging on and using the computers in the network suite. They have also explored programming Bee-Bots both on-screen and through programmable toys, giving single-step instructions (algorithms) to navigate a short route or floor map. The aim of the lesson is to develop the children's ability to give precise multi-step instructions, which show their understanding of the importance of sequence when writing algorithms.

FOR MATHEMATICS: The aim of the lesson is also to develop the children's ability to estimate distances using non-standard units, as well as to understand quarter, half and full turns.

GROUPING/TIMING

The lesson will last one hour, not including a 10-minute outline to recap on what they know about giving instructions to Bee-Bot. We will go into the hall at about 1.30 and leave at about 2.45 in time for the afternoon break. The class will be split into groups of 3–4. Groupings should be based on the teacher's knowledge of the children and the children should be reminded about how to work well together. There will also be a teaching assistant to support the task who has been briefed on the aims of the lesson.

RESOURCES

The hall will be used for this activity as it allows the children to work with the Bee-Bots on the floor. However, the activity could also be done outside using chalk to create different routes on the playground surface or in small groups using an area of the classroom. Each group will need an A1 sheet of paper and large pencils (chalk if outside), erasers and a non-standard Bee-Bot measure. Each group will need a Bee-Bot. Also each group will need a set of algorithm playing cards with the various Bee-Bot instructions on them (Forward, Backward, Right Turn, Left Turn or arrows). As an alternative, Bee-Bot routes could be created from three-dimensional objects such as building blocks or found objects.

THEORETICAL CONTEXT

From Avril Loveless, 'The Role of ICT' (Chapter 2 in Loveless, 2003, p.45):

> Control technology offers the opportunity for an investigative approach to problem solving and a development in the complexity of giving and modifying instructions … They can learn the importance of testing systems to make them foolproof in all circumstances – procedures essential to designers and engineers.

NC/EYFS CONTEXT

> Understand what algorithms are; how they are implemented as programs on digital devices; and that programs execute by following precise and unambiguous instructions.

> Create and debug simple programs, using logical reasoning to predict the behaviour of simple programs.

SCHEME OF WORK CONTEXT

Lesson ideas Year 1 unit: Journeys – Robot Routes

YOUR OWN LEARNING NEEDS

Make sure I am confident programming multi-step instructions into Bee-Bot.

Make sure that I know how to model using the Bee-Bot non-standard unit measure to model the design and creation of a Bee-Bot route.

ORGANISATIONAL MEMORY JOGGERS

Make sure all of the Bee-Bots are working properly and have enough battery life for the activity. Remember to collect enough paper, large pencils and erasers. Make sure I have briefed the teaching assistant and that they are familiar with how to program Bee-Bot. Make sure the children know their groups for the activity.

OTHER ADULTS

Remember to copy the lesson plan and talk to the teaching assistant before the lesson takes place if at all possible. Give them access to a Bee-Bot before the lesson if necessary.

LEARNING OBJECTIVES/INTENTIONS

FOR COMPUTING: The key idea is that children understand that robots/computers can be controlled using instructions (algorithms) and that they can receive and respond to multiple instructions (algorithms). Children will also develop their understanding of the need for precision and correct sequencing when working with algorithms to program Bee-Bot to complete a given route.

FOR MATHEMATICS: Children develop their estimation skills using non-standard measures and use the vocabulary of quarter, half and whole turns.

DIFFERENTIATION

Children will be organised in mixed-ability groupings based on their previous work with Bee-Bots. Lower attainers may need to break the Bee-Bot route into two-step algorithms but challenge them to combine or extend this to a multi-step algorithm to complete the whole route. Higher attainers can be challenged earlier in the process to predict and develop multi-step algorithms to navigate through the route. Lower attainers can also record their algorithms using the adapted playing cards whereas higher attainers will be encouraged to record their algorithms by writing them down fully or in pseudo code.

LEARNING NEEDS – SEN

For the child with difficulties with motor control, remember to ensure that they are given more time to physically program the Bee-Bot.

LEARNING NEEDS – EAL

Children who have English as an additional language are all at different stages of acquiring English. Partner the children appropriately according to language needed to access the activity. Remember to check and re-check understanding of the task.

ASSESSMENT OPPORTUNITIES

Complete observation pro formas on targeted children or on the whole class profile as appropriate (see Chapter 7).

KEY QUESTIONS

Remember to focus on the language being developed for computing, i.e. can they predict and make a recording of their algorithms or say their algorithms before testing them with Bee-Bot? With higher attainers, can they write or record multi-step algorithms to predict the Bee-Bot's route. Can they identify and debug errors in their predictions and algorithms? Can they estimate distance accurately using the non-standard unit (Bee-Bot unit)? Can they use the appropriate language for turns (e.g. quarter, half, full turn, left, right).

LESSON FORMAT

10 minutes: Opening with demonstration on IWB/visualiser/flip chart use Bee-Bot unit to draw a simple route for Bee-Bot. Invite some participation from the children. Ask questions. Explain that they are going to create their own routes. Model the use of language (e.g. right quarter turn, left quarter turn) while drawing a route. Check and re-check understanding of the task. Share the learning objectives with the children.

15–20 minutes: In groups children devise and draw their routes for Bee-Bot on large sheets of paper.

10 minutes: Re-group and use one of the groups' Bee-Bot routes. Remind the children how to program Bee-Bot using the input direction keys. Explain to the children that you want to challenge them to program the Bee-Bot in as few attempts as possible, e.g. try and predict the algorithm to get Bee-Bot to the end of the route in one go.

20 minutes: Using the routes they have created children collect a Bee-Bot and predict the algorithm they think they need to help Bee-Bot complete the route. Encourage them to offer different solutions before trying it, listening to everyone's suggestions in the group. If there is time groups could swap Bee-Bot routes.

10 minutes: Plenary with contributions/questions from children. Allow the children themselves to demonstrate and talk through their work. Remember to allow for questions from across the ability range. Possibly also use photographs of the children working and their algorithms to highlight their achievements.

EVALUATING THE LESSON (1) – OPERATIONAL ISSUES

Note here any changes during the lesson which might affect the way you work on this unit in the future. Issues which might have arisen include any of the following:

- All children needed more time to share the equipment.
- The two 20-minute activities were fine as it occurred, but some children needed more support within the groups to make it work.
- The plenary was too rushed and there was insufficient time to draw the understanding together and revisit the learning objectives with the children.

EVALUATING THE LESSON (2) – LEARNING OUTCOMES

Note in this section any particular achievements which children demonstrated. Were you able to carry out the assessments planned for during the session?

EVALUATING THE LESSON (3) – NEXT TIME

What aspects of this work (if any) need to be repeated? How could you deepen understanding of the computing concepts behind the work? What will you do next time in the light of the organisational changes you had to make?

PRACTICAL TASK   PRACTICAL TASK   PRACTICAL TASK   PRACTICAL TASK

Identify a unit in the school's scheme of work for computing for the age group you are teaching. Find an activity which fits in with the current units of work being undertaken in either computing or any of the other subject areas. Follow the pro forma for the example lesson plan from above, identifying the cross-curricular links if relevant, and plan a lesson for your class. Alternatively download one of the free sample activities or units from the Switched On Computing scheme of work at **www.risingstars-uk.com/Subjects/Computing-and-ICT**. Consider how you might need to adapt this for your class and learners.

A SUMMARY OF **KEY POINTS**

> ➤ There are some key principles to focus on when planning to teach computing, including maintaining high expectations, having secure knowledge and understanding of the subject and designing opportunities for learners to develop their skills.

> ➤ You need to use a range of teaching strategies and resources, including e-learning (e.g. IWB, visualiser, digital camera to capture any assessment opportunities), planning for a purposeful and safe working environment and ensuring that other adults in the classroom are fully briefed.

> ➤ Effective planning is underpinned by some key questions, including asking what is known about children's current knowledge, skills and understanding, what is required by the curriculum, what are the objectives for children's learning and how any activity will be assessed.

> ➤ A comprehensive lesson-planning format is recommended that draws on these key questions and is closely related to the school's scheme of work for computing.

> ➤ Computing must be taught as a National Curriculum subject in its own right but meaningful links can be made to other subjects as in the example Year 1 lesson plan.

> ➤ When planning for computing, it is important to set out the context of the lesson, and to set clear learning objectives/intentions against which you can assess children's progress.

> ➤ Links to other subjects should be noted if relevant.

> ➤ Differentiation for children of all ability levels, for those with additional and special educational needs and children with English as an additional language promotes the inclusion of all children.

> ➤ The lesson should be evaluated to complete the planning cycle.

M-LEVEL EXTENSION > > M-LEVEL EXTENSION > > M-LEVEL EXTENSION

When you have the opportunity to observe your class teacher or other colleagues, ask to look at their planning and discuss how they set about planning the lesson you saw and the series of lessons that it was a part of. Ask how they planned the differentiation that you observed. After reflecting on your discussion, decide how you would differentiate this activity for children with different needs. What about those children with specific learning difficulties or particular needs, for example children with English as an additional language? Would they require any particular support or additional resources? Remember that you may also have in the same group or class children who are able, gifted and talented. When you have made your decisions, discuss your notes with your mentor/class teacher and ask for feedback specifically on planning when a colleague observes you teaching.

REFERENCES REFERENCES **REFERENCES** REFERENCES **REFERENCES** REFERENCES

Berry, M. (2014) *Switched on Computing*. Rising Stars UK. Available at **www.switchedoncomputing. co.uk.**

Cooper, P. and McIntyre, D. (1996) 'Effective teaching and learning', *British Educational Research Journal*, 22(5), December.

DfE (2011) *Teachers' Standards*. Available at **www.education.gov.uk/publications**.

DfE (2013) *National Curriculum in England: Primary Curriculum*. London: DfE. Available at **https:// www.gov.uk/government/publications/national-curriculum-in-england-primary-curriculum.**

Kyriacou, C. (2009) *Effective Teaching in Schools.* London: Nelson Thornes.

Loveless, A. (2003) *The Role of ICT*. London: Continuum.

QCA (2000) *ICT at Key Stages 1 and 2*. Available at **http://webarchive.nationalarchives.gov.uk/content/20090608182316/http://standards.dfes.gov.uk/schemes2/it/?view=get**.

Turvey, K. (2015) *Teaching Computing to Primary Age Children.* Sage Video Tutorial. Available at **http://bcove.me/oouug2wh**.

FURTHER READING   FURTHER READING   **FURTHER READING**   FURTHER READING

Bird, J., Caldwell, H. and Mayne, P. (2014) *Lessons in Teaching Computing in Primary Schools*. London: Sage/Learning Matters.

7
Assessment in primary computing

Chapter objectives

When you have completed work on this chapter, you will have:

- understood the place of assessment in the planning cycle;
- considered the main principles of assessment and how it is used in practice in computing and when digital technologies are used to support the teaching and learning of other subjects;
- thought about the main tools used and available to assess computing and children's use of digital technologies;
- looked at observing and profiling individual children, including considering a detailed pro forma for this purpose;
- examined how whole-class snapshots can help you to gauge quickly the range of attainment of the group you are working with.

Introduction

Assessment is vital because it allows teachers to track progress and plan appropriately for children to achieve. Without proper assessment and recording in a given subject, there is no real evidence or knowledge of where the children are up to, and planning becomes empty and meaningless. In the worst cases, it leads to the same activities being undertaken year on year by children who will underachieve because of it. In computing this means seeing the same basic word-processing activities going on at Year 6 as happened at Year 2 or perhaps as children repeatedly use Scratch throughout Key Stage 2 but make little progress with deepening their understanding of the principles of programming or computational thinking. The planning and assessment cycle is incomplete in a school where this occurs and the children make no real progress in the subject or in their use of digital technologies generally. It should be remembered that effective assessment is about developing contingencies for learning as Wiliam emphasises in his definition of formative assessment thus:

> An assessment functions formatively to the extent that evidence about student achievement elicited by the assessment is interpreted and used to make decisions about the next steps in instruction that are likely to be better, or better founded, than the decisions that would have been taken in the absence of that evidence.

(Wiliam, 2009, p.9)

It may be that the school in which you are placed is still working with paper-based assessments of children's work and progress. The suggestions for pro formas in this chapter make this assumption. However, it may also be that you are working in a school that stores examples of work electronically, possibly with the involvement of the children. It could be that the school keeps an electronic portfolio for each child or for a group of children. Either way, the online examples of children's work can be used to help you to make judgements about children's work and the progress of their knowledge, understanding and skills in the subject.

Principles of assessment

The principles which underpin good practice in assessment apply equally to computing as a subject in its own right and to children's use of digital technologies. As teachers, we are looking for ways to make judgements about achievement which, at the same time, allow us to identify a child's future learning needs. These methods of assessment, in turn, will allow us to plan efficiently and appropriately in order to create opportunities for pupils to consolidate their understanding, undertake further practice or take on new challenges. Ways of assessing children in computing, as in other subjects, include some or all of the following:

- observing how the child goes about tackling a piece of work;
- diagnosing difficulties which become apparent over a series of lessons;
- devising and asking questions that encourage children to explain or make explicit their understanding of key concepts in computing
- observing which planning strategies appear to work and allow the child to succeed in a given area;
- collecting significant pieces of work in a portfolio of development;
- noting the context of the work and any factors which were significant: the grouping, the time taken, the level of concentration, their understanding of the concepts involved;
- noting the views and understanding of the child about the piece of work and asking them what made the activity so successful/significant/challenging;
- feeding the information back into the planning process;
- when appropriate, making a judgement about the child's progress in terms of the key knowledge and understanding identified in the National Curriculum programme of study for computing;
- at all times keeping a clear focus on key learning objectives – this is very important as well as having a general awareness of other learning taking place.

Nevertheless, assessment and record-keeping in computing and ICT are complicated by the fact that meaningful work samples are harder to come by than in most other subjects, with the possible exceptions of PE and RE. Printouts of work by themselves are not useful. A final product such as a Scratch game that has been designed and programmed by the child may not in itself offer much evidence of the process with which the child has engaged. Digital technologies are also often used as a tool to present work in its best possible light. Any revealing errors and misconceptions are often lost along the way. The finished product is only the final element of a much longer, more complex process. The process itself is what provides the real assessment opportunities. To borrow an example from another subject, English, a writing sample which contains only the finished ('best') copy is similarly without any real use. Teachers need to go back through the draft book to understand the process the child went through and also discuss their work with them. The child also needs to see and understand this in order to move forward.

Assessing computing and capability with digital technologies

Some digital technologies do allow for processes to be explored. Word processors, for example, allow changes to be tracked and printed. Some record how many times the child accessed the online help in a particular software package. Browser software tracks the user through the various sites and links they follow. This might provide useful assessment information. In some local authorities and schools, there are systems which allow children to select pieces of work and store them in an electronic portfolio. Taken together, in context, these are useful tools for the teacher assessing a child's achievement and identifying their learning needs. If we add connectivity to the home computer into the equation we have a powerful, fluid record of achievement which is also accessible to parents and to children out of school hours.

Tutorial software, including software produced as part of an integrated learning system (ILS), can record the units of work which the child has covered and can produce tables, graphs and collections of statistics. These relate to the software itself and closely to the subject being taught. They are of very limited use in assessing the child's capability with digital technologies or in computing, however, and should not usually be presented as evidence of attainment in computing. They record particular progress through an onscreen worksheet or tutorial. The ability to use tutorial software only demonstrates the ability to use tutorial software. True capability or knowledge and understanding in any subject is much more than the ability to follow onscreen instructions and click on the button which says 'Next' or 'Continue'.

The most useful tool in assessment of computing and children's capability with digital technologies is the teacher's own observation of the child in all contexts and interaction with them about their work. In all of the resource settings we discussed in Section A, this presents real logistical difficulties and requires systematic planning and the use of other adults in order to carry it out effectively. Many schools, for example, operate an assessment week with samples being collected across the curriculum at the same time, in each class, in each half term. Extra adults are sometimes drafted in to support the class teacher in this work. Collection of evidence and observation related to computing and children's use of digital technologies could also be planned for in this way.

However, on teaching placement with all of the course demands being placed on trainee teachers and their mentors and tutors, any assessment activity has to be focused and manageable. The course requirements which follow the prescribed curriculum for initial teacher training will spell out the number of assessments to be made of children and at what particular level in each curriculum area.

It is important to bear in mind that a further difficulty is the collaborative nature of work with digital technologies and computing. It is sometimes hard to separate out the individual contributions to a joint project. There will be times when this is irrelevant and unnecessary. However, while collaboration itself is usually to be encouraged, there comes a time, at the end of a unit of work or at other key times such as the end of the year and, more formally, at the end of the relevant key stages, when a teacher will need to make a judgement about the extent to which children have grasped and understood important areas of knowledge and understanding outlined in the programme of study for computing. As Berry (2013, p.22) points out 'National Curriculum assessment has undergone considerable change for the new framework.' A National Curriculum review by an expert panel (DfE, 2011, p.9) recommended that descriptive levels of attainment should be disregarded as they can often 'inhibit overall performance' and even 'undermine learning' if applied to pupils too rigidly as labels. Despite this, Berry (2013, p.23) also notes that level descriptors have become 'ingrained in many teachers' professional practice, as well as in the systems schools have in place to monitor pupils' progress'. Berry goes on to point out (ibid.) that 'nothing in the DfE's guidance prevents schools from continuing to use levels to monitor progress.' This may well be the case in the short term but trainees should also recognise that the new programme of study for computing identifies new areas of knowledge and understanding as discussed hitherto and these aspects of the programme of study are not adequately captured by the disapplied level descriptors.

It becomes important therefore to develop skilled observations of individual contributions to partner work in computing in order to determine what children know and understand about computing and the extent to which they are able to apply this knowledge and understanding as they develop their skills with a range of digital technologies. Developing skills in monitoring children's progress in this way also protects quieter, less dominant children from being overlooked. However, it is also important to approach any assessment of children's learning, knowing what it is we are actually assessing. While this may seem an obvious statement, it is complicated by the fact that computing has several different facets of knowledge, understanding and skills notwithstanding the different contexts within which these different facets may be applied.

What is being assessed?

For the purposes of assessing children's progress in computing against the programme of study it is useful to look in more detail at the way the knowledge, understanding and skills can be categorised in the National Curriculum programme of study for computing. As we examined in Chapter 6, three key areas underpin the programme of study for computing, which are: Computer Science (CS), Information Technology (IT) and Digital Literacy (DL). Twining (2013) offers a clear definition and discussion of these at the following link: **http://edfutures.net/ICT_is_dead_-_long_live_ICT**. Also Berry (2013, p.6) breaks the programme of study down as represented in Table 7.1.

Table 7.1

	KS1	KS2
CS	Understand what algorithms are and how they are implemented as programs on digital devices and that programs execute by following precise and unambiguous instructions.	Design, write and debug programs that accomplish specific goals, including controlling or simulating physical systems; solve problems by decomposing them into smaller parts.
	Create and debug simple programs.	Use sequence, selection and repetition in programs; work with variables and various forms of input and output.
	Use logical reasoning to predict the behaviour of simple programs.	

		Use logical reasoning to explain how some simple algorithms work and to detect and correct errors in algorithms and programs.
		Understand computer networks including the internet and how they can provide multiple services such as the world wide web.
		Appreciate how [search] results are selected and ranked.
IT	Use technology purposefully to create, organise, store, manipulate and retrieve digital content.	Use search technologies effectively. Select, use and combine a variety of software (including internet services) on a range of digital devices to design and create a range of programs, systems and content that accomplish given goals, including collecting, analysing, evaluating and presenting data and information.
DL	Recognise common uses of information technology beyond school. Use technology safely and respectfully, keeping personal information private; identify where to go for help and support when they have concerns about content or contact on the internet or other online technologies.	Understand the opportunities [networks] offer for communication and collaboration. Be discerning in evaluating digital content. Use technology safely, respectfully and responsibly; recognise acceptable/ unacceptable behaviour; identify a range of ways to report concerns about content and contact.

Breaking down the programme of study in this way (Berry, 2013, p.6) is useful when assessing computing because it can help us to develop a clearer focus for what is being assessed. Thus it is possible to get a clearer idea of what to look out for and listen for in children's responses to tasks. For example, if we think back to the example lesson given in Chapter 6 (Robot Routes) it is clear that the main focus in this lesson was Computer Science. For example, the lesson was designed to develop pupils' understanding of what algorithms are and how they are implemented in programs. So in this lesson we were looking for how confidently the children could work with single- and multi-step algorithms as well as how effectively they were able to identify any errors in the algorithms they devised to get the Bee-Bot through the route they had designed. While the main focus of this lesson concentrated on working with algorithms and one element of the programme of study, other lessons and tasks we plan for pupils may well incorporate several aspects of the programme of study. Furthermore even in a lesson that is tightly focused on developing children's capabilities when working with algorithms, links can be made to digital literacy by asking children to think about other important applications of algorithms in computing, e.g. the inconspicuous use of searching algorithms to harvest data as people use social networks.

In Section B of this book you will find many other ideas for lessons and different approaches to the teaching of computing. Other examples require assessment of different areas of the programme of study for computing. For example, in Chapter 8, Computational Thinking and Programming, we look at how various programs such as Scratch could be used to teach programming and computational thinking. One example involves children in Key Stage 2 designing and programming their own game. Such activities offer the opportunity to assess children in multiple areas of the programme of study.

For example, with regard to the Computer Science element we would be assessing how effectively children were able to use computational thinking to 'design, write and debug programs that accomplish specific goals' in the game they are creating. However, there would also be an opportunity to assess elements of Information Technology, because in designing and building a game the pupils would need to make effective use of various graphics software to create and assemble the graphical objects and backgrounds for their game. Similarly, in terms of Digital Literacy, there would be the opportunity to teach pupils about the importance of respecting others' intellectual property and copyrights when sourcing any graphics or images they used in their game. So when assessing the pupils' final products or games the opportunity arises to assess numerous aspects of the programme of study (e.g. CS, IT and DL) and not just their programming skills in Scratch.

The examples which follow detail two very different forms of assessment. The first, individual profiling, provides a means of systematically tracking an individual child in some detail. The second, taking a whole-class snapshot, provides a means of assessing children's capabilities with digital technologies at a very basic level in order to gain a picture of where each child in the class is at a given moment in time. These need to be employed together in order to gain the maximum benefit in terms of the assessment and planning cycle. Also, these examples should not be seen as a blueprint. It may be necessary to adapt them according to the specific context or unit of work being assessed.

Individual profiling

Individual profiling of children in curriculum subjects provides a means of mapping their progress through the various work samples collected and observations made. It makes a link to the child's own view of their developing capabilities and a link back to planning, thus completing the planning and assessment cycle.

The pro forma in Table 7.1 is intended to be completed two or three times in a term and should take no longer than five or ten minutes, once it becomes familiar. Ideally, it should be completed with the child in discussion about a particular work sample. The number of these completed in a teaching practice would need to be negotiated in terms of the overall course requirements for assessment. The questions next to each of the cells provide an *aide-memoire* of how to complete the form. As you can see, the areas covered include the child's individual progress alongside notes about the school context and an opportunity to record the child's own response to the piece of work. It is intended that the same sheet is used for each child and that the columns are completed for each observation so that it is possible to check progress across the two or three observations made.

THE BIGGER PICTURE THE BIGGER PICTURE THE BIGGER PICTURE THE BIGGER PICTURE

When you are planning opportunities to assess computing or capabilities with digital technologies, remember that peer- and self-assessment strategies that are useful in other areas of the curriculum such as maths and English can also be helpful here. You may use talk partners in literacy and other subjects, and many teachers build on these relationships to extend them to peer assessment. However, it is important that any feedback shared between children is constructive and you will need to have agreed guidelines for the children to work to.

Table 7.2

Date	Comment
Name of child	
Computing context (computer in class/ network room, tablet/handheld device)	Was the child working in the network room or on one machine? What was it?
How the software/hardware was used	Using software stand alone or on the internet? Was a range of software used?
Type of activity (e.g. programming robot, editing an image, using an office tool, debugging an algorithm, using logical reasoning, online safety using the internet)	Describe what the child was doing
Unit of work	Which unit was the child studying?
Working with partner? Who?	Was the child working alone, with a peer, with the teacher, teaching assistant, parent helper or other adult?
Length of time	For how long?
Confidence with hardware/software	Rate the child's confidence with the hardware listed and/or with printers or other devices if relevant. Very, fairly, not very, needing support, etc.
Software navigation (use of menus)	As above but for navigation within the particular piece of software
File management: saving, opening, renaming work etc.	As above but for working with files, reopening them, knowing where to find work, etc.
Computing programme of study	What knowledge, understanding and skills have been developed in relation to the different elements of the programme of study for computing, e.g. CS, IT, DL?
Cross-curricular context: using digital technologies to support work in English, science, maths or a foundation subject	How was the child operating within the curriculum context? Did the computer support the subject? Were there particular difficulties? Did the use of ICT help to improve the outcome?
Child's view of their work	Ask the child about their view of themselves as a user of digital technologies. Were there significant things about this piece of work that pleased them?
Where next?	What activities, explanations or ideas could help to move the child's knowledge, understanding and skills forward?

RESEARCH SUMMARY RESEARCH SUMMARY **RESEARCH SUMMARY** RESEARCH SUMMARY

Cook and Finlayson (1999) argue for the involvement of the child in recording progress in ICT. Tunstall and Gipps (1996) place great importance on the need to feed back to young children, identifying it as a 'prime requirement for progress in learning'. Both of these statements imply interaction and active involvement in the assessment process on the part of the child. The active involvement of the child in the process of formative assessment can be achieved, according to Wiliam and Thompson (2007), by:

- **activating students as learning resources for one another;**
- **activating students as owners of their own learning.**

Taking whole-class snapshots

To gain a picture of the whole class over a shorter period of time in order to map out their skills, knowledge and understanding of computing and ICT, it would be useful to complete a very basic skills matrix. This is in no way suggested as a substitute for the detailed profiling and sampling suggested in the previous section. This gives you a quick overview on which you can build some basic planning. The more detailed observations of individual children will be needed to gauge more accurately the effectiveness of the planning in raising the achievement of the class. Also whole-class skills matrices like the one detailed below should be adapted to suit the unit being studied. The example below is a general skills matrix which could be used, for example, with a Year 3 class editing and manipulating images or word processing a blog post. The matrix can be adapted accordingly to suit different ages and different units of work. Think about how you might adapt the matrix to suit an activity involving children working with algorithms and programmable toys/robots or to gain a snapshot of children's responsible and safe use of the internet during an activity in the computer suite.

Make best-guess judgements on a consistent value scale in order to provide a snapshot of the children in the class. Remember that this is merely an *aide-memoire* to help you write a short comment on the form for the rest of the class. The best practice in assessment is the longer form where curriculum contexts are taken into account alongside technical skill development. Use the longer format for the identified children.

For the snapshot, use a 1–4 scale for, for example, mouse skills and keyboard skills, switching on/off, opening and saving, cutting/pasting, inserting graphics, etc., as follows: 1 (not at all confident); 2 (developing confidence and accuracy); 3 (accurate and confident); 4 (very accurate and confident).

Table 7.3

Name	Date	Mouse/ keyboard skills	Switch/ log on Switch/ log off	Open/ save	Cut/ paste	Graphics	Independence	General comment

Assessing Early Years

We saw in Chapter 3 that very young children are working in a different context, that of the Early Years Foundation Stage. The different areas of learning for planned activities were mapped out.

In the EYFS, the criteria will be the Early Learning Goals and the observations you make will be referenced to the 'prime' and 'specific' areas of learning:

Prime areas:

- communication and language;
- physical development; and
- personal, social and emotional development.

Specific areas:

- literacy;
- mathematics;
- understanding the world; and
- expressive arts and design.

From September 2008, children in the EYFS have been assessed against a comprehensive Early Years Foundation Stage Profile (QCA, 2008), the main purpose of which is to provide Year 1 teachers with reliable and accurate information about each child's level of development as they enter Key Stage 1.

The individual profiling sheet described above, adapted appropriately, is of potentially greater use in the Early Years setting than the 'whole-class snapshot'. With a more detailed observation sheet, the background to the activity and the grouping become the more significant fields in which to enter any observations. If you are working in this context, you may even find it easier than in the mainstream school since so much assessment and recording in the Early Years setting depends on collating team observations of children across a period of time in different situations.

The Tickell Review, *The Early Years: Foundations for Life, Health and Learning* (Tickell, 2011), recommended a number of changes for EYFS reforms. One of these is a reduction of the number of Early Learning Goals, from 69 to 17. Furthermore, in order to make the profiling system described above less burdensome, Tickell recommended that there are three definitions for each goal to explain 'emerging', 'expected' and 'exceeding' the ELGs. These reforms have not been implemented.

REFLECTIVE TASK

At Key Stages 1 and 2 or in the EYFS, use and adapt the pro forma for individual observations to look in detail at the work of three children of varying levels of attainment. Complete the pro forma during a unit of work from the school's computing scheme or from a subject scheme and activity that utilises digital technologies. Carry out three observations on each child. Collect work samples and cross-reference your observations with them. Did the assessment reveal any strengths and/or areas for development? How helpful was the assessment?

Were there questions which you wished to see answered which were not on the form? If yes, what were they?

Were you able to track development through the lessons?

How did you differentiate your questioning for the focus children?

THE BIGGER PICTURE THE BIGGER PICTURE THE BIGGER PICTURE THE BIGGER PICTURE

Digital technologies and ICT in general can not only be used as a direct support to the assessment of children's learning during planned activities, but it can also help teachers with their ongoing assessment for learning, their regular record-keeping and in reporting on children's progress to their parents. There are commercially available programs to support all of these applications, but many local authority admin systems now have data-handling functions to track individual pupils' progress, their attainment as measured through summative assessments, and other important data such as attendance records. You may find that your school has pro formas that it uses as part of its assessment procedures and these may be available on the school's intranet or virtual learning environment (VLE). Ensure that you are familiar with the assessment policy and any forms used, and that you understand how they are used. Before using any of them, discuss them with your mentor/class teacher or the assessment co-ordinator.

A SUMMARY OF **KEY POINTS**

➢ **Assessment is a vital part of the planning cycle.**

➢ **The principles and processes of good assessment apply equally to computing as a subject in its own right and to the application of digital technologies to support children's learning in other subjects.**

➢ **Computing can be assessed using ICT tools in software packages and by collecting examples of children's work, but the best way of assessing computing and ICT capability is via the teacher's own observation.**

➢ **Through questioning and by discussing their work with them, children should be involved in their own assessment.**

➢ **In profiling individual children's progress, it is important to record information on the context of the observations, including whether the child was working alone or with a partner or small group.**

➢ **Taking a whole-class snapshot can be a quick way of identifying the range of levels of capability present in your group/class.**

➢ **Individual observations can also be useful in assessment in the EYFS to assess/record progress towards the Early Learning Goals and in the planning cycle for the 'prime' and 'specific' areas of learning.**

M-LEVEL EXTENSION > > M-LEVEL EXTENSION > > M-LEVEL EXTENSION

Register and sign up for the Computing At School community at the following link: **http://community.computingatschool.org.uk/door**. Search the community for resources for assessing computing. Compare the different approaches in some of the resources you find. For example, compare and contrast the different approaches taken to the assessment of computing in these resources:

- M. Dorling and M. Walker (2014) *Progression Pathways Assessment Framework*. Available at **http://community.computingatschool.org.uk/resources/2324**.
- M. Berry and P. Kemp (2014) *Assessing Attainment in Computing*. Available at **http://community.computingatschool.org.uk/resources/2078**.

REFERENCES REFERENCES **REFERENCES** REFERENCES **REFERENCES** REFERENCES

Berry, M. (2013) *Computing in the National Curriculum: A Guide for Primary Teachers*. Available at **www.computingatschool.org.uk/data/uploads/CASPrimaryComputing.pdf**.

Berry, M. and Kemp, P. (2014) *Assessing Attainment in Computing*. Available at **http://community. computingatschool.org.uk/resources/2078**.

Cook, D. and Finlayson, H. (1999) *Interactive Children, Communicative Teaching: ICT and Classroom Teaching*. Buckingham: Open University Press.

DfE (2011) *Teachers' Standards*. Available at **www.education.gov.uk/publications**.

Dorling, M. and Walker, M. (2014) *Progression Pathways Assessment Framework*. Available at **http://community.computingatschool.org.uk/resources/2324**.

QCA (2008) *Early Years Foundation Stage Profile Handbook*. London: QCA.

Tickell, C. (2011) *The Early Years: Foundations for Life, Health and Learning: An Independent Report on the Early Years Foundation Stage to Her Majesty's Government.* London: DfE.

Tunstall, P. and Gipps, C. (1996) 'Teacher feedback to young children in formative assessment: a typology', *British Educational Research Journal*, 22(4), pp.389–404.

Twining, P. (2013) *ICT Is Dead – Long Live ICT*. Available at **http://edfutures.net/ICT_is_dead_-_long_live_ICT**.

Wiliam, D. (2009) 'An integrative summary of the research literature and implications for a new theory of formative assessment', in H.L. Andrade and G.J. Cizek (eds), *Handbook of Formative Assessment*. New York: Taylor & Francis.

Wiliam, D. and Thompson, M. (2007) 'Integrating assessment with instruction: what will it take to make it work?', in C.A. Dwyer (ed.), *The Future of Assessment: Shaping Teaching and Learning*. Mahwah, NJ: Lawrence Erlbaum Associates, pp.53–82.

FURTHER READING FURTHER READING **FURTHER READING** FURTHER READING

Brennan, K. and Resnick, M. (2012) *New Frameworks for Studying and Assessing the Development of Computational Thinking*. Available at **http://web.media.mit.edu/~kbrennan/files/ Brennan_Resnick_AERA2012_CT.pdf**.

Briggs, M., Woodfield, A., Martin, C. and Swatton, P. (2008) *Assessment for Learning and Teaching in Primary Schools*. Exeter: Learning Matters.

8
Computational thinking and programming

Chapter objectives

When you have completed work on this chapter, you will have:

- understood some of the technical and subject-specific concepts and vocabulary associated with computer science;
- developed your own knowledge and understanding of programming and how it relates to the primary National Curriculum;
- considered different pedagogical approaches to developing children's computational thinking through programming;
- explored a range of software and devices to support the creative development and application of children's knowledge and understanding of computational thinking and programming.

Introduction

As discussed in the Introduction to this book, there has been a shift in emphasis in the latest draft of the National Curriculum for England, with calls for children to be taught more about how computers work. It is argued that as well as learning to use applications children should be given the tools and understanding to create their own applications by learning some of the fundamentals of programming and computational thinking. In this chapter we will give an introduction to programming in the primary years and consider both what is meant by 'computational thinking' and how children's capacity for computational thinking can be developed within meaningful contexts. We stress the importance of developing appropriate pedagogies and contexts for developing children's understanding of programming and computational thinking. There are many interesting concepts and processes in the subject repertoire that is computer science but it is vital to consider their appropriateness for the children we are teaching as well as the ways in which they are introduced and developed.

We will examine the aspects of the new programme of study for computing in order to clarify some of the key concepts relating to programming and computational thinking. Key software will be introduced with examples of projects and discussion of different pedagogical approaches. Software for teaching programming and computational thinking generally falls into two categories which are text-based programming (e.g. Logo, Python, Small Basic) and visual-based programming (e.g. Scratch, Blockly, Flowol). We also examine the role that programmable toys can play in introducing programming and computational thinking early in children's development. While we focus on specific pieces of software and hardware, the pedagogical and computing principles can be applied to any of the other programming languages or environments that are being explored to teach programming and aspects of computer science in the primary classroom.

What do the programmes of study for Key Stages 1 and 2 include?

Key Stage 1

- Understand what algorithms are, how they are implemented as programs on digital devices, and that programs execute by following precise and unambiguous instructions
- Create and debug simple programs
- Use logical reasoning to predict the behaviour of simple programs

Key Stage 2

- Design, write and debug programs that accomplish specific goals, including controlling or simulating physical systems; solve problems by decomposing them into smaller parts
- Use sequence, selection and repetition in programs; work with variables and various forms of input and output
- Use logical reasoning to explain how some simple algorithms work and to detect and correct errors in algorithms and programs

(DfE, 2013)

One of the most significant changes in the programme of study for computing (DfE, 2013) in the National Curriculum is its reference to specific specialist language. This specialist language comes from the broader discipline of computer science and signifies the intent within this programme of study to help children understand the distinct nature of computational thinking and how it is utilised within society. Thus in order to develop this understanding in children it is important that as teachers we also have a sound understanding of what is meant by computational thinking and the various processes involved. We will now explore some of the definitions surrounding these processes and various terminology in order to unpick this aspect of the programme of study. The aim of these definitions is to provide teachers with user-friendly working definitions to help them to develop the necessary language when working with children. Consequently, these may differ significantly to the various academic definitions to be found within the discipline of computer science.

Defining terms

Computational thinking

We define computational thinking here broadly as ways of thinking that people engage with as they employ the processes and tools of computing to solve problems. Such problems might exist in the physical world (e.g. an automated vending machine, a pedestrian crossing) or in a simulated/imaginary digital environment of a computer game or a tablet/ smartphone app. That is, computational thinking is, in its broadest sense, a term that encapsulates a number of particular logical thought processes that people employ, often, but not exclusively, to utilise a range of computer hardware and software to transform ideas and imagined solutions into reality. However, it is important to note that computational thinking is a process that people undertake, not computers. Indeed, computational thinking as we will see need not involve computer software or hardware. For example, Cuny et al. (2010, p.20) define computational thinking in the following way:

Computational thinking is the thought processes involved in formulating problems and their solutions so that the solutions are represented in a form that can effectively be carried out by an information-processing agent.

All digital technologies are 'information-processing agents', from our PCs to our mobile phones and the programmable toys we will examine later in this chapter. But humans are also 'information-processing agents' and we can employ the logical reasoning processes encompassed by computational thinking to solve problems that do not involve computers. Computational thinking need not involve the actual hardware of computers and digital devices or the applications we use on digital devices. Importantly, as Csizmadia et al. (2015, p.5) argue, it should be emphasised that computational thinking

concentrates on pupils performing a thought process, not on the production of arte-facts or evidence. Computational thinking is the development of thinking skills and it supports learning and understanding.

This is important because, as we will examine throughout this chapter, if we are to help children to develop computational thinking, teachers have a vital role to play in ensuring the thought processes we want children to engage with are made explicit. There is a risk that as teachers we get so involved in teaching children how to use specific software that we forget the underlying purpose and thought processes involved. So what are some of the main thought processes involved in computational thinking?

Algorithmic thinking involving algorithms, inputs, outputs, sequencing and debugging

These concepts and processes are identified in the National Curriculum for computing and are fundamental in computing and Computer Science. A useful way to think about algorithms is that they are the way we teach computers to carry out our ideas or automate aspects of our world. For example, when we press a letter (input) on a keyboard while word processing, the computer reproduces the graphic shape of the letter (output) on the screen. This is because the computer has been pre-programmed (or taught) to carry out this action via a set of instructions (algorithms). The instructions (algorithms) link the turning on of a particular formation of pixels on the screen required for the letter (output), to the physical key or input on the keyboard. So in this context, an algorithm is a set of instructions designed to teach computers to execute tasks and ideas. To do this successfully the instructions that the computer processes need to be precise and in the correct order, which is why understanding the importance of sequence when writing algorithms is also highlighted in the programme of study. Imagine for a moment the multiple algorithms operating behind the scenes when you are using a simple word processing program not only to reproduce the graphic representations of the letters as you type but to know what you mean when you select a piece of text to cut, copy, paste, change the font style or size, insert a table, and so on. Understanding the importance of algorithms to computing gives one an appreciation of the complexity of what is involved behind the scenes of any application. Consider, for example, the algorithms that might be involved in translating the gestures (inputs) you use on your smartphone or tablet device into various outputs.

As we have already emphasised, computational thinking need not involve computer hardware or software. Think about the algorithms that govern our day-to-day activities such as getting up in the morning and going to work, changing a light bulb safely, cooking your favourite meal, making bread, cleaning your teeth, safely making a right turn on your bicycle and so on; that is, the list is endless. Much of our day-to-day routines, where we need to achieve a specific outcome, have underlying algorithms. There are many activities in the classroom you could use to develop children's understanding of the importance of algorithms in our daily lives and in computing as the following examples illustrate.

IN THE CLASSROOM

Watch the Sandwich Bot video by Philip Bagge on YouTube available at: **www.youtube.com/watch?v= leBEFaVHllE&feature=youtu.be**

This is a good example of a simple classroom activity you can carry out with children to help them understand the importance of sequence and precise instructions when creating algorithms to achieve a specific goal. As you watch, see if you can debug or identify the errors in the algorithms or instructions that the children give the Sandwich Bot. What types of errors do they make – sequence, precision, language? Identifying errors in our algorithms is known as debugging. In other words, when we debug our algorithms we are identifying the errors in order to correct them as they stop the algorithm from accomplishing the specific goal it has been designed to carry out. Think about other similar examples that you could use in the classroom to plan a lesson that illustrates the importance of sequence and precise instructions when writing algorithms or instructions to achieve a specific goal. For example, you could use a shirt, tie and jacket, and ask the children to devise an algorithm to instruct a human robot to put these on correctly.

Abstraction and decomposition

These are also terms that are introduced in the National Curriculum for computing. First let us consider some simple definitions of these terms. Abstraction is a process by which any unnecessary detail is omitted in order to help us solve a problem or achieve a specific outcome. It is not only used by computer scientists but by all disciplines in some way. For example, graphic designers use abstraction regularly, stripping away any unnecessary

Figure 8.1 UK traffic sign using abstraction to warn motorists of children crossing the road ahead

Figure 8.2 Pedestrian crossing problem

detail to communicate a message clearly. For example, consider the road sign warning drivers to take care because there are likely to be children crossing the road going to or from school or to a playground ahead (Figure 8.1).

Decomposition is the process of breaking down a more complex problem into smaller constituent parts in order to solve the bigger problem. Again this is a process that is used a lot by computer scientists and programmers but it is not unique to computer science. It is a process we can use in our day-to-day problem-solving. It is also used in mathematics. A familiar example from mathematics is what is often called the 'decomposition method of subtraction' which involves solving a complex problem that we cannot subtract in our head such as subtracting one three-digit number from another by breaking it down into smaller but constituent parts. That is subtracting the units, then the tens and finally the hundreds to solve the whole problem.

A useful way to begin to understand all of these terms and how they apply to computing is to analyse and engage with examples of computational thinking that are often taken for granted in our physical environment. For example, we can identify these aspects of computational thinking in a system and problem such as a pedestrian crossing (see Figure 8.2).

First let us decompose a pedestrian crossing into the various real-world problems that the crossing is designed to solve. They can be defined thus:

1. Bring the traffic to a stop safely.
2. Enable pedestrians to cross the road safely.
3. Enable partially sighted or blind pedestrians to cross the road safely.

As you can see we can identify at least three problems in this scenario and by doing so we have begun to use decomposition to break the problem down into its key components. Note also that sequence is vital. There is a clear order in which some of the problems need to be addressed. We are also beginning to use abstraction in this process, because we are identifying the important details that will help us to solve the problem while getting rid of unnecessary detail. There are various solutions to these problems that we could design which will have varying levels of safety and effectiveness. Let's consider them one by one:

PRACTICAL TASK PRACTICAL TASK PRACTICAL TASK PRACTICAL TASK

To solve the problem of bringing the traffic to a safe stop consider the two algorithms shown in Table 8.1 and decide which is better and why.

Table 8.1 Algorithms

Algorithm 1	Algorithm 2
Start	Start
When pedestrian button is pressed (Input 1)	When pedestrian button is pressed (Input 1)
Turn pedestrian wait sign on (Output 1)	Turn pedestrian wait sign on (Output 1)
Turn green light off (Output 2)	Turn green light off (Output 2)
Turn amber light on (Output 3)	Turn amber light on (Output 3)
Wait five seconds	Turn amber light off (Output 3)
Turn amber light off (Output 3)	Turn red light on (Output 4)
Turn red light on (Output 4)	

So Algorithm 1 is safer because the extra instruction to wait for five seconds while the amber light is on will give the motorist more time to slow down and stop safely.

Repetition and selection

These two terms are also highlighted in the National Curriculum for computing and can be interpreted quite literally. For example, we can take Algorithm 1 in our pedestrian crossing problem and abstract it further to represent it in a simple flow chart (Figure 8.3). In Figure 8.3 we have got rid of all unnecessary detail. Notice that at the start of the flow chart there is a *repetition* loop, and a point where a *selection* has to be made between Yes/No. Repetition and selection are vital in computing. Remember what this algorithm represents. The traffic light system has to be in a constant state of readiness for a pedestrian coming along at any time and pressing the button (Input 1) to cross the road. The repetition loop and Yes/No selection at the beginning of the algorithm is how this is achieved. The system is constantly asking the question 'Is Input 1 on?' If the answer to this question is no, it simply keeps asking the question 'Is Input 1 on?' until the condition of Input 1 changes. If the condition of Input 1 changes – someone presses the button to

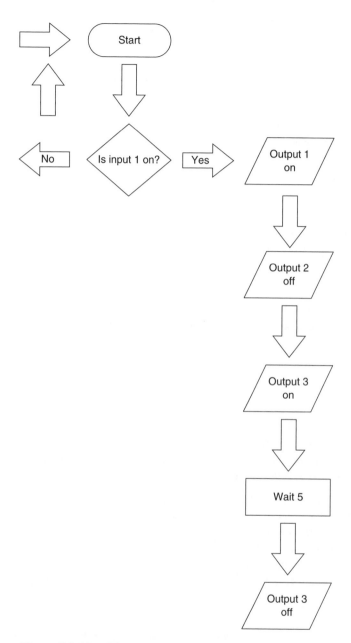

**Figure 8.3 Algorithm 1 bringing the traffic to a safe stop
expressed as a flow chart**

cross the road – then a different route through the algorithm is selected. Setting out the algorithm to solve this first problem, of bringing the traffic to a safe stop, in a flow chart in this way, helps us to see how the various logical reasoning processes of computational thinking are employed to solve a more complex problem in stages. We have employed decomposition, abstraction, repetition, selection, inputs, outputs and sequence to solve the first part of the more complex problem represented by a pedestrian crossing.

Table 8. 2 Algorithm to stop traffic and allow pedestrians to cross the road safely

Algorithm 1
developed to stop traffic and enable pedestrians to cross the road safely
Start
When pedestrian button is pressed (Input 1)
Turn pedestrian wait sign on (Output 1)
Turn green light off (Output 2)
Turn amber light on (Output 3)
Wait five seconds
Turn amber light off (Output 3)
Turn red light on (Output 4)
Turn wait sign (Output 1), amber light (Output 2) and red man off (Output 5)
Turn green man on (Output 6)
Wait 20 seconds
Turn green man off (Output 6)
Turn red man (Output 5) and amber light on (Output 3)
Wait 5 seconds
Turn amber light off (Output 3)
Turn green light on (Output 2)

We can now develop this algorithm further to address the second problem of enabling pedestrians to cross the road safely when the traffic has been stopped safely. In Table 8.2 the algorithm for achieving this specific goal has been written out in full but think how it might be expressed as a flow chart.

Table 8.2 is one possible solution to the first two problems of stopping the traffic safely and enabling pedestrians to cross. Think of a way that this algorithm could be improved and made safer. Is there a way of warning pedestrians that the green man is about to go off so that they do not set off across the road when there is not enough time to cross? For example, we could incorporate a flashing routine so that after a while the green man begins flashing to indicate that it will shortly turn off, or we could introduce new outputs in the form of a count down from 10 seconds, like is often found now in cities with wide and busy roads.

Computers, like humans, are capable of multi-tasking or carrying out more than one operation at the same time. So we can exploit this to address the third problem of making sure that the pedestrian crossing is also safe for partially sighted or blind people to use. As well as the various visual outputs such as the red/green man and red/amber/green traffic lights, pedestrian crossings have an audio output or signal that acts as a sign that it is safe to cross for those unable to see the visual signs. So it is possible to write a separate algorithm that would run in parallel to the main algorithm to control this audio output. Hence computer scientists sometimes talk of parallel or distributed algorithms. These are simply algorithms within the same system but controlling different outputs or aspects of the system and exploiting the computer's capacity to multi-task.

PRACTICAL TASK PRACTICAL TASK **PRACTICAL TASK** PRACTICAL TASK

Complete the pedestrian crossing problem by solving all three of the constituent problems within the system. For example:

1. **Bring the traffic to a stop safely.**

2. **Enable pedestrians to cross the road safely.**

3. **Enable partially sighted or blind pedestrians to cross the road safely.**

Express your solution to this problem using flow charts like in Figure 8.3 above. You may need to create extra features such as an audio output. When you have completed this task reflect on how you have used some of the different processes of computational thinking like decomposition, abstraction, repetition and selection.

IN THE CLASSROOM

To develop children's understanding of algorithms and the various processes we have discussed so far in this chapter, think about all of the day-to-day routines children might experience such as brushing their teeth in the morning, making a cup of tea, tidying their bedroom, doing the washing up, tidying up the classroom, caring for the classroom plants. Get the children to write the algorithms for some of these activities but then ask them to represent them as efficiently and succinctly as they can in flow charts. For example, you could create some classroom algorithms that you display as flow charts to help with the safe operation of equipment. Or you could create some eco-friendly algorithms to remind the class not to waste energy by leaving lights on and windows open when you leave the classroom to go out to PE or to assembly.

From this brief exploration of computational thinking and some of the associated concepts, it is possible to see how algorithms are fundamental to computing and why they have been emphasised in the computing programme of study. Clearly working with algorithms can be challenging when solving complex problems. We have begun to look at how we can get children engaged with computational thinking away from computers by thinking about the role that algorithms play in our daily lives and expressing these through various activities, including introducing them to flow charts. However, the National Curriculum for computing introduces algorithms in Key Stage 1, emphasising that children should understand what algorithms are and how they are implemented on digital devices. There are various child-centred ways of engaging young children at Key Stage 1 with algorithmic thinking and problem-solving, as we explore next.

Programmable toys and robots: introducing algorithmic thinking

Despite the recent shifts in the primary National Curriculum to encourage more teaching of aspects of computer science in the curriculum, this is not in fact new. Programming has been introduced into primary classrooms in the past from as early as Key Stage 1.

**Figure 8.4 Roamer® courtesy of Valiant Technology
at www.valiant-technology.com/**

Programmable toys such as Roamer Classic® (see Valiant Technology at **www.valiant-technology.com/uk/pages/roamer_home.php?cat=1&1)** are common devices that have been used in many primary schools since the 1970s to develop children's problem-solving skills and give children an understanding of the ways in which we can use computers to control or automate the world around us. To operate these toys or robots, children use the arrow keys and numerical values to input simple instructions to move the toys. Figure 8.4 is an example of the latest version called Roamer®. Problem-solving using programmable toys can also help to establish and develop some important mathematical concepts in young children such as an understanding of angle as rotation or turning, and the development of estimation of distance which is so important in mathematics when developing an understanding of linear measurement. Indeed the development of children's mathematical concepts underlies Papert's vision of the Logo programming language on which many programmable toys and interfaces are based (Papert, 1993).

Other programmable toys or robots such as Bee-Bot (Figure 8.5) have also become available. Programmable toys such as these are an ideal entry point for young and even pre-school children to begin to explore algorithmic thinking. That is giving simple instructions to devices and debugging or problem-solving when they do not behave in the predicted or expected way. Similarly apps are available for smartphones and tablets such as the iPad, which allow children to explore giving instructions and writing algorithms to program Bee-Bot in an on-screen game environment (Figure 8.5). The point at which teachers introduce the relevant vocabulary (algorithm, debug, quarter turn, whole turn, etc.) to young children should be left to the teacher's professional judgement based on their knowledge of the children. It is important to give children time to explore and play with programmable toys. However, it is also important for teachers to scaffold children's

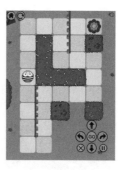

**Figure 8.5 Bee-Bot programmable toy (left) and
Bee-Bot app (right)**

learning with such devices. One way to do this is to use visual instruction cards which the children can use to plan and record the algorithms they are going to use. This way, there is then a record to refer back to and debug if there are errors in their algorithms. Another way is to use mini whiteboards and get the children to use their own code to record their algorithms.

PRACTICAL TASK PRACTICAL TASK PRACTICAL TASK PRACTICAL TASK

For examples of how you could incorporate activities with programmable toys into Key Stage 1 and lower Key Stage 2 to develop children's computational thinking see the video tutorial at the following link: **http://bcove.me/oouug2wh.**

After watching the video reflect on why it is important to use cards or some other way of recording the children's algorithms as they work with programmable toys.

Programmable toys also lend themselves to a range of pedagogical contexts and a search on the internet for teaching ideas will reveal a plethora of imaginative ideas of how to integrate the programming of such toys into the curriculum in meaningful ways. See, for example, Kristine Kopelke's resource *Making Your Classroom Buzz with Bee-Bots* (available at the following link: **http://elresources.skola.edu.mt/wp-content/uploads/2010/06/doc_669_2468_beebotguideA4v2.pdf**). Programmable toys and robots can be integrated into narrative role-play contexts, being adapted to take on a character from a popular children's book. Or they can be used within various games scenarios such as number mats and treasure hunt maps to name but a few. While there are many different activity and games mats available to accompany Bee-Bot and other robots it is also possible to get the children involved in designing and creating their own games and scenarios. Getting young children involved in the designing and exploring of games-based scenarios with programmable toys or robots engages them in the exploration of algorithms as they encounter problems that require solving and debugging. This can provide a sound basis for the further development of computational thinking. Key processes of computational thinking – designing and debugging algorithms, being able to break problems down into their component parts – are relevant whether learners are trying to navigate a Bee-Bot

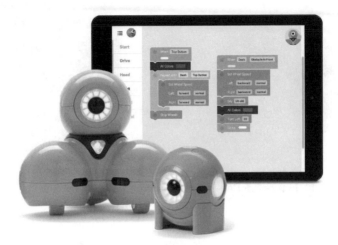

**Figure 8.6 Dash and Dot programmable robots courtesy
of Wonder Workshop**

through a maze on the classroom floor or write a programme to simulate a satellite orbiting the Earth on the computer. Computational thinking is required to solve the simplest of programming tasks to the most complex. Programmable toys have become much more sophisticated and also more affordable in recent years. One example of this is the Dash and Dot robots **(https://www.makewonder.com/dash)** which are floor robots that can be controlled using visual-based programming interfaces (e.g. Blockly) via a smartphone or tablet device. Again, such robots offer the potential for integrating programming activities into a range of imaginative scenarios which can then be used to develop children's computational thinking. Using a visual blocks programming interface such as Blockly (Figure 8.6) also means that the child can record their algorithms and take screenshots of them for discussion with the teacher and other children. This is important as it is through dialogue like this that the teacher can explore the child's computational thinking together with the appropriate vocabulary, and support them in developing it further.

IN THE CLASSROOM

A Year 3 class have been doing some work on road safety. They have been writing and improving simple algorithms to help them cross the road safely. The have created a 3D model on the classroom floor of a road with parked cars, trees and a pavement. Their task is to program Dash to simulate crossing the road safely. They have created algorithms using Blockly to get Dash to pause at the edge of the road, look both ways and cross the road, continuing to look and listen in both directions. The next problem they want to solve is to get Dash to check whether there is an obstacle (e.g. a car) in the road to the right or the left so that Dash only crosses the road if the road is clear.

There are many programmable toys and robots available, too numerous to introduce here. However, in principle, as well as providing opportunities for children to explore these devices in open-ended playful contexts, it is important for teachers to scaffold children's learning about algorithms and their significance in computing, including the need to develop the analytical skills to debug and use logical reasoning while programming the devices. For further ideas on suitable activities with programmable toys and robots explore the Barefoot computing website at the following link: **http://barefootcas. org.uk/**.

From Logo to Scratch

Seymour Papert and Cynthia Solomon, mathematicians and computer scientists, created the text-based programming language Logo, to enable children to explore mathematical concepts and develop problem-solving skills in much the same way that children initially acquire and develop language skills, that is through immersion in practice. There are various versions of Logo software available or, as it is also referred to, Turtle Graphics software (e.g. MSWLogo, FMSLogo). In the Textease Studio CT version, instructions or algorithms can be written straight onto the screen or in the command line to control the turtle's movement around the screen (see the video tutorial at the following link: **www.youtube.com/ watch?v=jOY6OVNnq1M**). Figure 8.7 illustrates a simple simulation of a satellite orbiting the Earth in Textease TurtleCT, which uses Logo as its programming language.

In Figure 8.7 the satellite has been made into a controllable object in the turtle settings. Consequently the algorithm repeat 180 (fd 1 rt 2) is applied to determine the direction and movement of the satellite. So for every step forward (fd 1) the direction of travel turns 2 degrees to the right (rt 2). As this is repeated 180 times, the satellite travels through 360 degrees back to its starting point. Logo, like Scratch, is what is often termed

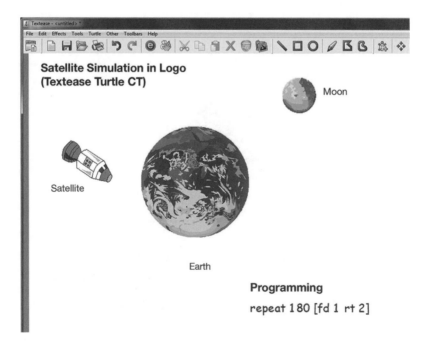

**Figure 8.7 Simulation illustrating a simple algorithm
in Logo (Textease Turtle CT)**

a 'low threshold, high ceiling' programming environment (Resnick, 2012). That is, it is easy to make things happen on the screen simply by using text-based commands such as forward (fd), backward (bk), right 90 (rt 90), left 90 (lt 90) and so on. Of course, Figure 8.7 is a simple simulation that could be developed much further but there are many possible applications for Logo including more complex simulations, graphics applications using the turtle to draw as it travels, game creation and animation. See the list of links at the end of this chapter for more examples of how Logo can be developed further.

Let us look now at the same scenario of the satellite orbiting the Earth but this time using Scratch to control the satellite (Figure 8.8).

Figure 8.8 illustrates the Scratch programming language. To programme in Scratch, users drag and click together various blocks into a logical sequence to form an algorithm. In the example given, the first block is an 'event' block (when green flag is clicked), the second block is known as a 'control' block because the instruction (repeat 180) is applied to everything within it (it is a repeating loop). The darkest blocks in Figure 8.8 are known as 'motion' blocks because they determine the various motion paths that the object being controlled takes around the screen. The instruction to 'set rotation style' to 'don't rotate' means that the satellite will remain in its current orientation when the program is activated and it orbits the Earth.

Scratch was developed by Mitchell Resnick and researchers at MIT Media Lab. Resnick describes the rationale behind its design as being to make the programming environment 'more tinkerable', as he describes it (2012, p.4):

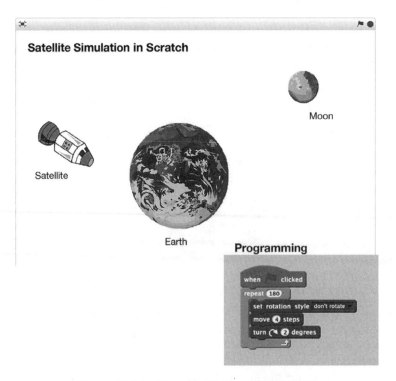

Figure 8.8 Satellite simulation using Scratch

To create programs in Scratch, you snap together graphical blocks into stacks, just like LEGO bricks, without any of the obscure syntax (square brackets, semi colons etc.) of traditional programming languages.

Thus the programming blocks together with the graphical interface are designed to make it easy for learners to get started and experiment to find out 'what would happen if?' Again the theory is that it gives learners a low threshold in terms of getting started with exploring and learning how to program but can also be used to challenge the learner as they create more sophisticated scenarios requiring more complex logical and computational thinking. However, facilitating progression in children's computational thinking can be pedagogically challenging, as we will explore next.

Pedagogies for progression in computational thinking

In this section we want to consider in more depth how children's computational thinking might be developed through different pedagogical approaches to a programming environment such as Scratch. It is beyond the scope of this book to give readers a course in Scratch programming and there are already many excellent online resources available to support teachers in the development of their own knowledge of Scratch, including useful video tutorials to get teachers or children started.

Indeed, the wealth of online video tutorials and support resources available for Scratch could arguably be problematic in terms of the pedagogical issues of developing children's computational thinking with Scratch. An important part of learning for young children is through practice and mimicking more knowledgeable others within any discipline. But this is problematic if it does not progress so that children begin to use their knowledge to express their own ideas or develop their own creativity through programming. Resnick and Siegel (2015) have recently expressed their own concerns about the ways in which Scratch is being used and taught by some as a technical skill that does not then progress beyond a technical proficiency. They argue that programming should be conceived as 'a new type of literacy and personal expression' (Resnick and Siegel, 2015). Some of the issues surrounding the pedagogy and purposes of teaching programming to young children today echo arguments from the past. For example, research carried out into the use of Logo programming in education back in the 1980s found that 'children's programs often displayed production without comprehension' together with 'rote use of chunks from other children's programs or those of the teacher' (Pea, 1983, p.5).

PRACTICAL TASK   PRACTICAL TASK   **PRACTICAL TASK**   PRACTICAL TASK

Watch the video by Miles Berry at the following link: **www.youtube.com/watch?v=TV0MqrmLpgU**. Another good starting point is the Scratch website for educators, which you can explore at the following link: **http://scratched.media.mit.edu/**.

So how can we ensure progression and development in children's computational thinking when using a tool such as Scratch and how can we ensure that children go on to use programming as an expressive and creative tool as Resnick suggests (2015)? It is clear that children's learning of programming and computational thinking needs to be scaffolded by the teacher from time to time in order for them to develop both a level of technical proficiency but also a deeper understanding of the computational processes they are engaging with. So how can we scaffold children's learning within this context?

Follow this link to the Scratch profile **http://scratch.mit.edu/users/JeremyBurton/**. There are two versions of the Orchard Game. The first version has no bugs in it. Play this to get an idea of how the game works. Now try the Orchard Game – Debugging Activity. In this version of the game, the creator has deliberately made some basic errors in the programming which need debugging. He has also provided some comments that you can open to help you if you get stuck. Try remixing this game to correct the errors in programming.

The screenshot in Figure 8.9 illustrates a project called Orchard Game created by Jeremy Burton. In the game, apples randomly clone themselves and fall from the trees. The main character, Skye (output) moves left and right across the screen in response to the arrow keys (inputs) to collect the apples in her basket as they fall. Each time an apple goes

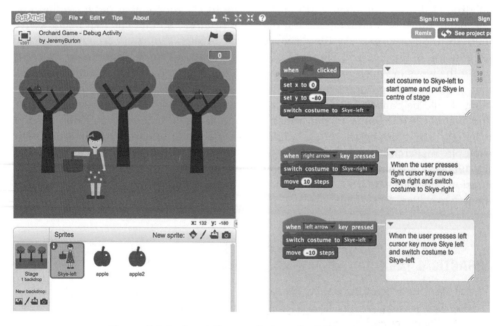

Figure 8.9 Orchard Game – Debug Activity, courtesy of Jeremy Burton

into the basket the score (variable) increases by one but if they hit the ground the score decreases by one. The score is one application of the concept of variables within a computer program. Essentially variables in a program simply store information monitoring changes in the state of a system, hence the label of variable. Another example is a vending machine which will use variables in its programming so that it registers when a product is sold out and can switch on an output to alert the customer that the product is not available. The version of Orchard Game in Figure 8.9 is what is known as a debugging activity in that the game is not working correctly.

There are many video tutorials on YouTube of how to create various games in Scratch. There are also many step-by-step walkthroughs of how to recreate various games. Pedagogically it is clear that when learning how to use any program, children will need to build their repertoire of commands in order to understand how to code or program and gain some level of technical proficiency. However, it is vital that they also understand why a certain piece of code within any program leads to a particular outcome within the system or game being designed. While following instructions on how to achieve certain outcomes within Scratch may be appropriate to get children familiar with the programming environment, this is ultimately limiting as following others' instructions or video tutorials may actually require little computational thinking or problem-solving. The pedagogical model provided by Burton's Orchard Game – Debugging Activity does actually require the learner to engage with solving the problems in the programming and offers a good pedagogical model for both building technical proficiency and deepening their understanding of the processes of computational thinking.

Once children are familiar with the basics of a programming language like Scratch they can be engaged in tasks that will require a deeper level of analysis and begin to challenge them to use computational thinking to a greater degree. For example, evaluating others' computer games that they enjoy playing can prompt further enquiry and discussion, identifying which bit of code or programming relates to which outputs within the game. In this way they can see how the various problems within the game have been solved and consider whether they have been solved in the most efficient or effective way. An important aspect of computational thinking is efficiency as the more unnecessarily complex a piece of code or algorithm the higher the chance of it conflicting with other algorithms in the programme which need debugging.

Ultimately, to develop higher levels of computational thinking children will need exposure to extended projects which require them to design their own games, simulations or scenarios. Much useful work can be done away from the programming environment or computer, getting children to design and devise their own ideas for games. Indeed games and software companies spend a great deal of time researching their potential audiences for any new software or games they design and create. The process of designing and creating a new piece of software or game is multidisciplinary as successful software products require careful research of the target audience, effective design and high quality graphics as well as effective programming and various testing of the final artefact. This process can offer an effective pedagogical model for children to engage with and can also be embedded within other areas of the curriculum. For example, a task might be to research, design and create a simulation that illustrates the water cycle. Another example might be to create an interactive and animated environment for younger children based on a favourite children's picture book. In order to tackle more open-ended design-based tasks children will need to engage in a number of key processes and it is useful to think about how the teacher can plan for these. For example, if getting children to design and create a new game or simulation, think about how you could incorporate into your planning, opportunities for the children to:

- collaborate to discuss their ideas;
- sketch or storyboard the different scenarios;
- source or create their own high-quality graphics and audio;
- identify the various algorithms required to control the various inputs and outputs behind their ideas;
- program their simulation/game;
- carry out user testing of their game/simulation;
- evaluate and debug any aspects that can be improved; and
- re-test the simulation/game.

IN THE CLASSROOM

A class of Year 4 children are analysing the game Hungry Monkey by Natalie Perkins (see the following link: **https://scratch.mit.edu/projects/21416773/**). In this game a monkey moves right and left, controlled by the arrow keys on the keyboard. On the up arrow the monkey jumps up and tries to reach the bananas hanging from the trees. If the monkey touches a banana, it disappears and the score increases by 1 point. The children are decomposing the game to identify the problems that the creator had to solve to make it work properly. For example:

1. Make the monkey move left and right according to the arrow keys.
2. Make the monkey jump.
3. Make the bananas disappear if the monkey touches them.
4. Make the background music play.
5. Keep the score each time a banana is eaten.
6. Switch the background to the game over screen when all of the bananas have been eaten.

When they have decomposed the game into its various problems and discussed how they could approach solving these as a class they try solving these problems using incomplete or bugged versions of the game, e.g. **https://scratch.mit.edu/studios/653644/**. As a progression the children also discuss how the Hungry Monkey game could be improved and developed further. For example, how could the task be made more difficult and the game more exciting for the user?

As you can see from the list above, a more creative and design-based project like this would need to be planned over a number of lessons, but would give children the opportunity to collaborate, develop and implement their ideas in a creative and multi-disciplinary approach which would also support the development of their digital literacy alongside their computational thinking.

The important aspect to remember when programming with children is that merely learning a programming language for its own sake can be limiting. Whatever programming language we are using, a key aim is also to build the children's relational understanding of what it means to be a computer scientist or a programmer and how this also connects with the wider world. Consequently children should be engaging in computational thinking both at the computer and away from the computer, utilising the tools creatively to realise their ideas and solutions to practical and imagined problems. Such aims need to be built into a whole-school approach to computing so that children's knowledge, understanding and skills are built on throughout the primary phase through appropriate challenges and appropriate pedagogies that require them to engage in the various aspects of computational thinking outlined earlier in this chapter. For more ideas about how programming with Scratch can be embedded in the curriculum see the *Literacy from Scratch* website **www.literacyfromscratch.org.uk/index.htm**.

Alternatives to Scratch

Although Scratch is a common tool for developing children's knowledge and understanding of programming, there are many other programming environments that are worth noting. Kodu (**www.kodugamelab.com**) is a programming environment that enables users to create their own games and narrative environments using visual programming blocks. Similarly, MIT App Inventor enables users to design and build apps for mobile devices (**http://appinventor.mit.edu/explore/index-2.html**) Some of these are featured in Chapter 9 on Physical Computing. It is we think important that children experience different types of programming environments if they are to gain a deeper understanding of the processes of computational thinking and how it can be manifest and exploited to different purposes and in different ways. Earlier in this chapter we discussed how useful flow charts can be both in computing and in developing children's understanding of algorithms. We conclude this chapter with a closer look at programming software based on flow charts.

Flowol

Other educational software that has been used in primary schools for a while to teach aspects of programming and computer science is Flowol (**www.flowol.com/**) and its extension software Mimic Creator. The concept behind these two pieces of software is not unlike Scratch. Like Scratch, this software can be used to program and control preloaded simulations or for children to create their own games and simulations. Firstly let us examine Flowol in more detail.

In Flowol, a 'mimic' is simply an on-screen visual simulation of a physical scenario, system or game which is programmed using flow charts. Figure 8.10 is an example of Flowol's preloaded Lighthouse mimic. In the screenshot all of the inputs and outputs are in the 'on' state. In Flowol, then, the mimic is essentially a graphic representation of a scenario with various 'hotspots' on the simulation that allow the inputs and outputs to be toggled between their 'on' and 'off' states as we have illustrated in Figure 8.10. So how is the mimic programmed?

Firstly we will examine some of the underlying algorithms that would be needed to automate a lighthouse and then illustrate how these would be represented using Flowol's flow-chart programming environment.

A lighthouse's warning lamp generally flashes on and off throughout the day and the night, with the foghorn warning being added in conditions of poor visibility. Consequently, let us begin with the algorithm for the warning lamp. Because Flowol uses

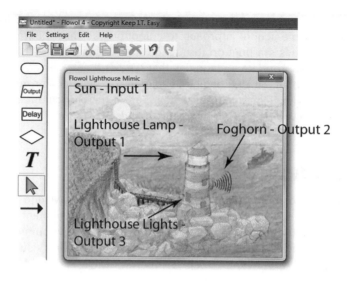

**Figure 8.10 Flowol Lighthouse Mimic showing inputs
and outputs**

a flow-chart programming environment, once the program is started it will continue to run as a series of flow-chart loops. So the algorithm to make the warning lamp flash could be written simply as follows:

Start

Turn output 1 on (Lighthouse Lamp)

Delay 1 second

Turn output 1 off (Lighthouse Lamp)

Delay 1 second

This algorithm is represented in the first flow chart – 'Lighthouse Lamp' – in Figure 8.11. Notice that there is an arrow from the last 'Delay 1' box back to the 'Start' of this program forming a loop, which will continue to run as long as the programme is in operation. So what about the Foghorn output and how this is controlled or programmed?

The algorithm for the Foghorn is in many ways similar to the Lighthouse lamp in that the computer needs to be instructed to turn this output on and off repeatedly during times of poor visibility. Consequently if you look closely at the third flow chart in Figure 8.11, labelled 'Foghorn Sub-routine' you will notice that the majority of this flow chart is very similar to the algorithm and flow chart for the Lighthouse Lamp. For example:

Start

Turn Foghorn on

Delay 1 second

Turn Foghorn off

Delay 1 second

However, in Flowol the Foghorn program has been written as a sub-routine because it would only be called on to run if there is poor visibility. Furthermore this is one example

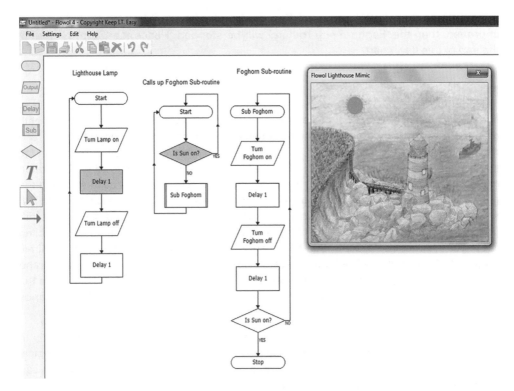

**Figure 8.11 Flowol Lighthouse Mimic with example of
flow-chart programming**

of how the process of selection can work in programming. Consequently, the visibility of the sun (Input 1) in the mimic is what activates the Foghorn. In Figure 8.11, the flow chart labelled 'Call up Foghorn Sub-routine' has been paused at the point where the programme checks whether the sun is visible or not. In programming and algorithmic terms this is often referred to as an 'if, then statement', or in Flowol the rhombus shape is referred to as the decision symbol. As the Sun (Input 1) is visible in Figure 8.11 then the program remains in the loop, constantly asking the question and checking if Input 1 is 'on'. If the Sun (Input 1) is clicked on the screen so that the sun is no longer visible (its 'off' state) then the program would 'select' and follow the 'no' path of the flow chart and activate the 'Foghorn Sub-routine'. What is also evident from analysing the flow chart programming is that it is helpful to break the various programs down into their component parts or 'decompose' the problem being solved by each of the different parts of the algorithm. In doing so we can use logical reasoning to solve the various problems faced.

Of course, programmers often remark that computers do exactly as you tell them but often not what you expect, and if you look closely again at the 'Foghorn Sub-routine' you will notice that there is another vital piece of this third flow chart (Figure 8.11). Once the computer has entered the 'Foghorn sub-routine' it is essential that it continues to monitor the visibility of the sun in order to turn off the Foghorn when the visibility improves. Consequently, at the end of the 'Foghorn Sub-routine' there is another 'decision symbol' or 'if, then statement' used to check the Sun Input. If the Sun Input is not on then the program will continue to loop (repetition) around the Foghorn flow chart, turning the foghorn output on and off. If the Sun Input is 'on' indicating visibility has improved, then the 'Foghorn sub-routine' will be stopped. Hence the 'Stop' symbol at the end of this flow chart.

Mimic Creator

Mimic Creator is an additional piece of software that works with Flowol and allows children to create their own mimics (programmable simulations or scenarios). Children can design their mimic or system and use graphics software to create a background image in which all of their inputs and outputs are represented in the 'off' state as we illustrated in Figure 8.11 using the Lighthouse mimic. A graphics package is then used to create the graphical representations of the inputs and outputs in their 'on' state, which are then layered over the background image. Essentially, Mimic Creator is used to assemble the different graphical inputs and outputs of the mimic ready to be programmed and controlled in Flowol. There is not space within this chapter to give a detailed introduction to Mimic Creator, but it can offer a useful progression once children are familiar with Flowol and have had experience programming the pre-installed mimics with flow charts. It offers the opportunity for children to design, develop and simulate their own automated scenarios or games.

In summary, the flow-chart approach to programming is a useful tool educationally in computing because it can help visually illustrate the importance of sequence and logical reasoning when writing programs. While running their programs in Flowol, children can speed up, slow down or pause the program, enabling them to track where the program may have an error that needs debugging. When a program is run in Flowol the various stages of the program are lit up making visible the processing of the algorithm (in this case a flow chart) by the computer. This can help children to understand the significance and importance of processor speeds in computers and what is actually going on within any computer program as it runs behind the screen.

A SUMMARY OF **KEY POINTS**

Throughout this chapter we have discussed a range of software and hardware, but it is always vital to consider the principles behind why teaching children how to code or program is important. We have stressed that:

> ➤ Beyond learning how to program in a particular language, children should be encouraged to develop their computational thinking skills, which we have seen involve: being able to solve problems by breaking them down or decomposing them into their constituent parts; writing and debugging algorithms; and using logical and sequential thinking when programming devices or simulations.

> ➤ Whatever software or programming environment is being explored – from working with programming blocks to flow charts or text-based programming languages – there are fundamental processes such as logical reasoning and working with algorithms, which underpin this aspect of computing and are therefore made explicit in the programme of study for primary computing.

> ➤ Computing is multi-disciplinary in nature, which concurs with Livingstone and Hope's review of this area of the curriculum (Livingstone and Hope, 2011). That is, effective programming and

computing is a creative endeavour in which children will also need to draw on their digital literacy skills to create artefacts that others want to engage with and to solve problems drawing on their own and others' resilience and ingenuity. Whether designing and creating a new game in Scratch or designing and developing an app for a smartphone with a program such as App Inventor, children will need to draw on a range of skills, knowledge and understanding. This will at times involve: engaging with the process of design to develop their ideas; applying their digital literacy skills to manipulate various digital media assets such as images and sound; developing their computational thinking as they work out what algorithms they need to make a game, app or program work; and testing and evaluating what they have created to identify any bugs or ways of improving their work.

➢ The role of the teacher and their pedagogical strategies in promoting and helping children to synthesise these dispositions and capabilities should not be underestimated.

M-LEVEL EXTENSION   > >   M-LEVEL EXTENSION   > >   M-LEVEL EXTENSION

Find out more about how to assess the various elements of primary computing introduced and discussed in this chapter. Consult the following resources as a starting point:

- M. Berry (2013) *Computing in the Primary Curriculum: A Guide for Primary Teachers*. Bedford: Computing at School. Available at **www.computingatschool.org.uk/**.
- K. Brennan and M. Resnick (2012) *New Frameworks for Studying and Assessing the Development of Computational Thinking*. Available at **http://web.media.mit.edu/~kbrennan/files/ Brennan_Resnick_AERA2012_CT.pdf**.

REFERENCES REFERENCES **REFERENCES** REFERENCES **REFERENCES** REFERENCES

Bagge, P. (2012) *Sandwich Bot*. Available at **https://www.youtube.com/watch?v=IeBEFaVHIIE**.

Berry, M. (2011) *Scratch Fish Demo*. Available at **www.youtube.com/watch?v=TV0MqrmLpgU**.

Berry, M. (2013) *Computing in the National Curriculum: A Guide for Primary Teachers*. Bedford: Computing at School. Available at **www.computingatschool.org.uk/**.

Brennan, K. and Resnick, M. (2012) *New Frameworks for Studying and Assessing the Development of Computational Thinking*. Available at **http://web.media.mit.edu/~kbrennan/files/ Brennan_Resnick_AERA2012_CT.pdf**.

Burton, J. (2013) *Orchard Game*. Available at **http://scratch.mit.edu/users/JeremyBurton/** (accessed 11 January 2014).

Csizmadia, A., Curzon, P., Dorling, M., Humphreys, S., Ng, T., Celby, C. and Woolard, J. (2015) *Computational Thinking: A Guide for Teachers*. Available at **www.computingatschool.org.uk**.

Cuny, J., Snyder, L. and Wing, J.M. (2010) 'Demystifying Computational Thinking for Non-computer Scientists'. Unpublished manuscript in progress, referenced in **https://www.cs.cmu.edu/~CompThink/resources/TheLinkWing.pdf**.

DfE (2013) *National Curriculum in England: Primary Curriculum*. London: DfE. Available at **https://www.gov.uk/government/publications/national-curriculum-in-england-primary-curriculum**.

Kopelke, K. (2012) *Making Your Classroom Buzz with Bee-Bots*. Available at **http://elresources.skola.edu.mt/wp-content/uploads/2010/06/doc_669_2468_beebotguideA4v2.pdf**.

Livingstone, I. and Hope, A. (2011) *Next Gen. Transforming the UK into the World's Leading Talent Hub for the Video Games and Visual Effects Industries*. London: NESTA. Available at **www.nesta.org.uk/publications/assets/features/next_gen**.

Papert, S. (1993) *Mindstorms: Children, Computers and Powerful Ideas*, 2nd edn. New York: Perseus.

Pea, R. (1983) *Logo Programming and Problem Solving*. Paper presented at symposium of the American Educational Research Association, 'Chameleon in the Classroom: Developing Roles for Computers', Montreal, Canada. Available at **http://hal.archives-ouvertes.fr/docs/00/19/05/46/PDF/A39_Pea_87d_CCT_TR_MS.pdf**.

Perkins, N. (2014) The Hungry Monkey. Available at https://scratch.mit.edu/projects/21416773/

Resnick, M. (2012) *Mother's Day, Warrior Cats, and Digital Fluency: Stories from the Scratch Online Community*. Available at **web.media.mit.edu/~mres/papers/mothers-day-warrior-cats.pdf**.

Resnick, M. and Siegel, D. (2015) *A Different Approach to Coding: How Kids Are Making and Remaking Themselves*. Available at **https://medium.com/bright/a-different-approach-to-coding-d679b06d83a#.l34rk9ntk**.

Turvey, K. (2015) *Teaching Computing to Primary Age Children*. Sage Video Tutorial. Available at: **http://bcove.me/oouug2wh**.

USEFUL LINKS

Barefoot Computing: **http://barefootcas.org.uk/**

Codeclub: **https://www.codeclub.org.uk/**

Computing at School: **www.computingatschool.org.uk/**

DfE Expert Advisory Group: **https://sites.google.com/site/primaryictitt/home**

Flowol 4: **www.flowol.com/**

Kodu Game Lab: **www.kodugamelab.com/**

Mit App Inventor: **www.appinventor.org**

Simon Haughton's website: **www.simonhaughton.co.uk/scratch-programming/**

Terrapin Tools for Thinking: **www.terrapinlogo.com/project-ideas.php#Anchor-project3**

Textease Turtle CT: **www.textease.com/turtle/**

FURTHER READING   FURTHER READING   FURTHER READING   FURTHER READING

Passey, D. (2015) 'Computer science (CS) or information and communication technologies (ICT): the curriculum needs both', in A. Brodnik and C. Lewin (eds), *IFIP TC3 Working Conference 'A New Culture of Learning: Computing and Next Generations': Proceedings*. IFIP, Vilnius University, Vilnius, Lithuania, 1–3 July, pp. 26-44. Available at **www.ifip2015.mii.vu.lt/file/repository/IFIP_Proceedings.pdf**.

9
Physical computing

Chapter objectives

When you have completed work on this chapter, you will have:

- understood how computational thinking and programming is embedded within the physical world and devices to solve problems, automate and control aspects of our environment;
- considered how to develop children's understanding of physical computing;
- examined a range of software and devices that can be used to get children actively and creatively engaged in physical computing activities;
- understood how developing children's understanding of physical computing addresses the National Curriculum for computing.

Introduction

In this chapter, we look at how physical computing can offer rich opportunities for children to develop a broad and deep understanding of the significance and application of computing in the wider world and society. By physical computing we mean the exploration and creation of physical objects or systems which have elements of computing embedded within them. Craft and Dare (2012, p.6) characterise physical computing as the use of electronic and digital components to 'mimic, augment and surpass the body's own sensory capabilities, detecting changes in light, sound, temperature, pressure and so on.' So, for example, think of the many familiar real-world objects or environments we interact with every day that have computers embedded within them such as vending machines, lifts, toys, mobile phones, TV remote controls, cars. Physical computing offers significant promise to many fields of human endeavour and none more so than biomedical engineering where it has brought hope for people paralysed with spinal injuries as this BBC report illustrates (2015): **www.bbc.co.uk/news/health-34335514**.

There are now many educational resources available that can be used to develop children's understanding of the ways in which computers can be utilised to express our designs and ideas physically or automate and interact with our physical world and environment to solve problems. We discussed earlier in Chapter 8 how programmable toys can be used to develop children's understanding of computational thinking as they create and explore different algorithms through programming and controlling toys and robots. However, programmable toys and robots tend to be closed systems in which the inputs and outputs have been pre-determined by the makers. In this chapter we focus on some of the more open-ended resources which lend themselves to creative and imaginative projects with primary aged children in which they can explore the integration and control of electronic components in systems, models or artefacts they design and create themselves. As we have discussed before, these approaches emphasise the interdisciplinary and creative nature of computing (Loveless, 2009; Livingstone and Hope, 2011; Craft and Dare, 2012; Halverson and Sheridan, 2014; Resnick and Siegel, 2015).

What do the programmes of study for Key Stages 1 and 2 include?

In Chapter 8, Computational Thinking and Programming, we focused on the Computer Science elements of the programme of study as a whole. We reproduce these here because they are relevant to this chapter but we have also underlined the aspects of these that relate more specifically to physical computing. For example:

Key Stage 1

- <u>Understand what algorithms are, how they are implemented as programs on digital devices</u>, and that programs execute by following precise and unambiguous instructions
- Create and debug simple programs
- Use logical reasoning to predict the behaviour of simple programs

Key Stage 2

- <u>Design, write and debug programs that accomplish specific goals, including controlling or simulating physical systems</u>; solve problems by decomposing them into smaller parts
- Use sequence, selection and repetition in programs; work with variables and various forms of input and output
- Use logical reasoning to explain how some simple algorithms work and to detect and correct errors in algorithms and programs

(DfE, 2013)

From a young age, children have a fascination with how things work. If we are to encourage this and develop their understanding of what algorithms are and how they are implemented on digital devices (KS1), then giving them the opportunity to explore physical computing and how this is manifest through electronics in digital devices is important. In terms of progression through primary school, we might expect children to become more confident and competent at working with and controlling digital components as their understanding of this aspect of computing develops. However, it should be acknowledged that this is ambitious and requires a whole-school approach that allows children to build on their experiences in order to design, write and debug programs to control and simulate physical systems (KS2). This is not something that is achieved within the scope of a single lesson but across numerous lessons and experiences which give children plenty of time to explore, experiment and build on their knowledge. This has implications for pedagogy but it is also important to build on children's wider cultural and out-of-school experiences and interests, which we turn briefly to now.

The broader context – the 'maker' movement

It is worth pausing for a moment to consider the broader context within which we are teaching because although the way we teach computing in primary schools is dependent on the resources we have to draw on in school, opportunities to make connections with the children's out-of-school experiences and cultural lives are also vital. In recent years there has been a significant growth of what is often referred to as the maker movement (Halverson and Sheridan, 2014). Many towns and cities now hold annual Digital Maker Faires, where children, young people and adults come together to explore a range of electronic components and digital technologies to incorporate into their own creative projects. Halverson and Sheridan (2014, p.497) refer to Maker Faires as events that 'combine the features of science, renaissance, and craft fairs, including live demonstrations, showcase booths, product sales, and opportunities for attendees to create their own projects'. Anderson (2012) makes the claim that we are witnessing a new industrial revolution with the growth of people and communities interested in and participating in digital making via the burgeoning 'makerspaces' that are emerging. Similarly, Craft and Dare (2012, p.7) argue that the burgeoning array of low-cost digital components and tools have created the ideal conditions 'for new kinds of creative exploration and expression'.

PRACTICAL TASK PRACTICAL TASK PRACTICAL TASK PRACTICAL TASK

Find out about the Crumble controller by watching the video at this link: **https://vimeo.com/94097687**.

To get a feel for what the maker movement is all about and a simple project that could be adapted for the primary classroom, read the following blog post (Burton, 2015) about a morning spent at the Brighton and Hove Maker Faire: **http://jeremysblog.co.uk/digital-education/crumble-monster/**. Find out if there is a Digital Maker Faire or a makerspace in your own locality. If possible, make time to arrange a visit to find out more about the wide range of resources and ideas available to support physical computing activities in the primary classroom.

Think about how you could adapt the Crumble Monster activity for the primary classroom if you had access to the Crumble Controller kit.

Six year-old learning to solder at the Brighton Maker Faire

Getting into components and terminology

Like we did in Chapter 8, to build your knowledge and understanding of physical computing, we will examine more closely a familiar object that we tend to take for granted. It can also be a useful approach in the primary classroom to get the children to think about everyday objects that have some aspect of computing embedded in them and analyse more closely how the object actually works. For example, think about a simple front or rear bicycle light (Figure 9.1). Bicycle lights have become much more sophisticated and many now have a range of settings. Some incorporate a rechargeable power unit that plugs into your desktop or laptop computer via USB for charging, with lights (outputs) to indicate when it is fully charged. Most bicycle lights have different settings such as on-and-off flashing routines or random routines whereby the LED outputs (Light Emitting Diodes) inside the light turn on and off in a randomised sequence. How is this achieved?

Figure 9.1 shows the anatomy of a bicycle light. Many of the components such as LEDs (light emitting diodes), batteries, the circuit board and switch will be familiar. What may be less familiar to some and certainly to many of the children we teach is the small chip known as a microcontroller. All electronic devices that have different modes of operation (e.g. flashing routines, randomised routines) have a microcontroller embedded in the circuit somewhere. So what is a microcontroller? A microcontroller is defined by Wikipedia (2016) as:

A small computer system on a chip – a single integrated circuit containing a processor core, memory, and programmable inputs/outputs.

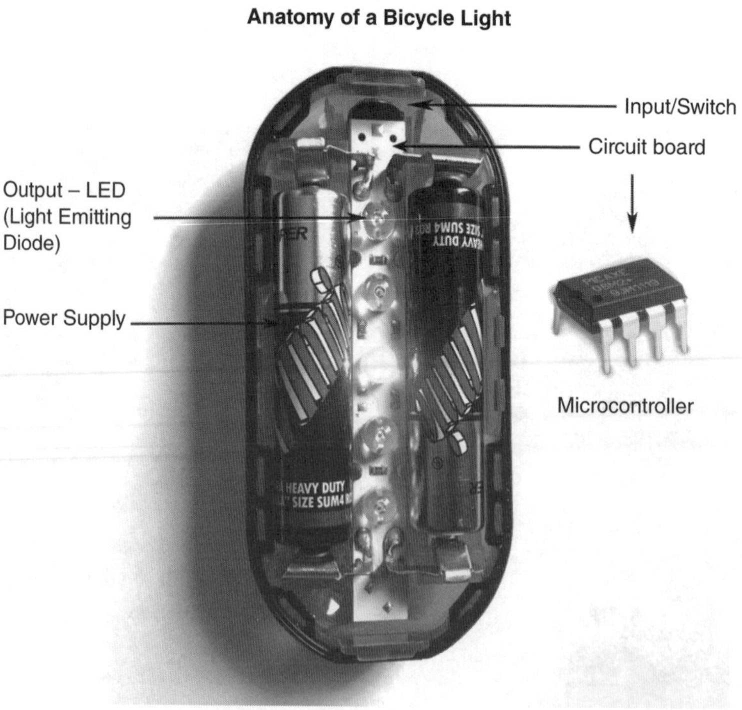

Anatomy of a Bicycle Light

Figure 9.1 Inside of a bicycle light

If you look closely at the image of the microcontroller in Figure 9.1, you will notice it has four pins on each side of its main body. These are the input/output pins that will be integrated into the circuit on the circuit board processing information from the inputs (Switch) and sending information to the various outputs (e.g. LEDs) . The memory and central processing unit (CPU – a sort of on-board clock) are integrated within the main body of the chip. Because the microcontroller has memory and a processor it is able to store and process algorithms which means it controls the LED outputs' modes of operation (e.g. all LEDs on, LEDs flashing, random LEDs and so on). A microcontroller is like having a very small computer embedded within a physical device, enabling us to program that device to behave in certain ways. Microcontrollers come in different sizes with different numbers of inputs and outputs, different sized memories and different capacity processing speeds. However, modern manufacturing processes mean that they can be very small and even microscopic.

IN THE CLASSROOM

A Year 5 class are studying the topic Light in science. Linked to this they are also considering different aspects of light such as how we use light to keep us safe in the winter. As part of the computing curriculum the teacher has collected a selection of different kinds of bicycle lights and the children have been comparing these. Some older lights only have one mode of operation (on/off) and older types of bulbs, whereas others have a number of LEDs and multiple functions. The children and the teacher discuss whether all of these lights have computing embedded in them or only some. They consider whether any digital information is being processed inside the devices. For example, the children notice that the switches (input) on some of the newer types of light respond to a short click and a long click e.g. click and hold. The children are also investigating some lights that no longer work and have taken them apart to see more closely what is inside. When they have investigated the lights and explored their different modes and patterns of operation they try to write down and explain the algorithms controlling some of the lights using flow charts.

In the first half of this chapter we have focused on developing our own knowledge and understanding of physical computing. Taking discarded devices apart and thinking about how they work as described in the example from classroom practice above is a good way of fuelling children's natural curiosity about computing and small digital devices such as phones. However, a word of caution is also vital. As teachers we should always assess any risks involved in the activities we plan to carry out with children and taking things apart can involve increased exposure to risks. For example, small components carry risk of choking and discarded computers and devices may have power units that retain a residual electric charge and therefore remain an electrical shock hazard even when unplugged. You also need to take care in case any battery acid has leaked if taking apart small electrical devices like bicycle lights. If you are going to disassemble a digital device with children as part of a lesson, then please consider the age appropriateness of this and carry out a thorough risk assessment before doing so.

In the second half of this chapter we examine a range of resources and approaches that can be used in the primary phase to support children to incorporate physical computing in their own projects and extend their own capabilities as digital makers.

Children as makers

We want now to focus on how as teachers we can draw on a range of resources and approaches to deepen children's understanding of physical computing as well as support them in developing the kinds of dispositions and skills needed to become increasingly creative with the ways in which they incorporate elements of physical computing into their own ideas and projects. As we stressed in the second half of Chapter 8, supporting children to design, develop and create their own games in different programming environments is something that needs to be developed over time and the same is true for extending this approach into aspects of physical computing. There is an ever increasing range of resources available to support physical computing projects and it is impossible for us to cover the whole range here, but the principles relating to physical computing apply whatever equipment or resources are being used. Teachers and schools need to make careful decisions about the scope and potential that different platforms and hardware offer for their children. It can be useful to consider how open the systems on offer are in terms of what opportunities and activities they afford. All of the systems and hardware we feature in the second half of this chapter bring different educational opportunities but also have limitations. An effective teacher is one who understands both the opportunities and limitations as discussed below.

Lego WeDo

Lego offers a range of construction kits that can be linked to and controlled by a computer through various interfaces, allowing children to progress to a point where they can devise their own systems or robots that incorporate various light, sound, distance and tilt sensors (inputs) as well as motors, buzzers, LEDs and various outputs. For example, there is a range of Lego WeDo Kits, which can be controlled using the Lego visual programming language (Figure 9.2).

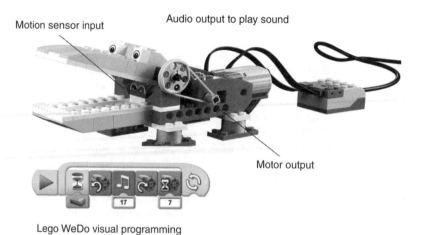

Motion sensor input

Audio output to play sound

Motor output

Lego WeDo visual programming blocks

**Figure 9.2 Lego WeDo Hungry Alligator kit and example
of visual program. Images courtesy of LEGO® Education www.LEGO
education.com © 2014 The LEGO Group**

In the example of the Hungry Alligator kit (Figure 9.2) the algorithm represented by the short visual program blocks illustrated is:

When the start key is pressed

Wait until motion is sensed

Turn the motor anticlockwise (7 tenths of a second)

Play sound 17 (a crunching noise)

Turn the motor clockwise (7 tenths of a second)

Repeat

The various programming blocks are combined to create programs that control the outputs and inputs embedded in the alligator. As we saw in Chapter 8 with Scratch, the blocks snap together in a sequence and the repeat block encapsulates the section of the program that is to be repeated much like the loop in the flow chart program we examined earlier. Lego WeDo can also interface and be programmed with Scratch. There are various Lego robotics and control systems available for different levels of competence and study. For example, the Lego Mindstorms products also offer the opportunity for children to build and control their own robots and controllable systems (**http://mindstorms.lego.com/en-gb/default.aspx**).

In order to design, develop and create their own physical and robotic models with Lego which can then be programmed and controlled children will need to develop significant experience over time, sometimes working with kits such as the WeDo example in Figure 9.2 and at other times devising their own controllable models or systems. For example, they could be given the task of using a Lego WeDo tilt sensor and building a simple game controller to integrate with a Scratch game they have designed and created. Have a look at the short video exploring the use of a tilt sensor to create a game controller joystick at **https://vimeo.com/129700065**. Similarly, have a look at the vimeo video channel from the teacher Mr Dowman which features a range of Lego WeDo projects, including some of his own inventions, at **https://vimeo.com/channels/927510**.

Makey Makey

Another device worth exploring for introducing children to aspects of physical computing in school is Makey Makey (see **www.makeymakey.com/**). Makey Makey is described as an Invention Kit. At its simplest Makey Makey is an input/output device that enables the user to imagine and create new ways of physically interacting with computer programs. So, for example, it could be linked to Scratch to create a physical interface for an onscreen game that children have created and programmed.

PRACTICAL TASK PRACTICAL TASK **PRACTICAL TASK** PRACTICAL TASK

Watch the introductory video to Makey Makey at the website link above. Read the Quick Start Guide at the following link **http://makeymakey.com/howto.php**. If possible, borrow a Makey Makey from your school or university resource centre. Make a console of inputs with whatever materials are available to control the outputs at the following sites:

- **www.kongregate.com/games/emst/idaft**
- **http://makeymakey.com/bongos/**
- **http://makeymakey.com/piano/**
- **www.freetetris.org/game.php**

When you have explored Makey Makey, think about how you could incorporate it into a physical computing project in your own classroom

The educational potential of a device like Makey Makey lies in its open-ended design. At its simplest it merely emulates common inputs found on a computer keyboard. As such it can be incorporated within any computer program to bring a physical element to its design. Furthermore, there are also numerous craft materials that can be utilised in the process. The photo shown in Figure 9.3 is an example of how Makey Makey can be incorporated as an extension activity into a Scratch project. Katie den Heijer, a primary computing specialist studying at Brighton University, created the project as part of a physical computing module in which she was tasked with creating a resource that could be used to develop children's computational thinking and model the ways in which computing can be embedded in our physical world. The physical game console to go with

**Figure 9.3 Mole in a Hole game with physical interface
by Katie den Heijer**

the Mole in a Hole game has been made using simple materials and copper sticky tape to create a circuit linking the moles to the arrow key inputs via Makey Makey. Each mole is mounted on a simple concertina paper spring which means the moles can be pushed like a switch to complete the circuit and create the input for the Scratch game. She has also created an online resource with various materials to illustrate how the resource could be used in the primary classroom, which can be found at the following link: **http://moleina hole.weebly.com**

Making a mobile phone app

Possibly the most familiar example of physical computing that has become embedded within many people's and young children's lives is the mobile phone or smartphone. But how do apps work and how are they made? The following classroom case study highlights a piece of software – App Inventor (**www.appinventor.org**) – which can be utilised in the primary classroom creatively to develop children's understanding of how programs such as apps work and are embedded in physical devices.

IN THE CLASSROOM

Lis Bundock and Pippa Totraku, Senior Lecturers in Primary Computing at the University of Brighton, led an app-making project at a local partnership school. The aim of the project was to build on the children's experience of programming with Scratch and use the open source software, MIT App Inventor, to explore how computational thinking is embedded within mobile devices and smartphones. App Inventor has a similar visual blocks programming language to Scratch, which is used to design, build and test apps on android smartphones. The project targeted children in Year 5 and 6, as this is a critical age when children, especially girls, make decisions about their aspirations to pursue computer science and ICT-related careers, which was another key aim of the project.

The school-based sessions ran for three hours a week over a ten-week period. The facilitators drew upon a range of teaching methods including face-to-face, online tutorials, web-based resources and practical workshops to ensure that all children could learn at their own pace. Prior to any programming, the children explored their understanding of computer science, computational thinking and the purpose of apps and their effectiveness. They then developed a range of core programming skills that provided them with the foundations necessary for designing, creating and testing their own mobile phone apps.

Motivation and engagement were high as children developed apps that reflected their own personal interests. Examples of some of the apps were: 'Shake the Beat' that you shook to play random songs that the pupils had recorded; 'I'm Bored' that worked as a Magic 8 ball and offered random ideas on what to do; and a 'Sound Box' that played sound bites of musical instruments. At the end of the project, the children connected their learning by taking the phones home to share and celebrate their apps with family and friends.

Let us have a closer look at how App Inventor works by analysing part of one of the apps that the children in this project created, 'Sound Box'. The screenshot in Figure 9.4 illustrates the design interface of App Inventor, which is used by the children to design the various mobile phone screens for their app and then assemble the various digital

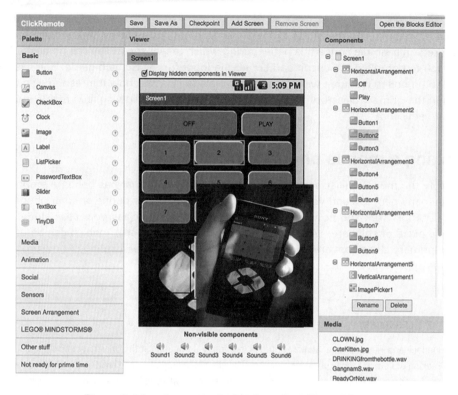

Figure 9.4 App Inventor design interface 'Sound Box'

assets that will be utilised such as sounds, images, buttons, backgrounds and so on. From this it is possible to see that before children proceed to this stage of constructing their app and assembling the digital assets, it is essential for them to have evaluated and discussed a range of different apps, paying attention to the layout and design of the various screens as well as the function of various components and the overall purpose of the app, as discussed in the example of classroom practice above. Much of this kind of work can be done away from the computer or software.

Once the children have designed and created the various digital assets (screens, images, buttons, sounds, animations and so on) they are brought together using the App Inventor software (Figure 9.4). Once all of the components for the app have been assembled in App Inventor they can be programmed using the Blocks Editor. This is where the programming of the various components and assets of the app (inputs and outputs) takes place and is similar to the Scratch in that it utilises graphical blocks that snap together to determine how the various buttons and digital assets that make up the smartphone app should behave.

Raspberry Pi

Other resources for the exploration of physical computing and electronics include the low-cost Raspberry Pi computer (**http://elinux.org/Raspberry_Pi**). Raspberry Pi is a small single board computer that can be linked to a keyboard, monitor and network and runs on the open source Linux operating system. It is referred to as single board because all of the components are contained on one circuit board as can be seen in Figure 9.5. Raspberry Pi also supports various programming languages including Scratch and, for more advanced users, a language called Python. The educational advantage of the Raspberry Pi is that it is an open and expandable system. By this we mean that the components are visible and not encased within a metal container like most of the computers we are used to using (see Figure 9.5). This means that children can start to become familiar with the components within the computer and begin to develop an understanding of their functions. In addition, Raspberry Pi can be integrated with other physical components. For example, it is possible to connect numerous peripherals such as expansion boards. An expansion board – also sometimes referred to as a 'breakout board' – is an electronic circuit board which allow users to connect LEDs, motors and various sensors to the Raspberry Pi which can then be programmed and controlled either using the Scratch or Python programming languages.

Let's consider in more detail what Raspberry Pi offers educationally. It is fair to say that you need to take some time setting up Raspberry Pi. The philosophy behind this computer is that users become familiar with the workings of the computer so it is not designed to simply take out of the box, plug in and go. It is necessary to spend some time downloading the operating system and configuring the SD card (1). Although this may seem daunting at first for those not used to tinkering with computers, it is not as difficult as it sounds and there are numerous start-up demonstrations that can be found on YouTube as well as the helpful and detailed start-up guide available via the official Raspberry Pi website at the following link: **www.raspberrypi.org/quick-start-guide**. This also creates an opportunity to discuss with learners the role of operating systems. An operating system is 'a collection of software that manages computer hardware resources and provides common services for computer programs' (Wikipedia, 2013). Every digital device requires an operating system for applications software to run on them. Most of

Figure 9.5 Raspberry Pi computer. Adapted from original image courtesy of Paul Beech and www.raspberrypi.org

the digital devices such as smartphones, tablets, laptops and desktop computers come with the operating systems pre-installed (e.g. Windows, Android, Mac OS X, Linux, etc.). Installing the operating system on the Raspberry Pi is an opportunity to explore and discuss the function of operating systems with learners rather than merely taking for granted this aspect of computer architecture. Once the operating system has been downloaded and installed on the SD card (1), the Raspberry Pi is ready to connect and use. Firstly it needs a power supply and this can be supplied via a micro USB lead (2) connected to another computer's USB slot. Some mobile phone chargers can also be used to supply power to the Rasberry Pi (see **www.raspberrypi.org/quick-start-guide** for further guidance on this). The Raspberry Pi is connected to a TV or computer monitor via the HDMI output (5) and the USB inputs (4) are used for connecting the mouse and keyboard. Once the initial set-up has been completed the process does not need to be repeated and the Raspberry Pi can operate as a fully functioning computer. Various software (e.g. Scratch, Python) come pre-installed within the operating system as does a simple web browser which can be used for searching the Internet when Raspberry Pi is connected via an ethernet cable (9). Again solving the problem of connecting the Raspberry Pi to the internet is an educational opportunity which learners can be fully involved in.

Perhaps where the Raspberry Pi offers the most opportunities for learning about how computers can actually work to control and automate our environment is in the capacity to expand the Raspberry Pi system. If you examine Figure 9.5 again closely you will notice a set of pins, which are labelled General Purpose Input/Output or GPIO pins (8). It is possible to buy connectors which connect these input and output pins to a solder-free breakout board into which wires can be pushed as well as various other electrical components such as light emitting diodes (LEDs), push switches and various other sensors which can then be programmed and controlled. See the short video at the following link which illustrates RaspberryPi used to program an LED simulation of a pelican crossing: **https://vimeo.com/126906876**.

While this is not the kind of activity you would undertake with the whole class it would be worthwhile to establish a computing development area in your classroom where children could explore this application of computing to simple electronics and begin to explore how computing is embedded in various automated systems through the use of various electrical components. There are some helpful blogs that outline how to exploit the RaspberryPi in these ways. For example, Simon Walter has a series of tutorials on how to use Scratch to control the GPIO pins on a Raspberry Pi available at the following link: **http://cymplecy.wordpress.com/2013/04/22/scratch-gpio-version-2-introduction-for-beginners/**.

In the Classroom

A Year 6 class have set up a maker area in their classroom with a Raspberry Pi, a breakout board and LEDs. They have simulated a traffic light system with the LEDs and have written a program to help Scratchy the cat cross the road when the traffic lights are on red. Watch the short video at the following link: **https://vimeo.com/126906876**.

Further resources for physical computing

There are other low-cost devices similar to Raspberry Pi which can be used with children to explore computing and electronics. For example, the Picaxe microcontroller products (**www.picaxe.com/What-Is-PICAXE**) are based on the same principles of an open system and can be used to develop various electronics projects which can then be programmed. Picaxe also make various pre-assembled electronic kits such as the dice kit below (Figure 9.6). With the dice project the object is to program the LEDs to light to produce random numbers like traditional dice. The dice is activated by the push button. Picaxe offer a range of cheap kits that introduce children to programming and electronics. For example the Simple PIC Kit involves three traffic light LEDs and the Safety Light Kit uses high intensity LEDs which are programmed to flash in various sequences to create a pedestrian or cyclist safety light. The Picaxe microcontrollers embedded in the kits connect to a computer via a USB port and can then be programmed using Logicator which is a flowchart programming language not unlike Flowol that we discussed earlier in this chapter. The kits can also be programmed with Flowol.

Another device that has recently been introduced is the BBC micro:bit. Again it is a small microcontroller device much like the Crumble we introduced at the start of this chapter. The BBC micro:bit has been given free to schools in the UK, one for every Year 7 child. Although this has been targeted at the beginning of secondary education it could be used in primary education. The micro:bit has LEDs built into the device which can be programmed, as well as integrated switches, inputs and sensors. Find out more about the micro:bit at the following link: **https://www.microbit.co.uk/**. Similarly, another device that integrates a range of components (switches, sensors, audio speaker) in a single device is the Picoboard. Again this is a useful device for developing physical computing projects with children (see **https://learn.sparkfun.com/tutorials/using-the-sparkfun-picoboard-and-scratch**).

Open systems like the ones we have explored in this chapter can be used to develop children's understanding of how computing hardware and software is used to both monitor and control our physical environment, as well as to create and invent apps or digital devices.

**Figure 9.6 Picaxe electronic dice kit. Image courtesy
of Revolution Education Ltd www.picaxe.com**

Building children's hands-on experience of the range of electronic input devices such as light, sound and motion sensors and their respective output devices such as LEDs, motors and buzzers can offer insights into computer science for children. However, such experiences have to be built over time. There are of course pedagogical and classroom management implications concerning the exploration of physical computing. As we suggested earlier, it is unlikely that teachers will have the resources to explore some of these projects together with a whole class. The advantage of programming environments such as Scratch or App Inventor is that it is possible for a whole class to be working on similar projects at the same time, for example during a session in the computer suite or on a class set of laptops. However, working with physical objects such as Lego WeDo, Makey Makey or Crumble devices or exploring programming and electronics with Raspberry Pi lend themselves much more to focused group work where the teacher can scaffold the children's learning and problem-solving as appropriate and over a longer period of time. Despite this, even with only a few devices available, once the children understand what is possible with these devices, there is a great deal of designing and making that can be done before connecting to the device. For example, to design and create a games controller or a physical interface for their Scratch games not every child needs a Makey Makey. The children could take turns to test their games interface and improve them.

We have covered a range of devices in this chapter and provided an introduction to the creative potential of physical computing. However, there is no doubt that new devices will appear as components become more affordable and interest in creating and inventing with digital technologies becomes more accessible. As Halverson and Sheridan (2015, p.503) comment:

> *Bringing the maker movement into the education conversation has the potential to transform how we understand 'what counts' as learning, a learner, and as a learning environment.*

That is, learning through doing and making is given new meaning in a digital age where hopefully creativity and inventiveness with digital technology can be valued. Given the growth and increasing power of digital devices connected via networks we also believe that it is vital for children to begin to understand the power and potential of physical computing as more and more ways of embedding computing into the physical world emerge and are invented. The potential of the internet to shape the way we engage with our physical world has begun to be explored further. That is, while the internet is essentially a communication tool, it not only enables us to communicate with other people, but can facilitate increased digital interaction with our physical environment as the objects we engage with can be programmed to respond in different ways.

REFLECTIVE TASK

Watch the video *What Is the Internet of Things?* (FW Thinking , 2013) at the following link: **www.youtube.com/watch?v=LVIT4sX6uVs**. Think about how we engage with the internet has changed over the duration of your life. What is your response to some of the future predictions regarding the 'internet of things' highlighted in this video? Think about the ways in which algorithms are currently used to build computational thinking into our physical environment as discussed in Chapter 8. What could be some of the moral and ethical issues underlying the predictions made in the video *What is the Internet of Things?*

If children are to develop a critical understanding of the ways in which computing may be embedded in the physical world they need to develop an understanding of the way such devices work. It should be clear from this chapter that this is a multidisciplinary endeavour encompassing working with art, design, materials and electronic circuits at the very least. We hope that the range of resources and ideas presented in this chapter have given readers an introduction and insight into the increasing opportunities for physical computing as a creative endeavour in primary school.

A SUMMARY OF **KEY POINTS**

> Physical computing involves the application of computing and computational thinking across a range of potential disciplines (Design and Technology, Art and Design, Media, Science, Engineering).

> Physical computing involves a deep understanding of how a range of electronic components and various media can be utilised to interact with and control our physical world.

> Physical computing offers children opportunities to develop a range of dispositions – creativity, invention, ingenuity, problem-solving and collaboration – as they work together on different design and make projects.

> Children need practice, time and support to develop their understanding of physical computing.

M-LEVEL EXTENSION > > M-LEVEL EXTENSION > > M-LEVEL EXTENSION

Find out more about Raspberry Pi (**www.raspberrypi.org**) or Crumble Controller (**http://redfernelectronics. co.uk/product/crumble-kit/**). Familiarise yourself with the different components of the single board computers and their function. Carry out further research online to discover the kinds of projects they have been used to develop. Think about how you could integrate a Raspberry Pi or the Crumble Controller into a developer area into your classroom to enable children to explore the potential of such devices and develop their understanding of physical computing.

REFERENCES REFERENCES **REFERENCES** REFERENCES REFERENCES REFERENCES

Anderson, C. (2012) *Makers: The New Industrial Revolution*. New York: Crown.

BBC News (2015) 'Paralysed man moves legs using brain reading device'. Available at **www.bbc. co.uk/news/health-34335514**.

Burton, J. (2015) *Crumble Monster*. Available at **http://jeremysblog.co.uk/digital-education/ crumble-monster/**.

Craft, B. and Dare, E. (2012) *Physical Computing*. London: Goldsmiths, University of London.

Den Heijer, K. (2015) *Mole in a Hole*. Available at **http://moleinahole.weebly.com/**.

DfE (2013) *National Curriculum in England: Primary Curriculum*. London: DfE. Available at **https:// www.gov.uk/government/publications/national-curriculum-in-england-primary-curriculum**.

FW Thinking (2013) *What Is the Internet of Things?* Available at **www.youtube.com/watch?v= LVIT4sX6uVs**.

Halverson, E.R. and Sheridan, K.M. (2014) 'The Maker Movement in education', *Harvard Educational Review*, 84(4), pp.495–504.

Livingstone, I. and Hope, A. (2011) *Next Gen. Transforming the UK into the World's Leading Talent Hub for the Video Games and Visual Effects Industries*. London: Nesta. Available at **www.nesta. org.uk/publications/assets/features/next_gen**.

Loveless, A. (2009) 'Thinking about creativity: developing ideas, making things happen', in A. Wilson (ed.), *Creativity in Primary Education*, 2nd edn. Exeter: Learning Matters.

Resnick, M. and Siegel, D. (2015) *A Different Approach to Coding: How Kids Are Making and Remaking Themselves*. Available at **https://medium.com/bright/a-different-approach-to-coding-d679b06d83a#.l34rk9ntk**.

USEFUL LINKS

Crumble Controller: **http://redfernelectronics.co.uk/product/crumble-kit/** and **http://4tronix. co.uk/blog/?p=894**

Geek Gurl Diaries: **www.geekgurldiaries.co.uk**

Lego Mindstorms: **http://www.lego.com/en-gb/mindstorms/?domainredir=mindstorms.lego.com**

Lego WeDo and Scratch: **http://info.scratch.mit.edu/WeDo**

Makerspaces: **https://www.makerspaces.com/**

Makey Makey: **www.makeymakey.com/**

MIT App Inventor: **www.appinventor.org**

Picaxe Micro-controllers: **www.picaxe.com/What-Is-PICAXE**

Raspberry Pi: **www.raspberrypi.org**

Raspberry Pi Wiki Hub: **http://elinux.org/Raspberry_Pi**

FURTHER READING FURTHER READING FURTHER READING FURTHER READING

Philbin, C. (2014) *Adventures in Raspberry Pi*. Chichester: Wiley.

10
Web literacy (including coding for the web)

Chapter objectives

When you have completed work on this chapter, you will have:

- understood some of the key concepts and terminology associated with the web;
- developed your knowledge of web literacy and how this relates to the National Curriculum;
- considered pedagogical approaches to developing children's web literacy;
- explored a range of software tools that can support the development of children's knowledge, understanding and skills in relation to web literacy.

Introduction

In 1989, while working at CERN, Englishman Tim Berners-Lee wrote a proposal for what was to become the World Wide Web. The response from his manager at the time did not foretell the impact this innovation was to have on the world. 'Vague, but exciting' was the feedback that was handwritten on the draft document (World Wide Web Foundation, 2016a).

During the opening ceremony for the 2012 Olympic Games, Berners-Lee made a typically self-effacing appearance in a section that celebrated the invention of the World Wide Web. The slogan 'This is for everyone' was displayed in flashing LED lights around the stadium, making reference to Berners-Lee's commitment to protecting an open web, accessible to all and free from corporate or government control (World Wide Web Foundation, 2016b; TED, 2014).

The knowledge, understanding and skills related to the web are commonly referred to collectively as 'web literacy'. The Mozilla Foundation, a non-profit organisation that shares Berners-Lee's commitment to protecting an open web (Mozilla, 2016a), run education campaigns to promote understanding of the World Wide Web (herein referred to simply as 'the web') and all that it has to offer. They have produced a very useful Web Literacy Map that clearly identifies its many different facets (Mozilla, 2016b). Spending some time exploring this map is a worthwhile exercise for teachers.

This chapter will help you to develop your understanding of the technologies upon which the web relies and will present some suggested starting points for teaching children about these technologies. Issues of online safety arise in this chapter – including ethical and legal questions concerning copyright – but are dealt with more fully in Chapters 17 and 18.

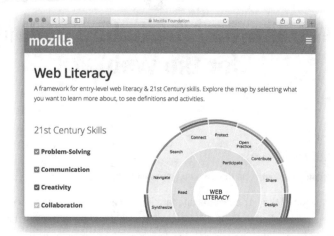

Figure 10.1 Click on a segment of the map for more information

What do the programmes of study for Key Stages 1 and 2 include?

Key Stage 1

- use technology purposefully to create, organise, store, manipulate and retrieve digital content
- recognise common uses of information technology beyond school
- use technology safely and respectfully, keeping personal information private; identify where to go for help and support when they have concerns about content or contact on the internet or other online technologies

Key Stage 2

- understand computer networks, including the internet; how they can provide multiple services, such as the World Wide Web, and the opportunities they offer for communication and collaboration
- use search technologies effectively, appreciate how results are selected and ranked, and be discerning in evaluating digital content
- select, use and combine a variety of software (including internet services) on a range of digital devices to design and create a range of programs, systems and content that accomplish given goals, including collecting, analysing, evaluating and presenting data and information
- use technology safely, respectfully and responsibly; recognise acceptable/unacceptable behaviour; identify a range of ways to report concerns about content and contact

(DfE, 2013)

Mozilla's Web Literacy Map (Mozilla, 2016b) highlights three key dimensions of web literacy: reading, writing and participating. There are clear connections between each of these areas and the specific requirements of the computing programmes of study for Key Stages 1 and 2 shown above. Mozilla have produced some very useful activities and lesson plans to help teach the various aspects of web literacy (available at **https://learning. mozilla.org/activities**). These may require tailoring to your own specific context but they are an excellent starting point for teachers.

Understanding key terms and concepts

Equipping children with an understanding of the technologies that power the web will help them to make more informed and discriminating judgements about how they use it, thereby helping them to stay safe online and maximise the value of their web browsing. It can also enable them to become creators of content for the web, opening up a wider range of learning opportunities. In order to achieve this it is important that teachers have a sound grasp of key concepts and an understanding of relevant terminology.

The distinction between the internet and the web

The internet and the web are often referred to as though they were one and the same thing. This is not the case, though they are closely related. Put simply, the internet is a global network of computers, connected by cables, satellites and other wireless technologies. This network provides the hardware and communication technologies that facilitate the web but it also facilitates other digital technologies that we utilise on a daily basis, such as e-mail, voice-over-internet (VoIP) services and digital file sharing. The BBC has produced a simple 'Bitesize' guide to the internet that could be used in the classroom (available at **www.bbc.co.uk/guides/z3tbgk7**).

The web is the diverse but interlinked mass of data that we access – via the internet – in a form generally referred to as 'web pages', although the metaphor of a 'page' (taken from the world of print media) has started to look less appropriate as the web content we consume becomes increasingly dynamic and responsive to the range of devices that we use to access it. Another BBC Bitesize guide explains how the web works (available at **www.bbc.co.uk/guides/z2nbgk7**).

HTML

Hypertext Markup Language (HTML) is the language of the web. The content of webpages – headings, paragraphs, lists, links, images, etc. – is 'marked up' using a system of tags that wrap around these pieces of content. These tags are used by *web browsers* and *search engines* to identify these different elements of content. Later in this chapter we will explore this system of tags in more detail.

CSS

Cascading style sheets (CSS) is a layer of code added on top of *HTML* that defines how the various elements of content within a webpage should be presented by a web browser. For instance, it can be used to set the font size, weight and colour for the various elements of text within a webpage. It can also be used to manipulate the layout of content within a page: for instance, presenting a list of links as a tabbed menu across the top of the page. An introduction to writing CSS code is provided later in this chapter.

HTTP

Hypertext Transfer Protocol (HTTP) is a data transfer protocol. In simple terms, a data transfer protocol is a set of rules for moving data around on a computer network. HTTP essentially enables web browsers and web servers to communicate with each other.

Web server

Web servers host websites. When a user enters an address (*URL*) into the address bar of their web browser the web browser sends an HTTP request that is passed to a web server that then responds by sending back the requested webpage (an HTML document). If the webpage includes embedded media files (e.g. images, audio, video) or references other files, such as *CSS* style sheets or *JavaScript*, these assets will also be sent to the user's web browser. All this data is temporarily stored (or 'cached') on the user's computing device.

Web browser

A web browser is a piece of software that runs on a computing device. A web browser can communicate with web servers over the internet using HTTP, giving access to the wealth of data that is collectively referred to as 'the web'. Modern web browsers usually share common features such as back/forward navigation, tabbed browsing, access to browsing history, private browsing modes (which in theory don't store website data on the user's device) and quick access to search engines such as Google or Bing.

It is important to note that these days access to the web is offered on a wide range of devices, including mobile phones, tablets, TVs, laptops, games consoles and even wristwatches. Web browsers exist that are optimised for each of these device types. The most widely used web browsers on desktop and laptop computers are Microsoft's Internet Explorer, Google's Chrome, Mozilla's Firefox and Apple's Safari but other browsers, such as Opera, are commonly used on other kinds of devices, including mobile phones.

Search engine

The web consists of an enormous amount of data and therefore quickly finding relevant information is a potentially challenging problem. Search engines are designed to help solve that problem. A search engine is a program that searches for items in a database through the use of keywords. Search engines use 'web crawlers' to index the data that exists on the web. These web crawlers collect data – for instance, how many other websites link to a particular webpage – that is then used to help serve up the most relevant and useful content when a user enters a particular set of keywords into the search bar of a search engine.

While Google now offers a wide range of software systems, they are most closely identified with their search engine, which has gained huge popularity due to its speed and ability to return relevant search results. Other popular search engines include Microsoft's Bing and Yahoo! Niche search engines offer features such as greater privacy (e.g. DuckDuckGo) or combining search results from multiple search engines (e.g. Dogpile) To help children at KS2 develop an understanding of how search engines work, take a look at the BBC Bitesize website (available at **www.bbc.co.uk/guides/ztbjq6f**).

URL

A Uniform Resource Locator (URL) is the address of a resource that exists on the web (that is to say it is stored on an accessible *web server*). If we know the URL for a website, webpage or other web-based resource then we don't need to use a search engine to find it; we can simply type the URL into the address bar of our chosen web browser and an HTTP request for that resource will be sent.

Understanding the structure of a URL can help us to navigate web resources more easily. URLs can be likened to a postal address written in reverse order. Figure 10.2 shows how a URL can be broken down. The last part of this URL is the file name of the resource with its file extension: *index.html*. From this we can deduce that this is a URL for a webpage (the *.html* extension tells us this as .html is the extension for a webpage). The part of the URL immediately before indicates that this webpage is located inside a folder (also known as a *directory*) called *resources*.

http://www.mywebsite.co.uk/resources/index.html

Figure 10.2 Breaking down a URL

The *mywebsite.co.uk* part of the URL is known as the domain name. If we were to remove all that comes after this part, the remaining URL should take us to the homepage of this website. The *.co.uk* part of the domain name (known as the top-level domain) is a fairly strong indicator that this is a UK-based site but it is important to understand that there is nothing to prevent an individual, organisation or business from setting up a website with a *.co.uk* domain when they are geographically located elsewhere. The domain name alone should not be taken as any kind of guarantee of the relevance of the website or the veracity of the information contained within it.

Web URLs begin either with *http://* or *https://* – the latter indicating a secure connection, meaning that in theory the data sent between the web browser and web server cannot be intercepted as it is encrypted. Understanding the difference between secure and insecure connections is an important aspect of online safety education. Submitting credit card details over an insecure (http) connection, for example, leaves the user more vulnerable to credit card fraud.

These days many web browsers do not require the *http://* or *www.* component when entering a URL in their address bar and by default don't display these when a website is loaded.

PRACTICAL TASK PRACTICAL TASK PRACTICAL TASK PRACTICAL TASK

Search for an image on the web. Can you open the image in a browser tab on its own? Look at the URL in the browser address bar – can you see the image file name and extension at the end? The extension is likely to be .jpg, .png or .gif (common image file formats on the web). Being able to find the URL for a specific media resource on the web can be very useful.

JavaScript

JavaScript is a client-side scripting language that enables web developers to enhance the interactive behaviour of websites. *Client-side* means that the code is executed in the user's web browser rather than on the web server that serves the website. JavaScript can, for instance, be used to validate the data entered by a user before it is submitted in an online form (e.g. checking that a password uses a mixture of letters and numbers and is of a certain length). It can also be used to create sophisticated applications that can run in a web browser (e.g. an online photo editor).

JavaScript programming can quickly become very complex but, with appropriate support, children at the upper end of Key Stage 2 may be ready to begin exploring some more simple uses of it within their own webpages. For learning resources relating to JavaScript see the list of useful links at the end of this chapter.

Server-side programming

Website data are often generated by code that runs on the web server before webpages are sent to a user's web browser. Web servers also often interact with databases which can store data to be used in a website. The combination of server-side code and data-base interaction allows websites to serve up dynamic content that is matched to a user's needs, such as a customised news feed in a social media website or a weather forecast for your local area. Programming languages such as Ruby, Python and PHP can be used to write server-side code.

It is unlikely that children of primary age will be ready to engage in server-side programming but it could be helpful for them to have a broad understanding of principles so that they can understand the dynamic nature of some of the content that they will encounter on the web. If you find yourself supporting a particularly capable child who has an interest in learning more in this area then you could guide them towards some of the online learning resources mentioned later in this chapter.

An introduction to HTML coding

A bit of HTML code is all that is required to create a simple webpage. This code can be written in any text editor that supports plain text format. This includes Notepad on Windows and TextEdit on Mac OS X – both of which are shipped as part of the standard software suites for these platforms – although a text editor designed for coding, such as Brackets (free download at **http://brackets.io**), will offer additional features that can make the process a lot more efficient and enjoyable.

The following is a quick primer to help you develop your own understanding of how to create simple web pages with HTML. Later in this chapter we will explore some good ways of introducing primary-aged pupils to HTML and CSS coding, making use of the best online resources available to support their learning. You may well find these interactive resources helpful in supporting your own subject knowledge development.

As mentioned previously, HTML code consists of tags that are used to 'mark up' the various elements of content within a webpage. Here is a simple example of the HTML tags that would be used to mark up the main heading in a webpage:

```
<h1>My first webpage</h1>
```

Here we're using the <h1> tag, which is used to identify the most important heading in a webpage. HTML tags are always enclosed in angle brackets. You can see that the tags wrap around the content. An *opening* tag is followed by the actual content (in this case some text), which is then followed by a *closing* tag. The closing tag is differentiated from the opening tag by the inclusion of a / inside the tag. The <h1> to <h6> tags are used to identify the various levels of heading within an HTML document.

A paragraph of text would be marked up using <p> tags, as follows:

```
<p> Pellentesque habitant morbi tristique senectus et netus
et malesuada fames ac turpis egestas. Vestibulum tortor quam,
feugiat vitae, ultricies eget, tempor sit amet, ante. Donec eu
libero sit amet quam egestas semper. Aenean ultricies mi vitae
est. Mauris placerat eleifend leo.</p>
```

To add a list to a document we could use the following markup:

```
<ol>
    <li>List item one</li>
    <li>List item two</li>
    <li>List item three</li>
</ol>
```

The <ol> tag indicates the beginning of an ordered list. This is followed by three list items that are marked up with <li> tags. Finally a closing <ol> tag indicates the end of the ordered list. To create an unordered list, simply replace ol with ul.

Using the tags discussed above we can begin to create a simple text document for the web:

```
<h1>About Me</h1>
<h2>My family and other animals</h2>
<p>I have 3 sisters. Two are older than me and one is younger.</p>
<p>We have a dog called Barney and two gerbils, called Bubble and
Squeak.</p>
<h2>My top 3 films</h2>
<ol>
    <li>Chitty Chitty Bang Bang</li>
    <li>The Fox and the Hound</li>
    <li>Monsters Inc</li>
</ol>
<h2>My hobbies</h2>
<ul>
    <li>Playing the guitar</li>
    <li>Birdwatching</li>
    <li>Building websites</li>
</ul>
```

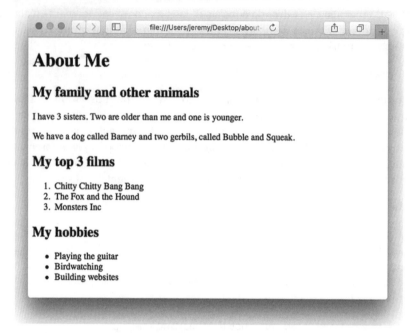

Figure 10.3 'About Me' webpage

This code generates the output shown in Figure 10.3 in a web browser.

HTML tags sometimes contain *attributes* and associated *values* that provide more information about the content element. A good example of this is when we want to add a hyperlink in our document:

```
<p>Visit <a href="http://www.myblog.co.uk">my blog</a> for more
details.</p>
```

In this case we are using the <a> tag (short for *anchor*) and the href attribute (short for *hyperlink reference*), to which we have assigned a value of *http://www.myblog.co.uk*. This is how we tell the web browser what the destination of our hyperlink should be. Note that values are assigned using = and should always be enclosed in quote marks.

An image could be added to our page using the following code:

```
<img src="my-image.jpg">
```

Note that in this instance there is no *closing* tag as there is no text content to mark up. The value assigned to the src attribute (short for *source*) specifies the image that we want to include.

Putting all of the above together we can create a simple HTML document:

```
<h1>About Me</h1>
<img src="photo-of-me.jpg">
<h2>My family and other animals</h2>
```

```
<p>I have 3 sisters. Two are older than me and one is younger.</p>
<p>We have a dog called Barney and two gerbils, called Bubble and
Squeak.</p>
<h2>My top 3 films</h2>
<ol>
    <li>Chitty Chitty Bang Bang</li>
    <li>The Fox and the Hound</li>
    <li>Monsters Inc</li>
</ol>
<h2>My hobbies</h2>
<ul>
    <li>Playing the guitar</li>
    <li>Birdwatching</li>
    <li>Building websites</li>
</ul>
<p>You can find out more about me on <a href="http://www.myblog.
co.uk">my blog</a>.</p>
```

The output is shown in Figure 10.4 in a web browser.

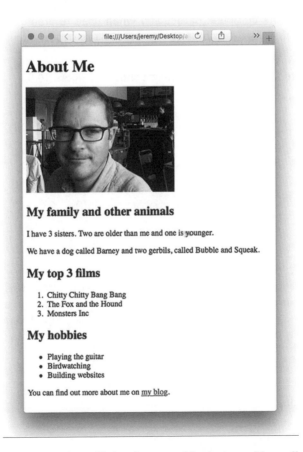

Figure 10.4 'About Me' webpage with photo and hyperlink

An introduction to adding CSS

Webpages produced using only HTML may be readable but they will lack the kind of design features that will make them really functional and visually appealing to the target audience. CSS allows us to add these important design features via style rules that can be applied to the different elements within a webpage or set of webpages.

Writing simple CSS style rules is something that children in upper Key Stage 2 are likely to be able to manage having mastered some basic HTML but it is worth noting that CSS can become quite complex, particularly when used to create more sophisticated page layouts, and therefore it is important to set realistic expectations of what might be achieved.

CSS rules are written using a simple syntax as shown in Figure 10.5.

Figure 10.5 CSS syntax

The *selector* identifies the HTML element that you wish to style. This is followed by a *declaration* - enclosed in curly braces - which includes a property and a value to be used by the target HTML element. Note the colon between the property and its value. Rules can include multiple declarations. Each declaration is terminated with a semi colon.

Here is an example of a CSS rule with three declarations:

```
h1 {
    font-weight: bold;
    font-size: 18px;
    color: #2a2a2a;
}
```

There is a wide range of CSS properties that can be set (visit **www.w3schools.com/css ref/default.asp** for a helpful list of CSS properties). A good place to start is with properties that style text.

Learning more

Interactive tutorial websites such as Playto (**https://learn.playto.io/html-css/lesson/0**), Codecademy (**https://www.codecademy.com/learn/make-a-website**) and Khan Academy (**https://www.khanacademy.org/computing/computer-programming/html-css**) offer excellent opportunities for teachers to develop their subject knowledge.

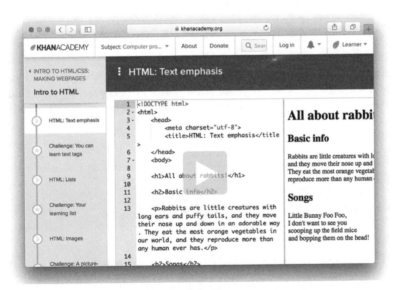

Figure 10.6 Khan Academy, Intro to HTML and CSS

Resources to support children's learning

Mozilla X-Ray Goggles

Exploring existing webpages using Mozilla's X-Ray Goggles (**https://teach.mozilla.org/tools**) can be a great way for children to start to develop some familiarity with HTML code. The X-Ray Goggles reveal the HTML that has been used to mark up elements within a webpage and can be enabled using an easy-to-install web browser 'bookmarklet'.

Once this has been installed you simply click it to enable the X-Ray Goggles on any webpage page you visit. The X-Ray Goggles not only reveal the underlying HTML code, they also allow the user to edit this code.

Children could use the X-Ray Goggles to remix a news article (e.g. from the BBC News website). They might start by locating the headline for the article (very likely marked up as an <h1> element) and then replacing this with their own headline text. After this they could try editing the paragraphs of text (almost certainly marked up with <p> tags. The X-Ray Goggles homepage features a sample activity, 'Hack the News', that is based on this idea. The challenge of replacing an image in a news article presents a good opportunity for children to learn about the construction of URLs (see above).

Once a webpage has been remixed with the X-Ray Goggles, it can be saved to a user's Webmaker account and a link to the saved remix can be shared with others. Links could be shared with the wider school community via a class blog or the school's website.

PRACTICAL TASK PRACTICAL TASK **PRACTICAL TASK** PRACTICAL TASK

Remix a news article on the BBC News site (http://www.bbc.co.uk/news) using the X-Ray Goggles. Set up a free Webmaker account and save your remix. Now share a link to your remix. Remember to remix responsibly!

Remixing webpages in this way will very likely prompt questions such as 'have I just hacked the BBC website?' This provides an opportunity for teaching the children more about how the web works. You can explain what a web browser is and how this stores

**Figure 10.7 Using Mozilla X-Ray Goggles to remix
a BBC News article ('public domain' photo sourced
using Creative Commons Search)**

web documents temporarily in a cache (see above). The version of the webpage that the child has remixed is this locally stored version and not the original version which remains untouched on the web server that hosts it.

This activity also presents opportunities to discuss responsible use of the web and the need for carefully checking the veracity of information found online.

Remixing with Mozilla Thimble

While the X-Ray Goggles allow children to start exploring the HTML code that is used to mark up the content of web documents, you will soon want to give them more freedom to create their own webpages. Mozilla Thimble (**https://learning.mozilla.org/tools**) offers a natural progression, providing opportunities for children to remix template HTML and CSS documents to create their own webpages. Alternatively, Thimble can be used by children to code web pages from scratch.

Children can get started with Thimble by remixing a simple Keep Calm and Carry On poster (see Figure 10.8 for an example remix) and can progress to more complex projects, for instance creating their own comic strip or movie poster. Thimble includes step-by-step tutorials for all sample activities and when children type their code, the editor offers up helpful coding hints and highlights errors. Educators can create their own Thimble activities and upload these to the Mozilla Learning site for others to remix.

As with the X-Ray Goggles, children's Thimble creations can be saved (if they are signed into a Webmaker account) and links to their webpages can then be shared. Providing a wider audience for the children's work can be a great motivator.

Activities such as those described above provide an excellent context for tackling important online safety issues, including copyright infringement. This relates to the expectations of the programme of study for Key Stage 2, which states that children must learn to 'use

**Figure 10.8 Using Mozilla Thimble to remix
a Keep Calm poster**

technology safely, respectfully and responsibly'. This would be a good opportunity to introduce Creative Commons licensing (visit **http://creativecommons.org** for more information) and 'public domain' media.

PRACTICAL TASK   PRACTICAL TASK   **PRACTICAL TASK**   PRACTICAL TASK

Using Mozilla Thimble, complete the 'Keep Calm' sample activity (available here: **https://learning.mozilla. org/tools**) and save your remix to your Webmaker account.

Other ways children can learn HTML and CSS

Whilst Mozilla's X-Ray Goggles and Thimble provide an excellent way for children to begin learning about the web and how webpages are coded, there are lots of alternative resources that can be utilised in and beyond the primary classroom. A growing number of interactive websites allow children to explore writing HTML and CSS code within the context of a guided online tutorial. These include interactive text editors where users can type code and receive instant feedback, creating a very powerful learning environment. They also often include audio-visual content that can help children develop understanding of more difficult concepts. The interactive tutorial websites mentioned previously, such as Playto and Codecademy, are not only valuable learning resources for teachers wishing to develop their subject knowledge but are also potentially suitable for use by children, particularly at the upper end of Key Stage 2.

Erase All Kittens (**https://eraseallkittens.com**) takes a novel approach to learning the languages of the web. In this interactive adventure the user has to learn about HTML and

Figure 10.9 Erase All Kittens, by Drum Roll:
an online platform game that teaches HTML and CSS

CSS in order to complete the different levels of the game. It offers the learner an immersive experience and a lot of fun. This may prove more appealing for some children than learning through a more standard tutorial-based approach.

IN THE CLASSROOM

Student teachers at the University of Brighton worked with children in Year 6, teaching them how to create their own webpages using HTML and CSS. In order to help them learn how to mark up elements in a web document, they created a giant HTML jigsaw. The children worked collaboratively to agree on the correct arrangement of the tags, attributes and values. This kind of activity, away from the computer screen, can help children learn from each other and presents good opportunities for identifying and correcting misconceptions.

**Figure 10.10 HTML jigsaw created by student teachers
at the University of Brighton**

THE BIGGER PICTURE   THE BIGGER PICTURE   THE BIGGER PICTURE   THE BIGGER PICTURE

This chapter has aimed to give an introduction to some important aspects of web literacy; however, as this is a broad topic there are inevitably areas that have been addressed either only very briefly or not at all. For example, understanding how to create accessible and effectively designed webpages is an important topic in its own right and is relevant to the expectations of the programmes of study. The Web Literacy Map produced by Mozilla, mentioned previously, is an excellent starting point for further exploration of wider issues and provides links to other useful learning resources. Further reading material is listed below.

A SUMMARY OF **KEY POINTS**

In this chapter we have highlighted the following:

➢ Equipping children with an understanding of web technologies will help them make more informed and discriminating judgements about how they use it.

➢ Developing your own understanding of key concepts and terminology relating to web technologies is a necessary step in enabling you to support the development of children's web literacy.

➢ A range of interactive learning resources is available online that can be utilised by teachers to develop their understanding of HTML and CSS.

➢ A variety of online tools exist that can be used to develop children's knowledge, understanding and skills in relation to the web.

➢ Remix projects can provide good opportunities for exploring relevant online safety issues.

M-LEVEL EXTENSION > > M-LEVEL EXTENSION > > M-LEVEL EXTENSION

Being able to build content for the web by coding with HTML and CSS is just one area in which primary-aged children can become more web literate. Develop your understanding of other dimensions of web literacy by exploring Mozilla's Web Literacy Map (https://learning.mozilla.org/web-literacy or see above).

REFERENCES REFERENCES **REFERENCES** REFERENCES **REFERENCES** REFERENCES

DfE (2013) *National Curriculum in England: Primary Curriculum*. London: DfE. Available at **https://www.gov.uk/government/publications/national-curriculum-in-england-primary-curriculum**.

Mozilla (2016a) *We're Building a Better Internet*. Available at **https://www.mozilla.org/en-US/mission/**.

Mozilla (2016b) *Web Literacy*. Available at: **https://learning.mozilla.org/web-literacy**.

TED (2014) *A Magna Carta for the Web*. Available at **https://www.ted.com/talks/tim_berners_lee_a_magna_carta_for_the_web?language=en**.

World Wide Web Foundation (2016a) *History of the Web*. Available at **http://webfoundation.org/about/vision/history-of-the-web/**.

World Wide Web Foundation (2016b) *About Us*. Available at **http://webfoundation.org/about/**.

USEFUL LINKS

Codecademy: Make a Website: **https://www.codecademy.com/learn/make-a-website**

Erase All Kittens: **https://eraseallkittens.com**

Khan Academy: Intro to HTML/CSS: **https://www.khanacademy.org/computing/computer-programming/html-css**

Mozilla WebMaker: **https://webmaker.org**

Playto: HTML/CSS tutorials: **https://learn.playto.io/html-css/lesson/0**

W3Schools: **www.w3schools.com**

Web Design for Kids: **http://webdesign.tutsplus.com/series/web-design-for-kids--cms-823**

FURTHER READING   FURTHER READING   **FURTHER READING**   FURTHER READING

Belshaw, D. (n.d.) *The Essential Elements of Digital Literacies*. Available at h**ttp://digitalliteraci.es/
assets/sample.pdf**.

November, A. (2008) *Web Literacy for Educators*. London: Sage.

Savage, M. and Barnett, A. (2015) *Digital Literacy for Primary Teachers*. Norwich: Critical Publishing.

11
Digital media/digital literacies

Chapter objectives

When you have completed work on this chapter, you will have:

- understood how digital media may be explored and produced across the curriculum as well as in specific subject areas;
- understood how working with digital media is a key way to meet the requirements of the National Curriculum for promoting digital literacy as well as providing wider authentic learning opportunities;
- examined a range of software and devices that can be used to get children actively and creatively engaged in digital media production activities.

Introduction

In earlier chapters we saw how the National Curriculum requires teachers to help pupils to develop computational thinking. We suggested a range of ways in which this can be supported in the classroom. In this chapter we are examining another key aspect of the computing curriculum, one which requires educators to ensure that

> ... pupils become digitally literate – able to use, and express themselves and develop their ideas through, information and communication technology – at a level suitable for the future workplace and as active participants in a digital world.

(DFE, 2013)

This statement reflects the many forms of literacy which exist beyond print and acknowledges the fact that children are experiencing digital media in their everyday interactions with each other and with the wider world, from the earliest years. It also clearly equates knowing about wider digital literacy with preparing children adequately for future employment as well as a way to become fluent and expressive in different media. We should state at the outset that print and media literacy are not mutually exclusive aims for the children we teach. Arguably, children encounter more reading now than ever before, once the plethora of screens and devices which they and their parents and carers use are factored in alongside more traditional books and printed materials. The need for children to be confident readers and writers in print has never been greater, along with the need to be critical, creative and culturally aware in their uses of such texts. However, print literacy *by itself* as a standard definition for *all literacy* is a reductive definition in a world in which audio, still and moving images are all dominant forms of communication. An inclusive definition of literacy which takes in digital texts and media and acknowledges that they sit alongside one another in the wider world is a definition which is likely to provide rich learning opportunities which reflect experiences, in computing certainly, but also in many other curriculum areas at the same time, as we will see. It is also one which acknowledges that literacy is about how *all* messages which convey meaning are shared and read, a facet of the new literacy studies, about which James Gee has written over a number of years. His book *Literacy and Education* (2015) provides a highly accessible account of this process and is useful background reading to the digital literacy aspects of the National Curriculum for computing. The notion of digital literacy is also helpfully explored by Doug Belshaw in his e-book, *The Essential Elements of Digital Literacies* (2014).

This chapter will look at ways to work with media in the primary classroom in order to develop digital literacies by organising them into sections devoted to: *working with still images*, *working with moving image texts* (film and animation) and, finally, *working with audio and music*. This is not to say that we do not acknowledge the overlapping and combined ways in which these media operate. In all cases the emphasis will be on practical ways to work which build on children's existing knowledge of digital literacy as consumers of these 'everyday literacies' (Lankshear and Knobel, 2011) order to develop and foster their ability to produce texts across a variety of forms of media (Buckingham, 2003).

What do the programmes of study for Key Stages 1 and 2 include?

While the word 'media' in the programmes of study is largely absent (the exception being in one small part of the orders for Maths), there are several instances where work on digital images and audio or moving images can find a location in the prescriptions of the National Curriculum. Aside from the general requirement that schools meet the aim to ensure pupils 'are responsible, competent, confident and creative users of information and communication technology' there is ample opportunity in media production to meet the following aims from the programmes of study.

Key Stage 1

- Use technology purposefully to create, organise, store, manipulate and retrieve digital content
- Recognise common uses of information technology beyond school

Key Stage 2

- Select, use and combine a variety of software (including internet services) on a range of digital devices to accomplish given goals ...

(DFE, 2013)

Some of the terminology and ways of thinking about these media are common in wider society and have a cultural currency with children and young people. They will not be as unknown initially to them as the some of the specialist vocabulary explored in earlier chapters specifically on computing. Nevertheless, these media do have their own rules and conventions and expressive manipulations of their own grammar systems. Still images work in specific ways by the nature of their composition, the choice of shot and the surrounding text (if there is any) which may alter or even subvert its meaning. Likewise, music and digital audio content has its own rules and conventions and there are further lessons to be learned about the grammar of moving image texts, in live action versions or in animated form. However, all of these can be understood readily in well planned, creative and purposeful activity in primary schools. The word 'creative' is important here because it implies an act of making and communicating which also generates original content, allows for children to have some agency over their activity and involves them in fashioning an outcome that can be read and seen in the outside world. If nothing else, producing content in this way, frequently but not exclusively located in the creative arts and humanities, can indeed meet the aim for the curriculum of preparing children for 'future workplaces' and 'active' participation in a world in which the media are the dominant mode of communication and a source of employment.

Part 1: Still digital images

Beginning then with still image media, we can start by stating that images, patterns, shapes and colours are key features of children's early learning. Logos and icons are increasingly important in making sense of the world, from choosing breakfast cereal to operating computer software. Children learn to communicate and interpret visual imagery and ICT has a significant contribution to make to the development of visual literacy which, in turn, is a key element of digital literacy.

In the same way the opportunity to *make* digital images, as opposed only to *reading* and *understanding* them, has multiplied as the number and range of devices which are capable of taking pictures has grown. At the time of the first editions of this text, digital cameras were the dominant device for the taking of still images. While they are still available and used widely in professional activities, the phone, smartphone and tablet device have all but supplanted the lower end of the camera market. It cuts across many socio-economic divides as even the least expensive communications devices have some form of image-making on them. Children see them in use in everyday situations and know the potential for making and sharing images. Add to this the convergence of various forms of interacting with such devices, the ways in which the market leading operating systems Apple, Android and Windows all begin to have commonalities of approach in terms of touch, icons and the like, and you have a huge number of possible ways of making images.

Devices

In a digital camera, or on a smartphone or tablet, the image is taken, or 'captured', but then it is also processed and stored as a file within the device itself (Ang, 2008). In a digital camera, processed images are often held on a memory card and while there is no absolute standard for this, the SD card is increasingly ubiquitous. From this medium the images may be transferred to a computer, usually by a USB cable or on recent computers by inserting the memory card into a drive on the computer. Phones and tablets often bypass the need for storing images on cards as the images are automatically uploaded to a cloud-based storage facility via wi-fi or data networks. Inevitably an issue related to using these devices in schools will be the fact that in the wider world, they are usually intended for use by a single consumer, an account holder. Tablets in particular need to be set up for classroom use in such a way that work with images is protected across a number of users and accessible without complicated workarounds by busy teachers. Happily, many tablet suppliers including the bigger names are increasingly opening their devices for multiple users on networks.

Image-making policy

At this point it is important to introduce a note of caution on the kinds of still image work which is possible in school. Unfortunately, the ease with which images can be recorded, transferred and stored by digital cameras, phones, smartphones and tablets has led to their misuse by unscrupulous individuals. Both trainees and serving teachers need to be aware and respectful of parental concerns about images of their children being taken. Schools will have their own policies in respect of photography, frequently guided by their local authority. A regular strategy is for the school to obtain written parental permission for their child to be involved in digital photography at the beginning of each school year or when the child enters the school. The understanding will be that the images are used only in the course of educational activity. Before using a digital camera in school, it is vital to ensure that you will be complying with your school's policy on making images with and of children. Naturally this also applies to moving images.

Images for record-keeping and personal curation

From the perspective of the teacher's own professional needs, a digital camera can be a helpful ally. Some learning opportunities which teachers and serving teachers create are, by their very nature, ephemeral but may indeed represent a significant achievement on the part of the child. For example, a picture of the outcome of a design technology project, or a photograph of PE or a dance or drama production will serve as a helpful record for assessment purposes. It is certainly quicker to create than a written account, and is likely to convey what was happening much more clearly.

For a teacher's own continuing professional development, photographic documentation can bring to life their work in the classroom and their contribution to the wider life of the school. It is also first-hand testimony, evidence in a form that is much more convincing than a written claim can be.

Additionally, children know that they can create images for themselves and they are aware that they and adults put themselves in the picture with 'selfies' and the like outside of school. Knowing this, perhaps they could be encouraged to keep their own visual records of their work. They are growing up in a world in which they will be increasingly expected to have some idea about *curating* their experience (cf. Potter, 2012), so why not connect this to the life of the school? If the digital policy allows for it, children could store images on the school server of their achievements in portfolio areas. As they grow older, they will soon be recording aspects of their personal life (if they are not already) in social media and some of the skills and dispositions towards this form of activity could be useful in their learning and reflection.

Image editing/graphics software

Depending on the context in which children are using images in the classroom it might be necessary to edit them in some way. This can be done in very simple editing software or at a higher level. In the everyday use of these images editing might only consist of simply cropping or resizing the image. These are tasks for which there are very many simple tools which come free with all manner of hardware from computer and laptop through to smartphone. The photo viewer application, for example, standard on an iPad and many other similar devices, provides a range of simple editing tools which children might wish to use or experiment with. In addition to cropping and resizing, a great many filters are built in for colour adjustment, light reduction or enhancement. Likewise, the standard Windows or Mac operating system editors work in this way with images associated with them. If you are working on images which you have taken from a digital camera, once they are dragged off the memory card on which they are were taken and into the computer, double clicking them opens up the world of simple editing.

In addition to working with images in this way, children may, of course, also be introduced to software which allows them to make their own images, on the phone, on the tablet or on the computer, manipulating simple painting tools; there have been many produced down the years which are bespoke for primary classrooms.

Drawing and painting packages each have different strengths and limitations. One of the key differences is in the storage mechanism for the images created and manipulated within them. Painting programs produce bitmap images. Bitmap images are minutely detailed, essentially recording separately every pixel (tiny dot) displayed on the screen, including blank areas. This results potentially in very large documents.

Drawing programs, sometimes called vector graphics programs, work in a different way. Drawings are stored as a series of vectors. These are mathematical descriptions of lines determining their magnitude and direction from the points at which they originate to their ends – and including all the curves and changes of direction in between. This is a more economical way of describing a simple image, and it results in smaller file sizes.

There has, however, been considerable convergence in graphics software. Most graphics programs are now painting programs which also support drawing features, such as lines, arrows and shapes. Drawing features have also been included in other software applications. For example, most word processing software supports a range of drawing functions which enable the user to incorporate diagrams and other line art into their documents. Children will doubtless have experimented with this and these tools are things which might be familiar to you. Indeed the photo editing within Word (for Mac or PC) is now very sophisticated. As with all the choices you make with these kinds of tools, the work that you ask them to do in such packages needs to be purposeful and somehow connected to what they are doing.

Practical tasks with image editing software

There are many different image file formats, though one you may have heard of, the JPEG (Joint Photographic Experts Group – an agreed international standard) is very common. Because of the different ways the different file types store data, they are vastly different in their size and the amount of storage they take up. It is worth exploring the characteristics of different image file types using image manipulation software such as those which are free on Mac or PC like Preview, or, if you have access to it, software such as Adobe Photoshop Elements or even the full version. Alternatively, the free utility PixResizer (**http://bluefive. pair.com/pixresizer.htm**) is specifically designed to support the resizing of images and their subsequent saving in alternative file formats. Compare the differences in file size of the same image saved in different sizes in different formats. Paste an image into a graphics or word processing program and enlarge it significantly. What do you notice? Could you explain what is happening, and why, to children? Could they research this themselves?

Teachers need to be competent and confident users of primary graphics software in order to facilitate children's learning. This does not mean that they need to know the answer to every technical question, but they do need a working knowledge of the software so as to be able to plan, support and assess appropriate activities. They also need to have strategies to support the children in their discovery of how the software works, as well as to assist with problem-solving.

Teaching with and about graphics software involves teachers:

- Preparing resources such as a sheet to support early mathematics work, a prepared graphics document in which children may explore and reinforce early symmetry work, or illustrations to accompany a wall display. Some of these examples focus on using ICT as a tool for teaching and learning in another curriculum area, while others focus on the teaching and learning of computing.
- Enhancing or extending children's learning in other ways, such as on the importance of presentation in communication. In some instances, the focus will be on teaching and learning in computing (e.g. aspects of digital literacy such as optimising images for different publication formats; e.g. the web or a printed poster) while in others ICT will be used as a resource in the teaching and learning of another curriculum area (e.g. creating a presentation on a history trip for a whole-school assembly).
- Making explicit links between related knowledge, skills and understanding. Graphics software has applications across the range of the primary curriculum and as a consequence may provide opportunities to make explicit links in knowledge, skills and understanding in mathematics and art, for instance.
- Demonstrating or intervening, for example demonstrating a new skill such as altering the size of painting tools or intervening to assist a child to delete multiple copies of a saved image to save memory space.

The list below attempts to identify the knowledge, skills and understanding that teachers need in order to teach effectively with and about graphics software. Many graphics programs support only a subset of these functions. This is no reflection on their usefulness – in most instances, simplicity is a strength. However, it does signal that teachers must be aware of the capabilities and limitations of any program as these will be significant in the choice of software for any teaching and learning activity.

Painting and drawing programs:

- creating, opening, closing, deleting and printing documents;
- selecting file type and saving documents;
- selecting page size, margins and page orientation;
- inserting, modifying and deleting background colours and textures;
- selecting, modifying and utilising tools from the tool bar (spray, round brush, shapes, line);
- utilising fill;
- utilising the pipette/choose a colour tool;
- utilising undo/redo;
- selecting, modifying and utilising the text tool (font, font size, colour);
- selecting areas (for cropping, scaling, reshaping, deletion);
- selecting, modifying, utilising and saving repeated images (stamps);
- selecting and utilising more advanced features such as tiling, flipping and rotation;
- switching grid on and off;
- utilising zoom/magnifier and understanding how it differs from image resizing;
- inserting, deleting, manipulating and saving imported images;
- exporting images/drawings to other applications;

- clearing the screen;
- utilising help;
- altering defaults;
- customising set up;
- connecting alternative input devices (overlay keyboards, touch screens, graphics tablets);
- protecting documents.

Figure 11.1 Shape-based worksheet designed using the drawing features (Microsoft Word)

The use of graphics software provides a quite different aesthetic and kinaesthetic experience compared with traditional art media. The outcomes produced are also different and there is a completely distinct physical experience associated with creating outcomes. Some children may be frustrated at the difficulties associated with using the mouse or trackpad, iPad or other tablet device as a drawing tool; others may delight in the potential to create difficult shapes, such as curves, exactly as they wish them to look. In order to develop understanding and inform choices, children need a range of experiences on which to base their decisions.

Drawing and painting software facilitates a range of starting points for graphic activities, from a blank screen to a photographic image to be manipulated and developed. Similarly, the sheer variety of tools, editing functions and effects available provide challenges in

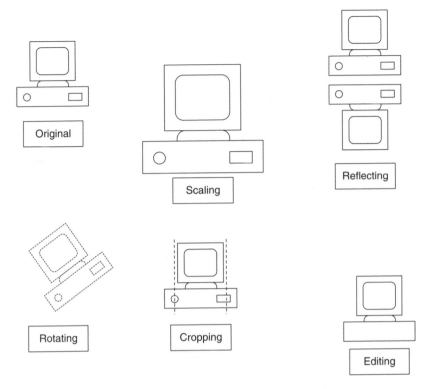

Figure 11.2 The effects of common editing functions (Microsoft Word)

themselves. The range of tools, editing functions and effects can, however, be limited in order to promote specific learning outcomes. Use of graphics software provides an opportunity to introduce and develop children's understanding of related technical issues such as file size and file extensions in a relevant and meaningful context.

Most graphics software allows users to undo the previous action. Many primary packages, though not all, support repeated undoing. This feature allows children to use the software to explore and experiment with effects in ways which are not possible with traditional art media. Comparisons may be made between alternatives to inform choices. Children should be encouraged to take risks. Regular saving of work can provide a similar security, allowing children to return to an earlier stage in their work and follow a different pathway. Graphics software can provide children with access to tools, editing functions and effects which may be difficult or impossible to achieve with other arts resources commonly available in primary schools. Children may be able to develop their understanding of watercolour painting and painters by simulating watercolour effects and similarly investigate the potential and limitations of pop art.

Graphic representation is an important area of communication. Experiencing the creation and manipulation of electronic images assists children to interpret the graphics they encounter, be they sporting goods manufacturers' logos or sophisticated film animations. Similarly, the electronic nature of some graphics enables global sharing and exchange through e-mail and the internet. Graphics software does not in any way replace children working with the traditional range of art media; rather, it increases the choices available. In certain situations the software features or even the nature of the outcome, in electronic format for instance, may make it the appropriate selection.

Progression of knowledge, skills and understanding

Graphics work will focus on the development of children's graphical communication and interpretation skills as well as software skills. Very young children may use touch screens and concept keyboards to control the software, developing their understanding of the relationship between their actions and the effects on the screen. A range of early language, number and science activities can be supported, for instance using fill tools to colour in prepared drawings – the boat red, the fish orange and the seaweed green. With adult help children might draw party hats on digital photographs of themselves. With increasing independence, children will be able to engage in a range of painting and drawing activities, such as producing a new label for their tray or coat hook.

Children will be increasingly able to make their own choices about the creation, manipulation and presentation of images, extending their repertoire of knowledge, skills and understanding through structured activities and interventions. Older children will be able to make appropriate choices related to the task and its audience. The variations in both software and the intended outcomes make ordering and ascribing particular skills and techniques difficult. Consideration is more appropriately focused on the development of knowledge and understanding which underpins the use of skills. In addition to directly teaching a limited range of skills, it is important for the teacher to encourage children to explore the software purposefully for themselves, to think of an effect that they want to create and then discover how to achieve it.

When you are planning graphics work, it is helpful to incorporate practical activities into real-life situations around school and in the community. For example, many schools take part in charity and fundraising events, such as sponsored walks or silences and end-of-term or summer fairs that are open to parents, friends and other members of the community. There are lots of opportunities for older Key Stage 2 children to get involved in organising these. Think of the possibilities in drawing a plan to show where the stalls will go, designing signage and instructions for each stall, price lists and menus for customers requiring refreshments, and posters and fliers advertising the event.

Sourcing images and ethical use

In addition to taking, drawing and painting their own graphics images, children can source prepared images or photographs from a variety of locations. Websites, CD-ROMs and scanning are common sources of images produced by others. Children often find it daunting to begin with a blank screen or even to work on something which they have taken as a photograph, for fear they might spoil it in some way (though this is of course a useful point in any discussion about saving files and non-destructive editing). The manipulation of an existing image can be a useful starting point, or a teaching and learning activity in itself where the emphasis is on exploring the features of the software. It is important to remember that any image other than clip art is likely to be subject to copyright. Children should also be taught about Creative Commons and how to source such images through image libraries such as Flickr (see **www.flickr.com**), carrying out an advanced search for images that are available under Creative Commons.

Essentially these are images whose creators give consent for others to use their work as long as there is no commercial or financial gain involved and the original creator is acknowledged. There are different kinds of Creative Commons licences which can be explored with children (see also **http://creativecommons.org/**). In addition to this, children should be taught that they have a responsibility to use images ethically. For example, while a classroom visitor may be content to have their photograph displayed on the wall of the classroom, they may not want it to be published on the school website or class blog. Consequently children should consider how the images they are sourcing will be used and published in order to ensure ethical and responsible use and that they have the appropriate permissions for how they intend to use the images.

Clip art, which is widely used in primary schools, is usually copyright-free artwork, although it may come as exemplar material as part of a program and so be licensed within that. Clip art is typically simple in execution and offered as GIFs or Windows Metafiles (.wmf) in order to minimise file size. Most word processing software now comes with a range of clip art. There are also websites from which free clip art can be downloaded, though these should be mediated by an adult as they frequently need some negotiation of pop-up advertising. Publishers of educational software also produce associated clip art images, e.g. Oxford Reading Tree.

Clip art may be used for a range of purposes, such as illustrating notices around the school, computer room and wet play area. Clip art images may also be a useful starting point for children to practise image-manipulation techniques in painting packages. However, clip art is to a certain extent a short cut to create visual impact; its originality lies with the artist who created it rather than with the child who imports it into their work.

Using scanners

Scanners allow digital images to be made of hand-drawn diagrams, existing photographs, autumn leaves and everyday (flattish) objects such as scissors. Scanners also come with software which enables images to be captured and saved in a range of file formats. They are also useful in generating electronic archived versions of work on paper for combining with other elements of a portfolio of work. The software will usually conduct a preliminary scan of the original when launched and allow the user to select and save just the parts of the image that are required. Scanners all accommodate images, and are usually provided with optical character recognition (OCR) software, which enables printed pages of text to be converted into a digital format that can be fed into word processing or text-editing applications. This technology has become very accurate, but it is not infallible, so documents should be checked before sent on or printed.

Scanners are useful for translating children's artwork, for instance, into an electronic format to allow it to be displayed on the school VLE. Similarly, scanned images can be the starting point for a range of activities. Children may scan leaves (see Figure 11.3), import them into a graphics package and manipulate them to produce a border for a poem. Alternatively, they could attempt to replicate a leaf using the drawing and painting tools

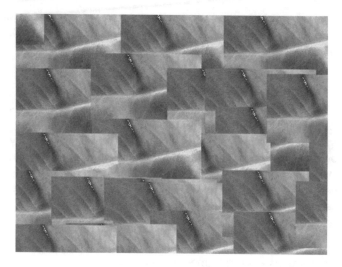

**Figure 11.3 Image created with a scanned leaf
and painting software effects (Dazzle, Granada Learning)**

in an activity designed to increase facility with these, displaying the scanned and the drawn images side by side. Due caution must be exercised to ensure that scanning does not breach copyright.

PRACTICAL TASK   PRACTICAL TASK   **PRACTICAL TASK**   PRACTICAL TASK

Use a scanner or a digital camera to produce a resource to support a science activity. How will you use the resource? How will you differentiate? How will you assess the resource's effectiveness?

Printing images

The large size of many graphics documents has implications for printing. Printers have memories into which documents are sent from the computer. Documents which are too large for the printer's memory will not print out. They will also prevent the printing of other documents sent subsequently to the printer until the problem document has been cleared from the print queue. Children may be disappointed to find that importing a number of graphic images into a word processing document, for instance, renders the file size too large to print. Problems with memory are usually associated with older printers. A further disappointment which children experience concerns the difference in what they see onscreen to what they see on paper and there is much useful learning and teaching in these differences.

Images, particularly those which are uncompressed or high resolution and therefore contain the most detail, take a long time to print out on conventional inkjet printers. Waiting for printing can be frustrating and time-consuming if such eventualities are not anticipated. Further, if a backlog of print jobs accumulates in the print queue because documents are taking time to print, the printer's memory may become overloaded, causing it to crash. Although the price of printers has fallen in recent years, colour printing is still expensive. Inkjet cartridges have only a small ink capacity and cost a lot. Colour laser printers have become more affordable but again their maintenance is not cheap. If very high-quality images are required, photographic-quality paper is available, but this too is expensive for regular use in schools. Nevertheless, if children are to work with images, then the likelihood is that at least some of their work should be printed, and schools need to take the consumables involved into account with their budgeting. This may or may not be within your control – it is always worth checking with the staff at the school about the policy on printing in colour before you send a whole class collection of images to a network printer.

Digital images and the core subjects

The ideas and activities introduced below are intended to give a feel for the range of ways in which graphics software and digital cameras can be utilised to support and enhance teaching and learning in mathematics, science and English. They are not intended to be comprehensive, merely to go some way towards illustrating the breadth of possibilities and to provide starting points for the customisation of ideas and the generation of others. Examples introduced under mathematics, for instance, may be just as applicable to one or more of the other areas.

Science

Children may use painting software to produce images which illustrate the effects of light sources, such as street lights at night, fireworks in the sky or sunlight reflected in water. The particular qualities of graphics software, which enable light colours to be easily imposed on top of dark ones, make ICT a suitable medium for such representations, allowing children to create an artistic effect otherwise only accessible to very practised artists.

Very often, science work at all levels requires illustration to aid communication. Graphics software enables images to be created, imported and modified as required. It also supports the addition of labels to aid identification and explanation. Posters may be designed to illustrate scientific understanding – the importance of a healthy breakfast or regular cleaning of teeth, for instance. Such posters can be created using traditional media, although graphics software allows revision and reorganisation to maximise presentational impact. It also enables children to incorporate images from a range of electronic sources including digital cameras. Digital cameras, tablets or smartphones can also be used to record key findings or observations from experiments.

Experience with graphics software in the manipulation of images, resizing or cropping for instance, is an important skill which can be applied to the incorporation of graphics across the range of generic applications, most notably word processing and desktop publishing.

Mathematics

Drawing programs may be used to support mathematical modelling activities. A teacher may prepare an electronic file containing a plan view of the classroom and the outlines of a range of furniture to be included. Children could explore possible arrangements.

Extension activities might include conditions (the computer cannot be located by a south-facing window) or additions (two new children are starting on Monday – where should the extra table and chairs be located?).

Graphics software sometimes includes a grid which can be switched on and off. Grids may help children use graphics software to develop their mathematical understanding of shape. A teacher may prepare graphics files incorporating a grid, lines of symmetry and shapes in one quadrant. Children can make use of the grid to help them draw the shape reflected or rotated (see Figure 11.2). Similarly, a teacher may use a regular shape on a grid to demonstrate rapidly and effectively the effect of increasing perimeter on area. The incorporation of images into mathematics work mediated through the interactive whiteboard presents particularly rich opportunities, simply because of the greater visual impact that an image commands in comparison with text.

Graphics programs can be used to produce repeating patterns for wallpaper or wrapping paper. The stamping facility in many paint packages enables a design to be rapidly duplicated and arranged. The suitability of various shapes for geometric sequences can be explored – an investigation that can be extended into consideration of Islamic art offering valuable opportunities for cross-curricular work.

English

Children's books are usually enhanced by their illustrations and logically their own writing will be made more attractive and perhaps clearer through the incorporation of digital images that they have composed. It is important that the pictures the children use do genuinely complement and enrich the text and are not just a technological version of the borders with which teachers encouraged children to decorate their work if they finished their writing quicker than anticipated. Talk to the children about how the words and pictures interplay to give meaning. Images can be imported into painting software – children may paint themselves into a Viking village scene, with appropriate clothing and props, for instance, and from there create a story of their life as a Viking.

PRACTICAL TASK   PRACTICAL TASK   PRACTICAL TASK   PRACTICAL TASK

Create a resource bank of photographic images that might be used in the classroom but which it may be impractical for the children to take themselves. For example, photographs of your town – the station, the marketplace, the park, key buildings such as the fire station and hospital – will be invaluable for a local study in geography. You will be able to use the photographs for whole-class work, perhaps on an interactive whiteboard, an online gallery within the VLE or on a personal blog, while the children will be able to include them in their reports or presentations.

Part 2: Moving images

Digital media production in schools has been made possible and accessible in recent years thanks to the proliferation of affordable equipment and software. Simple video editing software and the ease of sharing short film creations have given non-specialists access to areas which were previously in the domain of media professionals. As seen in the work in other chapters, a further set of possibilities has been opened up by the ease with which productions can be shared and exchanged through the medium of the internet or by swapping commonly formatted media files. It is also more than likely that some children in schools in which you work have begun to experiment with making both video and animation with cameras and/or on smartphones or tablets. They may never have considered editing these and perfecting them as short films but will undoubtedly have drawn on the wider culture of the moving image in designing and making them.

For formal educational settings, the production of digital video images of children and their work raises ethical considerations and internet safety issues. Sensible discussion of these safeguarding issues with school governors, parents, children, teachers and all stakeholders, together with an agreed protocol for making and distributing these productions, can result in children being given access to the very powerful medium of digital video within a school context. There are schools that regularly publish their children's work within password-protected areas in their local authority online learning environment. Others distribute material to parents on DVD. Some make sure that children can safely use the medium without being identifiable but that they can still engage with work such as animation or simple video production. In any case, simply closing the door, as noted above, denies children and young people access to a productive engagement with contemporary culture and further widens the gap between educational spaces and home.

RESEARCH SUMMARY RESEARCH SUMMARY **RESEARCH SUMMARY** RESEARCH SUMMARY

Whatever the means by which the concerns raised above can be addressed, there is little doubt that working with moving images in the classroom brings huge benefits in a number of areas of the curriculum and broadens our understanding of children's experience of literacy and the role of media in shaping learner identity. There are a growing number of studies and texts which explore this in more depth, including Becky Parry (2013), with a foreword by Jackie Marsh, and John Potter (2012), who reports on a digital video production project by children in Year 6 which was autobiographical in nature. In addition, Burn and Durran (2007) are an invaluable source of advice in the field for both live action and animation production.

Some curriculum uses of digital video

Some of the potential sites of this work in school settings include the following.

- Curriculum-based projects which allow children to make media productions of project work, either for assessment purposes (e.g. their portfolios) or for use within the school setting with other age groups (e.g. 'Make a movie which tries to explain gravity to a younger class').
- Autobiographical and/or creative productions which allow exploration of the medium in a more creative context, including the use of sound assembled for the project (see also Part 3 on audio below).
- Shorter clips produced with assessment in mind including peer- and self-assessment, e.g. for movement within a PE lesson. Shorter unedited pieces used to review movement on a shared space in the classroom (using the interactive whiteboard).
- Self-produced clips used to explore popular culture and emergent media literacy concepts, through parodies or references to popular programming on TV or online (in areas such as YouTube). Also used

to reinforce ICT concepts around media filetypes and simpler skills applicable across all digital media (cutting and pasting, etc.).

- Comparison of different tools of production from digital video cameras through to solid-state recorders (discussed later in this chapter), mobile phones and PDAs.

Whatever the location in the curriculum, there are teaching points to be made throughout about how moving images work together to make meaning. The pedagogical discussion which you have with children should be as much concerned with simple rules of moving image grammar and editing for clarity as it is with the curriculum content of the activity. If you are not confident in teaching some of these aspects of production, there is support for this online from organisations such as Learn about Film (**learnaboutfilm.com**) and the Film Space (**thefilmspace.org**).

Recent work on tablet film-making has revealed some interesting insights into how touch-screen mobile devices make some aspects of the work easier by conflating all of the tasks into one screen space, from initial planning and storyboarding, through to editing and, ultimately, screening. This research, 'Shoot Smart: Out of the Box', is showcased on the website of the Digital Arts Research in Education collaborative (DARE) (**darecollabo rative.net**) and was funded by Into Film, a charity established to inform and train children and teachers about the use of film in educational settings (**intofilm.org**).

THE BIGGER PICTURE   THE BIGGER PICTURE   THE BIGGER PICTURE   THE BIGGER PICTURE

When you are planning opportunities for peer- and self-assessment, remember that some subjects lend themselves to the use of digital video to support this. For example, in drama you could record improvisational exercises for children to discuss and make suggestions for improvement, and in PE you could film clips of movement sequences to review. Longer portions of team games could be filmed so that attacking shots, passes or defensive moves can be analysed. In English, debates can be filmed so that speaking and listening skills can be assessed, and in geography role-play activities about ethical issues can be recorded to review the quality of the arguments put forward by the characters.

Starting points for working with digital video production or animation

One of the key strategies for succeeding with digital video production or animation in the classroom is to begin with viewing and discussing film and moving image texts with which the children are familiar. Working in this way draws attention to moving image as a form which has its own conventions and ways of making meaning. It might be that they have never thought about this and about the way a moving image can be constructed. Beginning with viewing and talking creates a critical space for considering the construction of the texts as well as their emotional impact. It gives a space within the curriculum for the informally gained knowledge about film and moving images to enter the curriculum. A number of authors in recent years have addressed this aspect of the process (Parry, 2013; Burn and Durran, 2007). At a technical level, discussing how edits work in a short sequence to produce meaning is something which introduces editing interfaces and the myriad possibilities of what Burn and Parker refer to as the 'multimodal mixing desk' (Burn and Parker, 2003).

In order to undertake video production in the classroom there are a number of starting points. Digital still cameras often include the facility to make short movies which can be quickly reviewed and used in a spontaneous way in an unedited form. This could be useful in lessons which require the facility to go back and review live action to make a learning concept explicit (a science experiment, a piece of classroom drama or performance – see the classroom example below – or a PE lesson on making shapes). For animation, the same kinds of cameras or tablets could be used (especially with appropriate grips) or web-cams which can be attached by USB cable (such as the HUE webcam). Indeed, whereas there was previously difficulty at the uploading stage, smaller solid-state digital video cameras are available which shoot a small amount of material for downloading directly to the computer via a USB connection for editing or via a small memory storage card. Simple editing interfaces allow children to add effects and to export a finished version.

The widespread and growing availability of tablet computers is a further source of useful equipment. They are capable of producing high-quality results in good definition and require that children are holding them steady. In this regard they are perhaps more useful than a smartphone or small handheld camera for younger children. They also have the possibility to enable children to frame action better than looking through a small eyepiece. Both Apple and Android products have a substantial array of editing software apps available meaning that the whole production can be enabled with one device for shooting, editing and exporting. The reading list will also contain a list of possible suppliers and sources of further advice for both live action and animation use in the classroom.

Figure 11.4 Frame from an animated poem see
https://vimeo.com/33357020

IN THE CLASSROOM - A VIGNETTE

A teacher has distributed lines from a poem to a Year 4 class, two to each of five tables in the classroom. The task is interpreting the lines in a rhythmic way, to perform them to the rest of the class. The teacher reminds them to think about each word and how it contributes to the whole, and to think about how the overall pattern of the piece reflects a particular form (in this case, Calypso). The class comes out table by table after a short time rehearsing and the children record each table's two-line performance in turn. The whole thing is played back on the interactive whiteboard in sequence and the children appraise the overall class performance in terms of its communicative and dramatic aspects. This has been a literacy lesson which has featured a huge amount of excitement, and allowed for speaking and listening activities exploring aspects of poetry and performance. Motivation has been high. There have been no worksheets. Nothing has been recorded in a written form, but the movies can be saved as part of the class portfolio on the school's VLE and the teacher has had time to review contributions for her own record keeping.

PRACTICAL TASK PRACTICAL TASK PRACTICAL TASK PRACTICAL TASK

Follow the link in Figure 11.4 to the animated poem 'I Carry Your Heart' – a poem by E.E. Cummings. This animation was created by primary student teachers to explore the potential of animation. Find a suitable short poem that you would like to animate. Think about how you would go about planning your animation. Create a storyboard to help you plan an animation. Animation can be very time-consuming, but think about how you could accommodate this by sharing out responsibility among a whole class for animating different parts of a poem.

Developing digital video work further

The next and slightly more complex stage of video production involves some editing and post-production. Once inside the computer, via USB cable or a memory card, software allows for the scenes to be trimmed to appropriate lengths and joined using a variety of transitions simply by dragging them and dropping them onto a timeline or working with them as whole clips. You may already be familiar with this from your own use of free software to edit clips and images on a smartphone or tablet. In any case, if you have used the free audio editing software Audacity, recommended in Part 3 below, you will be familiar with the timeline concept and also the idea that because, like sound, video is stored digitally, it can be manipulated, cut and pasted in the same way. Effects such as titles can then be added and the whole production can be exported as a finished file for exhibition on the internet, the LA or school VLE, or for distribution home on disk.

It is worth mentioning at the outset that sound is a big problem in all kinds of animation and video production by learners. An audience will put up with poor camerawork (to an extent) over poor sound. Sound quality, whether in the form of a soundtrack or speech to camera, is closely bound to an audience's ability to construct meaning from a video production. You should draw attention to this and investigate the possibility of using microphones in noisier settings to record crucial speech or dialogue. Using Audacity, it might be possible to clean up poorer audio after shooting. However, in the interests of keeping the process simpler, it should be a consideration at the beginning of any project.

There is free software available to edit on a PC (Windows Moviemaker Live). On a Mac, as part of the same suite of software which provides GarageBand for music production, there is also free and powerful video-editing software called iMovie. There are some difficulties with certain filetypes due to the ways in which these have been compressed. The key to working successfully with these and overcoming difficulties is, obviously, to practise their use in advance of working with a class of children.

Teachers must always have a view of the pedagogy and a reason for using any resource and software is no different. There are possible mappings onto all curriculum areas for digital video production and animation, which make it ideal for cross-curricular work in school. At the same time, there are powerful reasons for using it as a way to extend learner knowledge in an exciting and motivating context and in a form which is culturally significant and authentic for them.

As stated above, a key factor that you must consider is the extent to which you will enable improvements in the quality of children's work by engagement with the language and techniques of film-making.

REFLECTIVE TASK

Using Google (UK), search online for Dingwall Primary School's weblog. Here you will find videos made by children at Dingwall School in Scotland. If you cannot locate this resource, search on BAFTA – BE Very Afraid. Here you will be able to view work produced by students and exhibited on the web – with permission – by Stephen Heppell, who has been actively involved in championing children's creative use of technology, including digital video production, for a number of years (see also **Heppell.net**, 2011). Once you have some examples of children's video, try to respond to the following questions:

- **Which curriculum area (or areas) is represented?**
- **What genre is the film operating in?**
- **Has the teacher given the children input into film-making?**
- **What do you think the plan for this activity looks like?**
- **What skills would you personally require to carry out work like this with children?**

THE BIGGER PICTURE THE BIGGER PICTURE THE BIGGER PICTURE THE BIGGER PICTURE

When planning the use of digital video, a useful resource can be found at **www.filmstreet.co.uk**. Film Street is an organisation aimed at getting children involved in film-making, and the site includes video-based workshops, stop-frame animation and information about different animators and film-makers.

Animation production in education

It should be apparent by now that the applications of digital video to the curriculum are potentially wide and varied and offer something to all subjects of the curriculum. Animation in particular has a place in schools which is potentially highly significant. It is a form of cultural production with which children and young people are highly familiar and which is ubiquitous in their daily life. Two main kinds of experience are usually available, either working with stop-frame animation in which objects are moved steadily through frames in front of a camera, recording their changing position over time to create the illusion of movement, or the use of software to create and shoot the animation inside the computer itself, with no movement of objects in real space. This kind of production is enabled by software which borders on programming using, for example, Flash or HTML 5 or by user friendly mock-ups of film and animation stages such Moviestorm, the Machinima software for schools.

For stop motion animation, the more widespread availability of simple equipment to shoot animation productions (still digital video cameras, tablet computers, smartphones) and the presence in schools of many things to animate with (toys, Lego, classroom objects and more) combined with the availability of low-heat steady-light sources (cheap LED lights) make this, for some, an even more viable option than film-making with live action. Indeed, for schools with deep anxieties about children featuring in videos made at school or without a safety policy on such images, animation can circumvent the issue by having only objects visible in the frame.

Animation itself can be used to teach concepts of framing more widely, along with camera angle and so on. In addition to the organisations already listed above, advice and support can be found from others specific to the form such as **www.animationforeducation.co.uk**.

RESEARCH SUMMARY   RESEARCH SUMMARY   **RESEARCH SUMMARY**   RESEARCH SUMMARY

From Australia comes evidence that the use of animation production in learning concepts of science and other curriculum areas is particularly successful (Hoban, 2015).

From England there have been a number of projects which refer directly to children's experience of animation and machinima, some of which are reported on the website of the DARE collaborative (**www.darecollaborative.net**) and the Media Education Association (**www.themea.org.uk**). These include a year-long study into the pedagogical benefits of children engaging with animation production to learn about the teaching of poetry (and vice versa) at Key Stage 1; this was called 'Persistence of Vision' and was carried out by Cary Bazalgette, Becky Parry and John Potter (see the MEA website above).

Part 3: Digital audio and music

The intention of this section is to introduce a range of ways in which children can utilise digital audio creatively both in computing and in music education. However, throughout this chapter we emphasise the caveat that technology should not replace traditional ways of learning about and making music in the primary school but offer new opportunities to engage with the subject.

The importance of music and audio in people's lives is often underestimated. Indeed, creating, performing and listening to music are fundamental activities that can play a significant part in the emotional, social and intellectual development of the individual. The music industry has undergone radical change due to the digitisation of music and the ease with which music can be created, accessed and shared in compressed file formats such as MP3s. Powerful music composition programs connected to an electronic keyboard can enable children to engage immediately with the elements and language of music without necessarily understanding formal music notation. Similarly, the significance of audio seems to be enjoying a resurgence as new forms of expression and communication emerge, such as the podcast. The ease with which quality digital audio recordings can be created through a desktop or laptop computer puts these new forms of communication and expression well within the grasp of primary school children. This section will introduce a range of applications, and examine how these can be utilised to support children's learning in music specifically but also how audio in general can be utilised creatively across the curriculum.

As we noted at the start of this chapter, in the general aims of the National Curriculum for computing it is emphasised that the teaching of computing 'ensures that pupils become digitally literate – able to use, and express themselves and develop their ideas through, information and communication technology – at a level suitable for the future workplace and as active participants in a digital world' (DfE, 2013). A key aspect of digital literacy is the ability to make effective and appropriate use of digital audio whether for the sound track of a movie, the audio in a computer game or creating a musical composition. Much digital audio can also be shared with wider audiences using online services. The specific aspects of the programme of study which relate to this are highlighted as follows.

At Key Stage 1, the new programme of study for computing (DfE, 2013) states that, children should be taught to:

- use technology purposefully to create, organise, store, manipulate and retrieve digital content;
- recognise common uses of information technology beyond school.

At Key Stage 2 (DfE, 2013) children should be taught how to:

- make use of the opportunities offered by internet services for communication and collaboration;
- use technology safely, respectfully and responsibly; know a range of ways to report concerns and inappropriate behaviour;
- select, use and combine a variety of software (including internet services) on a range of digital devices to accomplish given goals, including collecting, analysing, evaluating and presenting data and information.

Composing and performing music

GarageBand is a piece of software that comes with Apple Mac computers and is available in other forms for tablet devices. Similar programs are available for the PC and online but GarageBand is particularly suited to music composition activities (see Figure 11.5). The software contains pre-recorded musical loops which can be previewed and then dragged onto the score, building up tracks and layers of music which can then be mixed using the dynamic and balance controls. However, the real creative potential of this software is in the way that live instruments including the voice can be recorded. This opens up a number of possibilities such as creating and recording a rap, a song or creating a

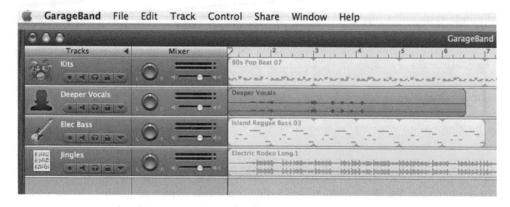

Figure 11.5 GarageBand Apple Mac – user interface

soundscape to accompany a poem written by a child or group of children. It is also possible to connect a midi keyboard to the computer so children can create, record and then orchestrate their own melodies.

THE BIGGER PICTURE   THE BIGGER PICTURE   THE BIGGER PICTURE   THE BIGGER PICTURE

When you are planning to use ICT to support children's learning in music, consider using the website **www.singup.org/**. This has a useful 'songbank' with ideas for lesson plans including using ICT to support the teaching of music and/or music plans.

There are a number of applications that work in a similar way to GarageBand, for example with children dragging pre-recorded samples and loops into their own compositions then adapting these by applying effects and editing them. These include Dance Ejay, Music Maker, RM Music Explorer and 2Simple Music Toolkit. However, as with any software for the classroom and as we have emphasised throughout, it is important that teachers recognise both the limitations and potential of a particular title and it is useful to ask some key questions.

- How far can any pre-recorded samples be adapted and changed?
- Is there any facility for recording and combining live instruments?
- To what extent can children generate their own melodies, rhythms or soundscapes?
- Does the software support any links between different types of media (sound, still/moving image, games)?

Another piece of software that is particularly flexible is Audacity, the freely available, cross-platform sound editor (see Figure 11.6). Although there are no sample sounds for children to use, they can record their own into the computer and then edit these by cutting and splicing them as well as applying effects.

Multiple layers of sound can also be built up to create complex textures of sound. This software particularly lends itself to spoken word and music projects such as creating a soundscape to accompany and add mood to a poem, story or computer game the children have created. The software is open source and can be downloaded at **http://audacity. sourceforge.net/**.

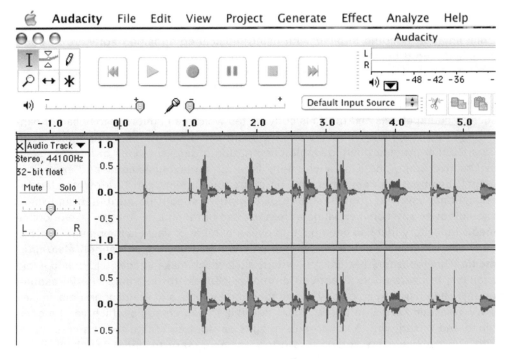

Figure 11.6 Interface of Audacity

IN THE CLASSROOM

A class of Year 5 children have been working with a trainee teacher, creating the words for a class rap on an anti-bullying theme. Over the course of a week, groups of the children use music composition software to set the words to music. The trainee teacher asks the children to think how they are going to accompany their rap. What kinds of instruments will they use? How will they make sure that as they build up the different layers of music, the all-important words and message they are trying to convey is not lost? What form will their rap take? Will they have a refrain that is repeated at intervals throughout or some other structure? How will the piece end: all instruments fading out together or phasing out the instruments one by one? As the children begin recording their rap, they make mistakes, which become evident as they listen to and evaluate their work as it progresses. At different stages, they decide to rehearse and practise coming in at the correct time before actually recording.

REFLECTIVE TASK

Consider this classroom example in relation to the programmes of study for music and computing.

What aspects of the programmes of study for both subjects could be addressed through the activity described?

Combining audio and visual

Once children become familiar with using musical composition software to compose and record music digitally, this opens up a number of possibilities for exciting projects combining audio with still and moving images. An important aspect of the programme of study for computing at both Key Stage 1 and 2 is using 'technology safely, respectfully and responsibly'. Children should be taught that digital audio such as sound effects and music is copyrighted which can limit how they can or cannot use other people's creative work, including audio/music. There are digital audio libraries that provide downloadable content under different kinds of licences such as Creative Commons. One such site is **http://freeplaymusic.com/** and another is **http://incompetech.com** where music and sound effects can be downloaded for educational use; the original source or composer should be attributed and there should not be any commercial gain from the use of the music. Another useful online media repository that has been built up over a number of years is maintained by Fred Riley and is available at the following link: **www.fredriley.org.uk/callhull/elearning/media**. This repository has links to various sites which make images, video and audio available to users under Creative Commons licences; for example, the Freesound project cited here is particularly useful for sound effects and atmospheric music (see **www.freesound.org/**). In this way it is possible to source audio which can be combined and mixed with the children's images or video to create the required mood and atmosphere. New software is often not necessary to initiate such projects. PowerPoint supports audio and this facility can be utilised in many ways. One idea might be to create an online gallery of children's artwork for a whole-school assembly by getting them to scan their work or photograph it. They could then create or choose an appropriate short piece of music to accompany their slide and artwork. Windows Movie Maker is available to download for PC users. Children could create their own pieces of music to accompany a short movie clip they have shot. The key to success with such projects initially is to try this out yourself first and to keep the pieces of music created to a manageable length. The impact of combining music and image is often rewarding and children enjoy experimenting with different types of music to create different moods.

Podcasts and podcasting

Podcasting is a method of publishing files to the internet, allowing users to subscribe to a feed and receive new files automatically by subscription, usually at no cost, whenever they log onto the internet. The latest update is automatically downloaded to the subscriber's preferred device, whether this is an MP3 player, tablet device or mobile phone. Again, there is a great deal of educational potential with this technology. Teachers might consider creating their own educational podcasts or children themselves could create a podcast to accompany a historical or geographical field trip to their local area. This could be shared more widely with the school community with software such as audioBoo (see **http://audioboo.fm/**). An audioBoo app can be installed on a tablet device or smartphone so that children can record their audio responses while out on a field trip. These are then uploaded to the school or class audioBoo site back in school so that it can be shared more widely. SoundCloud (see **https://soundcloud.com/**) offers a similar facility. Such software enables children to create and broadcast their own podcasts. Devices such as smartphones or tablets usually have a built in microphone and there are app versions of many of these software titles, such as SoundCloud, which can be used on them. Excellent advice on starting out with podcasting is available online at the WikiHow site (**www.wikihow.com/ Start-Your-Own-Podcast**).

In the Classroom

Follow this link: **https://audioboo.fm/boos/1332463-e-safety-broadcast**. Listen to the online safety broadcast that was made by Year 4 children. They created and composed the short audio advert using the software GarageBand. After a lesson discussing and exploring the issues of online safety their task was to plan and create a short audio advert to make other children in the school aware of online safety issues. These were then shared with other children in the school via audioBoo. Think about how this activity addressed some of the aspects of the computing curriculum.

Listening to and appraising music

Many primary school classrooms are equipped with interactive whiteboards, which again offer a wealth of opportunities for sharing and discussing ideas about music as they usually have good-quality audio integrated within the system. However, together with rich audio resources to enhance children's experience, there is also the capacity to use a range of media to explore musical ideas. For example, the interactive whiteboard could be used to create a graphic score which the class interpret using percussion instruments.

Alternatively, a class might be asked to appraise a particular Cézanne landscape. How does it make them feel? What is the mood? Is there a clue in the colours used? They could then go on to appraise different pieces of music and decide which is suitable for the painting. Indeed, the opportunity to bring together a rich array of digital media in one place can be a powerful tool in developing children's aesthetic appreciation of music through listening and appraising as this next classroom example illustrates.

In the Classroom

A music advisory teacher is giving a demonstration lesson with a Year 2 class. They are looking at how the elements of music can be used to depict a real event. They begin by performing a poem projected on the interactive whiteboard about a steam train. The teacher draws the children's attention to the sounds created in the poem. Next they watch and listen to a short video clip of a steam train as it blows its whistle and releases steam, finally coupling with its carriages and accelerating gradually out of the station. They talk about the different sounds they have heard in the sequence. In the main part of the lesson they create their own soundscape to accompany the video, using percussion instruments and body sounds, also discussing how to depict the gradual acceleration of the train through tempo. Finally, the teacher

---

introduces the children to a new piece of music – 'The Little Train of the Caipira' by Villa Lobos, which depicts exactly what they have been creating, using different instruments of the orchestra to represent the different sounds and manipulating tempo to illustrate the train gradually getting up to speed. The children listen carefully, identifying and appreciating the different elements of this piece of music, which they can now understand, having explored this event themselves through text, moving image and audio.

(Peter Walker, Advisory Teacher for Music, Brighton and Hove)

There can be no doubt that the range of ICT tools now available to the primary teacher offers new ways of enabling children to find out about a range of music. However, to make the most of these new opportunities a secure subject knowledge of music is essential in order to develop children's understanding further and use the technology effectively. You could seek further help from a teacher with responsibility for music in the school or from a relevant tutor or local authority advisor.

Some practical issues

There are some important factors concerning file types and saving work when using digital audio. Most software supports MP3 and WAV files. However, MP3 files compress the data more to give smaller file sizes, which is an important factor to consider if children's work needs to be transferred between machines or indeed uploaded to the school website or virtual learning environment. Audacity can be used to convert between file types. There are also numerous online converters available.

There is an array of software and hardware to support children's development of knowledge and understanding in music and the main focus of this chapter has been on those resources which lend themselves towards more creative uses of technology in music. For teachers to make effective use of ICT in music they must have a critical view of the technology and an understanding of the opportunities it affords both the teacher and the learner in relation to the development of their subject knowledge. It may be, for example, that it is far better for children to beat a real drum to a piece of music or song than create a rhythmic pattern in a computer program if we want to develop their ability to hold a steady beat. Similarly, to develop children's control of pitch they need plenty of opportunities to find their own voice through singing and performing live music together. However, we have also shown through this chapter that working with digital audio is a vitally important aspect in the development of children's digital literacy.

A SUMMARY OF **KEY POINTS**

➤ **There is a wealth of software and hardware that can be utilised to enrich and develop children's digital literacy when working with digital audio and still and moving images.**

➤ **Podcasts, video production, animation and more can support teaching and learning in a range of subjects as well as computing.**

➤ **Media production is a way for schools to fulfil the requirements for their pupils to have the opportunity to develop digital literacies in the computing curriculum.**

> ➢ ICT should not be used as a substitute for traditional ways of making music or making images; in both cases, they can be explored as another form of artistic practice.

> ➢ It is important for teachers to develop their own capabilities with digital media applications before implementing them in the classroom.

> ➢ A sound knowledge and understanding of the music curriculum should underpin any use of technology to support children's learning in music.

> ➢ Producing music and soundscapes, images and moving images can enhance literacy work with poems and stories and many other written forms in the curriculum.

> ➢ When producing images or moving images which feature children, you need to adhere to agreed school/LA protocols.

M-LEVEL EXTENSION > > M-LEVEL EXTENSION > > M-LEVEL EXTENSION

Choose a year group or key stage and look at the school's schemes of work for the age group in all subjects. Make a note of all activities that could benefit from the use of digital video to enhance teaching and learning, including assessment of these opportunities. Is it possible to develop these into a cohesive scheme of work that develops children's capability with digital media production progressively? Are there connections you can make between creating or manipulating digital media, and working with coding and programming?

REFERENCES REFERENCES **REFERENCES** REFERENCES **REFERENCES** REFERENCES

Ang, T. (2008) *Digital Photographer's Handbook*, 4th edn. London: Dorling Kindersley.

Audacity. Available at **http://audacity.sourceforge.net/**.

AudioBoo. Available at **http://audioboo.fm/**.

Belshaw, D. (2014) *The Essential Elements of Digital Literacies*. Self-published. Available at **http://digitalliteraci.es/**.

Buckingham, D. (2003) *Media Education: Literacy, Learning and Contemporary Culture*. Cambridge: Polity.

Burn, A and Durran, J. (2007) *Media Literacy in Schools*. London: Paul Chapman.

Burn, A. and Parker, D. (2003) *Analysing Media Texts*. London: Continuum.

DfE (2011) *Teachers' Standards*. Available at **www.education.gov.uk/publications**.

DfE (2013) *National Curriculum in England: Primary Curriculum*. London: DfE. Available at **https://www.gov.uk/government/publications/national-curriculum-in-england-primary-curriculum**.

Freeplay Music. Available at **http://freeplaymusic.com/**.

Gee, J.P. (2015) *Literacy and Education*. London: Routledge.

Hoban, G. et al. (eds) (2015) *Student Generated Digital Media in Science Learning*. London: Routledge.

Lankshear, C. and Knobel, M. (2011) *New Literacies: Everyday Practices and Social Learning*. Maidenhead: Open University Press.

Parry, B. (2013) *Children, Film and Literacy*. London: Palgrave.

Potter, J. (2012) *Digital Media and Learner Identity*. New York: Palgrave.

Riley, F. (n.d.) *Media Repositories for e-Learning*. Available at **www.fredriley.org.uk/callhull/elearning/media**.

Sound Cloud. Available at **https://soundcloud.com/** (accessed 20 January 2014).

FURTHER READING   FURTHER READING   **FURTHER READING**   FURTHER READING

Hague, C. and Williamson, B. (2009) *Digital Participation, Digital Literacy and School Subjects: A Review of Policies, Literature and Evidence*. Available at **www.nfer.ac.uk/publications/FUTL08/FUTL08_home.cfm**.

Pearson, M. (2005) 'Splitting clips and telling tales', *Education and Information Technologies*, 10(3), pp.189–205.

12
Writing with digital technologies

Chapter objectives

When you have completed work on this chapter, you will have:

- understood the ways in which writing with digital technology can support the aims of the National Curriculum for promoting digital literacy as well as providing wider authentic learning opportunities;
- examined a range of software and hardware that can be used to get children actively and creatively engaged in writing;
- considered the many different forms of writing which children engage with using digital technology.

Introduction

In earlier chapters we have seen how we can support pupils in developing computational thinking as part of their digital literacy development. We have also explored how a range of digital media activities can be used to develop these skills further in fulfilling the requirements of the computing curriculum. In this chapter we turn to the ways in which word processing, desktop publishing and collaborative writing can support learning in computing and in literacy.

Word processing is a key medium through which we communicate information using ICT. It is so completely ubiquitous in computing activity that it is hard to imagine a world without it. Although there is a strong focus on the necessary and essential skill of handwriting in the primary curriculum, keyboard input into computers (or tablets or smartphones) is one of the most common uses of ICT globally and probably remains the foremost implementation of ICT in our schools. Developments in technology and the ways in which we communicate have blurred the distinctions between word processing and desktop publishing (DTP) to the extent that there is usually now considerable overlap in functionality between the two types of software. Additionally, many word processors and desktop publishing packages have integrated multimedia elements – images, of course, but also sound, video and animation. The implication is that the same software can be used for presentation both electronically and in paper-based form. In addition, recent developments have seen the introduction of online collaboration tools such as wikis and synchronous word processing tools such as Googledocs which allows multiple users to edit a document online. Such tools are discussed more in Chapter 13, Social media – tools for communicating, collaborating and publishing.

Defining terms

Word processing software allows the entry, storage, retrieval and manipulation of text, and increasingly graphics and sound, in an electronic format. It facilitates a variety of processes which can support and enhance communication. Desktop publishing software, just to draw a distinction briefly, is more concerned with the *design* and *layout* of documents containing text and graphics, usually with publication in mind. While obviously content is important, to a greater extent than when word processing, the desktop publisher will have in mind the overall 'look' of the finished document and the impact that this will create. Hence, initially, desktop publishing on a computer was primarily the domain of professional designers in the press and elsewhere. However, the accessibility of DTP software, in terms both of cost and user interface, has increased to the extent that DTP is now within the reach of any computer user. Furthermore, the market-leading software in the field, Microsoft Word (for both PC and Mac) now contains a great many of the features of DTP within its screen space with "Design" and "Layout" available as menu pathways, blurring the distinction still further.

What do the programmes of study for Key Stages 1 and 2 include?

As we have seen previously, the aims of the National Curriculum emphasise that the teaching of computing 'ensures that pupils become digitally literate – able to use, and express themselves and develop their ideas through, information and communication technology – at a level suitable for the future workplace and as active participants in a digital world' (DfE, 2013). A key aspect of digital literacy is the responsible and safe use of technologies and with the ease with which it is possible to publish online it is also important to consider these ethical dimensions when creating and publishing text. The specific aspects of the programme of study which relate to this are highlighted as follows.

At Key Stage 1, the new programme of study for computing (DfE, 2013) states that children should be taught to:

- use technology purposefully to create, organise, store, manipulate and retrieve digital content;
- use technology safely and respectfully, keeping personal information private, and know where to go for help and support when they have concerns about material on the internet;
- recognise common uses of information technology beyond school.

At Key Stage 2 (DfE, 2013) children should be taught how to:

- use technology safely, respectfully and responsibly, and know a range of ways to report concerns and inappropriate behaviour;
- select, use and combine a variety of software (including internet services) on a range of digital devices to accomplish given goals, including collecting, analysing, evaluating and presenting data and information.

What do teachers need to know about word processing?

Teachers apply their knowledge, skills and understanding of word processing in two distinct ways. One is concerned with teaching and learning *with* and *about* word processing, and the other relates to the use of word processing to support more general aspects of their professional role.

It could happen that teachers use different word processors for these different purposes. Several word processors have been marketed specifically for primary age children, and feature facilities such as simple, easily modified interfaces, speech facilities and word banks. Alternatively, many schools have adopted Microsoft Word, possibly in one of its adaptable forms which enables the teacher (or child) to set levels of complexity for the interface. There are arguments in favour of both approaches. Some educators would prefer software designed for children, while others would argue that drawing children into the use of adults' 'industry standard' software has benefits.

Whichever word processing package is used in the classroom, teachers need to be competent and confident users themselves. This does not mean that they need to know the answer to every question about the detailed layout and design features. Rather they should have a working knowledge of the software so that they are able to plan, support and assess appropriate activities as well as predict likely difficulties and assist with problem-solving.

Word processing will impact in several different ways in the classroom:

- Selecting appropriate opportunities in which word processing software can facilitate, enhance or extend children's learning, such as the importance of presentation in communication. In some instances, the focus will be on teaching and learning in computing (how to enlarge text, make newspaper-type columns or add a border to a poster); in others ICT will be used as a resource in the teaching and learning of another curriculum area (writing for a specific audience).
- Making explicit links between related knowledge, skills and understanding. Word processing is closely associated with literacy and language work at all levels, and as a consequence has a contribution to make across the primary curriculum.
- Modelling appropriate use of ICT, for instance scribing and amending shared writing with the whole class or a group using the interactive whiteboard.
- Demonstrating or intervening, for example inserting an image into a word processing document, cutting and pasting, or deciding how and when to use the spell-checker. Explicit teaching of word processing knowledge, skills and understanding requires demonstration and intervention as with any other curriculum topic. Children may gain word processing skills by themselves, but without the guidance and direction of their teacher the acquisition of such capability will be haphazard.

To support their wider professional duties, teachers use word processing in a number of contexts.

- Preparing resources – such as an electronic writing frame to support writing in history, a word bank to support an individual child or a troubleshooting help-sheet or interactive display to improve children's independence when using the spell-checker. Alternatively, teachers may use ICT to prepare resources for activities which do not involve children utilising ICT, such as a shared text, a range of three differentiated worksheets or numbered lotto cards to support a group mathematics activity. Some of these examples focus on using ICT as a tool for teaching and learning (in another curriculum area); others focus on the teaching and learning of computing.
- Administering and managing – for example, correspondence with parents, creating and amending schemes of work or school policies, using templates to prepare weekly planning, recording children's progress and producing banners for display boards.

The list below attempts to identify the knowledge, skills and understanding of primary word processing software teachers need in order to teach effectively with and about word processing:

- creating, opening, saving, closing, deleting and printing documents;
- selecting font, font size, colour, style (italic, bold), line spacing and justification;
- inserting, deleting, selecting, cutting, copying, pasting and undoing;
- utilising help;
- inserting bullet points, tables, clip art, borders, shading and columns;
- altering page orientation (landscape, portrait), background colour, page size and margins;
- altering defaults;
- forcing page breaks;
- utilising tabs and indents;
- utilising spelling- and grammar-checkers (including how to switch on and off), thesaurus, print preview, highlighter and talking facilities (including how to switch on and off) and find and replace;
- connecting alternative input devices (overlay keyboards, touch screens);
- constructing and utilising on-screen word banks;
- inserting page numbers;
- inserting text, graphics, tables and documents from other applications;
- inserting symbols, headers and footers;
- creating macros and templates;
- utilising dynamic links between documents;
- customising the word processor;
- merging documents;
- formatting graphics;
- protecting documents.

As we have noted above, word processing software has become increasingly sophisticated in the range of features offered. In contrast, the interface has become progressively more user-friendly and accessible. As with any application it is important to have an understanding of the capabilities and limitations of the software in order to use it effectively. This is not to say that it is essential or even preferable to be familiar with all the possible functions of the software. If you consider your personal use of a word processor such as Microsoft Word, it is likely that on a regular basis you use only a small proportion of its functionality, while nevertheless using it as an effective and efficient aid to communication.

Word processors, like any category of software, are defined by their common features. These features could be listed, but it is important to understand that there may be good reasons to restrict the number of functions available. For example, if the software is to be used by young children who are not likely to wish to insert footnotes or track the modification of a document over time, then these facilities may not be included, so reducing the complexity of the interface. There are cut-down versions of Microsoft Word available for the tablet devices which children may encounter in schools where the resource base is moving away from desktops and even laptops.

In general terms, the key features of word processing software can be categorised as follows.

- *Editing.* Editing features allow the entry and manipulation of text or images, such as insertion and deletion at any point in the document, and cutting, copying and pasting to reorder and reorganise. It is important in the context of word processing for children to grasp the concept of provisionality: that anything created is easily modified or changed.

- *Formatting.* Formatting features allow the utilisation of a range of fonts, text sizes, text styles (such as italicising and emboldening), page size, page orientation (landscape and portrait), tables, boxes and other graphics options.
- *Tools.* There is a range of tools which complement and enhance the editing and formatting features of word processors. These include spelling and grammar checkers, speech capability, templates and word counting.

As indicated earlier, many word processors now incorporate desktop publishing and even multimedia and web-authoring tools – Textease Studio CT and Microsoft Word are examples. The advantage of such packages is that children (and teachers) are able to extend their ICT capabilities without the need to learn new software for specific tasks. Instead, they can build on their existing knowledge, skills and understanding.

Contribution of word processing to the writing process

The obvious context through which to explore the contribution word processing can make to teaching and learning is writing. If the writing process is broken down into its elements, then we can see what word processors offer at each stage.

The writing process can be considered to comprise:

- planning and drafting: the initial composition of the ideas, the facts, the emotions being communicated through the writing;
- editing: attention will be given to:
  - the structural aspects of writing, such as sequencing and style (text-level work);
  - the technical aspects of writing, such as sentence construction, punctuation, grammar and spelling (word and sentence level work);
- proofreading: the final revision to check for errors in spelling, punctuation and grammar, and for any omissions and repetitions;
- presentation: formatting the material to offer a neat, clear final copy. At this point – and probably not before – the focus will be on the layout and look of the writing.

When children write by hand, they must be resigned to a number of complete reworkings of their texts, or must address each element of the writing process simultaneously. While this latter is a valuable life skill in certain situations, it can also be a considerable challenge. For example, attention to presentation may detract from attention to the content. The fact that editing on the computer is provisional and facilitates presentation to such an extent can be key motivations for the use of a word processor in the classroom and beyond. We will now look at word processing's contribution in more detail.

Planning and drafting

Unless carefully guided, children tend to write sentence by sentence with little overview of the text as a whole, rarely rereading previous sentences to check the progress of the narrative. Indeed, many children find difficulty in retaining the thread of their thoughts while they also grapple with the physical aspects of writing, be they handwriting or keyboard entry. For some, the challenge of rereading their writing may prove a further distraction. The speech facility in some word processing packages can help some children to focus on the progress of their writing as a continuous whole, rather than as a series of disjointed statements. However, such facilities should not be relied upon and will not be appropriate for all children.

A range of text input strategies may be utilised in association with word processing software to enable children's speed of writing to better match with their thought processes. These include overlay keyboards, word banks and even voice recognition and are discussed in greater depth below.

Clearly, keyboard skills, particularly speed relative to handwriting, are also relevant. It is suggested that children engage in the writing process for longer when ICT is involved, thus producing extended and perhaps more sophisticated narratives.

The use of writing templates (electronic writing frames), an extension of the widely used non-fiction writing strategy, may assist children to produce writing, providing the support which they need in order to embark on the project.

Editing: structural aspects

Once text has been entered into a word processor, there is clearly much scope for revision and development to enhance the quality of the writing. Since making alterations will require thought and some manipulative skill, but not a lengthy rewrite by hand, children can experiment with a view to improvement. Text can be resequenced, rephrased, extended and enriched. Meaning can be clarified. Attention can be paid to style, structure, genre, audience and purpose. Alternatives can be explored and compared, and changes can be reversed. The act of writing becomes a process rather than an end point; a temporal dimension is introduced, with the opportunity for reflection, even research to influence subsequent amendments. Printouts can be a useful record of the stages of the process and can provide a teaching and learning opportunity in themselves. A text thus revised should far better reflect the writer's intentions than a first draft that has not undergone revision. Children will be encouraged to write more when the prospect of subsequent redrafting is not associated with the physical effort of copying out by hand.

However, children may not automatically use the editing possibilities afforded by word processors to improve the quality of their writing in this way. In practice, they are easily distracted by the technical editing opportunities associated with presentation rather than content. Refined outcomes depend on focused and explicit teaching and task-setting.

Editing: technical aspects

Perhaps the most obvious contribution that word processing can make to the writing process is the opportunity for children to focus in the initial stages of a writing activity (composing) on communicating ideas, safe in the knowledge that attention can be paid to grammar, spelling and punctuation (as well as structure and style) at a later stage. Word processors now incorporate functions to address each of these phases, but the built-in tools do not even have to be utilised for children to review and amend these aspects of their word-processed work. Frequently, a range of such secretarial adjustments can result merely from rereading the text, again safe in the knowledge that changes will not result in lengthy rewriting or untidy work. Often, this rereading and the selection of items for amendment can be done away from the computer on printouts. This arrangement serves to maximise effective use of computer resources, but equally importantly, it may be easier to see typographical errors on paper than on screen, especially when *proofreading* the final draft. If word processors are to provide the opportunity for children to write in a sustained and purposeful way, drafting and redrafting work, then children need access to the range of facilities word processing has to offer. This includes printing out and using drafts of writing in progress, rather than printing only when writing is judged to be finished. Pedagogic considerations should not be sacrificed to financial constraints.

Presenting

The options for presentation through word processing are practically endless, and nowadays it is in this area that the overlap with what was formerly the province of DTP software is most pronounced. Children can adjust the font and size of their text to be accommodated in the space available, in keeping with the genre of the work, the intended method of presentation (display on the wall or on a class blog, for instance) and the audience. Colour can be added, as can borders, backgrounds and bullet points. Text can be arranged in columns to replicate newspaper or magazine layout. One of the most significant developments in word processing software is the facility to incorporate images, be they clip art, children's compositions in drawing and painting software, digital photographs or images scanned or copied and pasted from other locations such as the internet (subject to copyright). We live in an age of changing and evolving literacies, in which children are surrounded by presentations of high quality, so it is important that they too have access to the means through which to communicate their ideas. Teachers similarly need to take advantage of presentation features to provide good models as well as visually engaging resources. However, care must be taken to ensure that children realise the value that teachers place on the content of writing relative to its presentation. While good presentation can significantly enhance communication, it is usually not the primary learning outcome of a writing activity.

There is evidence that for some children being able to word process their writing, at least some of the time, makes a substantial contribution to the development of self-esteem and confidence in their own abilities, a key determinant in children's progress. As previously indicated, the physical effort involved in handwriting at times may be an active deterrent to the creative process. For some children the struggle to provide tidy or even legible work may seem insurmountable. Access to a word processor may allow such children to produce writing which they feel can stand alongside that of their peers. They may also be enabled to communicate what they really want to say, but may not be able to commit effectively to paper by hand.

THE BIGGER PICTURE THE BIGGER PICTURE **THE BIGGER PICTURE** THE BIGGER PICTURE

When you are planning guided writing activities as part of the process of developing children's independent writing, these need not always be traditional 'literacy' texts. Guided writing techniques can be part of many other areas of the children's learning. For example, you may want to introduce children to the correct way to write up a science experiment or present the findings of a maths investigation or technology project. The move from short pieces of writing to extended writing does not have to take place solely in English sessions, but can be developed in history, geography or RE. Similarly, electronic writing frames, research-recording grids and other scaffolding methods can be useful in all subject areas, including when undertaking cross-curricular topic or theme work. Using guided writing in other parts of the curriculum reinforces the expectation that literacy skills are not just for use in English sessions, but are for all written work.

Progression of knowledge, skills and understanding

We have already alluded to the range of word processing software available, with the most significant contrast being in packages designed for children compared with those intended for adults working in business environments. This diversity in turn leads to there being variety in functionality among different word processors, and so differences in the ease with which particular outcomes are achieved. For example, Microsoft Word has a button to create bullet points which is situated clearly and conveniently, while finding a command for a bullet point in some children's word processors may be difficult. It is consequently problematic to attempt to identify skills development, and in particular to link skills development with levels of attainment or year groups. With this proviso in mind, however, it is possible to identify progression as children use a wider range of tools to improve both the quality of the content and presentation of their writing.

RESEARCH SUMMARY   RESEARCH SUMMARY   **RESEARCH SUMMARY**   RESEARCH SUMMARY

Helen Smith (as long ago as 1998) identified some specific and particular knowledge that young children need in order to use word processors. Many of these issues we take for granted and may assume that all children know instinctively. Some of this knowledge is quite different from that needed to write by hand, for instance:

- that the space bar must be pressed after each word, but not before punctuation marks such as full stops and commas;
- that the shift key provides access to capital letters and some punctuation;
- that the backspace can be used to correct errors;
- that text wraps around automatically onto the next line and that line breaks can be forced using the Enter/Return key.

She also details knowledge necessary for the basic editing of word-processed work:

- that the mouse is used to position the cursor (caret) and the importance of this;
- that arrow keys, page up, home, etc. can be used to move around the text;
- the use of strip highlighting for copying and pasting, cutting, etc.

To this should perhaps be added:

- **the value of the undo function.**
- **any variations to the above when editing text on tablet devices, which can differ significantly compared to using a fixed PC.**

What are the capabilities and limitations of word processing?

Document sizes and their implications

Text documents do not on the whole take large amounts of memory for storage. However, the inclusion of formatting features such as page borders, tables and images may considerably increase the size of a word-processed document. This will result in longer saving and retrieval times, especially on a slow network, saving to a server.

Text entry

Most text entry into word processing (and other) software is effected by use of the standard QWERTY keyboard. Supplementary technology such as overlay keyboards, touch screens and word banks can be deployed to support children entering text. In some circumstances, it is appropriate to use adult scribes (amanuenses). Voice input is available, too, and its accuracy has improved greatly of late. These alternatives to the keyboard often have an important role to play, particularly in SEND contexts. However, it remains that the keyboard itself is the predominant input mechanism for text.

Developing keyboard skills which facilitate text entry and other aspects of ICT use would seem to be a worthwhile investment for the future. Yet, despite the self-evident importance of text entry, there is little consensus about how keyboard skills should best be developed. Teachers have expressed concern over the inefficiency of 'hunt and peck' typing and, particularly in the early stages of keyboard use, the relative time required to enter text. It can be argued that children need to learn keyboard familiarity early on in their computer use, otherwise typing will take more time and concentration than handwriting the equivalent text. Timing is crucial because once habits are learned it is very hard to change them. If children do not develop skills which make word processing accessible as an activity, they will not be able to take advantage of the opportunities word processing provides to enhance communication. Keyboard skills do feature increasingly in Individual Education Plans (IEPs) of children with statements of special educational needs, particularly where the IEP also provides for the regular personal use of a portable word processor or computer.

Some knowledge, skills and understanding relating to text entry have already been discussed. There is a wide range of software available dedicated to the development of children's keyboard skills. In addition there are paper-based materials which provide keyboard familiarisation exercises. These can be used with word-processing software or even paper keyboards for children to practise either in the classroom or at home.

Most of these strategies focus on *touch-typing* – learning to use the full range of fingers to access the standard keyboard, with the aim of being able to use the keyboard without looking first to locate letters. When compared with the commitment required to gain some mastery of a musical instrument, for instance, touch-typing may not appear as such an unattainable goal, and some children will particularly benefit from practice in hand–eye co-ordination. However, touch-typing as taught to secretaries and other adults is based on the span and stretch of a full-size adult hand, and for younger children modified strategies will be more appropriate. These include:

- knowledge and use of the 'home' keys (*asdf* for the left hand and *jkl* for the right; *f* and *j* often have a raised dot or line on the keyboard to help the fingers in locating them);
- encouraging the use of the first fingers of both hands, and then of at least two fingers on each hand, the thumb for the space bar and the little fingers for the Shift key;
- the use of the number pad, usually located to the right of the keyboard, for the entry of numbers.

For younger children, stickers to replace the standard capital letters of the keyboard with their lower case equivalents are available and may simplify early familiarisation.

When schools are devising their schemes of work for computing and ICT, consideration should be given to the enhancement of children's keyboard skills and the identification of progression. Clearly there is an important role for teachers in the diagnosis and remedy of inefficient or ineffective keyboard techniques.

The physical demands that handwriting places on children and the consequent contribution word processors can make to writing when some of these are removed has already been discussed. However, it is worth remembering that some children (and adults) may prefer to write by hand or may prefer to do certain, perhaps more personal, types of writing by hand.

REFLECTIVE TASK

Think about your own use of word processing. Do you edit directly on screen or are there circumstances in which you prefer to prepare a handwritten draft or plan initially? Talk with other adults about their choice of approach. What implications do the differences you identify have for teaching children?

Some further adaptations to word processing in primary classrooms

Word banks are typically integrated within a children's word processor and, quite simply, facilitate the choice of appropriate vocabulary (and, by association, spelling). Word banks can be quickly prepared by the teacher to support specific activities; equally, a graduated range can provide differentiated support. For instance, a word bank of specific vocabulary could be used in the recording and reporting of a geographical or historical enquiry, enabling children to concentrate or articulating their understanding rather than being diverted by the spelling of new words. Equally, children may access personalised word banks.

Touch screens can be used in conjunction with word banks or Clicker to assist text or graphic entry. In these contexts, they may be crucial in overcoming physical obstacles posed to some children by the standard keyboard and mouse. Indeed software such as Clicker is now available in tablet format (Apple, iPad).

Adult scribes are used to assist children with emergent writing and there is no reason why this practice cannot be extended to word processing. This arrangement can provide another strategy to assist children during the composing phase of the writing, allowing them to concentrate on the communication of ideas. Equally, an adult scribe (or the teacher) could record contributions from a whole-class discussion, quickly printing and distributing them to groups to facilitate a follow-up activity.

Voice recognition software has been available for some time but has proved difficult to implement in practice, partly because of the necessity for the software to recognise the particular inflexions of individual users. This involves training the software by reading prepared texts and lists of words and phrases. The software builds up a profile of how words and sounds are pronounced by the user. Although invaluable in some special needs contexts, voice recognition software has yet to arrive in primary schools as a mainstream technology. The need to spend time training the software is one obstacle, but there is also the more mundane concern of background noise which will interfere with the process.

Speaking word processors

Most word processors designed for the primary school now incorporate a speech facility. They are usually referred to as 'talking' word processors. Since talk carries connotations of a dialogue or discussion, 'speaking' may be a more accurate description, but the increased interaction between a child and a word processor which has a speech facility does indeed carry some of the characteristics of conversation in which the child responds to what is being said.

Speaking word processors can be used to assist children's writing by reading back each sentence as it is completed, or the entire narrative so far, reminding children of what they have written and prompting them to take the writing forward. It is suggested that the writing of children who are still emerging as readers may as a result be more coherent. Similarly, the computer will read back what the children have actually written as opposed to what they thought or wanted to write, alerting them to opportunities for revision. This support clearly works to provide word-level feedback, too.

If used indiscriminately, speaking word processors can be a distraction both for children writing electronically and for those working close by. Children need to be clear how the speech can assist them to develop their writing and when and where not to use it. Choosing the appropriate settings (whole words or sentences, or individual letters and sounds) is also important. Explicit communication of learning outcomes and classroom protocols is essential for such tools to be used effectively – for instance, completing a first draft and then listening to the computer read the text to assist with the identification of errors and opportunities for improvement. Headphones may also be useful for individual work.

Teachers need to understand and make explicit to children the limitations of the speech facility. Words are uttered through the word processor by concatenating small chunks of recorded sound that correspond to the phonemes represented by letters or short combinations of letters. This can lead to the speech facility occasionally failing to pronounce properly words that are correctly spelled.

Spell-checkers and thesauruses

Spell-checkers can be useful to draw attention to possible errors, though they are far from infallible. Concern has been expressed about over-reliance on such tools which can act as a disincentive to children to improve spelling. Additionally, used indiscriminately, spell-checkers may not only want to correct spellings which do not require correction (e.g. are merely not within the spell-checker's memory) but more importantly provide a distraction to writers in the early stages of the writing process. Much time can be wasted adjusting and readjusting spellings, diverting children's attention from the ideas they are seeking to convey. Most spell-checkers allow for new words to be added and teachers should make use of this facility to ensure that the vocabulary associated with current curriculum work is recognised by the word processor. Some watchfulness should be used in encouraging children to add new words – perhaps these should first be checked by the teacher or teaching assistant, to avoid the obvious difficulties associated with inaccurate suggestions being offered by the spell-checker.

Spell-checkers, like speech facilities, may be easily turned off. It may be appropriate for children to complete their initial writing and only then use the spell-checker. Teachers must employ discretion about when and to what extent these facilities should be used.

A spell-checker may provide for a valuable learning experience in itself where unfamiliar words are suggested, particular if used in association with a dictionary or thesaurus, enriching vocabulary. Likewise, thesauruses can be used as part of a structured learning activity to promote independence.

Grammar- and style-checkers

For similar reasons to those discussed in relation to spell-checkers, grammar- or style-checkers, though generally helpful, need to be treated with some caution, especially in software which originated outside the UK, where syntactic conventions may be different. The grammar-checkers in many adults word processors were originally designed for the business market and the suggestions made reflect this. Additionally, they are unable to evaluate usage in context. Some grammar-checkers can be customised so that they will pick up particular errors and overlook others, and can be very useful for identifying overlong sentences or inappropriate use of apostrophes.

Word processing on laptops

Word processing software is frequently used in conjunction with laptops. However, it is important to consider health and safety issues and ergonomics when using small devices for carrying out such tasks with mobile technologies over a longer period of time.

On the other hand, word processing using portable computers can have a range of benefits for schools. Portable equipment by its very nature enables trips outside, to the hall or music room, and even home to be supported. In cramped classrooms, the possibility of using computer equipment on standard tables, rather than specially adapted and located furniture, can be attractive.

Portable word processors have proved effective tools for the support of struggling writers, often bringing associated gains in terms of improved behaviour and social confidence, particularly when used to provide differentiated support for children with SEND. Children gain confidence from the privacy and support provided by the technology. Portable machines have also been useful tools in encouraging parental involvement in children's writing, with children taking the equipment home to continue their writing.

Of course word processing is also undertaken on various smaller devices such as smartphones and tablets. This is discussed in more depth in Chapter 13.

Explicit skills teaching

One key area for children (and teachers) is their developing understanding of the scope and range of word-processing software – what is possible and what isn't. The swiftly evolving nature of the software and hardware means there is no lasting answer, but a developing appreciation of the possibilities goes hand in hand with a developing sophistication of use.

The nature of the ways in which we learn about the various functions of word processing (and other) software can lead to inefficient and ineffective practices. Much of the time we learn new skills by experimentation ourselves, by asking our peers or our teachers, by using built-in help, by observing others and by accident when we are trying to achieve something quite different. Some software also allows the same effect to be generated by a range of different strategies; for instance, in Microsoft Word, highlighted text can be copied by accessing the copy command from the edit menu, by using the copy icon on the standard tool bar, by using the keyboard shortcut Ctrl-C and by using the right mouse button to access a mini-menu of options, again including copy. Some of these may work in some other word processing packages and some may not. All are effective. Some are more efficient in terms of time and number of mouse clicks than others. Some suit some individuals and the ways in which they work better than others.

It is important sometimes to watch children working with word processing software and to note and confront inefficient and ineffective practices. For instance, many children access capital letters via the Caps Lock. This requires them to put on the Caps Lock, type the letter and take off the Caps Lock, a three-stage process. Very often children forget the final stage and may have typed several more words before they notice. Changing capitals to lower case letters once typed requires a quite detailed knowledge of some word processing software; it is just not feasible in others. In practice, children tend to delete the offending words and retype them. Time and continuity are lost. Use of the Shift key can be taught explicitly, either informally on a one-to-one basis or demonstrated to a whole class. This alternative makes the capitalisation of letters a two-stage process (Shift and the letter) and avoids unwanted capitals. Similarly, if children are typing in a number of figures, they may find the number keypad at the right-hand side of the keyboard easier than the numbers at the top of the keyboard. Many young children get into the habit of forcing their own line breaks via the Enter key or a mouse click when they notice they are getting towards the right-hand side of the typing area and do not realise that the text will wrap around automatically. This becomes a problem when children subsequently edit their text and the line breaks are not then in the best positions.

A regular 'tips' slot where children demonstrate useful strategies to their peers, or the teacher models a new idea, can easily and fruitfully be incorporated into classroom practice. It should not be assumed that children will learn word processing unaided. As in any subject, they will benefit from explicit teaching and guidance.

Children need to be aware of the limitations of software tools: that the spell-checker is not always right (likewise the grammar- or style-checker), that some words may not be in its dictionary and that some of its suggestions may not be appropriate. Some understanding of the clues that spell-checkers use to offer alternatives may be useful to enable children to make best use of such facilities. Similarly, the talking function may mispronounce words not in its memory, potentially giving children the false impression that something is incorrect.

Word processing and the core subjects

The ideas and activities introduced below are intended to give a feel for the range of ways in which word processing can be utilised to support and enhance teaching and learning in mathematics, science and English. They are not intended to be comprehensive, merely to go some way towards illustrating the breadth of possibilities and to provide starting points for the customisation of ideas and the generation of others. Examples introduced under mathematics, for instance, may be just as applicable to one or more of the other areas and vice versa.

Word processing and mathematics

Children can use word processing software to present the results of mathematical investigations. Writing can make a valuable contribution to the development and particularly the articulation of meaning and ideas, no less important in mathematics and science than in English-language development work. The word processor allows children to import graphs from graphing or database programs and images from painting and drawing packages or a digital camera. They can add commentary, perhaps to pose questions for their peers or to produce fact sheets to contribute to a whole-class reference document.

Of course, many graphing and database packages allow text to be added and amended for the recording and presentation of results. Children need to know that they can transfer their skills from one to the other, but also to recognise the potential limitations of such software; for instance, word banks or bullet points may not be available. Accordingly, children and their teachers need to make an informed choice.

Word processing and science

The strategies discussed for mathematics can similarly be applied to the teaching and learning of science. Children at all stages can use word processing software to assist with sequencing and sorting information. The degree of preparation and structuring required may vary with the development of the children. Young children may begin by using an onscreen word bank featuring images with text labels, to sort materials into hard and soft, for instance. An obvious extension for such an activity may be the writing of a sentence of explanation, with adult assistance as necessary.

Sequencing the stages of an investigation can be supported at a range of levels. Children can use cut and paste to sequence and resequence the elements of a prepared text. Children may enter their own text and use the facilities of the word processor to revise and reorder their work until they are satisfied. Activities such as these are appropriate for pairs or small groups, since the associated discussion and decision-making should be a fertile ground for rehearsing explanations, justifying opinions and articulating ideas.

One of the principal conventions of science is the systematic recording of investigations. Children begin early in their school careers to develop this skill and word processing can be used to support this writing in various ways. A word bank can be used to access new or difficult vocabulary, allowing children to concentrate on articulating their developing understanding. Electronic writing frames or templates, prepared files with headings and sometimes questions of a general nature which can be used in a variety of contexts or customised for particular activities can be useful.

Word processors can be useful tools when children are seeking information from data-bases. Children can make their own notes about what they have found, supplementing these as appropriate with images or text copied and pasted from electronic sources. Children may then use their notes in either an electronic or paper-based format to develop their work further.

The examples given above focus predominantly on using the features of word proces-sors to assist in the development of writing associated with science. Each of these can be taken a stage further by using the tools and facilities to improve the technical and presentational aspects of children's writing in science. The word processing and desktop publishing facilities of the software can be used to good advantage when children pro-duce posters to communicate important facts such as why we should clean our teeth or which foods we need for a healthy diet. Equally, information can be prepared in a word-processing document with a view to linking it with the work of others to form a multi-media document, for the school's VLE or to make a non-fiction talking book or reference guide for younger children. At this point it is particularly important that teachers are clear about their primary learning objectives which might reside in any combination of English, science and computing.

Word processing and English

Word processing has a range of features which support writing activities, some of which have already been discussed. Editing offers powerful possibilities, and may be structured in ways that develop both English and ICT capability. For example, under a heading such as *All about me*, young children can select and enter words, sentences and images from Clicker or an on-screen bank. Alternatively, or as an extension, children could delete descriptions from a prepared text which do not apply to them. Such an activity promotes skills in working with text on the screen.

A wide range of sentence-level literacy activities can be facilitated – for instance, highlighting direct speech from a prepared text. Some children might use the word processor to complete this activity, while others could use a highlighter and a printout, thus making practical and effective use of classroom resources. Likewise, a prepared text can be changed from reported to direct speech. Word-level work can involve inserting punctuation into a continuous narrative to produce sentences or using search and replace to substitute alternatives for *said*.

Shared text-level work on instructions may focus on simple instructional writing, such as *How we clean our teeth*, with the teacher fielding suggestions and acting as scribe as the class or group look on. The interactive whiteboard provides an ideal medium for modelling the writing and editing process. A more complex instructional text such as a recipe for shortbread biscuits can be supported at different levels according to need – a prepared list requiring reordering for some, a partial list or a blank sheet for others. Word processing allows children to insert, delete, reorder and present their work.

Prepared texts can be turned from prose into note form, or notes turned into prose. Interesting comparisons can result if one group of children perform the inverse task on the work of others (once it has been saved or printed). A competitive element can be introduced as children seek to use the fewest number of words while still conveying meaning. Debate on what is and is not considered to be important may ensue.

There are opportunities for work focusing on the importance of layout, for instance in the writing and presentation of poetry. The effects of inserting line breaks and capital letters, centring, illustrating or font selection and size can be examined. Cartoons and newspaper layouts can be supported at various stages. Teachers can prepare paper versions for planning and electronic templates to support some children with the layout of their work. Designing front and back covers and title pages for books can provide an alternative to the book review, although children can make use of a prepared electronic writing frame to support such writing.

Children of all ages can work with tables to compile ongoing lists of synonyms for common adjectives.

Many of the activities suggested above make use of prepared word-processed documents. Teachers should ensure that they manage the use of these carefully. Always have a backup copy and agree with the children how the prepared document will be used. Clearly, having the first pair of children making adjustments and then saving their work over the original is to be avoided. Protect the master document so that changes cannot be saved and encourage children to save the document with a new name before they do anything else or to print out their work and then close the document without saving.

PRACTICAL TASK   PRACTICAL TASK   PRACTICAL TASK   PRACTICAL TASK

Use the template facility of a word processing package to design:

- **headed notepaper for your home or school address;**
- **a lesson-planning pro forma;**
- **a writing frame to scaffold work in one of the core subjects.**

Consider whether and how each of these could be utilised electronically or as printouts.

Desktop publishing

Software is now available which enables the non-expert to produce high-quality desktop-published documents. Through the use of wizards, birthday cards, invitations, calendars and newsletters can be generated by following the onscreen instructions, inserting the required text or graphics as directed. Publisher, from Microsoft, is one example, though many of its functions are now available in later versions of Word itself.

THE BIGGER PICTURE   THE BIGGER PICTURE   THE BIGGER PICTURE   THE BIGGER PICTURE

When you are planning to use desktop publishing, remember that it is not just useful for literacy texts but also to publish children's work in other subjects, for example the results of investigations in maths, science and PE, and research projects in geography, history, RE and PSHE.

Many schools are now using such applications for half-termly newsletters, prospectuses, fliers, display banners and other publicity and display materials. They can also be usefully deployed in the classroom, for instance in newspaper activities. DTP software does not always allow for changes to be made easily, particularly in text. This mirrors the professional DTP process, where graphics and text are comprehensively edited and considered to be finished before being incorporated in the layout.

A SUMMARY OF **KEY POINTS**

➢ **Word processing addresses the Information Technology and Digital Literacy aspects of the National Curriculum computing programme of study (DfE, 2013), but it can support learning in all areas of the curriculum, especially the core subjects.**

➢ **Word processing and DTP can be used both in children's learning and to support aspects of the professional teaching role.**

➢ **Teachers need to be confident users themselves in order to use word processing and DTP to create a range of learning resources.**

➢ **They also need to be conversant with the features of word-processing programs designed for use by primary children, and to be aware of the capabilities and limitations of word processing.**

➢ **Word processing can support every stage of the writing process, but effective use depends on the explicit teaching of skills.**

➢ **Although many word-processing programs now incorporate DTP features, there are separate DTP programs for more advanced presentation needs.**

M-LEVEL EXTENSION   > >   M-LEVEL EXTENSION   > >   M-LEVEL EXTENSION

Word processing is such a fundamental aspect of ICT that we tend to accept it somewhat unreflectively as a given way in which we work with computers. However, as a primary teacher, it is important to consider that the word processing software that you use on a daily basis does not represent the only approach to what we have seen is a complex and involved creative process. Try to test out other word-processing software, particularly packages designed for children, and make comparisons with the application that you use regularly. Using the suggestions for Further Reading and your own research, start an evaluation of how word-processing skills can be properly developed as part of a scheme of work showing progression from the EYFS through Key Stages 1 and 2 to Year 6 and beyond.

REFERENCES REFERENCES **REFERENCES** REFERENCES **REFERENCES** REFERENCES

DfE (2011) *Teachers' Standards*. Available at **www.education.gov.uk/publications**.

DfE (2013) *National Curriculum in England: Primary Curriculum*. London: DfE. Available at **www. gov.uk/government/publications/national-curriculum-in-england-primary-curriculum**.

Smith, H. (1998) *Opportunities for ICT in the Primary School*. Stoke-on-Trent: Trentham Books.

FURTHER READING FURTHER READING **FURTHER READING** FURTHER READING

Abbott, C. (2002) *ICT and Literacy Teaching.* Reading: National Centre for Language and Literacy.

Andrews, R. (ed.) (2004) *The Impact of ICT on Literacy Education.* London: Routledge Falmer.

Archdeacon, T. (2005) *Exciting ICT in English*. Stafford: Network Educational.

Leask, M. and Meadows, J. (2000) *Teaching and Learning with ICT in the Primary School*. London: Routledge.

Loveless, A. and Dore, B. (2002) *ICT in the Primary School*. Buckingham: Open University Press.

Martin, F. and Asprey, E. (2001) *Double Click on Word Processing.* Oxford: Heinemann Educational.

Monteith, M. (ed.) (2002) *Teaching Primary Literacy with ICT*. Buckingham: Open University Press.

13
Social media – tools for communicating, collaborating and publishing

Chapter objectives

When you have completed work on this chapter, you will have:

- understood the ways in which careful use of social media can support the aims of the National Curriculum for promoting digital literacy as well as providing wider authentic learning opportunities;
- examined a range of social media that can be used to foster collaborative working;
- considered the many different forms of writing which children engage with using social media.

Introduction

Perhaps the greatest opportunities for cross-curricular work as well as deepening understanding of computing and ICT arise from the careful use of 'social media', those online environments which depend on communication, a shared understanding of ways of presenting ideas, resources and, ultimately, of self-publication/broadcast. These include blogs, wikis and social networking tools and many others. With careful use and regard for pupil safety, these environments can provide authentic and rich experiences for communicating, collaborating and publishing as well as learning about how the internet works. Most importantly of all, perhaps, social media in the world outside school is likely to be very much a part of the way of life of the children you encounter and teach, just as much as it is a part of yours. To varying degrees, and for better or worse, the children in your immediate care will have access to the wider social media spaces of the internet and they will certainly see their parents experiencing all-pervasive communicative media of many kinds. Even in poorer homes with lower ownership of equipment, the social media world makes inroads in the form of posting and commenting, private instant messaging, long-distance family relationships maintained through video call software like Skype or similar, and more. Encountering these spaces in a school setting can be a powerful way of educating about criticality and safety. Certainly, ignoring them altogether is a missed opportunity to enhance the digital literacy of the children you teach, one of the stated requirements of the National Curriculum for computing.

What do the programmes of study for Key Stages 1 and 2 include?

Working with social media across the programmes of study in a range of curriculum contexts to provide an authentic space for enquiry, discussion and collaboration is perhaps the most obvious use. However, there are many key elements of the National Curriculum for Computing and ICT which can be explicitly planned for, in order to meet the overarching stated aim of ensuring that pupils 'are responsible, competent, confident and creative users of information and communication technology'.

Key Stage 1

- Use technology purposefully to create, organise, store, manipulate and retrieve digital content.
- Recognise common uses of information technology beyond school.
- Use technology safely and respectfully, keeping personal information private; identify where to go for help and support when they have concerns about content or contact on the internet or other online technologies.

Key Stage 2

- Understand computer networks, including the internet; how they can provide multiple services, such as the World Wide Web, and the opportunities they offer for communication and collaboration.
- Select, use and combine a variety of software (including internet services) on a range of digital devices to accomplish given goals.
- Use technology safely, respectfully and responsibly; recognise acceptable/unacceptable behaviour; identify a range of ways to report concerns about content and contact.

(DfE, 2013)

Starting points for working with social media: What do teachers need to know? What is available to use?

For primary schools, the exploration and use of social media is often thought of as problematic in that many of them are open-ended, open-source and open-use (and therefore open to abuse). However, the tools which have emerged that make these sorts of sites possible have, on occasion, been adopted and adapted into safe environments for education. Such tools as 'blogs' or 'wikis' can and do form parts of VLEs enabling children to produce and edit their own online versions of themselves and their work which, in turn, invites communication from peers in the form of comments, questions, criticisms, etc. What social media offer are increasingly authentic publishing opportunities and rich environments for writing and exhibiting media production.

As noted in the introduction to the chapter, children of primary school age may well encounter some of the tools of 'social media' outside of school, even if these are not the same spaces which you use. They are also subject to rapid changes and patterns of use. Examples which younger learners may use more than Facebook include child-friendly spaces such as Club Penguin or Moshi Monsters which are not unlike social media in some of their functions. These may often have tie-ins to other forms of media products in a world in which media convergence is a given (see Jenkins, 2006). As far as Facebook is concerned, evidence suggests that the generation entering their teens now uses rapid sharing apps such as 'Snapchat' and simple blog publishing like 'Tumblr' instead of the more detailed and formal looking spaces of Facebook. Children whom you teach may well have seen parents, friends or siblings using these social media. Templates in all these spaces enable the creation of sophisticated-looking pages online. It should be stressed at the outset that all of these sites are places where the content is sometimes inappropriate. The onward links from people's pages, however innocent they appear at first, cannot all be vetted and verified. For this reason there is a tendency for such sites to be blocked for users in schools. However, the principle of one's own desktop and publishing space with the associated freedom to publish, comment and collaborate in a safe way is enshrined in many local and regional virtual or managed learning environments (VLEs or MLEs).

Outside the VLE and on the wider internet are a range of blogging services for education which allow for similar experiences of publishing for real audiences. Blogs are online journals or diaries, on any subject, often with rich media content (for more on this see Rettberg, 2008). 'Edublogs' is a blogging space especially created with education users in mind and is built on the same easy-to-use platform as one of the major free blog providers, WordPress.

The Edublogs homepage has a user-friendly interface and a series of useful global links, albeit dominated by educators and classrooms in the United States **(https://edublogs. org)**. The Edublogs dashboard (Figure 13.1) offers a user-friendly interface with a range of tools for creating content and personalising your blog. There are significant numbers of UK educators on there too who wish to administer a live writing and documenting presence for the work they undertake in their classrooms. The claims made for this are that it gives writing an 'authenticity' for the end-user. It's worth stating that it's also possible to be inauthentic in social media as much as it is anywhere else and that the technology by itself does not confer any useful agency on the children. Skilled, student-centred pedagogy brings out the best in the children by presenting them with huge opportunities to develop an audience and to reach out and engage with digital culture. The usual repeated caveats about safety are as important here as anywhere.

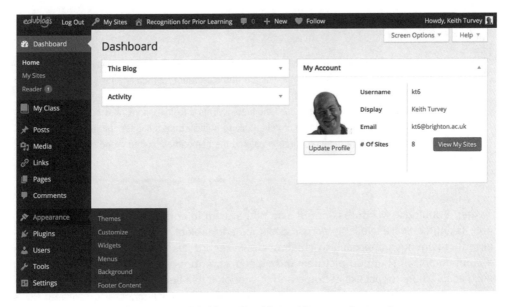

Figure 13.1 Edublogs Dashboard for creating and uploading content

---

IN THE CLASSROOM

One of the most recent and successful examples of blogging is the simple and effective structure devised by David Mitchell, a primary school deputy head teacher from Bolton, whose method, known as 'quadblogging', enables groups of up to four schools at a time to blog between each other over a four-week period, taking it in turns to be the focus and commentators on each other's work. The originating school has passed over a million hits and the main issue with blogs (that they start well but rarely stay maintained) is circumvented by the onward momentum and drive that inheres from having an audience and a purpose (see **www. quadblogging.com** (Mitchell, 2014)). Again, this is something which is worthy of investigation while keeping in mind that human agency is what keeps it going; the technology by itself confers no agency nor any guarantee of success in the venture.

A further example of the positive impact of blogging on writing comes from the work of Myra Barrs and Sarah Horrocks (2014). They studied the implementation of blogging for writing across the curriculum in an inner-city school, noting benefits ranging from increased motivation to write for a genuine audience to an extensive vocabulary (of a genuinely communicative kind, not simply a showcase of 'powerful' words).

Like many social media services, Edublogs are synchronised across devices and enable users to develop a sense of themselves as connected to the outside world and to their developing achievements as writers. For those children who are at the very earliest stages of writing whom you would nonetheless like to connect with other children and places beyond the school through social media, you could consider using a micro-blogging tool such as the phenomenally popular Twitter, where, as you probably know, users publish in short, 140-character pieces. This requires an active policy of policing and protecting younger users but it can be done very effectively as shown below.

IN THE CLASSROOM

Publishing in the form of a micro-blog of only 140 characters per post, Twitter has received some attention as a social media space which is of potential value in the classroom, particularly for younger learners. A teacher called Martin Waller used it with his class of six-year-olds who had a shared Twitter identity which he moderated, effectively making himself the firewall. This is a big responsibility but he has written of the very positive impact on the children of being able to publish their thoughts and actions to a wide audience, giving their writing a genuine purpose beyond the sometimes limited world of the classroom (see Waller, 2012).

Twitter, Edublogs, Wordpress could also all be used in conjunction with synchronised, note-taking software available across desktops and tablets, such as Evernote. A personalised and agentive approach to children's own record-keeping of their work would see a combination of snapped pictures and videos, scrapbooked electronically into spaces such as Evernote for access at home and at school. It has been successfully used in other settings and in other projects, such as Keri Facer and Helen Manchester's Learning Lives project (2012).

Other kinds of social media sites for sharing content

In addition to the communicative, self-curated and self-broadcasting social media sites such as Facebook and Twitter are the websites which provide hosting of user-generated content, such as, for example, Flickr; this may well be a photo-sharing website that you also make use of from time to time. Indeed, sites such as Flickr are a rich source of digital photographs, uploaded by users and given tags to make them searchable by others, including those uploading and using the same tags. Thus pictures of, for example, a trip to the Science Museum in London to view a gaming exhibition, 'Game on', could be uploaded to Flickr or similar and given label categories, known as 'tags', of 'London', 'Museum', 'Computer game', 'Science', 'Exhibition'. People viewing Flickr may search for the pictures which you have taken and uploaded by the tag you have used. Furthermore, you and your class may search for pictures taken of the same place – sometimes at the same time – for the purposes of onward communication, shared commentaries on public spaces, etc.

Furthermore, Flickr and similar sites are a way to share images between home and school with the caveat that you still require a shared internet policy to enable the publishing of pictures featuring children who may be recognised. The same sort of sharing and tagging applies to video images in sites such as YouTube which are popular exhibition spaces for digital video projects. Indeed the whole vexed issue of blocking YouTube or not is one which confounds many schools. Blocking is a way for many of protecting children from inappropriate content or, more likely, surprisingly offensive and inappropriate comments on highly appropriate content. There is no easy answer to this, but one approach is to recognise the unique repository of popular cultural and curriculum-related content on YouTube which is available feely. Inevitably, there is a high cost overhead in terms of your effort to police access to all this in real time (assuming YouTube is not blocked in your school). Many teachers simply arrive at the conclusion that they need to use their own time to download the source video file using one of the many converters available (such as zamzar.com) and show it to their class without any worries from linked content, offensive commenting on the clip or any adverts which are also worthy of blocking. For further reading on social media used in this way see Knobel and Lankshear (2010) and Lankshear and Knobel (2011).

The idea of co-authoring is extended into factual writing by the creation of online reference texts in wikis – collaborative writing tools. Thus Wikipedia has grown exponentially into an enormous reference resource, edited (and policed) by its creators to allow contributions from a wide range of co-authors, all of whom are writing from personal knowledge and experience. Although generally considered to be one of the safer sites for social software authors to visit, there is by no means universal understanding or approval of the site in formal educational circles. The tools which allow collaborative writing have, however, sometimes been adapted into wikis in shared areas in VLEs which creates genuinely interesting opportunities to work with peer learning, where more able writers may support less able ones.

A further social software tool which you should consider for your own personal use is one of the many sites which allow the tagging and categorisation of particular bookmarked websites. You can create an online collection of websites which you use regularly by tagging them with labels that enable you to locate them more frequently. Examples here would include Delicious and Diigo (which can be found by adding a .com to those names). The advantage over traditional bookmarking is that the list is synchronised across computers, tablets and smartphones. If you move location frequently, or use more than one computer in a day, these sites enable you to keep track of the useful resources you discover. There is also the possibility of enabling sharing of seeing what other people are finding through their use of a particular tag. As usual, one of the caveats here is a thorough exploration of the safety policy of the school and the site yourself to ensure that children are not at risk and that they will report to you anything that makes them uncomfortable. The other caveat is to remember that sites move and repurpose themselves; Delicious has been taken over twice for example. It is always worth checking resource recommendations and functionality for yourself. One suggested purpose of Delicious is to create group lists of resources in an online account administered at the school, perhaps one per class. Again, here, an important consideration will be the safety angle and not wishing to duplicate functions which may have been adapted into your local VLE already.

Conclusion

This brief survey of social media has attempted to provide you with some suggestions and starting points for an exploration of an area of great opportunity for schools to use. Social media allow for children to be productive in spaces which really do have an audience for whom they can learn to write and create. They afford the opportunity of learning beyond the classroom by connecting to other schools and other classes and, safety caveats notwithstanding, allow for your learners to develop a rich understanding of both the internet as it is used every day and of any of the subjects of the curriculum which you choose to make the subject of posts and creative activity.

A SUMMARY OF **KEY POINTS**

> Schools and their children are increasingly active in the online community, searching, retrieving, analysing and synthesising information as well as developing, trialling and publishing their own.

> There are clear benefits in working in linked spaces across synchronised devices.

> It appears that children and young people respond well to real opportunities to publish and to see their work online and experience the positive impact of others critiquing their work.

> Critical evaluation of web-based resources is vital to ensure suitability, accuracy and safety. Try any social media spaces yourself and/or seek the advice of other teachers using them through Twitter or blogs before you use them with children; always do so with permission from parents and school managers.

M-LEVEL EXTENSION > > M-LEVEL EXTENSION > > M-LEVEL EXTENSION

Consider the range of opportunities for the use of the internet in teaching and learning. What is the likely impact of the use of blogging and social software, possibly within a VLE, on your role in the classroom? How might this be a way to join subjects together in cross-curricular projects? What are the issues that must be taken into account when using the internet in this way?

REFERENCES REFERENCES **REFERENCES** REFERENCES REFERENCES REFERENCES

Barrs, M. and Horrocks, S. (2014) *Educational Blogs and Their Effects on Pupils' Writing*. London: CFBT Education Trust.

DfE (2013) *National Curriculum in England: Primary Curriculum*. London: DfE. Available at **https:// www.gov.uk/government/publications/national-curriculum-in-england-primary-curriculum**.

Facer, K. and Manchester, H. (2012) *Mapping Learner Lives: Final Report*. Manchester Metropolitan University Education and Social Research Institute.

Jenkins, H. (2006) *Convergence Culture*. New York: New York University Press.

Knobel, M. and Lankshear, C. (eds) (2010) *DIY Media: Creating, Sharing and Learning with New Technologies*. New York: Peter Lang.

Mitchell, D. (2014) Quadblogging site at **www.quadblogging.com** and **www.quadblogging.net** (older version with background).

Lankshear, C. and Knobel, M. (2011) *New Literacies: Everyday Practices and Social Learning*. Milton Keynes: Open University Press.

Rettberg, J.W. (2008) *Blogging*. Cambridge: Polity.

Waller, M. (2012) 'More than tweets: developing the "new" and "old" through online social networking, Martin Waller', in G. Merchant, J. Gillen et al. (eds), *Virtual Literacies: Interactive Spaces for Children and Young People*. London: Routledge.

FURTHER READING FURTHER READING **FURTHER READING** FURTHER READING

Buckingham, D. and Willett, R. (eds) (2006) *Digital Generations: Children, Young People and the New Media*. Mahwah, NJ: Lawrence Erlbaum Associates.

Gee, J.P. (2004) *Situated Language and Learning*. London: Routledge.

Merchant, G., Gillen, J. et al. (2012) *Virtual Literacies: Interactive Spaces for Children and Young People*. London: Routledge.

Potter, J. (2012) *Digital Media and Learner Identity: The New Curatorship*. New York: Palgrave Macmillan.

14
Graphing programs

Introduction

Graphical representations of data are everywhere: social media and websites, in newspapers, magazines, books, on television programmes and mobile devices. Children are constantly exposed to information communicated in this manner. If they are to interpret this in any meaningful way they need to develop appropriate critical knowledge, skills and understanding.

Graphing programs have been available in primary schools for many years. The range of features and functions supported by many graphing programs has also been significantly enhanced. Most recently, a plethora of web-based data collection and survey tools such as Google Forms and SurveyMonkey have enabled the easy collection and manipulation of data. Indeed, computer scientists and programmers have developed a range of data visualisation tools designed to communicate data in novel ways but which also require critical interpretation.

This chapter explores graphing tools and their potential for the enhancement and extension of children's knowledge and understanding of computing. However, this aspect of the computing curriculum also has significant cross-curricular applications. These will be explored and links made to other generic data-handling or visualisation software.

What are graphing programs?

Graphing programs facilitate the communication of information through graphical representation. They enable data to be entered, stored, presented and interpreted graphically in an electronic format. Some allow the rudimentary sorting of data, into ascending or descending order of frequency, for instance. Graphing programs do not, however, support sophisticated sorting, searching or modelling. Such data-handling activity requires database software, which will be examined in more detail in Chapter 15.

What do the programmes of study for Key Stages 1 and 2 include?

In the aims of the National Curriculum for computing it is emphasised that the teaching of computing 'ensures that pupils become digitally literate – able to use, and express themselves and develop their ideas through, information and communication technology – at a level suitable for the future workplace and as active participants in a digital world' (DfE, 2013). A key aspect of digital literacy is the responsible and safe use of technologies, which also applies when children are collecting data for representation in graphing programs. The specific aspects of the programme of study which relate to graphing programs and data visualisation are highlighted as follows.

At Key Stage 1, the programme of study for computing (DfE, 2013) states that children should be taught to:

- use technology purposefully to create, organise, store, manipulate and retrieve digital content;
- use technology safely and respectfully, keeping personal information private; know where to go for help and support when they have concerns about material on the internet;
- recognise common uses of information technology beyond school.

At Key Stage 2 (DfE, 2013) children should be taught how to:

- select, use and combine a variety of software (including internet services) on a range of digital devices to accomplish given goals, including collecting, analysing, evaluating and presenting data and information;
- use technology safely, respectfully and responsibly; know a range of ways to report concerns and inappropriate behaviour.

What do teachers need to know about using graphing programs?

In order to teach with and about graphing programs teachers need to be confident about their subject knowledge related to the handling of data. In this area there is a substantial and obvious overlap in terms of subject knowledge between science, mathematics and computing. Relevant issues include:

- choice of variables;
- types of data;
- grouping data;
- collecting and recording data;
- presenting data.

Many data-handling activities begin with a consideration of what data to collect. In science, the choice of variables is often a key teaching and learning objective. For instance, the growth pattern of a seedling may be explored by comparing its height at 9.00 a.m. each day over a three-week period. Two variables are involved here: seedling height and time. Alternatively, the investigation could be limited to one variable by measuring the height of a number of seedlings once only three weeks after sowing. The exploration would, in this instance, focus on the distribution of heights achieved. It should also be noted that there is potential for children to confuse the meaning of the word 'variable' as it is used in the process of scientific investigation compared to its usage in computing and programming.

There are three types of data: categorical, discrete and continuous. *Categorical data* fall into distinct named categories which do not overlap and cannot be ordered. For example, children's eyes may be blue, brown, hazel, green or grey. Where *discrete data* are concerned, the classes are defined by discrete whole numbers. An example might be the number of siblings class members have. *Continuous data* cannot be so easily segregated. The height of seedlings is measured on a continuous scale and each seedling's height is, potentially at least, slightly different from that of the others. The type of data collected influences how it is collected, recorded and presented in graphing software.

Before data are collected and recorded, decisions should be made about grouping. In the case of categorical and discrete data the categories or classes will usually be quite obvious. Where continuous data are involved there is a choice: either to record and then plot each individual item (each seedling's exact height) or to attempt to group the data into classes, effectively translating continuous data into discrete. For instance, rather than recording a seedling's height as 8cm, another as 8.5cm, another as 6cm, each of these three seedlings could be entered into the category 5.0–9.9cm, with other categories for 10.0–14.9cm, etc.

Decisions about the grouping of data will affect recording and presentation. To continue the example above, further decisions about accuracy, number of decimal places and use of rounding will be required, and a suitable recording format must be chosen. Data may be collected and recorded in a number of ways, counting and tally charts being the most common for categorical, discrete or grouped data.

Once data have been collected and recorded, consideration can be given to presenting them graphically. It is important that the choice of graph is consistent with the data type. Categorical and discrete data are conventionally represented by bar charts, with each bar representing one discrete category or number. Bar charts can be arranged horizontally

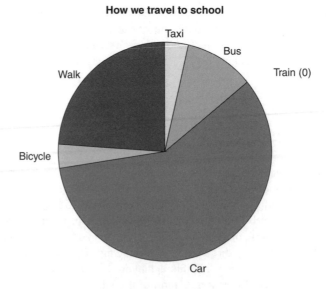

How we travel to school

**Figure 14.1 Pie chart with one category (Train)
having a zero value**

or vertically or as bar line graphs. Pie charts are also suitable for the presentation of categorical or discrete data, particularly where consideration of relative proportions is important – for example, in comparing the ways in which members of a class travel to school. However, caution should be exercised in the use of pie charts, especially where there are two or more categories containing similar or equal amounts of data, since it may be difficult to distinguish their relative size by eye. The representation of data sets where one or more category has a value of zero is also problematic, since these will not be represented on the pie chart.

Line graphs and scatter graphs are suitable for the presentation of continuous data. Continuous data may include two variables, for example the growth of a plant may be measured over time, with its height plotted against the day on which each reading is taken. Such graphs are sometimes called *xy* graphs. A scatter graph represents the actual

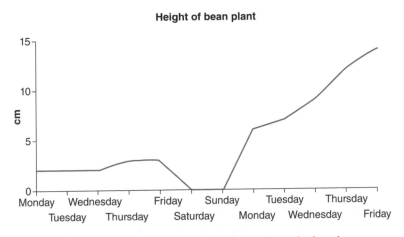

**Figure 14.2 Line graph showing the effect of a break
in data collection**

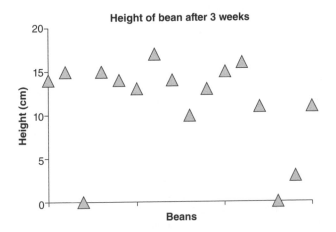

**Figure 14.3 Scatter plot showing distribution
of seedling heights**

data in this instance, whereas a line graph may be used to join the individual points to give some indication of rate of growth over time. However, children need to understand that joining such plots by a line represents an approximation. If data had been collected at intermediate points they would not necessarily fall directly on the line. Further, if some data-collection opportunities are missed, for instance over the weekend or half-term, the graphing program may interpret no data as having a value of zero. In this case, the line graph will return to the x-axis. Spreadsheets, which also enable graphs to be plotted from such data, may cope better with this situation.

Teaching with and about graphing programs involves teachers in the following:

- *Selecting appropriate opportunities* in which graphing programs can facilitate, enhance or extend children's learning, such as exploring the impact of graphically representing one set of data using a range of scales. In some instances the focus will be on teaching and learning in computing and ICT (how a graphing program can facilitate such an investigation), while in others ICT will be used as a resource in the teaching and learning of another curriculum area (the effect of choice of scale).
- *Exploring the full range of data-handling activities.* It is important that data-handling work does not always end with the production of a graph. In many instances data-handling work will begin with a graphical representation and learning will be focused on interpretation and analysis.
- *Making explicit links between related knowledge, skills and understanding.* Data-handling has applications in many areas of the primary curriculum; teachers thus have opportunities to make explicit and reinforce the links between children's previous experiences and new learning across the range of contexts.
- *Modelling appropriate use of ICT*, for instance, the joining of individual plots of data by a line graph to assist in the analysis of the pattern or trend the data represent.
- *Demonstrating and intervening*, for instance, intervening to assist a child to export a graph to the appropriate place in a word-processed record of a science experiment; similarly, demonstrating and discussing the potential difficulties of interpreting data represented in a pie chart.

The list below attempts to identify the knowledge, skills and understanding of graphing software teachers need in order to teach effectively with and about graphing programs.

Many graphing programs support only a subset of these functions. This is no reflection on their usefulness – in most instances it may be a strength. However, it does signal that teachers must be aware of the capabilities and limitations of any program as these will be significant in the choice of software for any teaching and learning activity.

- graphing program knowledge, skills and understanding;
- creating, opening, saving, closing, deleting and printing documents;
- adding, modifying and deleting data;
- plotting and replotting graphs;
- selecting and displaying graph types and visualisations, including more than one graphical representation of the same data;
- selecting and modifying constituent elements of graphs, such as changing the colours of bars in a bar chart to correspond with the data represented;
- selecting, resizing, cutting, copying and pasting graphs;
- selecting and modifying graph scales and autoscaling;
- selecting two-dimensional or three-dimensional representations;
- inserting graph titles, axes labels, key and text;
- selecting font and font size for graph and axes headings;
- exporting graphs into other applications;
- importing information from other applications, such as clip art;

- utilising help;
- altering defaults;
- customising the graphing program, switching off functions not needed;
- utilising alternative input devices (particularly data-loggers);
- selecting appropriate colours, patterns or visualisations depending on printer availability (black and white or colour);
- protecting documents.

There will be occasions on which other data-handling software, such as databases or spreadsheets, will be more suitable. Teachers need to be confident in making decisions about the most appropriate application for a particular situation.

What are the key features of a graphing program?

Graphing programs:

- produce graphs directly from data entered;
- offer a range of graph types;
- usually automatically select the scale;
- provide opportunities to reinforce the relationship between numerical and graphical representation of the same data;
- allow children to focus on using the information contained in a graph rather than the process of construction;
- do not replace children constructing graphs manually – this is an important developmental stage in the process of understanding;
- facilitate a range of learning outcomes – for instance, emphasis may be on data collection (planning, organising, recording, entering), interpretation, or on the effect of scale and choice of representation;
- facilitate work on equivalence and differences between graph types, such as bar charts, pie charts, bar line charts, line graphs, scatter graphs;
- facilitate work on progression in graphical representation.

Graphing programs can be divided into two categories:

- pictogram programs, which support early graphing activities and usually allow for the representation of data only as pictograms or block graphs;
- more sophisticated graphing programs, which support a range of graph types and functions.

In order to facilitate the exploration of the features and contribution of each of these, they will be referred to as pictogram programs and graphing programs respectively.

What do graphing programs contribute to teaching and learning?

One of the key advantages of working with graphing programs to handle data is that much of the time-consuming work of planning and plotting graphs is automated, allowing the user to focus on the information contained in the graph. Which is the most frequently owned pet in Year 3, and how does this compare with pet ownership of children in Year 6?

Other questions may then be raised, such as what might be the influences on choice of pet? What constitutes pet ownership where there is more than one child in a family? How is double-counting avoided? The emphasis should be on investigation and analysis as much as on representation.

An important aspect of work in handling data involves choosing the most appropriate graphical representation. Graphing programs facilitate immediate comparisons between the different graph types. Would pie charts be the most suitable method of representing the pet ownership information? What if some animals are owned by children in Year 3, but not by children in Year 6? Using graphing programs enables children to make independent choices of graph types, safe in the knowledge that the graph can be redrawn speedily if necessary. When hand-drawing is involved there may be a tendency for the teacher to direct children towards a shared class decision in order to avoid wasting time.

Most pictogram and graphing programs also enable data to be sorted at a simple level, for example into ascending or descending order of frequency. This can be a very useful facility, especially if there is a wide range of categories, or the scale is marked in intervals of two or five or ten. Using a sorting function does not obviate the need for children to be able to read information accurately from graphs; it can provide another opportunity for teaching or reinforcing that skill.

Graphing programs can be used to demonstrate the relationship between data, their recording in a frequency table and their representation or as a graph. Most programs allow the frequency table to be shown alongside a graph. Making these connections is vital if children are to handle data in a meaningful way.

Developing children's understanding of the equivalence of information represented in different graphs can be facilitated by showing, for instance, a horizontal bar chart, a vertical bar chart and a bar line graph side by side.

Graphing programs have autoscaling features which choose the scale of the graph, usually depending on the highest value or frequency. Most programs replot graphs each time new data are entered. In this way the development of a graph and the effect of each new piece of data can be powerfully demonstrated. Autoscaling often results in graphs where scales are marked in intervals of two, five or more. The construction and interpretation of such graphs are important stages in the progression of children's understanding of data handling. Sometimes the autoscaling feature can be disabled to enable children to make their own selections as appropriate.

Similarly, the connection between choice of scale and the effectiveness or impact of a graph can be explored. There can be valuable learning associated with attempting to 'misrepresent' information, choosing a scale that will make a small variation look large or a large variation look insignificant. This also brings in the ethical dimensions surrounding the ways in which such data is used. For example, when collecting data about other people children should be taught about their responsibilities in using and storing the data appropriately and responsibly. Almost any newspaper, magazine, website or TV news programme will contain some graphical representation of information. Making links with real-life applications of knowledge and understanding which children could otherwise view as quite abstract in nature can be a powerful learning tool.

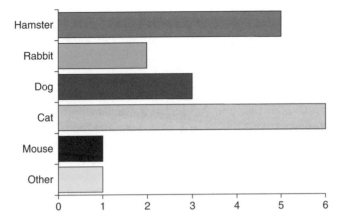

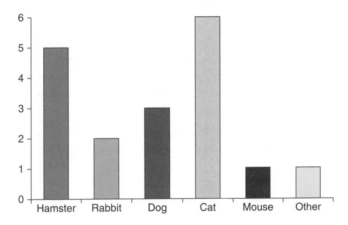

Figure 14.4 Horizontal and vertical bar charts showing the same data (CounterPlus, BlackCat)

Many of the issues discussed above, such as choice of graph type, equivalence, comparison and scale, also have relevance for the exchange and sharing of information. Additionally, if a group of children presents the results of a science investigation for display on the classroom wall, decisions need to be taken not only about the most suitable type of graph for the data but also about its readability at a distance. The advantages of a horizontal bar chart over the more common vertical, where the labels might more obviously correspond with the data, might also be explored. There are instances where two or more graph types may be equally appropriate and children can justify their personal selections and discuss the merits of each (see Figure 14.4).

Copying and pasting a graph into a report or other document is a useful function and many pictogram and graphing programs support this. Graphs can usually then be moved and resized as any other image. It is important that children know that they can transfer their skills in this way within and between applications.

Progression of knowledge, skills and understanding

Early data-handling activities will relate closely to children themselves and their own experiences. 'Ourselves' is a common theme and many pictogram programs such as Counting Pictures 3 (BlackCat) and Pictogram 3 (Kudlian Soft) have a predetermined range of relevant topics to select from, e.g. pets, favourite foods and hair colour. Having chosen a suitable focus, such as children's eye colour, and discussed the likely alternatives, the teacher can call up a blank pictogram on screen and ask each child in turn their eye colour. The children may need to consult with a friend and the teacher (or a child) can click or drag the appropriate icon to include the information in the graph. The pictogram will be built in front of the children and the connection between each child's answer and the appearance of an icon in the relevant column made explicit. This method of data collection is appropriate for young children and the immediate building of the graph reinforces the connection between the data (the answers the children give) and the graphical representation of the data (see Figure 14.5).

At its simplest, a pictogram drawn with a graphing program will consist of columns of icons indicating a one-to-one representation. The teacher can lead the children in counting to establish how many children in the class have blue eyes. There is no need for text labelling as each category is identified by an icon, although the software usually allocates a title based on the subject selected.

Pictogram programs have a variety of features which facilitate their use at various stages in supporting children's knowledge and understanding of data-handling. These might include:

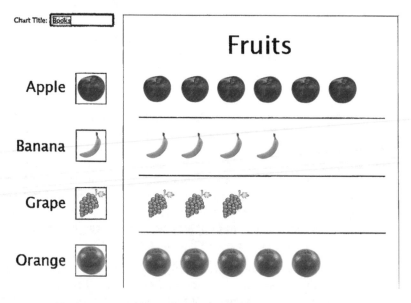

Figure 14.5 Building a pictogram (Pictogram 3 courtesy of Kudlian Software)

- *adding a scale* – reading from a scale requires a more sophisticated understanding of number than does counting icons;
- *adding axes* – the addition of *x* and *y* axes represents a stage in the development from a straightforward pictorial representation of data towards the more abstract model generally recognised as a graph;
- *transforming the pictogram into a block graph* – again, this is a development from the straightforward pictorial representation of data towards something more abstract in nature. Each block in a block graph clearly represents an individual piece of data, which distinguishes it from a bar chart in which the divisions between the data are not distinct. Pictogram 3 (Kudlian Soft) also supports bar charts, representing a further progression.

REFLECTIVE TASK

Following the compilation of a Year 1 class pictogram of favourite foods, what questions would you ask to probe and develop the children's understanding? How would you follow up the activity?

Programs such as DataPlot (Kudlian Soft), Counter (BlackCat), 2Graph and 2Count (2Simple Software) facilitate more sophisticated data-handling activities. Data are entered through a frequency table and a graph is drawn and redrawn as new data are added. Text labels are transferred from the frequency table to the graph and are necessary to identify and interpret the graph. There is a range of graph types to choose from, allowing children to experiment and select the most suitable. Scales marked at intervals greater than one can result, although such graphs can also be drawn in some pictogram packages. Options for saving, adding text and exporting to other applications are easily accessible. A further level of sophistication enables each axis to be separately titled and choices to be made about colours and/or patterns. Two- and three-dimensional representations are often possible and selection can be made from a wider range of graph types. Negative and decimal numbers are usually supported. Effective utilisation of graphing programs may facilitate the development of children's knowledge, skills and understanding of handling data independently of the motor skills required for the hand-drawing of graphs.

What are the capabilities and limitations of graphing programs?

Selecting appropriate graph types

Graphing programs do not automatically select the most suitable graph type to represent data. The choice remains with the user. Nor will the software warn against unsuitable selections. Teachers will need to ensure that children make appropriate choices based on the data. Many graphing programs automatically represent data as vertical bar charts unless another graph type is specifically selected. This default risks reinforcing the use of this most common graph type at the expense of a consideration of alternatives.

IN THE CLASSROOM

A trainee teacher had carefully prepared a lesson on graphing programs. His teaching objectives were appropriately described in terms of computing. He was familiar with the software and had selected data related to current geography work. He took the class to the ICT suite and proceeded to introduce the activity, describing the process. The children were required to access a graphing program, enter into it data relating to average temperatures across a year in a distant place and the UK, and produce pie charts for comparison.

The trainee teacher provided pairs of children with a help sheet he had prepared and the lesson proceeded. After 35 minutes, each pair had produced two pie charts. These were printed out and the class returned to the classroom. Questioning the children, however, suggested that they had little understanding of the information the graphs represented. Although the data had been chosen to relate to a current geography study, the links between that and the computing session had not been made explicit to the children. Further, there was little examination of the finished pie charts in order to interpret the data. This would in any event have been difficult using the graph type selected.

PRACTICAL TASK PRACTICAL TASK PRACTICAL TASK PRACTICAL TASK

Prepare a display to demonstrate:

- **an appropriate use of each of the graph types supported by a particular graphing program; or**
- **how to print a completed graph, including making appropriate selections to cater for the available printer; or**
- **children's top tips for using the particular graphing program you are focusing on.**

Frequency tables and tally charts

Most graphing programs allow data to be viewed through a frequency table as well as a graph. In many, the data are entered through the frequency table. This feature provides an opportunity for teachers to reinforce the correspondence of the information represented in these different ways. Counting Pictures (BlackCat) also has a tally chart function which can be used to facilitate the progression from simultaneous data collection and entry, as in the eye-colour example described previously, to recording and subsequent entry, for which the tally chart is the most frequently used mechanism.

PRACTICAL TASK PRACTICAL TASK PRACTICAL TASK PRACTICAL TASK

Plan a sequence of lessons to introduce the concept of tally charts for the recording of data. Choose a suitable subject context. Note how and why ICT can be used, making reference to assumptions about the availability and location of resources. Note prerequisite knowledge, skills and understanding with respect to mathematics and ICT.

3-D graphs

Most graphing programs have the facility to display graphs in three dimensions as well as two. The third dimension allows children to produce sophisticated-looking representations which compare with those they see on television or in the press.

However, the 3-D effect can be problematic for children when reading information from scales. This concern is particularly apparent in respect of bar charts. Children may experience confusion in deciding which lines to follow to read off information. Similarly, a bar with a zero value will still contain a block of colour. The interpretation of 3-D graphs may thus require explicit teaching. There is an argument for avoiding them altogether as strictly speaking the 3-D perspective distorts the areas that should represent the individual fields so that they no longer constitute an accurate proportion of the whole. This problem is most clearly evidenced by 3-D pie charts.

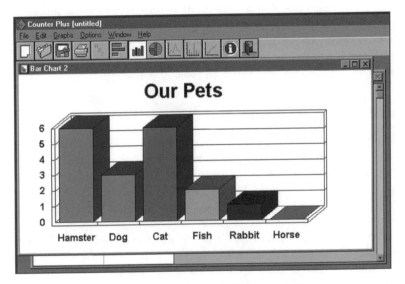

Figure 14.6 3-D bar chart showing category with zero value (CounterPlus, BlackCat)

Pictogram programs

Pictogram programs tend to have a limited range of possible graph subjects, such as pets, journeys to school or favourite colour, determined by the icons available. It is entirely appropriate that young children's data-handling experiences involve data which have some relevance to them, rather than the rainfall patterns in a distant location, for instance, and most of these are catered for. Some packages provide the opportunity for the range to be extended although this involves drawing appropriate pictures using the tools provided. Within each graph subject there is also a limited range of categories; 'hamster', for instance, may not always appear as a pet choice, although 'horse' often does. Again, these can be customised and software houses enhance their products over time, most welcoming feedback on such issues. Similarly, there may be restrictions on the amount of data that can be entered. With class sizes even in Key Stage 1 of around 30, such a limitation on numbers can be important as the result might be that it is impossible for a record to be entered for each child.

Selecting colours

Graphing programs often allocate predetermined colours to bars in bar charts; thus the first bar may be blue, the second green and so on. Clearly this may be problematic if the data have some link to colour – for instance, children's favourite colours, hair colour or eye colour – and there is a mismatch. A graphing program will not be helpful if it represents the number of people with blue eyes with a red bar. Better software will allow colours to be changed once the initial graph has been drawn up, but there is some software in which this option is not available.

Teachers need to ensure that they explore such issues when selecting software for particular tasks. The writers of the DataPlot (Kudlian Soft) software saw this as a potential difficulty and incorporated some programming that ensures that if data are identified by colour (e.g. eye colours, blue 6, green 3, brown 7), it is represented by those colours. The software also identifies hair colours such as ginger, fair and blonde and makes appropriate choices (assuming the colours have been spelled correctly).

Printing considerations

Most graphing programs make extensive use of colour. This helps children differentiate between different groups of data and aids the visual engagement with the graphic representation. However, when graphs are to be printed out this may become an issue. Colour printing is expensive. Printing a coloured graph in black and white usually results in various shades of grey. These may be difficult to distinguish. There are two potential solutions available to teachers and most graphing programs will support at least one of these. Sometimes it is possible to choose to print out a graph without any colour, enabling the children to colour in by hand. DataPlot (Kudlian Soft) provides an option to switch off the colour function. Alternatively, it may be possible to change the various colours to white, producing the same effect when printed out. Secondly, some programs provide a range of pattern options which can be selected instead of colours.

Links to other generic data-handling software

CounterPlus (BlackCat) allows multiple columns of numeric information to be incorporated and thus represented on the same graph, enabling comparisons to be made. This type of function is usually only possible using a spreadsheet.

Many software houses have linked ranges of data-handling programs, so that the transfer of children's skills from one to another is facilitated by familiar icons and functions. Kudlian Soft produce Pictogram 3 and DataPlot, facilitating progression from one to the other. Additionally, DataPlot is a constituent of DataSweet, which also includes the spreadsheet DataCalc as well as database software. Similarly, Counting Pictures uses the same icons as Pick a Picture, BlackCat's early database program.

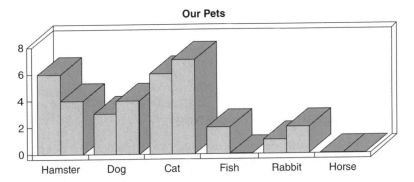

**Figure 14.7 Block graph and frequency table demonstrating
comparison between two sets of data
(CounterPlus, BlackCat)**

Common errors and misconceptions

Although using graphing programs reduces some of the demands on children relating to graphical representation of data, it is important to ensure that emphasis is placed on interpretation as well as presentation. The graph is not the end product. Children need to be able to analyse, discuss and summarise what the graph means. A display of the children's graphs alone indicates that this process may not have happened. The display will be far more convincing if it includes a record of the children's commentaries.

The scale of data-handling activities deserves consideration. The availability of ICT might prompt the collection of far more data than would otherwise be contemplated. This might be to its advantage, for instance in the monitoring of environmental conditions. However, caution should be exercised to ensure that the time taken to collect data does not distract from the teaching focus. On the other hand, especially for older children familiar with the basic principles of data-handling, it is important for the challenge to be authentic. Entering the colours of cars from the staff car park into graphing software to establish which shade is the most popular is poor use of the power of ICT to handle data.

Autoscaling can often be disabled to allow children to select their own scale and consider the implications of differing intervals.

Graphing programs and the core subjects

The ideas and activities introduced below are intended to give a feel for the range of ways in which graphing programs can be utilised to support and enhance teaching and learning in mathematics, science and English. They are not intended to be comprehensive, merely to go some way towards illustrating the breadth of possibilities and to provide starting points for the customisation of ideas and the generation of others. Examples introduced under mathematics, for instance, may be just as applicable to one or more of the other areas and vice versa.

There is extensive overlap between science, mathematics, English, computing and other subject knowledge, skills and understanding in this area of data handling. Teachers need to be clear about their primary teaching objective for any particular task or sequence of activities and maximise the opportunities for making explicit links between learning in the various curriculum contexts.

Graphing programs and science

Graphing programs have many possibilities in science for the recording and representation of experimental data. A number of possibilities have already been discussed. Most graphing programs allow text to be entered and displayed alongside graphs, and graphs can usually be copied and pasted into other applications, such as word-processing software.

Some activities will involve the collection, entry and representation of data, while others may start with prepared data looking for patterns, causal links and evidence to test hypotheses.

Environmental monitoring and sensing

Data-logging is the process of monitoring and recording environmental data such as temperature, light, movement and sound using sensors. The data are displayed through software which can be considered to be a special application of a graphing program, having many common features and functions, such as choice of graph types and scale.

Sensors (inputs) are linked to the computer through a buffer box interface (for example, from Deltronics) or through more portable equipment such as the LogIT Explorer, which provides an integrated interface between the sensors and the computer. The software, which is often supplied with the hardware or may be purchased separately (such as Junior Datalogging Insight from Longman Logotron), is used to set the timescale for the logging of the data, which can be very short or very long, and the intervals at which data are collected are automatically adjusted. Data-logging can take place with the interface connected to the computer, enabling the results to be simultaneously displayed on screen or, with LogIT, remotely (even outside) and subsequently downloaded.

Data-logging offers a variety of possibilities both inside the classroom and beyond. Key Stage 1 children can hold temperature sensors in their hands and watch the screen as the sensor warms up. Similarly, they can observe the instant and dramatic effects of clapping, singing or being very quiet near a sound sensor. Recording the sound levels in a classroom over the school day can provide interesting discussion as the teacher and children attempt to identify peaks and troughs and relate these to particular activities or incidents.

Older children may insert a temperature sensor into a defrosting bread roll and record data over a 24-hour period. (Temperature sensors fall into two broad technical categories and not all are appropriate for contact with damp conditions.) Two temperature sensors connected to the buffer box can record the temperature inside and outside a window overnight. Similarly, away from the classroom the temperature in the school pond may be monitored night and day over a week or even longer. Another long-term project might involve placing a movement sensor in a pot with a bulb while it sprouts, flowers and dies.

Data-logging can make a valuable contribution to children's data-handling experiences. Its principal advantages are:

- *speed* – data can be recorded more quickly than by hand;
- *electronic data entry* – the data recorded are automatically entered into the software, removing the time-consuming manual entry of data;
- *memory* – large amounts of data can be stored;
- *persistence* – data can be logged over extended periods.

Data-logging can be used to facilitate children becoming more scientific in their experimental technique:

- enabling the realistic repetition of experiments to achieve consistency in results and an appreciation of the concept of experimental error;
- enabling the testing of variables over greater ranges of values and similarly wider ranges of variables to be tested.

PRACTICAL TASK PRACTICAL TASK PRACTICAL TASK PRACTICAL TASK

Find out how to:

- **connect the sensors to the data-logging interface and the interface to the computer;**
- **select the duration and/or intervals of data collection;**
- **collect data remotely and download to the computer;**
- **save and retrieve collected data.**

Briefly outline activities involving the logging of environmental data suitable for Year 1, Year 3 and Year 5 children. Relate these to your school's scheme of work for science.

Graphing programs and mathematics

Graphing programs should contribute to the development of children's understanding of the graphical representation of data. Almost any activity involving graphs draws on children's existing mathematical knowledge and provides opportunities for reinforcement and extension work. As already indicated, graphing programs can make a substantial contribution where the speed and automatic function of the software enable teachers and learners to focus more specifically on a particular mathematical objective, be it choice of appropriate graph type or scale, the grouping of data or recording technique.

THE BIGGER PICTURE THE BIGGER PICTURE THE BIGGER PICTURE THE BIGGER PICTURE

When you are planning to teach children about data handling using graphing programs, make sure that you are confident with this area yourself so that you are able to deal with any misconceptions that children may have. Check out some of the useful revision sites such as BBC Bitesize to practise your own skills in this area. See Chapters 3 and 6 of *Primary Mathematics Knowledge and Understanding* (Mooney et al., 2012) for more on this.

Teachers can also make use of graphing programs to provide prepared documents as starting points. Children might use printouts for work away from the computer or complete activities involving data that has been pre-prepared. Such strategies maximise the contribution of limited ICT resources.

THE BIGGER PICTURE   THE BIGGER PICTURE   **THE BIGGER PICTURE**   THE BIGGER PICTURE

Some really useful interactive programs (ITPs) were developed to support the Primary National Strategy for Mathematics and, although the requirement to have regard for the strategies has been removed, these materials are still available. The ITPs were designed to support the modelling of various aspects of mathematics:

- *Data handling* (**www.taw.org.uk/lic/itp/itps/datahandling_2_9.swf**) **enables you to enter data into a table and then create a vertical or horizontal bar chart or a pie chart. Existing datasets can be amended to show the impact on the charts.**
- *Line graph* (**www.taw.org.uk/lic/itp/itps/line_graph_1_1.swf**) **enables you to enter data into a table or select from existing datasets and then create a line graph to represent the data. Data and values on axes can be changed to explore the impact on the graph.**

Graphing programs and English

Most media make extensive use of the graphical representation of data to communicate information. On at least some occasions there is an element of selection, either of the data themselves or of the means by which they are presented, in order to persuade the audience to reach a particular conclusion. If children are to engage with information critically they need a range of opportunities through which to explore the issues of selection and presentation of data – taking information presented in a local news story and reinterpreting it to support an alternative slant, for instance. This might involve the selective omission of data, choice of scale or even choice of graph type to accentuate or mask certain aspects.

PRACTICAL TASK   PRACTICAL TASK   **PRACTICAL TASK**   PRACTICAL TASK

Find out how to switch the autoscaling facility on and off. Represent one set of data using a range of scales and comment on the selection of the most appropriate. Collect a range of graphical representations of data from the media. Plan a speaking and listening activity to explore the issues associated with the impressions conveyed.

Children can develop and apply their knowledge of genre and the classification of literature by analysing the books in the class library. A range of data-handling questions arises relating to the selection, grouping and presentation of data. Similarly, children will be involved in prediction, articulating their ideas, supporting their views and decision-making. The results can be considered in the light of children's preferences. Further exploration might focus on the similarities or differences in girls' and boys' tastes.

RESEARCH SUMMARY RESEARCH SUMMARY **RESEARCH SUMMARY** RESEARCH SUMMARY

Phillips (1997) reviewed three experiments conducted by others into Key Stage 2 children's abilities to interpret graphical representations of information where ICT is involved.

In the first, children were asked to interpret a car's journey on a distance/time graph. They were able to identify when the car was travelling rapidly forwards, when stationary and when going slowly backwards, although very much more difficulty was experienced with associating these movements to time. In the second study, children were readily able to distinguish and interpret data-logging sensor readings for light, sound, movement and temperature on a time graph, telling the story of the various features of the data. The last involved children investigating paper spinners to determine the optimum length of wings to maximise distance travelled. Scatter graph plots were discussed and a line of best fit used to identify the V pattern in the data and consequently the optimum wing length.

Phillips contrasts these results with data which show poorly developed graphical interpretation skills among secondary children. He concludes that it takes time for children to develop graphical interpretation skills and that the increasing use of ICT for data-handling in primary schools is likely to increase the children's exposure to graphic representations with consequent positive effects. He cautions against well-presented but meaningless graphs which are all too easy to produce with ICT, highlighting informed decision-making in this respect as a key issue for intending teachers.

PRACTICAL TASK PRACTICAL TASK **PRACTICAL TASK** PRACTICAL TASK

Work that children undertake with graphing programs in the classroom will become more meaningful if it can be related to examples of the use of graphs in the world around them. Try to collect instances that the children may have encountered, for example voting on a TV game show or graphs in a newspaper. Discuss these with the children. Why are graphs used rather than text? Talk about how graphs can be manipulated – an example of breaks in a bar chart which result in differences in the bars being exaggerated is a good starting point.

A SUMMARY OF **KEY POINTS**

➢ **Effective teaching with graphing programs requires careful consideration of the selection, collection and recording of data.**

➢ **Graphing programs enable learners to focus on the interpretation of graphical representations of data.**

➢ **Graphing programs facilitate work on the equivalence and differences between graph types.**

➢ **Data-logging software can be considered to be a special application of graphing.**

➢ **Graphing programs have very specific features. For some data-handling activities, spreadsheets or other types of databases will be more suitable.**

M-LEVEL EXTENSION > > M-LEVEL EXTENSION > > M-LEVEL EXTENSION

Download a copy of *Mathematics: Understanding the Score – Improving Practice in Mathematics Teaching at Primary Level* (Ofsted, 2009) from **www.ofsted.gov.uk**. As you read it, think about teachers' use of questioning in areas of the mathematics curriculum, including handling data and the need for regular 'real-life' problems to develop children's skills in interpreting data. Start to devise a series of real-life problems for each year group from the EYFS to Year 6 that can be used to develop children's knowledge, understanding and skills in the area of handling data and that will generate datasets that can be used with graphing programs. For each investigation, write a list of relevant questions that will probe children's understanding and challenge them to use appropriate vocabulary in their responses. Can the same questions be used as part of your assessment of this aspect?

REFERENCES REFERENCES **REFERENCES** REFERENCES **REFERENCES** REFERENCES

DfE (2011) *Teachers' Standards*. Available at **www.education.gov.uk/publications**.

DfE (2013) *National Curriculum in England: Primary Curriculum.* London: DfE. Available at **https://www.gov.uk/government/publications/national-curriculum-in-england-primary-curriculum**.

Mooney, C. et al. (2012) *Primary Mathematics Knowledge and Understanding*. Exeter: Learning Matters.

Ofsted, (2009) *Mathematics: Understanding the Score*. London: HMSO. Available at **https://www.stem.org.uk/elibrary/resource/31194/mathematics-understanding-the-score**.

Phillips, R. (1997) 'Can juniors read graphs? A review and analysis of some computer-based activities', *Journal of Information Technology for Teacher Education*, 6(1), 49–58.

FURTHER READING FURTHER READING **FURTHER READING** FURTHER READING

Bennett, R. (2006) *Learning ICT with Maths*. London: David Fulton.

Clark-Jeavons, A. (2005) *Exciting ICT in Maths*. Stafford: Network Educational.

Frost, R. (2006) *Dataloggerama: Ways with ICT in Science Education*. Available at **www.rogerfrost.com/** (accessed 10 May 2011).

Higgins, C. et al. (2002, 2003) *ICT Connect* (Years 1–6). Oxford: Harcourt Education.

Loveless, A. and Dore, B. (2002) *ICT in the Primary School*. Buckingham: Open University Press.

Meadows, J. (2004) *Science and ICT in Primary Education: A Creative Approach to Big Ideas*. London: David Fulton.

Way, J. and Beardon, T. (2002) *ICT and Primary Mathematics*. Buckingham: Open University Press.

Williams, J. and Easingwood, N. (2003) *ICT and Primary Science*. London: RoutledgeFalmer.

Williams, J. and Easingwood, N. (2004) *ICT and Primary Mathematics*. London: RoutledgeFalmer.

15
Databases and spreadsheets

Chapter objectives

When you have completed work on this chapter, you will have:

- understood how databases and spreadsheets differ in the way data can be organised and then utilised for different purposes;
- thought about how database and spreadsheet programs can be used to develop children's knowledge, understanding and skills in interpreting and handling data;
- looked at how database and spreadsheet software can be used to enhance teaching and learning in computing;
- considered the cross-disciplinary application of knowledge and understanding of data handling software.

Introduction

Among the first purposes to which computers were widely applied was the systematic handling of data. That the modern world is so information-rich in so many ways is largely due to the facility with which computers can store and process large amounts of data. Through understanding the concepts underlying data-handling, children will not only develop computing and ICT skills, but also will become familiar with key principles through which knowledge and information are now managed. Working with data-handling programs can provide insights into how computers use different types of searching algorithms to sort and find information efficiently.

What are databases and spreadsheets?

Databases are structured stores of information. They allow large amounts of data to be stored, organised, sorted, searched and retrieved quickly and easily. They provide far more sophisticated interrogation than the graphing programs that we explored in Chapter 14. Databases as repositories of information abound, from the school library catalogue to television listings to government records, and almost all are now in digital format. In order to access, analyse, synthesise and interpret information, children need to develop appropriate knowledge, skills and understanding, including a basic under-standing of how computers utilise search algorithms to retrieve information efficiently. The electronic databases used in school take a variety of forms, from branching tree identification keys to multimedia CD-ROMs and various web-based databases, although CD-ROMs are much less utilised these days due to the internet and world wide web.

Spreadsheets are another kind of data-handling software that is widely used by adults. While they may share some features with databases, spreadsheets are usually not as adept for sorting and searching data, nor are they as effective for storing long text strings. However, where they come into their own is in the manipulation of numerical data, which makes them well suited to mathematical calculations and modelling.

As software development continues, the distinctions between many generic categories blur and fade. Spreadsheets may share many of the features and functions of databases. Similarly, many databases also incorporate spreadsheet functions. This chapter explores the variety, features and functions of databases and spreadsheets and their potential contribution to teaching and learning in the primary school. Clear links are made to other generic aspects of data handling.

What do the programmes of study for Key Stages 1 and 2 include?

Key Stage 1

- Use technology purposefully to create, organise, store, manipulate and retrieve digital content.
- Recognise common uses of information technology beyond school.

Key Stage 2

- Use search technologies effectively, appreciate how results are selected and ranked, and be discerning in evaluating digital content
- Select, use and combine a variety of software (including internet services) on a range of digital devices to accomplish given goals, including collecting, analysing, evaluating and presenting data and information

(DfE, 2013)

What do teachers need to know about using databases and spreadsheets?

Vast amounts of data are collected, from the various meanings of words, to the amount of rain that falls in a particular location, the daytime telephone numbers of families with children at a particular school and the school's annual repair budget. In order for these data to be of any use, they must be organised and stored in some way, usually as an electronic database. The choice of a database is important to ensure that information can be accessed and manipulated as required.

The types of data-handling software utilised in some primary schools can appear quite distinct from those employed in the world at large. However, there has also been a contrasting tendency for educational ICT to move towards 'industry standards'. The argument, used particularly in secondary schools, is that children should be encouraged to learn the software that they will encounter in the world of work. As an example, the RM spreadsheet Number Magic has many features which will be familiar to users of Excel. It is important to remember, though, that data-handling software used in schools is designed to facilitate learning about the processes and possibilities of data-handling as well as for the retrieval and manipulation of information. An important contrast is that educational databases usually incorporate presentation capability – the capacity to generate graphs – which may not be so critical for commercial or governmental databases.

A number of different types of data-handling programs are commonly used in schools, including:

- branching tree or binary databases;
- flatfile or tabular databases;
- relational databases;
- spreadsheets.

Each of these is structured differently to support different functions.

Branching tree or binary databases

Branching tree or binary databases facilitate the identification of objects, people or plants, for example, by the posing of questions relating to attributes which must be answered 'yes' or 'no' (a binary response). The answer to any question leads to a further question to be answered similarly until only one possible outcome remains (see Figure 15.1).

The structuring of information in binary databases can also provide insights into how binary searches are used in computing to find data or solutions to problems more efficiently. For example, we could play a simple *Guess My Number* game to illustrate this. If I think of a number between 0 and 50 and invite the children in my class to guess the number using questions to which I reply 'yes' or 'no' there are various strategies they could use for guessing my number. They could simply search for my number using a linear or sequential strategy, starting at 0 and one by one eliminating the numbers until they found my number. This would be fine if I had chosen a low number like 3, but if I had chosen a much higher number such as 35, it would be a very inefficient way of searching for my number. A more efficient strategy would be to choose the middle number of the range each time. For example if the number 35 is being guessed in the range 0–50 we could find the number in six questions thus:

Is it less than 25? No

Is it less than 37? Yes

Is it less than 31? No

Is it less than 34? No

Is it less than 36? Yes

Is it greater than 34? It must be 35

This strategy uses a binary search algorithm to locate a piece of data or information as quickly as possible in a set of data. This is something that computers have to do all of the time in relation to the data that is stored in a database. There are many activities away from the computer like this that can be used to illustrate how computers are used to store, organise and search data efficiently. A comprehensive resource (Bell et al., 2010) for further classroom ideas is available from the Computer Science Unplugged website at the following link **http://csunplugged.org/**.

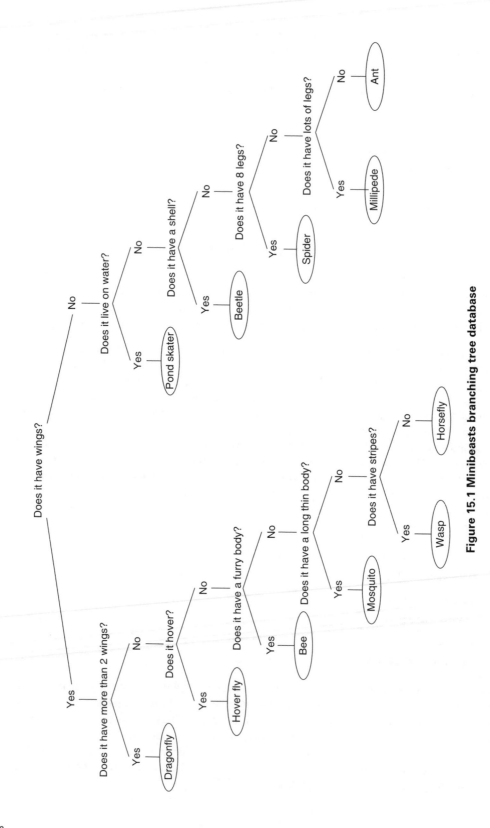

Figure 15.1 Minibeasts branching tree database

PRACTICAL TASK PRACTICAL TASK PRACTICAL TASK PRACTICAL TASK

Familiarise yourself with the activity *Battleships* (Bell et al., 2010, p.43) for exploring different types of searching algorithms. The resources and instructions for this activity can be found at the following link: **http://csunplugged.org/**. Try this activity out with a small group of children. Discuss their understanding of the underlying principles of how computers carry out efficient data searches.

Flatfile or tabular databases

Flatfile or tabular databases are perhaps the type of database that most readily come to mind when primary data-handling activity is considered. A datafile comprises a number of records, each containing data arranged in fields. Children will be able to relate to football cards as an analogy. The pack of cards is the datafile and each card is a record. In addition to the player's name, football cards usually include a photograph, the player's age, the name of the club they play for, the position they play, as well as dates of participation in major championships and national representation. Each of these categories is a field. Data are usually entered into a flatfile database through a form, which resembles a questionnaire and includes prompts for data to be added to each field.

Individual records can be viewed on screen (see Figure 15.2). The entire database can usually also be viewed in tabular format, with each column representing a field and each row a record. Sometimes this is called a spreadsheet view. However, the term is

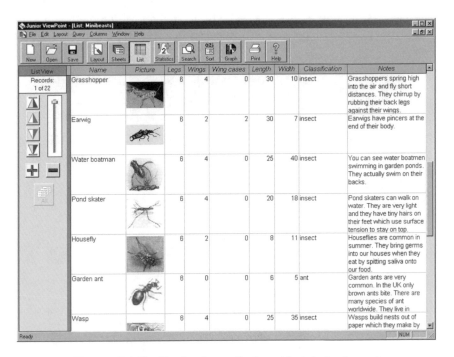

**Figure 15.2 Flatfile database displayed in tabular format
(Junior ViewPoint, Longman Logotron)**

misleading as the tabular format does not offer all of the functions of a spreadsheet. 'Table' or 'list' are better alternatives.

Relational databases

Relational databases have more complex structures than flatfile databases. Rather than data being organised as it is then entered into records and fields which then determine the types of interrogation activity the database will support, information is tagged. The tagging interrelates the information in the database. This organisational structure supports greater flexibility in interrogation. Some CD-ROM encyclopaedias and reference works are relevant examples of relational databases used in primary schools. They often feature menus, indexes, keywords and hyperlinks as ways of navigating substantial amounts of related information. It is unlikely that in a primary school the need will arise for teachers to teach and children to learn about the technical aspects of relational databases, but they will need to use them.

Spreadsheets

A spreadsheet appears as a grid made up of cells arranged in rows and columns. Each cell is identified by a co-ordinate conventionally comprising a letter for the column and a number for the row – A3, D4, for example. The column reference is given first. Data, often numeric, are entered into each cell by clicking and typing. The data can be searched, sorted, rearranged and presented in graphical format. More importantly, however, individual cells can be programmed to make and display the results of calculations. In the spreadsheet in Figure 15.3, the cell B12 has been programmed with a formula which instructs it to add 17.5 per cent VAT to the value in cell B10 and display the result.

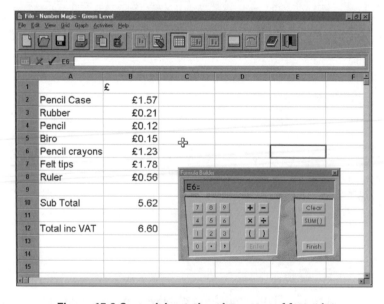

Figure 15.3 Spreadsheet showing entry of formula
(Number Magic, RM)

Teaching with and about databases and spreadsheets involves teachers in the following activities.

- *Selecting appropriate opportunities* – in which data-handling can facilitate, enhance or extend children's learning, such as through a research project that involves interrogating a database, or exploring number patterns and rules with a spreadsheet. In some instances, the focus will be on teaching and learning in computing – how a database can facilitate an investigation. In others, ICT will be used as a resource in the teaching and learning of another curriculum area, for instance using a CD-ROM to research the eating habits of minibeasts.
- *Selecting appropriate resources* – a search tool which enables safe searching of a website or a CD-ROM which supports beginning readers with audio and graphic clues. Both teachers and the children should also make informed choices about when it is worth going through the preparatory work to set up a database, rather than resorting to the quicker option of setting up a spreadsheet.
- *Preparing suitable resources* – although it is instructive for children to construct a database by determining their own fields and records, it may alternatively be appropriate for them to interrogate prepared resources. Many datafiles are commercially available, and may be supplied with the database software, but sometimes teachers will wish to prepare their own or customise existing ones to meet their objectives. Similarly, teachers will sometimes design databases in which children can then enter information they have researched or collected.
- *Exploring the full range of data-handling activities* – databases and spreadsheets are not just about the storage and retrieval of information: they facilitate hypothesising, decision-making, organising, analysing and synthesising.
- *Making explicit links between related knowledge, skills and understanding* – knowledge, skills and understanding of databases and spreadsheets have relevance across the primary curriculum. Teachers thus have opportunities to make explicit and reinforce the links between children's previous experiences and new learning across the range of contexts.
- *Modelling appropriate use of ICT* – for instance, how producing a branching tree database in electronic format enables modifications to be made quickly and easily, or how spreadsheet formulae can be replicated using the 'fill down' function.
- *Demonstrating and intervening* – for example, intervening to assist a child to identify the tallest child in a class by sorting height data in descending order, or demonstrating the effect of changing the price of an item in a spreadsheet budget.

The list below attempts to identify the knowledge, skills and understanding of database and spreadsheet software teachers need in order to teach effectively with and about these software packages. The list reflects the features of common software under each of the categories identified. Some software packages may support only a subset of these functions. This is no reflection on their usefulness – in most cases it is a strength, as it may not be helpful for the children to encounter a cluttered interface. However, it does signal that teachers must be aware of the capabilities and limitations of any program as these will be significant in the choice of software for any teaching and learning activity.

Branching tree or binary databases:

- creating, opening, saving, closing, deleting and printing documents;
- adding, modifying and deleting data and questions;
- plotting and replotting branching tree keys;
- inserting titles;
- selecting font and font size;
- exporting branching tree keys into other applications;

- importing information from other applications, e.g. clip art;
- utilising help;
- altering defaults;
- customising the branching tree program, e.g. switching off functions not needed;
- utilising alternative input devices, e.g. overlay keyboards;
- protecting documents.

Flatfile or tabular databases:

- opening, closing, deleting and printing existing datafiles;
- navigating through records using forwards and backwards;
- simple and complex sorting and searching (more than one condition);
- searching to retrieve data;
- plotting and replotting graphs/reports, including:

  - adding text, title, etc.
  - selecting graph type
  - selecting and modifying colours
  - saving
  - exporting graphs to other applications;

- entering data into a prepared datafile, including:

  - selecting a new record/answer sheet
  - entering, modifying and deleting data -saving;

- designing a new datafile, including:

  - opening a form/questionnaire designer
  - selecting font, font size, font colour, background colour
  - inserting and modifying questions, including making appropriate selections for style and format of answer supported:
  - words, numbers, dates
  - yes/no multiple choice;

- inserting text, images, borders, arrows;
- saving.

Relational databases (e.g. CD-ROMs):

- loading, including installation prior to first use;
- modifying computer display and volume settings;
- opening and closing;
- navigating using menus, hyperlinks, forwards, backwards, home;
- searching and retrieving information using menus, indexes, keywords and hyperlinks;
- playing audio and video;
- copying and pasting text and graphics into other applications;
- selecting and printing information;
- utilising help;
- critical evaluation.

Spreadsheets:

- creating, opening, saving, closing, deleting and printing documents;
- selecting worksheet and cell size;

- selecting font and font size;
- inserting, modifying and deleting row and column labels;
- inserting, modifying, moving and deleting textual and numerical data;
- inserting, modifying and deleting formulae and functions;
- using fill down and fill right functions to replicate formulae;
- inserting and deleting cells, rows and columns;
- formatting data, e.g. left alignment, centring around decimal point;
- searching and sorting data;
- adding, modifying and deleting borders and shading;
- selecting, modifying and displaying graph types;
- formatting graphs to include axes labels, key and text;
- exporting graphs and spreadsheets to other applications;
- importing information from other applications, e.g. clip art, data;
- utilising help;
- altering defaults;
- customising the spreadsheet program, e.g. switching off functions not needed;
- utilising alternative input devices, e.g. data-loggers;
- protecting cells and documents.

There will be occasions on which other data-handling software, such as graphing programs, will be more suitable. It may also happen that a data-handling project that, on a large scale, would be tackled through a database could in the context of a classroom activity be more easily implemented through a spreadsheet. Teachers need to be confident in making decisions about the most appropriate application for a particular situation.

What are the key features of databases and spreadsheets?

Branching tree databases:

- support sorting and classification activities at all levels;
- support data-handling activities across a range of subject areas;
- provide opportunities for developing and refining questioning techniques;
- do not replace children using paper- or book-based branching tree keys;
- facilitate the creation, revision and extension of branching tree databases;
- facilitate understanding of how computers search data efficiently;
- often support images as well as text.

Flatfile or tabular databases:

The structure of a flatfile database is determined by the choice of fields and the type of information they contain. These design issues in turn determine the ways in which the database can be used.

Flatfile databases:

- support searching to retrieve information, e.g. the names of the children in the class with blue eyes;
- support understanding of how computers can quickly and efficiently sort and search data;
- support more sophisticated searching, on two variables, e.g. the names of girls whose favourite food is pizza;

- support sorting by field, e.g. to see the distribution of hair colour across the class;
- support sorting and ordering a field, e.g. into descending order to find the name of the child with the smallest feet;
- provide graphical representation of enquiry results where this is appropriate, often called a report;
- support sorting and classification activities at all levels;
- support data-handling activities across a range of subject areas;
- facilitate the development of knowledge and understanding across a range of subject areas;
- provide opportunities for developing and refining searching and sorting techniques;
- often support data held as images as well as text;
- support the rapid retrieval of information.

Relational databases:

- support searching by keyword, index and menu;
- support complex or Boolean searching (see Chapter 17);
- support data-handling activities across a range of subject areas;
- provide opportunities for developing and refining search techniques;
- do not replace children using traditional reference sources;
- facilitate the development of knowledge and understanding across a range of subject areas;
- often support video, audio and animations, as well as images and text;
- support the rapid retrieval of vast amounts of information.

Spreadsheets:

- support data held as text or numbers;
- display and process numerical information;
- enable automated calculations and recalculations;
- support the graphical representation of information;
- support the organisation and reorganisation of data to identify patterns, gaps and correlations;
- support the use of graphs to identify errors in data;
- provide opportunities for developing and refining searching, sorting and modelling techniques;
- support the rapid retrieval of information;
- support rapid calculations;
- sometimes support searching to retrieve information, e.g. chocolate bars available for less than 40p;
- support sorting, e.g. displaying chocolate bars in order of unit cost;
- support data handling activities across a range of subject areas;
- sometimes support images for illustration purposes.

What do databases and spreadsheets contribute to teaching and learning?

In the wider world, the key characteristic of databases is that they facilitate the rapid retrieval of information. This feature is worth discussing with children as the link between the databases they use in the classroom and a commercial database may not be apparent. For example, it is important to discuss how databases are used by banks, the National Health Service (NHS) and the police. Similarly, discussing the ways in which consumer data is harvested and used commercially is important in developing children's understanding of the role that databases play more broadly in society.

Databases support the development of questioning skills in practical situations. Branching tree databases require very particular types of questions, to which the answer can be only 'yes' or 'no', but at the same time they call on children to apply their subject knowledge as well as skills of sorting and classification. Similarly, if children are to interrogate flatfile or relational databases effectively and productively they need to devise effective questions. Again, these are dependent on experience, knowledge and understanding of the data and structure of the database as well as of the subject itself.

An attribute of spreadsheets is their potential to support 'what if' questions. If the price of every item in the tuck shop is raised by 2p, will profits increase? The answer may appear obvious at first sight, but the children will quickly realise that other variables, such as the effect of the price increase to deter sales, will come into play and the model will need to be modified. Spreadsheets provide opportunities for children to make predictions and hypotheses and test them. For example, is the cheapest way to buy fruit in large pre-packed bags? A spreadsheet can be used to compare the costs of different fruit bought singly, loose and pre-packed from different shops. Decision-making is involved in all sorts of data-handling activity.

Similarly, children may consider what is the best way to interrogate a database to retrieve information. Will keyword searching lead to the required information most quickly? Would using the index lead to information which may not be found by a keyword search?

Databases are organised stores of information. Information collected by one individual or group is of value to others only if it is accessible. The preparation of data for entry into a flatfile database requires children to order and organise and classify material around the database fields. Structuring information has many applications and is a key skill in effective communication. Children can consider the audience for their data and associated tensions, such as quality versus quantity.

Data retrieval is rarely the final outcome of data-handling activity. Often it is the start. Data retrieved from any type of database can be analysed, interpreted, synthesised and presented. The presentation of data graphically is often the first stage in analysis and interpretation. It can also support the identification of relationships and potential errors and inconsistencies.

Progression of knowledge, skills and understanding

Branching tree or binary databases

Identification keys for plants and animals are the most obvious example of branching tree databases. The creation of branching tree databases which are as all-encompassing as this is a very sophisticated activity, requiring high levels of subject knowledge and understanding together with well-developed questioning skills. It is more appropriate to use a finite set of, perhaps, minibeasts and explore questions which will progressively lead to a positive identification. Does it have six legs? Does it have a hard, shiny shell? Does it fly?

Children need to use examples of prepared branching tree databases, electronic or otherwise, before they can consider designing their own. It is useful to begin by laying out the objects, or cards representing them, on a table or the floor for children to arrange and rearrange as they select and trial questions. Even with only eight minibeasts to contrast with each other, this may take some time. Children may also need to draw on reference material to facilitate their sorting. A considerable amount of work may be involved before the children are ready to use a branching tree program on the computer.

Some of the primary packages, such as FlexiTREE3 (Flexible Software Ltd), come with prepared examples. Children can test these and will soon realise that their datasets are restricted. Increasing the range of minibeasts will require more questions. An extension activity could be to try to reduce the number of questions necessary to differentiate between the minibeasts.

Flatfile or tabular databases

Junior ViewPoint (Logotron) is generic software which can be used across the curriculum. The example in Figure 15.4 provides an appropriate model for work with younger children as the amount of information to be entered of a textual or numeric nature is minimal, with some fields requiring selections to be made from multiple-choice lists by pointing and clicking.

In this example children will enter their own data, perhaps with assistance, into a prepared structure. Then, as a group or class, they can interrogate the data to answer questions (how many people have blue eyes?) or test hypotheses (taller people weigh more).

As with graphing, it is not always necessary or appropriate for children to collect and enter their own data into a flatfile database before they interrogate it, particularly if this information is sensitive as in the case of weight. They can also work productively with prepared datafiles. A number of software publishers sell prepared datafiles to support a range of curriculum areas. These have advantages which include effective design, accuracy of information, large numbers of records and saving teacher preparation time.

ALL ABOUT ME

1. What is your name?   Daniel

2. Are you a boy or a girl?   ☒ Boy   ☐ Girl

3. What colour is your hair?   ☐ Blonde   ☐ Black   ☒ Brown   ☐ Ginger

4. What colour are your eyes?   ☐ Blue   ☐ Grey   ☐ Green   ☒ Hazel   ☐ Brown

5. How tall are you?   142 centimetres

6. How much do you weigh?   28 kilogrammes

7. What did you weigh when   4.0 kilogrammes
   you were born?

**Figure 15.4 An 'ourselves' questionnaire making use of
multiple-choice data entry
(Junior ViewPoint, Longman Logotron)**

Children will need plenty of experience with databases before they can begin to design their own. Designing and preparing a database is a time-consuming activity and due thought should be given to long-term outcomes. A class may begin a database of plants and animals living within the school grounds, which could be monitored and expanded by subsequent classes, building into a valuable record of diversity and change over time. Trialling the design and checking the entries for errors are vital stages of the process. Such activity is generally recommended for the latter part of Key Stage 2.

Spreadsheets

Children can be introduced to spreadsheets through the functions they perform. For example, RM's Number Magic spreadsheet software comes complete with a number of prepared examples (see Figure 15.5). These will support a range of activities, mainly mathematics-focused, across Key Stage 2. Children can enter numbers into a spreadsheet set up as a function machine to determine what function the machine supports. The teacher may then draw the children's attention to the formula determining the function and encourage them to experiment with modifying the formula.

Another route into spreadsheet activity is making the link with calculators, placing emphasis on a spreadsheet's potential for supporting and facilitating calculations, especially those of a repeated nature. Children may begin by entering a number and choosing an operation to perform on that number, for instance adding 3. This process can be repeated focusing on emerging patterns, predicting and checking. At this level, spreadsheets have a number of advantages over calculators, the most pertinent being that

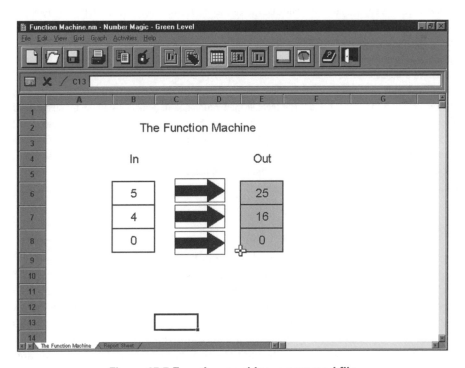

**Figure 15.5 Function machine, a prepared file
in RM's Number Magic**

they are easily checkable, by reviewing the formula for a calculation, or by graphing results to identify anomalies. It is important that the copying and pasting of formulae is not offered as a solution too soon, before the purpose and process of formula-writing has been understood. It is also important to make links to computer programming. In creating a spreadsheet with an embedded formula to model a particular situation, they are programming the computer and working with inputs, outputs and algorithms, albeit in a different context.

Children will need opportunities to become familiar with the navigation of spreadsheets, the entry of numeric and textual information, the display of numeric and graphical results, saving and printing.

Spreadsheets can then be used to extend children's knowledge and understanding of number facts and arithmetic laws, supporting mental calculation as children predict and check results as well as deriving generalisations, supporting early algebra work.

As we have seen, spreadsheets are ideal for modelling 'what if' scenarios. These can be applied to mathematic and scientific situations, particularly in Key Stage 2. Budgets are a popular focus as are modelling the effect of changing variables in science work. Graphical representation of spreadsheet data can be particularly powerful in this respect.

IN THE CLASSROOM

A Year 6 class was applying their mathematical understanding to the comparison of data from their school weather station with national information for the same period. In order to make comparisons they needed to calculate some weekly and monthly averages from their own data recorded on a daily basis. The teacher reminded the class that, anticipating making eventual use of it, the data had been recorded in a spreadsheet as they were collected. She reminded the children how to enter a formula to calculate the arithmetical mean rainfall over one week in March. The children carefully programmed formulae into other cells to determine median and modal values. The teacher then intervened to demonstrate how formulae could be copied and applied to other cells using the fill handle. A while later the teacher was intrigued to notice that some of the children were busy checking the spreadsheet's calculations with calculators. Questioning determined that this checking regime had been a group decision to ensure that formulae copied from one location to another were actually performing the intended operation.

Relational databases

Most CD-ROM databases make use of multimedia to a greater or lesser extent and whole new concepts in terms of resources have been developed in consequence. *Magic Grandad's Seaside Holidays* (Sherston) supports history teaching at Key Stage 1 by integrating text and images, together with spoken narration and historical video clips, to enable today's children to contrast holidays now with those experienced 50 or 100 years ago. This database requires some quite sophisticated information-handling skills if children are to search in it independently, although the format and navigation are clear and the teacher can control which resources are accessed.

To some extent classroom use of CD-ROMs has inevitably been overtaken by the access that schools enjoy to the internet. However, the authenticity of CD-ROM material, the sharp focus it gives through its content to the children's learning and the safe environment that is provided, all serve to make CD-ROMs preferable for certain purposes. CD-ROM databases are subject to editorial control by their publishers, in the same way as traditional media. No such quality monitors are exercised by the authors of most websites and information retrieved from these should be treated with due caution.

PRACTICAL TASK   PRACTICAL TASK   **PRACTICAL TASK**   PRACTICAL TASK

Design an A4 help sheet to help children navigate successfully in a specified CD-ROM. What are the key features of effective help sheet design?

What are the capabilities and limitations of databases?

Selecting appropriate databases

The different types of database discussed in this chapter support different types of data-handling activity. Teachers and children will need to make informed decisions about the most appropriate tool for a particular purpose. Again, this is no reflection on the suitability of a particular piece of software as no single program supports all the features and functions discussed.

Keyword searching

Effective keyword searching relies on the choice of appropriate keywords. For most children such selections will require thought, discussion and practice. Some words which have a wide range of applications may not be suitable. Effective keyword selection implies some background knowledge of the search subject. Refining techniques can be used to further narrow the focus of a search.

IN THE CLASSROOM

A group of Year 5 children had been charged with researching and presenting some information on the planet Earth as part of a class science study on the Earth and beyond. Two of the group decided that a CD-ROM encyclopaedia might be a good place to start. They input 'earth' into the search tool and a high number of matches were found. Beginning to explore these in a systematic manner, the children became confused as the first two hits related to soil types and electrical circuits. They had not considered that, even in science, the word 'earth' can have different meanings in at least three contexts: planet Earth, electrical earth and soil.

Spelling is another issue in keyword searching. Incorrectly spelled words are unlikely to prove effective in retrieving the desired information. Some CD-ROMs and websites provide support for children to help them check their spelling before conducting a search.

One of the strengths of relational databases is that a particular item may be retrieved by searching for any one of a number of keywords. Flatfile or other databases may be more restricted in this respect.

Hypertext literacy

Reading hypertext documents requires a range of skills – many of these have parallels with those associated with traditional texts while some are different. Many relational databases are navigable by index as with traditional reference material. The presence of hypertext links, however, means that children's reading of these texts is not linear – they may dart about from one narrative to another to another. Retaining a task focus throughout such a process can be demanding. Similarly, hypertext documents give no sense of geographical location within a text. Children may never know whether they have accessed everything on a particular subject.

CD-ROMs

CD-ROM databases should not be confused with the following:

- *CD-ROM talking books* – these make use of multimedia but their structure mirrors more closely the linear nature of traditional books. The subject focus of a talking book may be fiction or non-fiction (Oxford Reading Tree, Sherston and Living Books, Broderbund).
- *CD-ROM software* – CD-ROMs are used for the storage and transfer of software. Often when a school buys new software this comes in the form of a CD-ROM. The software is then copied onto the school's computer or network as appropriate and used from there.
- *CD-ROM games and resources* – some games and other resources also come in the form of CD-ROMs. These are not necessarily designed to be copied onto the computer's memory; if space is short, the resources may often be used direct from the disk. Tizzy's Toybox (Sherston) and Mighty Math Number Heroes (Riverdeep) are examples.

CD-ROMs and websites provide access to almost unlimited quantities of information. Sometimes this can be quite daunting as making appropriate selections to satisfy the needs of the task demands that children judge whether particular information is relevant to their enquiry as well as thinking how they might use it.

Copying

Many data-handling activities involve children retrieving information with a view to synthesising or applying it in some way. Teachers have long struggled with children copying information retrieved from reference sources, apparently without engaging with the material. One likely reason for this is that children have difficulty in making sense of the information. Often reference texts are designed with an adult audience in mind and make use of complex sentence structures and sophisticated vocabulary. Information can be useful only if children are able to read it. They also need to deploy associated higher-order reading skills, such as skimming and scanning text.

IN THE CLASSROOM

A Year 5 teacher was encouraging her class to make use of CD-ROM databases to support research across the curriculum. She was discouraged to note that many children merely copied down the text as it appeared on the screen or printed it off. She discussed this issue with the children and suggested a new strategy. Children could print entries or copy and paste them into a word processor, but must then read them through away from the computer, highlighting or underlining words that they did not fully understand and then looking them up. The children then replaced these elements of the text with their own words to form a narrative that had meaning for them. Some time later she drew one child's attention to the presence of the word 'tectonic' in his work, and was told that it was okay because he now knew what tectonic means.

Data accuracy

Effective interrogation of a database relies on the data held being accurate. It also relies on data being entered in a format in which they can easily be searched or sorted. If a child enters data on the number of their siblings into a flat file database as text, they could appear as '2brothers' or '2 buthrs'. The data would require considerable checking and modification before it could be used. The phrasing of questions as multiple-choice or yes/no wherever possible minimises the chance of such errors.

Flatfile databases and types of data

Flatfile databases can support data entered in a variety of formats, including:

- text, e.g. the name of a minibeast;
- numeric, e.g. the number of legs the minibeast has;
- dates;
- yes/no, e.g. does the minibeast live in the UK?
- multiple choice, e.g. the life expectancy of a minibeast:

  - a day
  - a week
  - a month
  - three months, and so on.

Where text entries are concerned it is usually possible to limit the length of answers to a specified number of characters. Numeric entries can similarly be limited to a predetermined number of digits, to reduce the chances of inaccurate data being entered in error. In large commercial databases the limits also serve to minimise the storage space needed – a factor which in the past was significant, but which is not so critical now. The use of multiple-choice and yes/no answers further reduces the risk of inaccurate entries or entries that are difficult to search or sort. Multiple-choice answers rather than open-ended text also make analysis easier.

Spreadsheets and the = sign

Teachers will need to ensure that they make explicit the role of the equals sign in spreadsheet formulae. It does not balance the equation, showing that one side is equal to the other, but provides a function, effectively instructing the software to perform the calculations that follow it. This may also be explained as 'the contents of this cell are equal to'. This is slightly different from the use of the equals sign with calculators, when the calculations are entered first and the = sign instructs the calculator to perform the functions.

Written algorithm:

10 + 4 = 14 (balance, both sides of the equation are equal)

Spreadsheet:

= B3 + B7 (function, add the contents of B3 to B7 and display)

Calculator:

10 + 4 = (function, now add 10 to 4 and display)

Professional use

Spreadsheets have various possibilities for teachers' professional use. Many teachers make a class list at the beginning of the year which they are able to use and reuse many times as mark sheets or for other records.

Data protection

Personal data are governed by the provisions of the Data Protection Act 1998 (as consolidated in the DPA 2003). Although this legislation was not formed with primary school data-handling activities in mind, teachers must ensure that they comply with its requirements where applicable. The key issues are ensuring that data are secure and cannot be accessed by unauthorised individuals and that they are not held any longer than necessary. See Section C of this book on the professional use of digital technologies for further information.

Privacy

The collection and interpretation of personal data about children raise issues of privacy and sensitivity – children's height and weight, for instance. Teachers have devised a number of strategies in this respect. Ourselves-type data can be collected for young children's teddies, while with older children it may be appropriate to discuss some of the issues raised or use datasets that come with the software.

Software selection and advice

Often software and ICT-related resources, such as talking books or non-fiction CD-ROMs, can be obtained from their publishers or software wholesalers on approval or a limited licence for trial purposes. However, with limited budgets and an ever-increasing range of products to choose from, the costs of mistakes can be higher financially and professionally. Software should be evaluated for content and for compatibility. Some software does not sit well with particular operating systems or other software items. It is important to determine whether a software package will cause such problems and, if so, whether the benefits of the software outweigh the problems of overcoming compatibility issues.

Professional and social networks of other computing subject leaders can be a good source of advice and support when purchasing software.

Printing issues

It is all too easy with some data-handling programs to print accidentally the entire file rather than the portion intended. Children may decide that it would be useful to print the information they can see on the screen, without considering that that may be a subsection of a very large document. Often it is necessary to detail exactly what is to be printed and to check it with Print Preview if such a facility is available. Sometimes copying and pasting into a word processor or other document may be useful.

The importance of interpreting data

Although using database programs reduces some of the demands on children involved in the manipulation of data, it is important to ensure that value is placed on interpretation and understanding rather than on the presentation of professional-looking graphics. Similarly, use of a database does not ensure successful teaching and learning. This will depend on appropriate task-setting, differentiation and intervention, as in any other teaching and learning situation.

Data-handling and the core subjects

The ideas and activities introduced below are intended to give a feel for the range of ways in which databases can be utilised to support and enhance teaching and learning in mathematics, science and English. They are not intended to be comprehensive, merely to go some way towards illustrating the breadth of possibilities and to provide starting points for the customisation of ideas and the generation of others. Examples introduced under mathematics, for example, may be just as applicable to one or more of the other areas.

There is extensive overlap between science, mathematics, English, ICT and other subject knowledge, skills and understanding in the area of data-handling. Teachers need to be clear about their primary teaching objective for any particular task or sequence of activities and maximise the opportunities for making explicit links between learning in the various curriculum contexts.

Data-handling and science

Databases are used extensively in primary science. Data can be collected from children's own observations ('Ourselves' is a good starting point) and experimental results, and then recorded for analysis. Alternatively, a spreadsheet might be used to predict and explore the effect of making changes to variables – for example, recording plant growth measurements against differing quantities of water, light and warmth.

Spreadsheets, and particularly graphs generated from them, can be equally valuable in highlighting errors. The concept of experimental error is often difficult to explore effectively in primary schools owing to the lack of opportunity for repeated experimentation.

However, data from a whole class's results entered, compared and analysed might high-light anomalies, leading to discussion and prediction of possible causes and perhaps improvements in experimental technique – the same group member operating the stopwatch each time, for example.

The properties of materials could be a research topic for the compilation of a class data-file resource. Fields might include what the objects are, where they come from and what we use them for, the field structure of the database providing a framework for the children's research. Such resources can be accessed for information later and added to by other classes to build enduring resources over which children have ownership.

CD-ROMs and websites can provide access to high-quality multimedia data. When the USA has a space mission, images are available to children in classrooms around the world as quickly as they are to NASA scientists. Such databases also provide a breadth of resources which would not be available otherwise – slow-motion video of spiders walk-ing or animations of the way the bones or muscles in the leg move as humans walk.

Data-handling and mathematics

Spreadsheets can be used to generate arithmetic and geometric sequences rapidly. Teachers may generate and print these to use away from the computer. A range of problem-solving activities can be supported in this way. For example, using a hundred square, colour in all the cells containing 7s (see Figure 15.6). What do you notice? Now colour all those with numbers ending in 3. What do you notice?

A branching tree database incorporating pictures may be used to support the sorting and classification of shapes with younger children. Does the shape have corners? Does it have four sides?

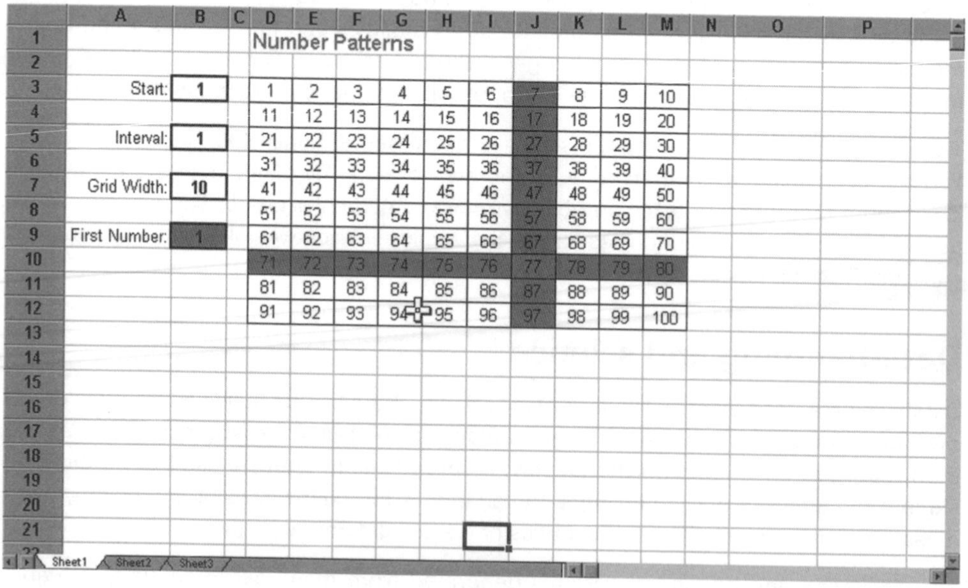

Figure 15.6 Using the number pattern function
(Number Magic, RM)

Mathematical investigations such as the shape of a farmer's field can be modelled using spreadsheets – creating the maximum area with the minimum fencing materials and exploring different shapes of field, working towards generalisations and early algebra.

Data-handling activities which have real relevance for children can be derived from school sporting activities. Recording the results from the netball or football league matches week by week can provide opportunities for statistical analysis, for example average goals scored per match and comparison of home and away results. Children can be charged with determining the placings of athletics competitors on school sports day, for example calculating the overall winner based on the average of three long jumps or throws of the rounders ball.

THE BIGGER PICTURE   THE BIGGER PICTURE   **THE BIGGER PICTURE**   THE BIGGER PICTURE

When you are planning work on databases and spreadsheets, it is helpful to incorporate practical activities into real-life situations around school and in the community. For example, many schools take part in charity and fundraising events, such as sponsored walks or silences and end-of-term or summer fairs that are open to parents, friends and other members of the community. There are lots of opportunities for older Key Stage 2 children to get involved in organising these. Think of the mathematics in making up a 'float' of change for each stall holder, serving customers and making change, and counting the takings at the end of the fair. A spreadsheet can be used to work out the profit after the floats and any expenditure on purchasing refreshments for sale have been deducted. Children could devise a database of sponsors to record donations or a spreadsheet that keeps a running total as the sponsorship money is collected.

Databases and English

Effective use of a range of databases in the primary school provides opportunities for the teaching and reinforcement of a range of higher-order language skills, such as keyword selection and the skimming and scanning of text.

A class database of book reviews searchable by author, subject matter and reading level may be a valuable ongoing resource. In a whole-school context, children may be involved in the process at varying levels. Older children may be called on to design and trial the structure of the resource. All children could be involved in adding records, with support varying from adult scribes to older children checking the entries for errors and inaccuracies. Similarly, all children might use the database to assist their selection of reading material.

Electronic dictionaries and thesauruses provide alternative reference sources. Some children find these easier to use than paper-based sources because of the combination of audio, images, text and hyperlinks. Most word-processing packages have their own built-in dictionaries and thesaurus.

REFLECTIVE TASK

To provide, in your own mind, a context into which children's work with databases might be lodged, make a list of the databases managed by national and local organisations (commercial, governmental, educational, leisure-related) that hold data about you. Its length may surprise you!

A SUMMARY OF **KEY POINTS**

➢ Databases enable interaction with data to explore meaning through relationships, patterns and modelling.

➢ There is a range of types of data-handling software commonly found in primary schools. These include:

- binary or branching tree databases
- flatfile or tabular databases
- relational databases
- spreadsheets.

➢ Good database design is essential if the data contained is to be used effectively.

M-LEVEL EXTENSION > > M-LEVEL EXTENSION > > M-LEVEL EXTENSION

Look back over the practical activities suggested in the chapter for helping children to understand the uses of databases and spreadsheets. Divide them into those that could take place in the classroom or other indoor space and those that would be best undertaken outside. How might you use the outdoor classroom and playground areas to best effect in your planning of this aspect? Is it possible to devise a scheme of work with links across a range of subjects that will develop children's capability in the use of databases and spreadsheets?

REFERENCES REFERENCES **REFERENCES** REFERENCES **REFERENCES** REFERENCES

Bell, T., Witten, I.H. and Fellows, M. (2010) *Computer Science Unplugged: An Enrichment and Extension Programme for Primary-Aged Students*. Available at **http://csunplugged.org/**.

DfE (2013) *National Curriculum in England: Primary Curriculum.* London: DfE. Available at **https://www.gov.uk/government/publications/national-curriculum-in-england-primary-curriculum**.

FURTHER READING FURTHER READING **FURTHER READING** FURTHER READING

Bennett, R. (2006) *Learning ICT with Maths*. London: David Fulton.

Clark-Jeavons, A. (2005) *Exciting ICT in Maths*. Stafford: Network Educational.

DfE (2011) *Teachers' Standards*. Available at **www.education.gov.uk/publications**.

Fox, B., Montague-Smith, A. and Wilkes, S. (2000) *Using ICT in Primary Mathematics: Practice and Possibilities*. London: David Fulton.

Leask, M. (ed.) (2000) *Teaching and Learning with ICT in the Primary School*. London: Routledge.

Leask, M. (ed.) (2001) *Issues in Teaching Using ICT*. London: Routledge.

Loveless, A. and Dore, B. (2002) *ICT in the Primary School*. Buckingham: Open University Press.

Meadows, J. (2004) *Science and ICT in Primary Education: A Creative Approach to Big Ideas*. London: David Fulton.

Way, J. and Beardon, T. (2002) *ICT and Primary Mathematics.* Buckingham: Open University Press.

Williams, J. and Easingwood, N. (2003) *ICT and Primary Science*. London: RoutledgeFalmer.

Williams, J. and Easingwood, N. (2004) *ICT and Primary Mathematics*. London: RoutledgeFalmer.

Section C
Digital Technologies and the
Professional Teacher

The rapid development of digital technologies brings a series of challenges to which teachers must respond. In this third section we provide an overview of three aspects of teachers' involvement with ICT which are critical for effective and positive use of digital technologies in the classroom. These are:

- professional use of digital technologies;
- online safety – including health and safety;
- ethical and legal issues.

ICT should be a teacher's helpful ally administratively, for example providing ready means for maintaining records of children's progress as well as offering diverse opportunities for the preparation of resources and furthering your own knowledge. In Chapter 16 on the professional use of digital technologies, we offer some ideas as starting points for both improved personal capability and continuing professional development.

The importance of online safety has been placed at the core of the new curriculum for computing, featuring prominently in the programme of study both at Key Stage 1 and 2 as illustrated in Chapters 10 and 13. Schools have a responsibility for promoting and teaching children about the safe and responsible use of the internet which we deal with additionally here in Chapter 17. Teachers also have a clear duty of care for the children in their classroom. Electrically powered equipment in the classroom brings a particular burden of responsibility for safe operation. It would be impractical to provide an exhaustive list of 'dos' and 'don'ts' in respect of health and safety, but Chapter 17 in this section includes guidelines on how to make your classroom as free from risk as possible, as well as referring you to appropriate interpretations of the relevant legislation.

The new ways of communication that digital technologies offer have raised a range of ethical and legal issues with which we as a society are grappling to come to terms. Many of these are not completely new problems – for example, there have always been opportunities for plagiarism or for the dissemination of undesirable material. However, the need to take a moral stand and deal with potential threats has been markedly accentuated by the speed and ease with which information can now be transmitted. The earlier chapters on the internet and social media (see Chapters 10 and 13) discussed some of the questions involved. In Chapter 18 on ethical and legal issues we turn our attention to two other significant areas for ICT in education – copyright and data protection – contributing to the promotion of positive values and attitudes in a pragmatic way and aiming to avoid unnecessary pitfalls.

The Teachers' Standards are also clearly addressed throughout Section C, focusing on some of the broader aspects of these. For example, Chapter 16, Professional use of digital technologies, focuses on your use of digital technologies to sustain your own ongoing professional development and as such is directly relevant to Teachers' Standards 3 and 8 as follows.

TEACHERS' STANDARDS

A teacher must:

3. **Demonstrate good subject and curriculum knowledge**

-   **have a secure knowledge of the relevant subject(s) and curriculum areas, foster and maintain pupils' interest in the subject, and address misunderstandings**
-   **demonstrate a critical understanding of developments in the subject and curriculum areas, and promote the value of scholarship**

8. **Fulfil wider professional responsibilities**

-   **make a positive contribution to the wider life and ethos of the school**
-   **develop effective professional relationships with colleagues, knowing how and when to draw on advice and specialist support**
-   **take responsibility for improving teaching through appropriate professional development, responding to advice and feedback from colleagues**

Chapter 17, Safety; online and off, deals with issues that have direct relevance to the safeguarding of the children in your care so have implications both for your own conduct as well as the children's. Similarly, Chapter 18 focuses on legal and ethical issues in the use of digital technologies and also has relevance for your own and the children's conduct. From this perspective these two chapters specifically address the following Teachers' Standards.

TEACHERS' STANDARDS

A teacher must:

1. **Set high expectations which inspire, motivate and challenge pupils**

-   **establish a safe and stimulating environment for pupils, rooted in mutual respect**

7. **Manage behaviour effectively to ensure a good and safe learning environment**

-   **have clear rules and routines for behaviour in classrooms, and take responsibility for promoting good and courteous behaviour both in classrooms and around the school, in accordance with the school's behaviour policy**
-   **maintain good relationships with pupils, exercise appropriate authority, and act decisively when necessary.**

In considering your wider professional and personal conduct as a teacher it is also vital that you are aware of the requirements and expectations of you as a professional, which are detailed in Part Two of the Teachers' Standards. All teachers, regardless of whether they are following a university- or school-led route into the profession, will be evaluated against the areas of the Teachers' Standards detailed in Part Two (DfE, 2011) which states as follows:

TEACHERS' STANDARDS

Part Two: Personal and professional conduct

A teacher is expected to demonstrate consistently high standards of personal and professional conduct. The following statements define the behaviour and attitudes which set the required standard for conduct throughout a teacher's career.

- Teachers uphold public trust in the profession and maintain high standards of ethics and behaviour, within and outside school, by:

  - treating pupils with dignity, building relationships rooted in mutual respect, and at all times observing proper boundaries appropriate to a teacher's professional position
  - having regard for the need to safeguard pupils' well-being, in accordance with statutory provisions
  - showing tolerance of and respect for the rights of others
  - not undermining fundamental British values, including democracy, the rule of law, individual liberty and mutual respect, and tolerance of those with different faiths and beliefs
  - ensuring that personal beliefs are not expressed in ways which exploit pupils' vulnerability or might lead them to break the law.

- Teachers must have proper and professional regard for the ethos, policies and practices of the school in which they teach, and maintain high standards in their own attendance and punctuality.
- Teachers must have an understanding of, and always act within, the statutory frameworks which set out their professional duties and responsibilities.

Much of the content in Section C of this book will raise issues concerning how you conduct yourself both personally and professionally, and is thus important to consider in relation to Part Two of the Teachers' Standards (DfE, 2011).

REFERENCES REFERENCES **REFERENCES** REFERENCES **REFERENCES** REFERENCES

DfE (2011) *Teachers' Standards*. Available at **www.education.gov.uk/publications**.

16
Professional use of digital technologies

Chapter objectives

When you have completed work on this chapter, you will have:

- thought about how you can sustain the development of your own knowledge, understanding and practice with regard to digital technologies;
- considered how you can use digital technologies to keep up to date professionally through networking with other professionals;
- examined how you can use digital technologies to improve your own efficiency as a teacher;
- begun to develop your own Professional/Personal Learning Network (PLN);
- understood the importance of maintaining a healthy work–life balance.

Introduction

In order to fulfil your wider professional responsibilities in a timely and effective way, you may consider using ICT to support you. This chapter begins by discussing how digital technologies can improve efficiency and then considers the use of ICT to support your ongoing professional development. There is a glut of information available to teachers through the internet and online professional networks. At times it can seem like there is too much information. For this reason it is important to build your own personal learning network to enable you to quickly and efficiently find the help or information you require. This is essential for maintaining your own work–life balance as a professional. This chapter briefly outlines some of the ways in which your own efficient and effective use of digital technologies might help to achieve this balance while also keeping your professional development up to date.

Personal capability

Selective use of digital technologies will repay the investment of time made to gain proficiency with the keyboard, other hardware and appropriate software. Facility with the keyboard remains particularly helpful. For those who want to develop typing skills, an electronic tutor such as Mavis Beacon or Accu-Type is invaluable. The course need not necessarily be followed to its conclusion but to a point when you are using most of your fingers and moving around the keyboard with some fluency. Despite the increasing accuracy of speech recognition facilities across devices, the keyboard remains one of the most common forms of input so fluency is vital.

In a similar way, cumulative benefit is derived from learning to use key software. Modern word processors, desktop publishing packages and spreadsheets have wide-ranging functionality. However, it is also reasonable to expect that teachers are able to use a range of media including video and audio. To a novice such software may seem daunting, but in time it will prove quicker to use them than rely on 'traditional' pen-and-paper approaches. Effective use of software can be time-saving and also open up educational possibilities. For example:

- using a template in your word processor so that a lesson plan can be called up repeatedly;
- using a spreadsheet to keep children's records that can readily be sorted into order and converted into graphical representations to demonstrate progress;
- using desktop publishing to produce professional-looking worksheets;
- using digital photography (both still and video) to record children's work;
- using the internet for classroom resources and to supplement your subject knowledge;
- modelling a mathematical algorithm with screen-capture software on a tablet device so children can practise at home with parents.

Further ideas are available on a number of websites, including Terry Freedman's useful ICT in Education website (see **www.ictineducation.org**/). If you need support with a particular piece of software or technique it is always worth doing a search online for help tutorials or YouTube video tutorials as there is an ever-expanding wealth of self-help tutorials available.

Professional development using ICT

In their work in the classroom, teachers will be supporting children in the use of digital technologies to source information. This is a key skill – the ability to access information is now critical. While reference is often made to a 'knowledge-based' society, there is a strong argument that as well as holding knowledge personally, it is also vital to know how to find unfamiliar information and knowledge when it is needed. Teacher professional communities, both online and face-to-face, provide an excellent network through which to find out about and access continuing professional development (CPD). Indeed teachers often report that the most effective form of CPD with digital technologies is that run by teachers through CPD networks and personal learning networks (Pachler et al., 2010). Hayler and Turvey (2015, n.p.) developed a model of professional learning 'that exploits the personalisation and connectivity that professional blogs can yield' to support student teachers in the development of their pedagogical practice. Increasingly, teachers find professional blogs a useful platform through which to share practice and critique research as can be seen from the emergence of sites such as Staffrm (**http://staffrm.io/stories/discover**) and Pedagoo (**www.pedagoo.org**/).

Teachers can help themselves professionally to keep up to date by using ICT in a variety of ways. the most important of which is accessing information via the internet and developing their own professional/personal learning network (PLN).

It is important to explore the potential of all new forms of developing technologies, both in your own teaching and to support your children's learning, so that you do not just rely on those with which you are currently familiar. You need to plan for how you will ensure that you keep up to date with the development of ICT and ensure that you can use as wide a range of new media as possible effectively in your teaching. Many teachers develop their own professional/personal learning networks (PLN) using social networking tools such as Twitter.

Watch the video *Building a PLN for Teachers* at this link: **https://vimeo.com/76499583**. In this video tutorial Jeremy Burton discusses the advantages of building your own professional/personal learning network through the use of social network tools such as Twitter. When you have watched the video, sign up for a Twitter account and research what hash tags or teachers might be appropriate for you to follow. For example, for general discussion about teaching and education you could search #ukedchat or #edchat. However, if you want to find out more about the use of digital technologies in education then search the hash tag #edtech or #edtechchat. Of course, like all social media, Twitter should be approached critically. It can be used to share resources or to engage in constructive discussion with fellow professionals. However, think carefully about how you maintain your own professional identity online. Sometimes people's online conduct can leave a lot to be desired, but this should not be an obstacle to accessing the benefits of engaging in social and professional networks.

There are a number of key sites with which all teachers should be familiar. A useful starting point is provided by the Department for Education site **www.education.gov.uk**, not just for its own content – which includes news and discussion of current issues in education – but for links it offers to other key national bodies.

Teachers' TV was a digital television channel for education professionals (heads, teachers, support staff and governors). Programmes covered a range of topics, ranging from the curriculum to more general themes such as tackling challenging behaviour. The effectiveness

Table 16.1 Teachers' TV sources

ABA Education Consultancy Ltd	**www.proteachersvideo.com**
Teach Pro Limited	**www.schoolsworld.tv**
Phoenix TTV Limited	**www.teachersmedia.co.uk/**
TSL Education Ltd	**www.tes.co.uk/video**
Laser Learning Ltd	**www.laserlearning.tv**
Axis 12 Limited	**www.teachfind.com/**
RAISEonline.Training	**www.eyfsonline.org**
Creative Education	**www.creativeeducation.co.uk/videos/**
Promethean Planet	**www.prometheanplanet.com/PDTV**

of the medium is that it is visual. Watching teaching and learning take place, supported by an informed commentary, provides insights that would be difficult to achieve through the written word alone. Teachers' TV ceased operation in 2011 but most of the resources are available elsewhere. Table 16.1 identifies a number of possible sources.

It is important that teachers should have access to inspection evidence, and foremost among sources for this is the Ofsted site at **www.ofsted.gov.uk**. The site provides access to all of the inspection reports carried out on schools and other educational institutions such as local authorities and teacher training providers. This is a huge repository of information. It would be difficult to conceive how it might be made so readily available and kept so up to date other than by the internet. It is also worth remembering that Ofsted produces, and posts on its website, reports on subject and curriculum issues aggregated from its findings in individual schools. This is authoritative research that complements material that teachers might glean from other sources.

There are many other governmental and quasi-governmental sites that hold helpful information for teachers. Most of these are very effective technically; they have been designed carefully and offer an interface that is attractive and intuitive. Not surprisingly, privately produced sites, which tend to offer curriculum resources rather than statutory information and administrative support, can be of less consistently high quality in terms of both content and presentation. They reflect the somewhat anarchic nature of the internet, and it is worth being circumspect about material when the provenance is uncertain.

Sites referred to in the text were current in February 2016.

Professional bodies and subject organisations

There are a number of professional bodies and subject organisations that can support you in your ongoing endeavour to keep your professional knowledge, understanding and skills up to date. Some of these organisations are free to join and offer a rich resource and wealth of experience to draw upon. Many of these organisations also hold annual conferences or regional meetings which are ideal opportunities to network and meet with fellow colleagues at various stages in their career. The details provided in Table 16.2 are not exhaustive and focus mainly on computing and ICT. All subject areas have their own professional bodies, and we list some of those associated with the core subjects at the end.

Table 16.2 Professional and subject associations for teachers

Name	Description	Web and Twitter
Naace (Educational Technology Association)	'Naace is the ICT association. We are a community of educators, technologists and policy makers who share a vision for the role of technology in advancing education. Our members include teachers, school leaders, advisors and consultants working within and across all phases of UK education.'	**https://www.naace. co.uk/@Naace**
CAS (Computing at School)	'The mission of Computing At School is to provide leadership and strategic guidance to all those involved in Computing education in schools, with a significant but not exclusive focus on the Computer Science theme within the wider Computing curriculum.'	**www. computingatschool. org.uk/ @CompAtSch**

MirandaNet	'The MirandaNet Fellowship is a non-profit professional organisation that was established in 1992 by Professor Christina Preston. At that time it was clear that a one-day training session for teachers about using computers in schools was not enough. Then the sudden advent of the World Wide Web and more accessible use of the Internet offered the opportunity for educators to go on sharing policy and practice in the emerging field of computers in teaching and learning when workshops had finished.'	**http://mirandanet. ac.uk/ @MirandaNet1**
ITTE (Association for Information Technology in Teacher Education)	'ITTE is an association of teacher educators who share an interest in improving learning through the application of digital technology in teaching and through the effective teaching of ICT as a subject. Our concerns include: the pedagogical application of digital technology by all teachers; developing the teaching of computing and digital capability; and the effective use of digital technology in teacher education itself.'	**www.itte.org.uk/ @ITTEorg**
BCS (Chartered Institute for IT, formerly British Computer Society).	'BCS, The Chartered Institute for IT, is committed to making IT good for society. We use the power of our network to bring about positive, tangible change. We champion the global IT profession and the interests of individuals, engaged in that profession, for the benefit of all.'	**www.bcs.org/ @bcs**
ATM (Association of Teachers of Mathematics)	'The Association of Teachers of Mathematics (ATM) was established in 1952 to encourage the teaching and learning of mathematics by relating more closely to the needs of the learner. ATM is a registered charity and has a membership of approximately 3000 individual teachers, schools and institutions.'	**www.atm.org.uk/ @ATMMathematics**

NATE (National Association for the Teaching of English)	'NATE works to:
	
	• Promote standards of excellence in the teaching of English from Early Years to University
	• Promote innovative and original ideas that have practical classroom outcomes
	• Support teachers' own professional development through:
	
	  – Access to current research
	
	  – Publications
	
	  – National and regional conferences
	
	• Provide an informed national voice on matters concerning the teaching of English and its related subjects
	• Encourage sharing and collaboration between teachers and learners of English and its related subjects'
		www.nate.org.uk/ @NATEfeed

ASE (Association for Science Education)	'The Association for Science Education (ASE) is the largest subject association in the UK. As the professional body for all those involved in science education from pre-school to higher education, the ASE provides a national network supported by a dedicated staff team. Members include teachers, technicians and advisers.'	**www.ase.org.uk/ home/ @theASE**

Another valuable source of support and ideas is the various TeachMeets that are organised and held throughout the country. According to Wikipedia:

> *A TeachMeet is an organised but informal meeting (in the style of an unconference) for teachers to share good practice, practical innovations and personal insights in teaching with technology.*

TeachMeets are excellent for meeting up with other teachers from your locality to share ideas and practice with. The emphasis is on the informal sharing of practice although it does not always have to be focused on the use of digital technologies. Search on the internet for any TeachMeets in your own area or explore this link to find a TeachMeet close to you: **http://teachmeet.pbworks.com/w/page/19975349/FrontPage** .

It should be clear from this chapter that there is a wealth of information and support available beyond the immediate locality of your own school or placement. While it is important to recognise and utilise the wealth of experience that may be available within your school context, the careful and critical engagement with online professional networks such as those featured in this chapter can also be invaluable in supporting your professional practice and sustaining your ongoing professional development. It is important, however, to strike a balance between engaging in online professional development and remaining focused on your professional role. From time to time it is worth critically reviewing your PLN. For example, think about how many people you are following on Twitter and if you are using this tool as productively as you can. If you are following too many people you can lose focus. Similarly, it may be more productive to belong to only one or two subject associations based upon your career aspirations and developmental needs. Teaching is a demanding job so you need to prioritise areas for professional development in order to maintain a healthy work–life balance.

A SUMMARY OF **KEY POINTS**

> ➢ You can develop your personal ICT capability by improving your own basic skills and by learning to use key office and educational software.

> ➢ You can make use of ICT to support your professional learning by using a range of websites and social networking tools to keep you fully informed of new initiatives and technologies.

> ➢ Developing your own professional/personal learning network (PLN) through social media can be an efficient way to build a supportive professional development network.

> ➢ It is important to critically review your online professional networks in order to maintain a healthy work–life balance.

M-LEVEL EXTENSION > > M-LEVEL EXTENSION > > M-LEVEL EXTENSION

Find out more about any courses available to you now and in your first few years. Look out for any open access webinars that you may be able to participate in. For example, many education conferences now run parallel online facilities that enable those at a distance to participate via a video link or webinar. Spend some time following an education conference from a distance using online links such as a video link and the Twitter conference hash tag. Reflect critically on this experience. Did you learn anything from participating online? How useful was this activity for your ongoing professional development?

REFERENCES REFERENCES **REFERENCES** REFERENCES **REFERENCES** REFERENCES

Burton, J. (2014) *Building a PLN for Teachers*. Available at **https://vimeo.com/76499583**.

DfE (2011) *Teachers' Standards*. Available at **www.education.gov.uk/publications**.

Freedman, T. (2016) *ICT in Education*. Available at **http://ictineducation.org/**.

Hayler, M. and Turvey, K. (2015) *Connecting Personal and Professional Learning Narratives in Teacher Education: Implications for Policy*. Conference paper, European Educational Research Association, Budapest. Available at **www.eera-ecer.de/ecer-programmes/conference/20/contribution/33638/**.

Pachler, N., Preston, C., Cuthell, J., Allen, A. and Pinheiro-Torres, C. (2010) *ICT CPD Landscape: Final Report*. Coventry: Becta. Available at **http://dera.ioe.ac.uk/1769/**.

Pedagoo (n.d.) Available at **www.pedagoo.org/**.

Staffrm (n.d.) Available at **http://staffrm.com/stories/discover**.

FURTHER READING FURTHER READING **FURTHER READING** FURTHER READING

Arthur, J. and Cremin, T. (2010) *Learning to Teaching in the Primary School*, 2nd edn. Abingdon: Routledge.

Duffty, J. (2006) *Primary ICT: Extending Knowledge in Practice*. Exeter: Learning Matters.

17
Safety; online and off

Chapter objectives

When you have completed work on this chapter, you will have:

- understood the key areas of risk associated with the concept of online safety;
- considered some of the resources available to develop a proactive approach to developing children's awareness of online safety issues;
- examined the importance of managing your own online identity and conduct to protect your professional reputation;
- considered your responsibility for managing health and safety issues that can arise from the use of technologies in education;
- developed strategies to promote children's safe use of the Internet in teaching and learning.

Introduction

In this chapter, we introduce the important and ever-shifting issues surrounding the safe use of technologies and the internet. We want to highlight the constantly changing nature of this area, as rapid advances in technological devices and the ways in which people communicate and connect via communications networks mean that new risks go hand in hand with burgeoning opportunities (Livingstone et al., 2011). Schools, teachers, parents and children all need to work together to ensure children can safely make the most of the opportunities offered by new technologies. However, schools and teachers in particular have an important role to play in facilitating children's digital literacy and safety skills, which in turn has implications for teachers' professional knowledge and understanding, as we consider in this chapter. This chapter also builds on Chapters 10 and 13 in Section B, which highlighted the different ways of developing children's digital literacy in relation to the internet and social media. As such the online safety element of this chapter relates specifically to the National Curriculum programme of study for computing (DfE, 2013) which states:

Pupils should be taught to:

- KS1 – Use technology safely and respectfully, keeping personal information private; know where to go for help and support when they have concerns about material on the internet.
- KS2 – Use technology safely, respectfully and responsibly; know a range of ways to report concerns and inappropriate behaviour.

In the second half of this chapter, we also address more general health and safety considerations that apply to the use of technologies in schools as well as schools' legal responsibilities with regard to health and safety.

The bigger picture

There are many new varieties of electronic text and forms of communication emerging as technology develops. Blogs, vlogs, instant messaging, mobile phone texting, wikis, tweets and social networking sites provide ever-expanding possibilities for sharing information, images and other media. The use of such tools is only just beginning to be explored in educational contexts and there has been concern about privacy and about who can access information outside a person's chosen contacts. One of the risks is that, without hearing or seeing the other person, children cannot identify them or know if their motivation for making contact is innocent. However, it does not have to be a stranger to the child who puts them at risk – peers or indeed family members in some circumstances could be a source of risk.

Social networking can provide a forum for 'cyberbullying'. This is a term used to describe the use of the internet or mobile networks to harass others. It is extremely upsetting for victims because it intrudes into their private space and it can appear that there is no escape. Incidents can take place at all times of day or night, and at any location, even within the safety of the home. There is guidance for schools on managing this issue in the document *Cyberbullying – Safe to Learn: Embedding Anti-bullying Work in Schools* (published by the DCSF in 2007 and available via **https://www.kidscape.org.uk**). The Child Exploitation and Online Protection (CEOP) Centre is a useful resource for guidance on cyberbullying and the safe use of the internet and social networking. While the issues of cyberbullying and the grooming of children by online predators are great cause for concern these risks do not represent the whole picture.

Identifying the risks

A good starting point as a student teacher is to ensure that your own knowledge and understanding of the risks associated with the internet and other communications technologies is up to date. Some of the dangers inherent in the use of the internet or mobile communications networks are widely known and acknowledged. For example, issues such as online grooming of children and young people, or cyberbullying, understandably garner much attention in the media and are a particularly acute concern to children, parents, teachers and the wider community alike. However, equally pervasive is the plethora of wholly inaccurate and pernicious information available online. This includes versions of history which serve extreme political views and are represented as fact (Holocaust deniers, for example). Furthermore, Livingstone et al.'s (2011) comprehensive European survey of children and young people's use of online networks identifies a far more nuanced picture of newer risks emerging via user-generated content, including hate sites, pro-anorexic sites, self-harm sites, drug forums and suicide sites. Childnet International (2014) have developed a range of useful resources for trainee teachers focusing on the issues of online safety, in which they classify the risks in terms of four broad areas (often referred to as 'the four Cs'):

- *Conduct.* Often children and adults have a false sense of anonymity when online which can lead them to conduct themselves in ways that are inappropriate, putting themselves and others at risk. It is important therefore for children to understand the impact their online activity could have, in order to fully understand the importance of keeping their own and others' information private.

- *Contact.* This includes this risks of online grooming and cyberbullying. It also includes the safe management and review of their online contacts.
- *Content.* This includes any inappropriate material such as pornographic, hateful or violent content. It also includes any material that may be dangerous, illegal, age-inappropriate, inaccurate or biased. Under this category plagiarism and copyright issues are also considered as children, like adults, can put themselves at risk through the illegal use of copyright material.
- *Commercialism.* This includes issues such as junk e-mail, personal privacy and commercial exploitation of children and young people through aggressive marketing strategies and premium rate services.

PRACTICAL TASK PRACTICAL TASK **PRACTICAL TASK** PRACTICAL TASK

Watch the 'Know IT All' video presentation for teachers available from the Childnet International website at **www.childnet.com/resources/know-it-all-for-primary/teachers-presentation**.

When you have watched each chapter of this video presentation, discuss your response with other student teachers on your course. Ensure that you understand your responsibility to report to the designated child protection officer in school any disclosure which indicates a child may be at risk. You should also make careful notes of any disclosure which you should sign and date.

Developing a proactive stance towards online safety

There are various strategies that schools use to ensure, in the first instance, that children are kept safe while using the internet in school. Internet safety policies exist to ensure, as far as possible, safe access and responsible use of the internet for learners within school. All schools making use of the internet should have an appropriate policy, often called an acceptable use policy (AUP) or a responsible use policy (RUP), which clearly outlines the potential benefits and risks and how these are managed within the school. Policies are usually written and reviewed in consultation with parents and there are model versions available from government websites for education and parents' information sites. Student teachers should familiarise themselves with how these policies operate in their schools and seek further advice from the senior management and/or ICT subject leader.

Since most access to the internet in schools is now supplied under contract by regional broadband consortia (RBCs), the filtering of inappropriate content is often carried out remotely by the local authority or RBC itself. Teachers can often report sites which they feel are harmful, and these are added to the list for blocked access. It may also be appropriate to request the unblocking of sites – as it is quite possible that harmless yet educational sites can be blocked due to the software not discriminating between key words and words contained within words (Sussex, for example). Encouraging a culture where children feel able to report things they see which make them feel uncomfortable fosters a responsible attitude and begins to educate learners about how they would deal with these issues in the wider world beyond the classroom. It is also important to remember that no filtering system is guaranteed to filter out all potentially harmful content.

While the provision for filtering and blocking content together with clear expectations and policies with regard to acceptable internet use in schools can be useful tools in a proactive stance towards online safety, it is questionable whether, in and of themselves, these can empower children and young people to keep themselves safe online beyond school. Increasingly, children are faced with a plethora of online tools and facilities. These are accessed through mobile technologies such as phones, iPads and other tablet devices and MP3 players offering connectivity to the internet, social networks and online applications. In addition, domestic and public spaces are increasingly equipped with both secure and open wireless connectivity, which again can be accessed through a range of devices and applications.

RESEARCH SUMMARY   RESEARCH SUMMARY   **RESEARCH SUMMARY**   RESEARCH SUMMARY

There have been two major research studies into online safety: the Byron Review (2008), and the EU Kids Online study (Livingstone et al., 2011). A vital message emerging from these two research studies into online safety is that it is no longer adequate for teachers and schools to only take a banning and blocking approach to inappropriate content or activity on the internet. Livingstone et al. (2011) found that 38 per cent of 9–12 year olds were using social networking sites under age and the authors of the review question the usefulness of blanket age limits altogether. It is clear that policing the internet, whether in school or in the wider society, is not in itself sufficient, as Byron points out:

> Children and young people need to be empowered to keep themselves safe – this isn't just about a top-down approach. Children will be children – pushing boundaries and taking risks. At a public swimming pool we have gates, put up signs, have lifeguards and shallow ends, but we also teach children how to swim.
>
> (Byron, 2008, p.2)

Livingstone et al. (2011) also focus on the need to empower children and young people to keep themselves safe while making the most of the rich opportunities offered by online collaboration tools. However, they also stress the changing nature of the risks associated with the internet and mobile networks, and the importance of 'listening to children to learn what new risks they are experiencing' (Livingstone et al., 2011, p.29). Against this backdrop, it is clear that schools and teachers have an important role to play in equipping children with the critical knowledge, understanding and skills to keep themselves safe online in school and beyond. As discussed in Chapters 10 and 13, the use of the internet in schools together with the access to a range of online collaboration tools within the relatively safe environment of a VLE, places schools in a unique position to address issues of online safety with children.

There is a rich source of materials for supporting teachers in the teaching of online safety in primary schools as you will find by exploring websites such as Childnet International and their Know IT All resources (**www.childnet.com/resources**). Similarly, the Child Exploitation and Online Protection Agency (CEOP) has a lot of useful advice and resources to support teachers in addressing the issue of online safety (*www.ceop.police. uk/*). CEOP operate the Thinkuknow website which again has a wealth of resources for education (**https://www.thinkuknow.co.uk/**). CEOP also have a responsive mechanism

Figure 17.1 CEOP Report Abuse Button

by which children, young people and adults can report abuse when using social media such as Facebook or Messenger. It is important to ensure that children are familiar with the CEOP Report Abuse Button (see Figure 17.1) and how it connects to the CEOP safety centre (**www.ceop.police.uk/safety-centre**).

If you are asked to teach an online safety lesson as a student teacher or NQT you should always seek local advice from other colleagues and read the school's safeguarding policies very carefully to ensure you are familiar with procedures. You should also have an established relationship with the children you are teaching so that you are able to evaluate their responses accurately. Discussing the more sensitive issues of online safety can make some children feel uncomfortable so it is advisable also to teach such lessons when you have support from a teaching assistant who also knows the children well and can offer appropriate support. It is not at all advisable that a new trainee deliver an online safety lesson that looks at the dangers of online grooming with a class of children. However, at some point in your early career you may be required to plan and teach such a lesson. The next practical task is designed to help you begin to think about how you would prepare for this.

PRACTICAL TASK   PRACTICAL TASK   **PRACTICAL TASK**   PRACTICAL TASK

Watch the following video by CEOP, *Jigsaw: for 8–10 year olds*, at **https://www.youtube.com/watch?v=_o8auwnJtqE**. The video from CEOPs Thinkuknow education programme is designed to help children understand the importance of protecting their personal and private information. It could be used to teach them the importance of setting their online profile to private and emphasising the importance of only talking to people they know and trust in real life. When you have watched this film, think about and discuss with another teacher the following questions:

- How might you use this video as a teaching resource, e.g. as a one-off lesson or as part of a series of lessons on online safety?
- What issues might arise from showing this video to the children?
- Who else might you involve in a lesson based on this resource (e.g. another experienced teacher, a teaching assistant, some invited parents)?
- How would you follow up this lesson?
- How could you involve parents to make sure that the messages and learning from the lesson are followed up positively?

For further ideas and resources to support your teaching of online safety in primary schools, Burton (2016) worked with a network of primary school teachers to curate an online resource of the most useful links that the teachers draw on to support their teaching and professional development in this area. These can be found at the following link: **www.theslate.org/learn/e-safety/**.

As a trainee or NQT you can also do a great deal of online safety work with children to equip them with the knowledge, understanding and skills to keep themselves safe online. In Chapter 10, Web Literacy, we examined how children's web literacy can be developed by helping them to understanding how web technologies work. Children will use the internet throughout the curriculum both in and out of school. In school the promotion of safe use of the internet can also be reinforced by following some general principles of good practice.

The internet and especially the world wide web can be enthralling – the temptation for random exploration can be hard to resist. Teachers will need to manage children's tasks in order to ensure both their safety and the productivity of the activity. Use of bookmarked sites only, tightly focused tasks and time limiting can be appropriate strategies.

Reading level and language issues

The vast majority of web pages are aimed at an adult audience and may thus be difficult for some primary children to comprehend. There are a number of strategies teachers can deploy in order to provide material which is accessible to children, including:

- the use of a search tool such as Ask Kids, which is designed to select sites which answer the query posed at an appropriate reading level;
- reviewing any websites to be used before the lesson;
- utilising web pages specifically written for children;
- utilising web pages recommended by other teachers;
- utilising children's work on school web pages.

Teachers may also be concerned about American web pages which display not only differences in vocabulary but also differences in the spellings of words. Children are exposed to US (and Australian) vocabulary through television, as are adults, and appear to have little difficulty with comprehension. Alternative spellings may provide more of a challenge, although they can also provide a teaching and learning opportunity. Teachers can make explicit the differences and discuss these with children – for instance, searching for information on the theme of 'colour' in a US-based search tool may be unproductive, although a parallel search using the US spelling could also be attempted.

Currency and authenticity

There is a lot of concern about the currency and authenticity of materials available on the world wide web. The potential to access up-to-the-moment satellite weather photographs, breaking world news stories, images from space as they are received from missions or real-time videos of bird eggs hatching is exhilarating. However, there are lots of websites which are not regularly maintained and in which the information displayed may be outdated. This can be frustrating and schools must also do their bit to ensure that their own web pages are current. Many web pages include information giving the date on which they were last updated. This can be a useful guide.

Authenticity is often harder to assess. Anyone can upload information to the world wide web or circulate it via e-mail, newsgroups or listservs. There is no editing process, as there is with any published book, newspaper or magazine, and thus material, particularly from unfamiliar sources, must be viewed critically. It may be partial, misleading or inaccurate. Comparing information from the internet with that from other sources for substantiation and corroboration can be a teaching and learning objective in itself. Some high-quality websites are subject to an editing process, such as the BBC **(www. bbc.co.uk)** and newspapers (e.g. **www.guardian.co.uk)**. Children need to be taught about these issues so that they can be critical and discerning in their use of content.

IN THE CLASSROOM

A class of Year 4 children are exploring the following website **http://zapatopi.net/treeoctopus/**. They have identified that the site and the content of the site is not authentic but they are analysing the strategies that have been used to make this appear an authentic website. For example, they identify the use of formal style of language and technical vocabulary. They then go onto to discuss how they can cross reference to other sources to try to validate the authenticity of the web page. Think about how you could use a site like this to develop children's knowledge and understanding about how to question and validate the information they find on the world wide web.

Advanced search techniques

Another way to promote children's safe use of the internet is through teaching them how to search more efficiently and effectively. Most search tools support both keyword and categorised searching. For many users, especially when starting out, search tools can be frustratingly unproductive. Perseverance and the use of some advanced or Boolean searching strategies will usually turn up something useful. The term 'Boolean' originates from the nineteenth-century English mathematician George Boole because the search strategies themselves are based on a form of logic that he developed.

Boolean searching involves the use of operators such as AND, OR and NOT. These can be used to refine searches by combining or excluding words or phrases:

- AND narrows a search such that only sites that contain both keywords will be displayed, e.g. information AND technology;
- OR widens a search to include sites containing one or other, or both, of the keywords used, e.g. information OR technology;
- NOT narrows a search by excluding sites containing the keyword which follows it, e.g. information NOT technology.

Often the Boolean operators must be in upper case, although it is important to check in the search tool being used. Some tools use the plus and minus sign (+/–) to provide similar functions. Other useful strategies supported by a number of search tools include:

- the use of quotation marks around phrases, such as "information technology" – this will ensure that only sites in which the words appear in this order are found;
- wild cards, which are symbols that can be entered at the beginning or end of keywords or phrases, such as 'tech', and the search engine will then look for matches which contain words beginning with tech, but with a range of endings, such as technology, technologies, techniques and technical. The symbol used varies between search tools.

Search tools vary enormously. They also develop and change. It is worthwhile exploring the guidance given by the tools themselves – there is usually a wealth of information pointing towards more efficient and effective use. You could also use the website **www.searchenginewatch.com** which is a comprehensive listing of search engines together with tutorials and rankings of the various services.

Professional issues for teachers

If student teachers and teachers are to keep up to date with both the new risks and opportunities that developments in new forms of communication might yield, then their own safe and critical use of such technologies is to be welcomed. Furthermore, social networking sites and tools are used by many student teachers to keep in touch with friends and family while away from home. They are also a useful tool for forming new friendships and networks both professionally and socially. However, it is the tendency of these social and professional networks to converge that can pose risks to students' and professional teachers' reputations alike.

You should take care over what information you share online, including any photographs of your social life. Remember that children and their parents may look you up online. They might also request to become friends with you on social networking sites. To protect your professional reputation, ensure that you understand the privacy settings you use for any online content you upload or any online communities you participate in. Consider carefully what information you include in any online profiles, professional or personal.

It is important to follow all relevant guidelines on communicating with children and their parents/carers, for example on using your own personal mobile or any mobile phone issued by the school, the local authority or nationally. Many schools do now use various text-messaging services to update parents on events at school or even their child's progress. However, this is very different from using your own mobile phone to contact parents. Many schools have a school mobile phone for use on trips or contacting parents in case of emergency. However, common sense also dictates that in the case of a serious emergency the child's immediate safety should come before the need to follow any school protocol regarding what mobile phone to use.

With the increasing emergence of digital mobile technologies such as smartphones and tablet devices such as iPads, innovative teachers and schools will want to explore the educational potential of these devices. You need to remember that such devices can store a great deal of personal and professional data, which needs to be managed effectively and safely to ensure the protection of those in your care and, ultimately, your own professional reputation.

PRACTICAL TASK PRACTICAL TASK **PRACTICAL TASK** PRACTICAL TASK

Visit the KnowITAll for trainee teachers website at the following link **www.childnet.com/kia/trainee teachers**.

Work through the two sections Social Networking Guide for Teachers, and Teachers and Technology Checklist, and use the checklists to carry out an audit of your own knowledge and understanding. Audit your own 'digital identity' by carrying out a search on your name using public search engines. After consulting this material, make some time to discuss your response with other trainees on your course.

Health and safety

So far in this chapter we have examined the safety issues surrounding the use of the internet and new forms of communication tools. However, there are also a number of traditional health and safety considerations that apply to the use of computers and other aspects of ICT equipment in schools. There are legal requirements that student teachers need to be aware of. However, the extent to which legislation deals with specific aspects of the use of ICT in schools is limited and so we will also cover some practical considerations which contribute to the sense of responsibility for health and safety that every good teacher will have in her classroom.

Legal requirements

Under the Health and Safety at Work etc. Act 1974 and the Management of Health and Safety at Work Regulations 1999, employees – which includes classroom teachers – must:

- take reasonable care of their own and others' health and safety;
- co-operate with their employers;
- carry out activities in accordance with training and instructions;
- inform the employer of any serious risks.

While the current health and safety legislation resides primarily in documents issued by the Health and Safety Executive (see Further Reading), and while ultimate responsibility lies with senior leaders, teachers need to think beyond the strictly legal to consider what constitutes good practice.

Room layout

Only a few primary schools were designed from the outset to accommodate computers, and so in many cases the siting of equipment is at best a compromise with the overall physical arrangements of the classroom. The convention in the primary school originally was for computers to be dispersed around the school, usually one, two or possibly three to each classroom. Where they are positioned among the desks, tables, chairs, bookshelves and cupboards will to some extent be dictated by circumstances, but even so there are guidelines worth following. None of these is more than common sense, but they bear summarising.

It is important that the computer is positioned so that the monitor is not subject to reflection, either from artificial light or from sunlight. Not only is glare distracting, but it may also cause headaches and strain if users are subjected to it for long.

The computer should be as close to a power supply as possible, keeping the length of electrical flex to a minimum in order to reduce proportionately the risk of someone tripping over it. If the cable supplied is too long, and an alternative of more appropriate length is unavailable, it is preferable to loop and tape or tie the surplus together (but to minimise the build-up of a magnetic field the loop should not be too tight).

For convenience, many schools have bought trolleys so that computers can be moved easily from room to room. These are fine as long as they are designed well with the work surface at an appropriate height for the children – which won't be the same throughout a primary school – and with sufficient area for the 'footprint' of your equipment. The dimensions merit checking as trolleys may not have convenient workspace for overflow, especially if the expectation is for more than one child to be using the computer at any time. Again, attention must be paid to ensure that cables are not flapping loosely around the system.

The question of space often becomes even more acute in those schools that have decided to dedicate a room to an ICT suite. The challenge is to accommodate children and computers in a room that was in all likelihood designed with only children in mind. Rows of computers are often arranged around the wall, with little space for writing or source materials – or a co-worker.

Additionally, turning to face the teacher is hard for the children. Possibly associated with a lack of space may be problems caused by excessive heat and humidity. Computers give off a significant amount of heat and fumes, especially if grouped together, and consideration of improved ventilation may become important. Schools may need to give consideration to the installation of air-conditioning units.

THE BIGGER PICTURE   THE BIGGER PICTURE   **THE BIGGER PICTURE**   THE BIGGER PICTURE

When you are planning to reorganise your classroom, keep in mind the requirements of health and safety (of both children and adults, including your own!). Take advice from other teachers and senior staff, and the site manager or caretaker. Also, bear in mind the safeguarding agenda, for example don't cover external or corridor windows and glass panels in doors completely with displays or posters. It is considered safer for children to have sightlines available, and it is also in your best interests as it reduces the possibility of any misunderstanding or false allegations. Always adhere to school policies in these areas.

Setting up the computer

Linking the components that make up a single computer system, one that is either new or has been dismantled for a move, is not difficult and there is no reason to be disconcerted by this task. However, as with all electrical equipment, there is a potential hazard if care is not taken, and the obvious precaution is to ensure that the equipment is disconnected at the mains before making any adjustments to the cables that make up the system.

Computers in operation are not drawing much power from the mains, which means that a single computer, monitor and peripherals can share just one socket without problem. However, a gang, rather than a splitter (which is more likely to become dislodged if leads are accidentally bumped), should provide this access. Also, one gang per socket is the rule, and gangs should not be daisy-chained. In a room in which several stations are planned, professional advice should be sought. Both tidiness and safety will dictate that mains leads, and any data cables for networking, should be concealed in trunking, with as little flex as possible lying on the work surface.

Data from the computer to the monitor are run through an RGB cable, RGB representing red, green and blue – the colours used to make up the picture on the screen. Usually, the cable has 15-pin D-shaped connectors at either end, with the direction of the cable made obvious by the configuration of the pins.

The same is true for the connection of other peripherals. Computer manufacturers over the last few years have gone out of their way to make clear which device goes into which socket, often using colour coding to assist. The keyboard and mouse, which are standard input devices, often have reserved sockets. However, they may alternatively be supplied to connect through USB (universal serial bus) ports. These are a more efficient alternative to the older nine-pin serial port (which you will still find on some computers). Most peripherals – printers, cameras, memory sticks, scanners – are now manufactured with USB connections.

They are usually efficient and require no manual installation of supporting software. All of the above makes the assumption that the equipment is sound and in good working order. Old or frayed leads must be replaced, and you must be vigilant in watching for any accidental damage, such as cuts to plastic insulation or wear to plugs, that may have been sustained. If repairs, rather than connecting and setting up ICT equipment, are involved, then professional help should be sought.

Danger, children at work

Teachers must be clear that, while ultimate legal duty for health and safety in the classroom lies with employers, in practice they are responsible for the safe operation of computers in their classrooms. A cable that has not been correctly attached is a potential hazard and on a daily basis only the teacher is in a position to check this. For the same reason, none of the setting up discussed in the previous section should be delegated to primary age children.

Apart from electrical safety, computer equipment is often heavy and should be moved only by an adult. Yet children are going to be the main computer users in your classroom, and so they too need to know how to work efficiently and safely at the computer. For older Key Stage 2 children this may extend to switching the computer on themselves, and perhaps even to switching on at the mains too. However, the teacher must be on hand to supervise either of these tasks.

Monitors have improved considerably in quality over recent years but it is still not advisable for children (or adults) to sit in front of a screen for extended periods. There is no substantive evidence that eyesight is adversely affected by spending a long time in front of a VDU (visual display unit), nor is the level of radiation emitted close to breaching safe levels set out in international recommendations. However, reading a screen for long periods without a break can cause a headache.

Teachers need also to be aware of rare, but serious, effects that can arise. A few people suffer from photo-sensitive epilepsy which is triggered by flickering light. However, they can often still work successfully with a monitor, especially given that the quality of this equipment has improved so substantially over the last decade. Similarly, some people experience skin irritations as the result of working with monitors. The cause of this response may be a range of factors, possibly attributable to the computers drying out the atmosphere, in which case air flow and humidity into the room should be improved.

Another reason to discourage extended time in front of the computer is to make it practical for the user to maintain good posture. Slouching, while generally unattractive and unhealthy, will also be detrimental to the relationship of the user's wrists with the keyboard. The lower arms should be held off the desk and be about horizontal. Children in the classroom are unlikely to be using a computer continuously long enough to be susceptible to repetitive strain injury, but if they can be encouraged to sit properly at the computer from early on it will stand them in good stead for the future. For similar reasons, an ergonomic chair with adjustable height and backrest is recommended. This will enable children – who vary tremendously in height – to sit with their feet on the floor (or on a rest) and with their thighs parallel to the ground.

Newer technologies

In recent years there has been an influx of various technologies in the classroom, including interactive whiteboards, visualisers, laptop charging stations or trolleys, handheld devices and more recently tablet devices such as iPads. All of the general safety issues raised in this chapter also apply to varying degrees with these newer technologies. Trailing cables, the location and storage of equipment, together with the length of time spent using technological equipment must be managed effectively by the teacher to minimise any risks to children. Equipment with powerful light sources such as visualisers and data projectors linked to interactive whiteboards must also be monitored carefully to ensure that children or teachers are not exposed to glare. It is important when using the interactive whiteboard that both teachers and children are aware of the potential danger of staring directly into the light source. Standing to one side rather than directly between the board and the data projector when facing the class reduces this risk.

Mobile devices such as handheld devices and iPads can also pose new safety issues. The fact that these devices are light and carried around easily can lead users to use the devices while on the move. Although the technology may be mobile, children should be discouraged from using such equipment on the move.

A SUMMARY OF **KEY POINTS**

> **New technologies and applications, whether virtual or real, bring new opportunities and new risks.**

> **Children need to be empowered to make safe use of new communications technologies within and beyond the school environment.**

> **Teachers, children and parents need to work together to develop awareness of online safety and the skills to protect themselves.**

> **There is a wealth of online safety support and materials available to schools, teachers, parents and children.**

> **There is a range of strategies that teachers can use to promote the safe use of the internet.**

> ➤ Trainees and NQTs need to monitor and maintain their own high standards of conduct when using social media.

> ➤ Under relevant legislation, you must take reasonable care of your own and others' safety, cooperate with your employer regarding health and safety, carry out acts in accordance with training/instructions provided, and inform the employer of any serious risks.

> ➤ You must take care where ICT equipment is placed in your classroom and how you and your children use it.

M-LEVEL EXTENSION > > M-LEVEL EXTENSION > > M-LEVEL EXTENSION

Consider whether any of the health and safety recommendations provided in this chapter, included in the examples in other chapters of the book and raised by the reference materials and further reading suggestions provided below apply more widely than in ICT. What other subjects are likely to need similar levels of attention to the safeguarding of children? How can you increase your awareness of health and safety issues now and when you are awarded QTS?

REFERENCES REFERENCES **REFERENCES** REFERENCES REFERENCES REFERENCES

Burton (2016) *E-Safety.* Available at **www.theslate.org/learn/e-safety/**.

Byron, T. (2008) *The Byron Review: Safer Children in a Digital World.* London: DCSF. Available from **www.education.gov.uk/publications/standard/publicationdetail/page1/DCSF-00334-2008**.

Child Exploitation and Online Protection Centre (CEOP) Available at **http://ceop.police.uk/**.

Childnet International (2007) *E-safety: An Introduction for Trainee Teachers.* Available from **www.childnet.com/kia/traineeteachers/trainers.aspx**.

Childnet International (2011) *Know IT All for Trainees and NQTs.* Available from **www.childnet.com/kia/traineeteachers/**.

Childnet International (2014) Supporting Young People Online: Information and Advice for Parents and Carers. Available at **www.childnet.com/parents-and-carers**.

DCSF (2007) *Cyberbullying – Safe to Learn: Embedding Anti-bullying Work in Schools.* Available from **www.kidscape.org.uk**.

DfE (2013) *National Curriculum in England: Primary Curriculum.* Available from **https://www.gov.uk/government/publications/national-curriculum-in-england-primary-curriculum**.

Livingstone, S., Haddon, L., Görzig, A. and Olaffson, K. (2011) *EU Kids Online: Full Report.* London: LSE. Available from **www.lse.ac.uk/media@lse/research/EUKidsOnline/Home.aspx**.

Search Engine Watch (2016) Available at **www.searchenginewatch.com**.

FURTHER READING FURTHER READING **FURTHER READING** FURTHER READING

Acts and Regulations – see **www.legislation.gov.uk**.

DfE (2011) *Teachers' Standards.* Available at **www.education.gov.uk/publications**.

Health and Safety Executive (2006) *Working with VDUs Revision 3.* Downloadable leaflet from the HSE website **www.hse.gov.uk**.

Health and Safety Executive: **www.hse.gov.uk/services/education/index.htm**. For information on classroom risk assessment, school trips, work-related stress, slips and trips in school and a range of resources.

18
Ethical and legal issues

Chapter objectives

When you have completed work on this chapter, you will have:

- understood some of the legal obligations on the use of digital content;
- considered some of the legal requirements regarding copyright in relation to the use of digital technologies and content;
- examined the different kinds of licences that can be assigned to digital content, including Creative Commons licences, and the implications of these for education;
- understood your legal obligations with regard to digital content and the Data Protection Act 1998 (as consolidated by the DPA 2003).

Introduction

The rapid development of ICT has presented a range of new social and legal challenges. Some of the ethical questions that are raised have already been considered throughout this book. However, the innovatory opportunities for learning, working and leisure presented by digital technologies have further consequences for the legal framework in which they operate, and the rapid pace of change has added an additional layer of complexity to these tangled arrangements.

This chapter aims to provide an awareness of some of the issues involved. However, it is not intended to be a comprehensive guide, and if you have a concern over a particular circumstance in which the legitimacy of an action might be debatable, it is sensible to seek further advice.

Copyright

Even before the advent of computers the question of copyright was a vexed one for schools. The current legislation in the United Kingdom is, though, unequivocal and thorough. It applies to anything published (including text and artistic production, which might itself be literary, musical, graphic or dramatic in nature). It extends, too, to other technological media apart from computers, such as films, audio and televised programmes. In short, the likelihood is that anything you might want to copy is covered by the legislation.

Some of the confusion over copyright for schools may originate in the concept of 'fair dealing' which is embodied in the Copyright, Designs and Patents Act 1988 (this Act still forms the basis of the legislation in this country, though its impact has been modified by EU harmonisation). Becta's helpful guidance (Becta, 2000) summarised this idea succinctly:

> *'Fair dealing' is really a permitted form of defence if accused of infringement, limited to particular purposes of which the best known is 'research or private study', but case law has established that producing multiple copies for classes is certainly not 'private study'.*

The inference is clear. Educational institutions are not in any way exempt from copyright legislation. However, many schools and colleges have paid a fee to the Copyright Licensing Agency (CLA). This provides limited rights to make copies of some copyright material. Copying is restricted to works published by organisations that have joined the scheme, but this in fact covers most British publishers (a major exception, however, is printed music). More restrictive, though, is the scope of the CLA scheme in applying only to printed material. The exact allowance for copying (usually photocopying) differs between institutions and has been varied in recent years; it would be sensible to check your school's current agreement to ascertain precisely what is permitted.

If we switch our focus more particularly to ICT, the same principles apply. In practice, a computer program should be regarded as a literary work, with its authors and distributors enjoying the same rights and privileges as if they had produced a book. Software publishers are usually very careful to stipulate what the purchaser has bought. In general, buying software only gains title to a licence to install and use the software, not to the software itself. The text of the licence will give details about how many copies of the software may be made. The starting point is that only one will be allowed, in order that data may be transferred to a computer's hard disk. However, it is often possible to buy at economic rates licences to cover a whole site or multiple stations within a purchasing institution.

Teachers have an obligation to ensure that software-licensing conditions are not breached in their school. In some circles the conditions under which software has been purchased are broken with the excuse that additional, illegal copies are not hurting anyone because the transmission is electronic; no physical material is appropriated. However, the disk and packaging are negligible elements of the software bundle. What is at stake is the author's intellectual property, and an unauthorised copy represents its theft. Apart from the ethical argument against software theft, there is also the highly pragmatic consideration that, especially among smaller educational publishers, loss of revenue will jeopardise future development of material.

Several organisations are involved in monitoring the use of software to ensure that breaches of copyright are avoided. Foremost of these in the United Kingdom is the Federation Against Software Theft (FAST), which has its website at **www.fastiis.org**. FAST does not simply act to police software use, however; it is a valuable source of advice and support to computer users.

The internet poses considerable challenges to the enforcement of copyright law, not least in the difficulty of monitoring all the material that is held and available for download. Nevertheless, copyright laws do apply. Even if copyright ownership is not declared, it should be reckoned as applicable, unless its rightful owner has explicitly placed the material in the public domain.

Creative Commons

As discussed so far, issues surrounding copyright are complex which can sometimes lead to teachers and children understandably becoming over cautious in their use of ICT when creating content. In order to address this issue much digital media and content is also made available under different types of copyright licences courtesy of the organisation Creative Commons which you can find out more about at the following link: **http://creativecommons.org/about**. Work that is made available under Creative Commons remains the intellectual property of the person who created the original content, but the various different copyright licences allow the owner to be more specific about the permission they grant for others' use of their content. For example, work that is licensed as 'CC BY-NC' or 'Attribution-NonCommercial' indicates that the owner gives permission for others to 'remix, tweak, and build on' the work 'non-commercially'. In this case any new work that incorporates, for example, someone else's digital audio must acknowledge the original creator of the audio and be non-commercial. For more detail about different types of licences visit the following link: **http://creativecommons.org/licenses/**.

PRACTICAL TASK PRACTICAL TASK **PRACTICAL TASK** PRACTICAL TASK

Most search engines allow you to carry out an advanced search in which you can search for digital assets that have been made available under creative commons copyright permissions. Using a photo-sharing website such as Flickr (see **www.flickr.com/**) find out how to carry out an advanced search for images that are available with Creative Commons permissions.

THE BIGGER PICTURE THE BIGGER PICTURE **THE BIGGER PICTURE** THE BIGGER PICTURE

There is a useful website that gives information about poetry that is out of copyright or where living contemporary poets have given permission to have their work performed in videos for the site, including poems by Michael Rosen, Roger McGough, Francesca Beard and Benjamin Zephaniah. Set up by Michael Rosen when he was the Children's Laureate (2007–9), Perform a Poem is an e-safe site for sharing children's poetry performances. The site, a joint project between Booktrust and the London Grid for Learning (LGfL), is also available to be hosted by other UK grids that are part of the National Education Network. For more information, see the website **http://performapoem.lgfl.org.uk**.

Another useful site providing free access to online resources is Project Gutenberg, which has a choice of over 33,000 free e-books for a variety of platforms, including a 'children's bookshelf' (see **www.gutenberg.org**).

Teachers will need to determine how best to introduce children to the concept of copyright. While this is a more urgent question in secondary schools, the increase in computer use, particularly at home, by primary age children means that breach of copyright as well as plagiarism from the internet or CD-ROM may well arise in your classroom. While it may not be appropriate to introduce a formal system of referencing to young children, spending time to explain why sources should be acknowledged will only be to their long-term benefit. Also teaching children about different licences and Creative Commons is a good way of getting them to engage with the issues when they are creating their own content with digital media. For example, what kinds of permissions do they think they would give others with regard their own content?

Data protection

Teachers and schools need to know of their obligations regarding data confidentiality. These duties are enshrined in data protection legislation. In essence, this dates back to the Data Protection Act 1984, which was introduced in response to growing concern about the impact of advancing computer technology on personal privacy. Considering its vintage, it was far-sighted, providing both rights for individuals and a demand on organisations (or individuals) who hold and use personal information to adopt responsible practices, even for data such as names and addresses, which might not be considered to be particularly sensitive.

Ironically, the original Act was limited to information held on computer, which exempted data records held by 'traditional' methods on hard copy. Another difficulty with the 1984 Act, which perhaps could not be foreseen, was that the growing internationalisation of computer use through the internet would facilitate unscrupulous transfer of data to locations outside of UK jurisdiction. Partly to improve the regulations in these areas, but also partly in response to an EU directive issued in September 1990 aimed at harmonising legislation across the member states, the 1984 Act was replaced by a revision, formulated in 1998 and taking effect in March 2000.

Like the original Act, the current legislation is based on eight principles. The detail of these has been rearranged from the earlier requirements, primarily to accommodate the new eighth principle. The list was summarised by the Information Commissioner as follows:

> ... *anyone who processes personal information must comply with eight principles, which make sure that personal information is:*
>
> * *fairly and lawfully processed;*
> * *processed for limited purposes;*
> * *adequate, relevant and not excessive;*
> * *accurate;*
> * *not kept longer than necessary;*
> * *processed in accordance with the data subject's rights;*
> * *secure;*
> * *not transferred to countries without adequate protection.*

(ICO, 2007)

There remain exemptions to the Act. These include personal data held in connection with domestic or recreational matters and personal data that the law requires the user to make public, such as the electoral register. On the other hand, the principles provide for individuals to be able to access data held about themselves and to insist on the data being corrected if they are erroneous.

Schools are subject to the Data Protection Act, and it is difficult to envisage a school not being registered. Staff who keep records on children on a home computer, and, indeed, under the 1998 Act, paper records, come under the scope of the legislation and their schools should be aware of this.

A SUMMARY OF **KEY POINTS**

➢ **Copyright applies to anything published in any medium.**

➢ **Many schools and colleges have paid a fee to the CLA; this provides limited rights to make copies of some copyrighted materials.**

➢ **A computer program should be regarded as a literary work, with the same protection.**

➢ **Children should be taught about copyright and the ethical use of their own and others' content.**

➢ **Schools are subject to the Data Protection Act 1998.**

➢ **You need to comply with the eight principles of the Act.**

M-LEVEL EXTENSION > > M-LEVEL EXTENSION > > M-LEVEL EXTENSION

Find out more about how copyright and data protection apply to schools. How can you teach children about copyright in ways that they can understand so that they are well prepared for the next stages of school and for lifelong learning? How will the requirements of data protection legislation apply to you as a primary teacher in your dealings with children's personal information and records? How can you incorporate within Citizenship the development of children's understanding about their data protection rights, their rights to privacy, and the reasonable measures that they should take to protect themselves from sharing too much information about themselves online?

REFERENCES REFERENCES **REFERENCES** REFERENCES **REFERENCES** REFERENCES

Becta (2000) *Copyright and ICT Information Sheet* (no longer available).

Creative Commons – see **http://creativecommons.org/**.

Flickr – see **http://www.flickr.com/**.

ICO (Information Commissioner's Office) – see **https://.ico.org.uk**. Summaries and the full text of the Data Protection Act can be downloaded from this site.

Project Gutenberg – see **http://www.gutenberg.org/**.

Rosen, M. with Booktrust (2014) *Perform a Poem*. Available from **http://performapoem.lgfl.org.uk/default.aspx**.

FURTHER READING FURTHER READING **FURTHER READING** FURTHER READING

Acts and guidelines – see **www.legislation.gov.uk**.

Copyright Licensing Agency (CLA) – see **www.cla.co.uk** for information on copyright compliancy.

Federation Against Software Theft (FAST) – see **www.fastiis.org/** for information on software rights.

Self-assessment questions

Chapter 1 – Organising digital technologies in your classroom

1. You may hear teachers in schools talking about ICT initiatives using the following acronyms. What do they stand for?

    (a) NGfL
    (b) RBCs
    (c) NOF
    (d) VLEs

2. What is the 'skills gap'?

3. List three models of logon practice that you might encounter in schools.

4. Why is it important for children to save their work before printing?

5. Whole-class demonstrations of new software or introductions to new skills are recommended. What are the main drawbacks of the alternative 'cascade' model?

6. Match the following examples of hardware/peripherals that can be used to support children with additional and special educational needs to their descriptions:

    (a) Concept keyboard
    (b) Touch window
    (c) Big keys
    (d) Trackball

    (i) An inverted mouse system based on a large ball
    (ii) A large-format keyboard for children with fine-motor control difficulties
    (iii) A device attaching to the front of a monitor that acts as a touch screen or replacement mouse
    (iv) A device creating touch-sensitive areas to be created on a flat board, allowing users to input text/commands

Chapter 2 – Planning for digital technologies across the curriculum

1. In what ways could the use of a wiki or Googledocs support the writing process?

2. Where you are using a three-part mathematics lesson, how can the use of digital technologies support each part?

3. For each of Key Stages 1 and 2, give two examples of the use of digital technologies to support science.

4. Match the uses of digital technologies with the appropriate foundation subject:

(a) Art and Design
(b) Geography
(c) History
(d) Design and Technology
(e) Music
(f) RE/PSHE/Citizenship
(g) PE
(h) Languages

    (i) Record and assess children's own compositions
    (ii) Use a drill-and-practice vocabulary program
    (iii) Use a digital camera to record in the locality
    (iv) Use the internet to find out about other cultures and faiths
    (v) Use painting software to explore colour, pattern, texture, line and tone
    (vi) Use videos of movements and actions to develop ideas
    (vii) Undertake a virtual museum tour
    (viii) Use a programmable robot to learn about control devices

Chapter 3 – Planning to use digital technologies in the Early Years Foundation Stage

1. Whose theories underpin the organisation of Early Years settings?

2. How did he believe that young children refine their growing understanding?

3. What did he call the environment in which this takes place?

4. How can the use of digital technologies support talk in the EYFS?

5. In which prime or specific area of learning would each of the following uses of ICT support children's development?

- Experiencing a story via the interactive whiteboard
- Using graphics software to experiment with shape and colour
- Using the internet to find out about other countries and cultures
- Handling a range of ICT equipment requiring various fine-motor skills
- Sharing and collaborating in the use of ICT equipment
- Using software that develops counting/number identification

Chapter 4 – Digital display technologies

1. What are IWBs?

2. What are visualisers?

3. What factors must be taken into account when siting the components of the IWB setup?

4. What are some of the identified benefits of using display technologies such as visualisers or IWBs?

Chapter 5 – Mobile technologies

1. Match the mobile technologies with their key features.

    (a) PDA
    (b) Smartphone
    (c) Laptop or notebook
    (d) Tablet device
    (e) MP3 player/DAP

    (i) Has all of the functionality of a desktop but is portable
    (ii) Has a touch-sensitive screen but can also be operated with a pen-shaped stylus input device
    (iii) Personal organiser with additional functionality, including versions of office software, internet connectivity, sound recording facility and photographic capability
    (iv) Mobile phone with many applications, including internet access, camera, games, and communication via social networking
    (v) Originally only for music files, now capable of other media, for example storing still images and video playback

2. Explain how mobile technologies contribute to 'anytime, anywhere' learning.

Chapter 6 – Planning for primary computing as a subject

1. Why are the following aspects important when thinking about planning in the light of new technologies?

    - High expectations
    - Designing opportunities for learners to develop and practise their computing skills

2. What are the three main areas that underpin the National Curriculum programme of study for computing?

3. Test yourself on the definitions of the following terms: algorithm; input and output; selection; decomposition; debug; variable.

4. Which four aspects of context should be included in a longer-format lesson plan?

5. How can you brief another adult supporting you in the classroom?

6. List three types of possible differentiation that you might make in your planning.

7. How can you ensure that you are well prepared for a lesson?

8. Which three elements should be evaluated at the end of a lesson?

Chapter 7 – Assessment in primary computing

1. Why is assessment a vital part of the planning process?

2. Why are samples of children's work insufficient as a record of progress in computing?

3. What is individual profiling of children in computing?

4. List six of the important elements of the context of an observation of a child's work in computing.

5. How can a whole-class snapshot support formative assessment?

6. Which assessment strategy described in this chapter would be most appropriate for use in the EYFS and why?

Chapter 8 – Computational thinking and programming

1. Define computational thinking in a way that is accessible to a non-specialist.

2. Identify 3–4 applications of computer science in our physical environment.

3. How are the program languages Scratch and Logo different?

4. What strategies could teachers use to ensure there is progression in the development of children's computational thinking through programming?

5. How can flow charts be used to support children's computational thinking?

Chapter 9 – Physical computing

1. Define physical computing.

2. Match the following with their descriptions below:

   (a) Light emitting diodes (LED)
   (b) Microcontroller
   (c) Central processing unit (CPU)
   (d) General purpose input and output (GPIO)

       (i) A single chip usually containing an integrated circuit, inputs/outputs, a central processing unit and memory
       (ii) The part of a microcontroller that carries out the instructions from a program relating to the inputs and outputs (a kind of digital clock)
       (iii) The part of a microprocessor or computing device that connects to inputs and outputs in a system
       (iv) A type of output that emits light

3. Why can Raspberry Pi be referred to as a single board computer?

Chapter 10 – Web literacy (including coding for the web)

1. What is the difference between the internet and the world wide web?

2. What is a web browser?

3. Define the elements of the following URL: **http://www. ofsted.gov.uk/reports/**

4. What aspects of a web page do the following HTML tags identify

    (a) \<h1\>content here\</h1\>
    (b) \<p\>content here\</p\>

5. How do HTML and CSS differ?

Chapter 11 - Digital media/digital literacies

1. What are the main purposes of graphics software?

2. In settings with older hardware setups, what might be the problems with printing from graphics software?

3. There are many benefits of using digital video in schools. However, its use raises some issues. What are these?

4. When editing films, what features does editing software allow?

5. When considering what software to use to support composing and performing music, what important issues should you consider?

6. What is a podcast?

Chapter 12 – Writing with digital technologies

1. What is the difference between word processing and desktop publishing?

2. Explain the three key features of word-processing software:

    • Editing
    • Formatting
    • Tools

3. What are the four stages of the writing process that word processing can support?

4. List six ways of text entry into a word processor.

Chapter 13 – Social media – tools for communicating, collaborating and publishing

1. To what should teachers give careful regard when considering using social media in the classroom?

2. What is the name that has been given to a form of blogging which enables groups of up to four schools at a time to blog between each other over a four-week period, taking it in turns to be the focus and commenters on each other's work?

Chapter 14 – Graphing programs

1. What are graphing programs?

2. When would it be better to use a database?

3. What are the three types of data that you might collect?

4. What are the potential drawbacks of the following?

   - A pie chart
   - Line graphs

5. What are the two categories of graphing programs?

6. Give examples of where a program with a set colour order may be inappropriate if not adjusted.

Chapter 15 – Databases and spreadsheets

1. What are databases?

2. What are spreadsheets?

3. What are the four main types of data-handling programs commonly used in schools?

4. Match the type of software with its possible use:

   (a) Branching tree or binary databases
   (b) Flatfile or tabular databases
   (c) Spreadsheets
   (d) Relational databases

      (i) Contain data arranged in fields, usually input through a form
      (ii) Contain complex data that are tagged to enhance flexibility of interrogation and may have menus, indexes, keywords and hyperlinks
      (iii) Facilitate the identification of objects, people or plants by posing yes/no questions about their attributes
      (iv) A grid of cells arranged in rows and columns where data and formulae can be entered prior to searching, sorting and presenting graphically

5. What do the following terms mean?

   - Keyword searching
   - Hypertext literacy

6. List the formats of data that can be supported in a flatfile database.

Chapter 16 – Professional use of digital technologies

1. In which two main ways can you improve your personal ICT capability?

2. How can you use ICT in support of your own professional development?

Chapter 17 – Safety; online and off

1. What are 'the 4 Cs' of online safety identified by Childnet International?

2. What are the four main duties placed on you as an employee by the Health and Safety etc. at Work Act 1974 and the Management of Health and Safety at Work Regulations 1999?

3. Which body provides regular updates and guidance on health and safety?

Chapter 18 – Ethical and legal issues

1. Two organisations involved in the monitoring of copyright are CLA and FAST. Give their full titles and say which aspects of copyright they oversee.

2. What are the eight basic principles of data-protection legislation?

3. How are Creative Commons licences useful for teaching children about copyright and intellectual property?

Answers to self-assessment questions

Chapter 1 – Organising digital technologies in your classroom

1. The acronyms stand for:

   (a) NGfL: National Grid for Learning
   (b) RBCs: regional broadband consortia
   (c) NOF: New Opportunities Fund
   (d) VLEs: virtual learning environments

2. The 'skills gap' is the perceived difference between the ICT knowledge, skills and understanding of children who are experienced in using ICT at home, including PCs and gaming consoles, and teachers who are lacking in confidence and have a lower level of ICT capability.

3. The three models of logon practice that you might encounter in schools are:

   - the whole class with the same username and password into a general area for saving work;
   - group logon names/passwords;
   - each child has a unique username/password.

4. It is important for children to save their work before printing in case they lose their work or the printer fails.

5. The main drawbacks of the 'cascade' model are:

   - the teacher and/or child who are shown first may be wrongly perceived as the 'ICT experts';
   - ICT may be seen as something separate from the rest of children's learning.

6. Match the following examples of hardware/peripherals that can be used to support children with additional and special educational needs to their descriptions.

   (a) Concept keyboard – (iv) this is a device creating touch-sensitive areas to be created on a flat board, allowing users to input text/commands.
   (b) A touch window – (iii) this is a device attached to the front of a monitor that acts as a touch screen or replacement mouse.
   (c) Big keys – (ii) this is a large-format keyboard for children with fine-motor control difficulties.
   (d) Trackball – (i) this is an inverted mouse system based on a large ball.

Chapter 2 – Planning for digital technologies across the curriculum

1. A wiki or a Googledoc could support the writing process by enabling children to write collaboratively on a shared document both in school and at a distance.

2. Where you are using a three-part mathematics lesson, the use of digital technologies can support each part as follows.

- Mental maths starter – resources can be varied by using the IWB.
- Main/group activities – a range of software can be used to explore number patterns, practise and assess skills, handle data, develop subject knowledge in various aspects of maths, transform shapes, develop logical thinking and problem-solving skills.
- Plenary – strands of the lesson can be drawn together by the use of electronic media.

3. Check the answers that you gave for each of Key Stages 1 and 2 in the section on planning to use digital technologies in science.

4. The uses of digital technologies match with the appropriate foundation subject as follows.

   (a) Art and Design – (v) use painting software to explore colour, pattern, texture, line and tone.
   (b) Geography – (iii) use a digital camera to record in the locality.
   (c) History – (vii) undertake a virtual museum tour.
   (d) Design and Technology – (viii) use a programmable robot to learn about control devices.
   (e) Music – (i) record and assess children's own compositions.
   (f) RE/PSHE/Citizenship – (iv) use the internet to find out about other cultures and faiths.
   (g) PE – (vi) use videos of movements and actions to develop ideas.
   (h) Languages – (ii) use a drill-and-practice vocabulary program.

Chapter 3 – Planning to use digital technologies in the Early Years Foundation Stage

1. Vygotsky's theories underpin the organisation of Early Years settings.

2. He believed that young children refine their growing understanding through innate 'inner speech' that they verbalise and test/retest in their interactions with others.

3. He called the environment in which this takes place the 'zone of proximal development'.

4. The use of digital technologies can support talk in the EYFS by providing starting points and stimuli for the inner dialogue and talk in the zone of proximal development, for example in imaginative and role-play scenarios.

5. The areas of learning that each would support are as follows.

   - Experiencing a story via the interactive whiteboard – communication and language.
   - Using graphics software to experiment with shape and colour – expressive arts and design.
   - Using the internet to find out about other countries and cultures – understanding of the world.
   - Handling a range of ICT equipment requiring various fine-motor skills – physical development.
   - Sharing and collaborating in the use of ICT equipment – personal, social and emotional development.
   - Using software that develops counting/number identification – mathematics.

Chapter 4 – Digital display technologies

1. IWBs are touch-sensitive boards that allow teachers and children to engage directly with material projected onto a screen from a computer via a data projector.

2. Visualisers enable the live presentation and modelling with artefacts (e.g. documents, books, objects, pictures, tools) by way of a powerful overhead camera which can also be used to record events and processes (video).

3. Factors that must be taken into account when siting the components of the IWB set-up include whether it is fixed or mobile.

If mobile:

- the need to be recalibrated after being moved;
- the vulnerability of the components;
- security from theft;
- health and safety, for example trailing wires.

If fixed:

- the position of the board on the wall, for example its height;
- the space needed for it to be interactive;
- the position of other light sources, for example windows;
- the positioning of the computer or laptop for classroom activities;
- the secure positioning of the data projector.

4. Key identified benefits of using IWBs and visualisers are:

- capacity to vary the pace of learning;
- enhanced modelling;
- potential to improve quality of interactions;
- opportunity to improve quality of assessment due to more effective questioning;
- can redress balance between making resources and planning.

Chapter 5 – Mobile technologies

1. The mobile technologies match with their key features as follows.

   (a) PDA – (iii) Personal organiser with additional functionality, including versions of office software, internet connectivity, sound recording facility and photographic capability.

   (b) Smartphone – (iv) mobile phone with many applications, including internet access, camera, games and communication via social networking.

   (c) Laptop or notebook – (i) has all of the functionality of a desktop but is portable.

   (d) Tablet device – (ii) has a touch-sensitive screen but can also be operated with a pen-shaped stylus input device.

   (e) MP3 player/DAP – (v) originally only for music files, now capable of other media, for example storing still images and video playback.

2. Mobile technologies can contribute to 'anytime, anywhere' learning by extending the classroom so that learning is not restricted to the school day or site – it can take place at home, in the evenings or at weekends or even in the holidays.

Chapter 6 – Planning for primary computing as a subject

1. The following aspects are important when thinking about planning in the light of new technologies.

- High expectations – it is important to have high expectations of all children in order to ensure that all are appropriately challenged. Your expectations must be based on knowing what children's knowledge, skills and understanding are already.
- Designing opportunities for learners to develop their computing skills – whether planning for computing as a subject or ICT within another subject, you must always keep in mind that the learning should be purposeful rather than just allowing children to engage with the technology.

2. The three main areas that underpin the National Curriculum programme of study for computing are computer science, information technology and digital literacy.

3. Check your definitions against those given in the chapter.

4. The four aspects of context that should be included in a longer-format lesson plan are:

- the school/class context;
- the theoretical context;
- the National Curriculum or Early Years Foundation Stage context;
- the scheme of work context.

5. You can brief another adult supporting you in the classroom by:

- talking to them about the lesson beforehand;
- giving them a copy of your planning;
- making clear their role in the lesson/any assessment that is taking place.

6. Three types of possible differentiation that you might make in your planning are:

- for children of different abilities;
- for those with additional or special educational needs;
- for children with English as another language.

7. You can ensure that you are well prepared for a lesson by:

- planning likely timings;
- checking resources;
- reviewing your own learning needs;
- listing organisational memory joggers.

8. The three elements that should be evaluated at the end of a lesson are:

- operational issues;
- learning objectives/intentions;
- what you would do/change next time.

Chapter 7 – Assessment in primary computing

1. Assessment is a vital part of the planning process because, without proper assessment and recording in a subject, there is no real evidence or knowledge of where children are up to and planning becomes empty and meaningless. This can lead to activities being repeated inappropriately. Assessment allows teachers to track progress and plan for children to achieve.

2. Samples of children's work are insufficient as a record of progress in computing because the final copy of the work and printouts do not show the drafting process and may hide any misconceptions. Children often

work collaboratively and only by observing individual children working can the teacher really assess their capabilities accurately.

3. Individual profiling of children in computing is a means of mapping their progress linking work with detailed observations by the teacher and taking into account the child's own views of their developing capabilities. It includes identification of next steps in learning, thus completing the planning cycle.

4. The important elements of the context of an observation of a child's work in computing include:

    - the hardware being used;
    - the software being used;
    - the relevant unit of work;
    - any other curriculum links;
    - whether they were working independently or with a partner/group;
    - the date/timing of the activity.

5. A whole-class snapshot can support formative assessment because it can help you to gain a picture of the ICT capability of the whole class at a particular time to support your planning. It could help you to group children appropriately and to plan relevant work for each group; it is therefore a useful part of the planning/ assessment cycle.

6. The assessment strategy most appropriate for use in the EYFS is individual profiling because observations of individual children fit in with the style of assessment prevalent in the EYFS and it allows you to assess/ record progress towards meeting the Early Learning Goals in all six areas of learning.

Chapter 8 – Computational thinking and programming

1. An accessible way of describing computational thinking is that it is the way of thinking that people engage with as they employ the processes and tools of computing to solve problems.

2. The following are examples of the application of computer science in our physical environment:

    - traffic lights at a pedestrian crossing;
    - a drinks vending machine;
    - an automated entry and exit point for a car park.

3. Logo is a text-based programming language whereas Scratch is a visual-blocks programming language.

4. Strategies to develop children's computational thinking through programming are:

    - Children should be discouraged from copying chunks of code without understanding what they do as it is vital that they also understand why a certain piece of code within any program leads to a particular outcome within the system or game being designed. Getting children to explain chunks of code and what they do is important.
    - To develop higher levels of computational thinking children will need exposure to extended projects which require them to design their own games, simulations or scenarios.

5. Flow charts can be used to support children's computational thinking by helping them to sequence events and then to write algorithms. Some programming software also uses flow charts as the programming interface.

Chapter 9 – Physical computing

1. Check your definition of physical computing by re-reading the introduction to the chapter.

2. The components match with their descriptious as follows:

    (a) Light emitting diodes (LED) – (iv) type of output that emits light.
    (b) Microcontroller – (i) a single chip usually containing an integrated circuit, inputs/outputs, a central processing unit and memory.
    (c) Central processing unit (CPU) – (ii) the part of a microcontroller that carries out the instructions from a program relating to the inputs and outputs (a kind of digital clock).
    (d) General purpose input and output (GPIO) – (iii) the part of a microprocessor or computing device that connects to inputs and outputs in a system.

3. Raspberry Pi is a small single board computer that can be linked to a keyboard, monitor and network and runs on the open source Linux operating system. It is referred to as single board because all of the components are contained on one circuit board.

Chapter 10 – Web literacy (including coding for the web)

1. The *internet* is the global network of computers, connected by cables, satellites and other wireless technologies. The *world wide web* is part of the internet and is made up of hypertext pages that include text, images, sounds and animations interconnected by hypertext links, providing information, news, opinion, archive material, music and video.

2. A web browser is a piece of software that allows the user to locate, view and navigate web pages.

3. The elements of the URL http://www.ofsted.gov.uk/reports/ are:

    (a) http = hypertext transport protocol;
    (b) www = world wide web;
    (c) ofsted.gov.uk = the domain name of the organisation's server being accessed;
    (d) /reports/ = the directory or path on the server.

4. The HTML tags identify

    (a) <h1>content here</h1> = main heading of the web page
    (b) <p>content here</p> = a paragraph of content

5. HTML is used to determine the structure of web pages (e.g. headings, lists, paragraphs) whereas CSS is used to determine the style of content and how it is presented (e.g. format of text).

Chapter 11 – Digital media/digital literacies

1. The main purposes of graphics software are to enter, store, retrieve and manipulate images and their constituent elements, line, colour and texture.

2. In settings with older hardware setups, the problems with printing from graphics software might be the large size of graphics files that can fill up limited printer memory, preventing documents from printing out/backlogging printer queues.

3. The problems of using digital video in schools include that, under the safeguarding agenda, publishing images of children introduces ethical and internet safety issues. Trainees should find out about and adhere to the school's and/or local authority's policies and protocols.

4. When editing films, editing software allows:

   - scenes to be trimmed to length;
   - scenes to be joined together along a timeline;
   - titles to be added;
   - music and sound effects to be added.

5. When considering what software to use to support composing and performing music, the important issues that you should consider are as follows:

   - Does it include any pre-recorded samples and how far can these be adapted or changed?
   - Does it have a facility for recording and combining live instruments, including the voice?
   - Does it support any links with different types of media, for example other audio material, still images, video clips, etc.?

6. A podcast is a sound (or video) file that can be transferred onto mobile devices or computers, providing a method of publishing files to the internet that allows users to subscribe to a feed and receive new files and updates automatically. Although the word subscriber is used, this does not mean that there is necessarily a cost.

Chapter 12 – Writing with digital technologies

1. *Word processing software* focuses more on the entry, storage, retrieval and manipulation of text, with some formatting features allowing the inclusion of graphics and sound to enhance the layout and presentation of the final document. *Desktop publishing software* focuses more on the design of the documents and usually has less emphasis on the text content; often, designers require a final version of text to be provided before laying out the pages with the graphics and design features.

2. The three key features of word-processing software are:

   - editing – this allows the entry and manipulation of text, including insertion, deletion, correcting, cutting, copying, pasting, etc.;
   - formatting – this allows the use of different fonts, text sizes, styles, page size/orientation, and use of colour, bullets, tables and boxes, etc.;
   - tools – there is a range to support the functions described in editing and formatting, including checking of spelling, grammar and style, speech capability, use of templates, and word count.

3. The four stages of the writing process that word processing can support are:

   - planning and drafting;
   - editing (both structural and technical);
   - proofreading;
   - presentation.

4. Ways of text entry into a word processor include:

   - via a standard QWERTY keyboard and a mouse;
   - via an overlay keyboard;

- using a touch screen;
- using a word bank;
- using voice-input/recognition software;
- with the help of an adult scribe (amanuensis).

Chapter 13 – Social media – tools for communicating, collaborating and publishing

1. Teachers should show careful use and regard for pupil safety when using social media but these environments can provide authentic and rich experiences for communicating, collaborating and publishing as well as learning about how the internet works.

2. The term used to describe this form of blogging is 'quadblogging'.

Chapter 14 – Graphing programs

1. Graphing programs facilitate communication of information through graphical representation, enabling data to be entered, stored, presented and interpreted graphically.

2. It would be better to use a database when the data-handling requires sophisticated sorting, searching or modelling.

3. The three types of data that you might collect are:

- categorical, for example eye colour;
- discrete, for example number of siblings;
- continuous, for example heights of growing seedlings.

4. The potential drawbacks of the following are:

- pie charts – they are unable to record a zero value and it can be confusing when there are similar values that are difficult to judge by eye;
- line graphs – gaps in data collection may be interpreted as a zero value.

5. The two categories of graphing programs are:

- pictogram programs – these usually represent data as pictograms or block graphs only;
- more sophisticated graphing programs – these support a wider range of graph types and functions.

6. Examples of where a program with set colour order may be inappropriate if not adjusted include:

- eye colour;
- hair colour;
- favourite colours;
- colours of cars, bedroom walls, football strips, front doors, etc.

Chapter 15 – Databases and spreadsheets

1. Databases are structured stores of information that allow large amounts of data to be stored, organised, searched and retrieved quickly and easily.

2. Spreadsheets are another kind of data-handling software sharing some features with databases but are more appropriate for the manipulation of numerical data and therefore well suited to mathematical calculations and modelling.

3. The four main types of data-handling programs commonly used in schools are:

   - branching tree or binary databases;
   - flatfile or tabular databases;
   - relational databases;
   - spreadsheets.

4. Match the type of software with its possible use:

   (a) Branching tree or binary databases – (iii) facilitate the identification of objects, people or plants by posing yes/no questions about their attributes.
   (b) Flatfile or tabular databases – (i) contain data arranged in fields, usually input through a form.
   (c) Spreadsheets – (iv) a grid of cells arranged in rows and columns where data and formulae can be entered prior to searching, sorting and presenting graphically.
   (d) Relational databases – (ii) contain complex data that are tagged to enhance flexibility of interrogation and may have menus, indexes, keywords and hyperlinks.

5. The following terms mean:

   - Keyword searching – a feature of database software requiring the user to select a keyword to be the focus of a search; keywords must be carefully chosen and correctly spelled.
   - Hypertext literacy – the skills required to read and navigate hypertext documents.

6. The formats of data that can be supported in a flatfile database are:

   - text;
   - numeric;
   - dates;
   - yes/no;
   - multiple choice.

Chapter 16 – Professional use of digital technologies

1. The two main ways that can you improve your personal ICT capability are:

   - by developing your keyboard skills;
   - by learning to use key software, including both office/admin programs and educational software.

2. You can use ICT in support of your own professional development by using key websites to keep you up to date and to source resources and find out required information. You can also build a PLN (professional/personal learning network) using social media tools.

Chapter 17 – Safety; online and off

1. The '4 Cs' of online safety defined by Childnet International are:

   - *Conduct* – sometimes children and adults have a false sense of anonymity when online which can lead them to conduct themselves in ways that are inappropriate, putting themselves and others at risk.
   - *Contact* – this includes online grooming and cyberbullying.
   - *Content* – this includes any inappropriate material such as pornographic, hateful or violent content. It also includes any material that may be dangerous, illegal, age-inappropriate, inaccurate or biased. Under this category plagiarism and copyright issues are also considered as children, like adults, can put themselves at risk through the illegal use of copyright material.
   - *Commercialism* – including issues such as junk email, personal privacy and commercial exploitation of children and young people through aggressive marketing strategies and premium rate services.

2. The four main duties placed on you as an employee by the Health and Safety etc. at Work Act 1974 and the Management of Health and Safety at Work Regulations 1999 are to:

   - take reasonable care of your own and others' health and safety;
   - co-operate with your employer over health and safety issues;
   - carry out all activities in accordance with training/instructions provided;
   - inform your employer of any serious risks.

3. The Health and Safety Executive (HSE) provides regular updates and guidance on health and safety.

Chapter 18 – Ethical and legal issues

1. Two organisations involved in the monitoring of copyright are:

   - Copyright Licensing Agency (CLA) – printed materials; issuing licences to make copies of these;
   - Federation Against Software Theft (FAST) – monitors software use; gives advice to computer users.

2. The eight basic principles of data-protection legislation are that personal information must be:

   - fairly and lawfully processed;
   - processed for limited purposes;
   - adequate, relevant and not excessive;
   - accurate;
   - not kept longer than necessary;
   - processed in accordance with the data subject's rights;
   - secure;
   - not transferred to countries without adequate protection.

3. Work that is made available under Creative Commons remains the intellectual property of the person who created the original content, but the various different copyright licences allow the owner to be more specific about the permission they grant for others' use of their content. Teaching children about Creative Commons can help to develop children's understanding of copyright and intellectual property.